Åsa Tricosa

Ziggurats

16 elegantly seamless knits

sweaters :: cardigans :: tutorials

Åsa Söderman

Til min mand.

Åsa Tricosa Ziggurats :: 16 elegantly seamless knits
   1st Edition Published 2018 by Åsa Söderman
   2nd Edition Published 2019 by Åsa Söderman

Text © Åsa Söderman of Åsa Tricosa
Photography: © Åsa Söderman and Knud Haakonssen (where not stated otherwise)
Additional photography: © Sabine Bach, Emanuel Borsboom, Bob Dietrich, Karin
Emma Karlsen, Kaire Kitse, Sol Rencorcet, Annabel Young
Photo Editor (cover): Mark Monckton at www.markmonckton.co.uk
Technical Editing, Patterns: Kitty Wunder
Technical Editing, Tutorials: Charlotte Monckton at www.charlottemonckton.co.uk
Copy Editing: Maria Skrzypiec
Special thanks to Jeannette Gustavus for proofreading
Schematics: Cathy Susko
Layout and Book Design: Ewa Opalinska Shephard at www.zingcreative.eu

For pattern corrections please visit **www.asatricosa.com/errata**

Paperback ISBN: 978-3-9819688-0-4
E-Book ISBN: 978-3-9819688-1-1

A catalogue record for this book is available from the British Library

The text of this book is composed in Bonobo and Myriad Pro
Printed in the UK by Bell & Bain, Glasgow.

Distribution
   Shephardess Press - www.shephardesspress.com
   Remarkable Yarns - www.remarkableyarns.com - USA & Canada

www.asatricosa.com

Contents

Introduction

Åsa Söderman, known to the knitting world as Åsa Tricosa, is a pattern designer who delights in solving tricky knitting problems. Her designs feature her own innovative techniques and a pure pared-back style, centred around warm functionality, clean lines, flawless craftsmanship and an understated Scandinavian elegance.

She finds her inspiration in the creative generosity and flair of the knitting community, and in turn enthuses others to 'knit with abandon'. Her ardent desire is to share her signature Ziggurat method for truly seamless sweaters and cardigans. She teaches it with missionary zeal all over Europe and North America.

Born and raised in Sweden, Åsa has lived in New York, Boston, Sussex, Singapore and Scotland. She has now knitted her way to Germany, where she lives with her Danish husband.

You can find her designs at www.asatricosa.com, and on Ravelry.

('Åsa' rhymes with Tricosa – in most languages. Söderman rhymes with not much at all.)

The Ziggurat Method

The Ziggurat method was born, like much good knitting, from a selfish impulse. I wanted sweaters that fit, that suited me, and a method that took the suspense and guesswork out of the equation.

The essential elements are:
- a nicely shaped neckline that curves in the back
- set in sleeves knitted contiguously with the shoulders and body
- integrated buttonbands
- integrated pockets
- integrated everything
- no seaming

What is more, I wanted all of this with the possibility of some stripes, and with absolutely minimal cutting and joining of skeins.

What emerged, after much zigging and zagging, was my Ziggurat method. The method has been refined and honed over the years, and is now ready to face its public. Like many creators and designers, I have a missionary streak; I wish to share my discoveries, tools, and inventions with fellow knitters.

This book is my invitation for you to knit well-fitting sweaters with precisely worked out details; to explore and adapt the patterns as you become more experienced. It is also an invitation to discover the beauty of some of my favourite yarns from both commercial and indie dyers.

Come and learn to Ziggurat. And knit with abandon!

How to Ziggurat

Ziggurats are ancient Assyrian and Mesopotamian temples, built as stepped pyramid towers, and an architectural construction that seemed to me a fitting representation of the zigging steps I had embarked upon. While mulling over the name, I happened upon a Zikkurat poster on display at the British Academy and took it as a sign.

The method has gone through much fine-tuning since its inception, but the basic zigging has stayed the same.

If you already enjoy knitting top down, I do not have to sing its praises. But it is important to remember that there are always different ways to knit things, and the more tools we have as knitters, the more interesting and exciting (not to mention well-fitting) knits we can create.

How is Ziggurating different?

Well, for a start, if you knitted the most basic Ziggurat pullover from a large cone of yarn, you would at the end have only six yarn ends to weave in – one at the shoulder cast on, one at the hem bind off, one at each underarm, and one at each cuff. You would also have a well-shaped sweater with fine finishing details.

The other main difference is in the adaptability of the patterns – they are extremely customisable. I have discovered that what I most like to wear is simple shapes, containing large areas of stocking stitch. Now, stocking stitch is perhaps not the most exciting thing to knit, but knitting excitement is to be had in other ways. This is where the finely tuned details come into play – a peekaboo contrast hem, a lined cuff, a hidden pocket. I especially have a thing for pockets (some Ziggurat pockets are decidedly only for the most adventurous and patient knitters, but there are options for all levels of knitting, including a very simple afterthought pocket). All these optional extras make the patterns infinitely changeable, and as challenging as you would like them to be.

How to use the book

Each pattern has comprehensive written instructions. Follow these from start to finish, possibly with the help of the photo tutorials section of the book, and you should end up with a well-fitting sweater.

If you are new to Ziggurating, I recommend a close look at the Ziggurat Steps tutorial (page 188). The moves are sometimes unexpected and unusual. At times it may be better to follow the instructions blindly, rather than ask yourself how it all will come together. This approach does not work for all people, as some knitters (and I am one!) really want to understand where they are heading before plunging in. Nevertheless, some things become clear only in the doing, so I venture to suggest doing what it says, and having faith that it will work.

The beginner

Follow the instructions blindly. Trust that even odd-looking moves will eventually bring you a beautifully shaped and well-fitting sweater. When enthusiastic but sometimes bewildered knitters seek advice in my Ravelry group, the common advice from more seasoned Ziggurateers is 'Close your eyes and knit'.

The Mayhem DK cardigan is a good pattern for a first Ziggurat knit – it works up quickly in DK yarn, and it is completely straightforward as it has no buttonbands and no waist shaping. It is also a flattering shape on all kinds of bodies. If you would like a bit of challenge, knit the hidden Mayhem pocket. If you prefer to keep things simple, you can skip the pocket altogether.

Another cardigan, Jadeite, is also a straightforward knit if you skip the advanced pockets and opt for plain cuffs, and are ready to take on buttonbands and buttonholes.

Among the pullovers, you could try Simple Summer Ziggurat or a plain version of Sammelsurium with simple rolled collar, hems, and cuffs.

All of these are good for beginner Ziggurateers, but choose one that makes your heart sing! It is only knitting, and there is plenty of guidance through the steps.

The adventurous knitter

You too can follow the instructions blindly. But hopefully you will be tempted to steal a pocket from one design, borrow the split hem from another and perhaps add your own stitch pattern or colour work, using one of the patterns in this book merely as a starting point. Most of the patterns are intentionally quite basic, but offered in a wide variety of gauges. This way you are likely to find one that suits your particular yarn and gauge.

The Coucou tunic with its intricate tuck, cable cuffs and collar, may be a good pattern for the adventurous knitter. The double-knitted pockets with buttonband edging (Pocket 3D) offer another good challenge. Chatoyant, with its underarm gusset and lined hem, is also an interesting knit. As is Vaudeville tunic, with split, double-knitted hems, striped linings for the cuffs, and a welt pocket.

Choosing a size

One beauty of knitting our own sweaters is that we do not have to put up with off-the-shelf sizing: we can tailor our projects to fit our bodies.

For a good and flattering fit, you should choose size based on your shoulder measurement, not your bust size. Measure a well-fitting sweater or t-shirt from shoulder seam to shoulder seam in front and above the bust (garments often stretch across the back, so it is usually better to measure in front). For semi-dropped shoulder sweaters, determine your Ziggurat size based on a tailored model such as Sammelsurium (page 118).

Bust size can then be adjusted to suit. Most of the patterns include optional bust darts; these instructions can be used to add bust darts to any sweater as long as you take the issue of placement into consideration. This is just one way to adjust for bust size. In the Ziggurat Steps Tutorial (page 188), you will find additional tips on how to modify the patterns for a good fit, and also in the Hints & Tips Tutorial (page 196).

Tools

No particular tools other than yarn and circular needles are required. The initial steps of a Ziggurat sweater require you to loop the cable of the needle, so a long and flexible cable is highly recommended. It is also a good idea to have additional circulars to hand, especially if you plan to add pockets to your pullover or cardigan. A crochet hook may be useful for picking up and knitting stitches, but is not essential.

Now, cast on already!

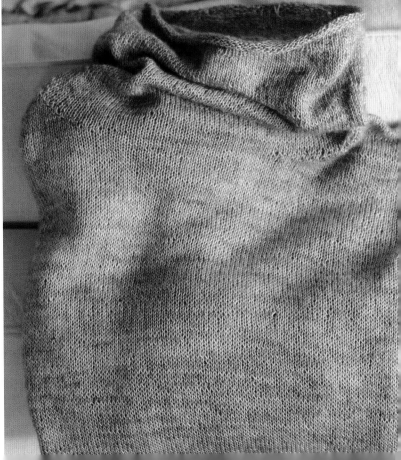

Patterns

Coucou is a comfortable, slightly flared Ziggurat, featuring a contrasting cable neckline, a cute tuck, and a dainty pocket. Sleeves are three-quarter length and also finished with a contrasting cable.

There are various options for the tuck: A two-coloured triangle tuck for intrepid knitters; a plain tuck for those who are less adventurous; and a more traditional gather. Coucou is knitted with Suilven from Ripples Crafts. Another magic yarn blend, Suilven has wonderful lustre and drape, the kind of drape that neither clings nor loses its shape – perfect for the little tuck at centre back.

TO FIT SIZE
81 (86, 91, 97, 102) [107, 112, 117, 122, 127] cm
32 (34, 36, 38, 40) [42, 44, 46, 48, 50] inches

BALLERINA NECK
With cable edging

FIT
Tailored shoulders, fitted at bust, gently flaring to hips

YARN
Ripples Crafts Suilven (Fingering, 60% Merino, 20% Silk, 20% Yak,
366 m (400 yds) per 100 g)
MC Slice of Lime, 3 (4, 4, 4, 4) [4, 5, 5, 5, 5] skeins
Small amounts of **CC1** Carnations; **CC2** Red Red Wine

APPROX YARDAGE
1150 (1200, 1250, 1350, 1400) [1450, 1500, 1600, 1650, 1750] m
1250 (1300, 1400, 1450, 1550) [1600, 1650, 1750, 1850, 1900] yds

ALTERNATIVE YARN SUGGESTIONS
Nature's Luxury Farouche, Rohrspatz & Wollmeise Blend, Rohrspatz &
Wollmeise Pure

NEEDLES & NOTIONS
3 mm (US 2.5) circular needle, 80 – 100 cm (32 – 40")
or size to obtain gauge
2.75 mm (US 2) circular needle, 80 – 100 cm (32 – 40")
2 cable or double pointed needles
Stitch holders; stitch markers

BLOCKED GAUGE
26 sts x 36 rows on 3 mm (US 2.5) needle = 10 cm / 4"

SAMPLE SIZES
Green (RIpples Crafts Suilven): Size 36 without bust darts weighs
300 g/10.5oz, including **CC**
Mauve (Rohrspatz & Wollmeise Pure, extrem romantisch): Size 40
with Middling bust darts weighs 345 g/12 oz (with **CC** only on
pocket and tuck)

Coucou

STEP 1: CAST ON & RIGHT BACK SHOULDER

With **MC**, using longtail cast on and 3 mm (US 2.5) needle, cast on 86 (90, 94, 98, 102) [104, 106, 108, 110, 114] sts.
Setup Row (WS): P14 (14, 14, 15, 15) [15, 16, 16, 17, 17], turn.
R1 (RS): Sl1^, pm, k8 (8, 8, 8, 8) [8, 9, 9, 10, 10], turn.
R2 (WS): Sl1^, purl to m, rm, p1^, p1, turn.
R3: Sl1^, pm, k4 (4, 4, 4, 4) [4, 4, 4, 5, 5], turn.
R4: Sl1^, purl to m, rm, p1^, p1, turn.
R5: Sl1^, pm, knit to last 2 sts (working any sl1^ as k1^), sl1wyb, k1.
R6: Purl to m, rm, p1^, p1, turn.
R7: Sl1^, pm, knit to last 2 sts, sl1wyb, k1.
Work **Rows 6 & 7** once more.
Final Row (WS): Purl to m, rm, p1^, purl to end.

86 (90, 94, 98, 102) [104, 106, 108, 110, 114] Back sts

STEP 2: LEFT BACK SHOULDER

R1 (RS): K1, sl1wyb, k12 (12, 12, 13, 13) [13, 14, 14, 15, 15], turn.
R2 (WS): Sl1^, pm, p8 (8, 8, 8, 8) [8, 9, 9, 10, 10], turn.
R3: Sl1^, knit to m, rm, k1^, k1, turn.
R4: Sl1^, pm, p4 (4, 4, 4, 4) [4, 4, 4, 5, 5], turn.
R5: Sl1^, knit to m, rm, k1^, k1, turn.
R6: Sl1^, pm, purl to end (working any sl1^ as p1^).
R7: K1, sl1wyb, knit to m, rm, k1^, k1, turn.
R8: Sl1^, pm, purl to end.
Work **Rows 7 & 8** once more.

STEP 3: WORKING ACROSS BACK

R1 (RS): K1, sl1wyb, knit to m, rm, k1^, knit to last 2 sts, sl1wyb, k1.
86 (90, 94, 98, 102) [104, 106, 108, 110, 114] Back sts
R2 (WS): Purl.
R3: K1, sl1wyb, knit to last 2 sts, sl1wyb, k1.
R4: Purl.
Work **Rows 3 & 4** again x 1 (1, 2, 2, 2) [2, 2, 2, 3, 3].
Work **Row 3** once more.
Final Row (WS): Purl to last 2 sts, p2tog, pm, p&p8 (8, 9, 9, 9) [9, 9, 9, 10, 10] sts along edge (for first half of Left Sleeve Cap).

8 (8, 9, 9, 9) [9, 9, 9, 10, 10] Left Cap sts
85 (89, 93, 97, 101) [103, 105, 107, 109, 113] Back sts

Slide stitches off needle tips to rest on the cable.
Set these stitches aside, continue to next step without turning.

STEP 4: LEFT FRONT SHOULDER

nM1 = neck increase
Setup Row (WS): Loop cable, p&p13 (13, 13, 14, 14) [14, 15, 15, 16, 16] sts (for Left Front Shoulder) in the cast on of Left Back Shoulder,

and remember to pick up second st in line with faux seam.
13 (13, 13, 14, 14) [14, 15, 15, 16, 16] Left Front sts
R1 (RS): K8 (8, 8, 9, 9) [9, 10, 10, 10, 10], turn.
R2: Sl1^, purl to end.
R3: K4 (4, 4, 4, 4) [4, 5, 5, 5, 5], turn.
R4: Sl1^, purl to end.
R5: Knit to 2 sts before loop (working any sl1^ as k1^), sl1wyb, k1, turn.
R6: Purl.
R7: Knit to 2 sts before loop, sl1wyb, k1, turn.
R8: Purl.
R9: K2, nM1R, knit to 2 sts before loop, sl1wyb, k1, turn.
14 (14, 14, 15, 15) [15, 16, 16, 17, 17] Left Front sts
R10: Purl.
Works **Rows 9 & 10** again x 4 (4, 5, 5, 5) [5, 5, 5, 6, 6].
18 (18, 19, 20, 20) [20, 21, 21, 23, 23] Left Front sts
Final Row (WS): K2, nM1R, knit to 2 sts before loop, ssk, pm, p&k8 (8, 9, 9, 9) [9, 9, 9, 10, 10] sts (for second half of Left Sleeve Cap), knit to m, sm, sl1wyb, knit to last 2 sts, ssk, pm, p&k8 (8, 9, 9, 9) [9, 9, 9, 10, 10] sts (for first half of Right Sleeve Cap).

16 (16, 18, 18, 18) [18, 18, 18, 20, 20] Left Cap sts
8 (8, 9, 9, 9) [9, 9, 9, 10, 10] Right Cap sts
18 (18, 19, 20, 20) [20, 21, 21, 23, 23] Left Front sts
84 (88, 92, 96, 100) [102, 104, 106, 108, 112] Back sts

Slide stitches off needle tips to rest on the cable.
Set these stitches aside, continue to next step without turning.

STEP 5: RIGHT FRONT SHOULDER

nM1 = neck increase
R1 (RS): Loop cable, p&k13 (13, 13, 14, 14) [14, 15, 15, 16, 16] sts (for Right Front Shoulder) in the cast on of Right Back Shoulder, and remember to pick up second st in line with faux seam.

BOX A

sM1 = sleeve increase   nM1 = neck increase

RS ROWS
R1: K2, nM1R, (knit to 1 st before m, sl1wyb, sm, sM1L, knit to m, sM1R, sm, sl1wyb) twice, knit to last 2 sts, nM1L, k2.

WS ROWS
R2: Purl.

R4: P2, nM1Lp, purl to last 2 sts, nM1Rp, p2.

13 (13, 13, 14, 14) [14, 15, 15, 16, 16] Right Front sts
R2 (WS): P8 (8, 8, 9, 9) [9, 10, 10, 10, 10], turn.
R 3: Sl1^, knit to end.
R4: P4 (4, 4, 4, 4) [4, 5, 5, 5, 5], turn.
R5: Sl1^, knit to end.
R6: Purl to loop, working any sl1^ as p1^, turn.
R7: K1, sl1wyb, knit to end.
R8: Purl to loop, turn.
R9: K1, sl1wyb, knit to last 2 sts, nM1L, k2.
14 (14, 14, 15, 15) [15, 16, 16, 17, 17] Right Front sts
R10: Purl to loop, turn.
Work **Rows 9 & 10** again X 4 (4, 5, 5, 5) [5, 5, 5, 6, 6].
18 (18, 19, 20, 20) [20, 21, 21, 23, 23] Right Front sts
Work **Row 9** once more.
19 (19, 20, 21, 21) [21, 22, 22, 24, 24] Right Front sts

Final row (WS): Purl to 2 sts before loop, p2tog, pm, p&p8 (8, 9, 9, 9) [9, 9, 9, 10, 10] sts (for second half of Right Sleeve Cap), purl to end.

16 (16, 18, 18, 18) [18, 18, 18, 20, 20] sts for each Sleeve Cap
18 (18, 19, 20, 20) [20, 21, 21, 23, 23] sts for each Front
84 (88, 92, 96, 100) [102, 104, 106, 108, 112] Back sts

STEP 6: SLEEVE CAPS & BODY
You will now increase for the sleeves and neck.
(See Helpful Table for an overview of all increases.)

REFER TO **BOX A** FOR ROW INSTRUCTIONS
Work **Rows 1 & 2** x 10 (10, 8, 9, 10) [11, 11, 10, 11, 9].
36 (36, 34, 36, 38) [40, 40, 38, 42, 38] Sleeve sts
28 (28, 27, 29, 30) [31, 32, 31, 34, 32] sts for each Front

Works **Rows 1 & 4** x 2 (3, 4, 4, 4) [4, 4, 5, 4, 6].
40 (42, 42, 44, 46) [48, 48, 48, 50, 50] Sleeve sts
32 (34, 35, 37, 38) [39, 40, 41, 42, 44] sts for each Front

STEP 7: JOIN FRONTS TO KNIT IN THE ROUND
Joining Row-Round 1 (RS): K2, nM1R, (knit to 1 st before m, sl1wyb, sm, **sM1L**, knit to m, **sM1R**, sm, sl1wyb) twice, knit to last 2 sts, nM1L, pm (=Nm), k2, *(turn work over so WS is facing) borrow last st for cast on loop, crochet cast on 19 (19, 21, 21, 23) [23, 23, 23, 23, 23] sts, replace loop onto LN (make a final chain st but not around the needle), turn work over so RS is facing, join to Left Front, knit to m, sm.*

You are now at Left Front Sleeve.

42 (44, 44, 46, 48) [50, 50, 50, 52, 52] Sleeve sts
85 (89, 93, 97, 101) [103, 105, 107, 109, 113] Front sts
84 (88, 92, 96, 100) [102, 104, 106, 108, 112] Back sts

Joining Round 2: Knit to Nm, rm, ssk, knit to end of cast on, make loop in bar and place on LN, k2tog (the first st of Left Front and the loop), knit to 1 st before m.

42 (44, 44, 46, 48) [50, 50, 50, 52, 52] Sleeve sts
84 (88, 92, 96, 100) [102, 104, 106, 108, 112] Front sts
84 (88, 92, 96, 100) [102, 104, 106, 108, 112] Back sts

STEP 8: SLEEVE & BODY INCREASES
Continue to work sleeve increases and also introduce body increases.
The round begins 1 stitch before Left Front Sleeve marker.

REFER TO **BOX B** FOR ROUND INSTRUCTIONS
Work **Rnds 1 & 2** x 8 (8, 9, 7, 7) [6, 7, 6, 5, 7].
58 (60, 62, 60, 62) [62, 64, 62, 62, 66] Sleeve sts

INTRODUCE BODY INCREASES
Work **Rnds 3 & 2** x 3 (2, 2, 2, 2) [3, 3, 4, 5, 5].
64 (64, 66, 64, 66) [68, 70, 70, 72, 76] Sleeve sts
90 (92, 96, 100, 104) [108, 110, 114, 118, 122] Front/Back sts

Work **Rnds 3 & 4** x 0 (1, 1, 2, 2) [3, 3, 4, 5, 5].
64 (66, 68, 68, 70) [74, 76, 78, 82, 86] Sleeve sts
90 (96, 100, 108, 112) [120, 122, 130, 138, 142] Front/Back sts

Work **Rnd 3**.
66 (68, 70, 70, 72) [76, 78, 80, 84, 88] Sleeve sts
92 (98, 102, 110, 114) [122, 124, 132, 140, 144] Front/Back sts

Final Rnd: Knit to 2 sts before Left Front Sleeve m.

BOX B

sM1 = sleeve increase   bM1 = body increase

ODD (SLIP-STITCH) ROUNDS
Rnd 1: (Sl1wyb, sm, sM1L, knit to m, sM1R, sm, sl1wyb, knit to 1 st before m) twice.

Rnd 3: (bM1L, sl1wyb, sm, sM1L, knit to m, sM1R, sm, sl1wyb, bM1R, knit to 1 st before m) twice.

EVEN (PLAIN) ROUNDS
Rnd 2: Knit.

Rnd 4: (bM1L, k1, sm, knit to m, sm, k1, bM1R, knit to 1 st before m) twice.

STEP 9: SEPARATING SLEEVES & BODY

Separation Rnd 1: *Pm, k2, rm, place all sts to next m on holder (= sleeve sts), rm, *(turn work over so WS is facing) borrow last st for cast on loop*, crochet cast on 8 (8, 9, 10, 11) [10, 11, 11, 10, 11] sts, pm, cast on 7 (7, 8, 9, 10) [9, 10, 10, 9, 10] sts, *replace loop onto LN (make a final chain st but not around the needle), turn work over so RS is facing*, knit to 2 sts before m, work from * to * once more, knit to m.

You are now at Left Front Sleeve.

107 (113, 119, 129, 135) [141, 145, 153, 159, 165] Front/Back sts

Separation Rnd 2: *Rm, ssk, knit to m, sm, p1, knit to end of underarm cast on, make loop in bar and place on LN, k2tog (next st and loop), knit to m*, work from * to * once more.

106 (112, 118, 128, 134) [140, 144, 152, 158, 164] Front/Back sts

STEP 10: BODY & SHAPING

Continue in stocking stitch over body stitches only.
The round begins under Left Sleeve.
Note: *Two stitches under each arm are worked in a cord pattern that creates a faux side seam (TwSl on alternate rounds).*

REFER TO **BOX C** FOR ROUND INSTRUCTIONS

AT THE SAME TIME - WAIST SHAPING

Please read through the entire step before proceeding, as a few things happen at the same time or overlap, beginning with the TUCK.

- Tuck
- Optional Bust Dart
- Pocket – worked before waist shaping is complete

TUCK OR GATHER

- Gather
- Monochrome Tuck
- Two-Colour Tuck

The two-colour tuck was created for the adventurous knitter.
For a little less adventure, knit the monochrome version.
For a walk in the park, forgo the tuck altogether. To achieve some swing in the back, instead add a bundle of stitches for a charming gather.

REFER TO **TUCK TUTORIAL** FOR TUCK INSTRUCTIONS
Instructions for the simple Gather and placement of the Tucks follow below. See Tutorials for step-by-step Tuck instructions.

BOX C

BODY & SHAPING

Rnd 1: Knit.

Rnd 2: (Sm, TwSl, knit to m) twice.

Decrease Rnd: Sm, k2, k2tog, knit to Tm1, RLI, sm, knit to Tm2, sm, LLI, knit to 2 sts before side m, ssk, sm, k2, k2tog, knit to 2 sts before m, ssk. 4 sts decreased, 2 sts increased

Increase Rnd: Sm, k2, RLI, knit to Tm1, RLI, sm, knit to Tm2, sm, LLI, knit to side m, LLI, sm, k2, RLI, knit to side m, LLI. 6 sts increased

ALTERNATIVE SIMPLE GATHER

The Gather adds 20 sts into the 10 Centre Back sts over two rounds. The third round places Tuck markers (Tm) for further increases.
   Gather Rnd 1: K49 (52, 55, 60, 63) [66, 68, 72, 75, 78] sts, pm (=Tm), (kfb) 10 times, knit to end of rnd.
   Gather Rnd 2: Sm, TwSl, knit to Tm, sm, (kfb, k1) x 10, knit to m, sm, TwSl, knit to m.
   Gather Rnd 3: Knit to Tm, rm, k10, pm (=Tm1), k10, pm (=Tm2), knit to end of rnd.

Continue with Bust Darts and Waist Shaping as instructed below, starting with a BOX C **Rnd 2**.

MONOCHROME TUCK PLACEMENT

Tuck Rnd 1: Sm, k49 (52, 55, 60, 63) [66, 68, 72, 75, 78], work Tuck as instructed in Tutorial section.

TWO-COLOUR TUCK PLACEMENT

Tuck Rnd 1: Sm, with **MC** k49 (52, 55, 60, 63) [66, 68, 72, 75, 78], work Tuck as instructed in the Tutorial section.

106 (112, 118, 128, 134) [140, 144, 152, 158, 164] Front sts
126 (132, 138, 148, 154) [160, 164, 172, 178, 184] Back sts

AT THE SAME TIME

When Gather or Tuck is complete, work BOX C **Rnds 1 & 2** to 5 cm / 2" from underarm.

AT THE SAME TIME OPTIONAL BUST DARTS

Optional Bust Darts may be placed here or a bit lower. See BOX D.
Note: If you are trying to stretch your skeins, this is a good place to set the body aside to work the sleeves before finishing the body.

AT THE SAME TIME WAIST SHAPING

At 5 cm / 2" from underarm, begin waist shaping.
You are decreasing along the sides while also adding stitches to the Tuck.

WAIST DECREASES

Work **Decrease Rnd & Rnd 2**.
104 (110, 116, 126, 132) [138, 142, 150, 156, 162] Front sts
124 (130, 136, 146, 152) [158, 162, 170, 176, 182] Back sts

Continue with **Rnds 1 & 2**, working **Decrease Rnd** every 8th rnd again x 2.
100 (106, 112, 122, 128) [134, 138, 146, 152, 158] Front sts
124 (130, 136, 146, 152) [158, 162, 170, 176, 182] Back sts

WORK STRAIGHT

Work **Rnds 1 & 2** x 4.

WAIST INCREASES

Work **Increase Rnd**.
102 (108, 114, 124, 130) [136, 140, 148, 154, 160] Front sts
128 (134, 140, 150, 156) [162, 166, 174, 180, 186] Back sts
Continue with **Rnds 1 & 2**, working **Increase Rnd** on the next 18th round x 3, then the next 20th rnd once.
110 (116, 122, 132, 138) [144, 148, 156, 162, 168] Front sts
144 (150, 156, 166, 172) [178, 182, 190, 196, 202] Back sts

BOX D

OPTIONAL BUST DARTS

Place your darts at approx 5 (6, 10, 10) cm / 2 (2.25, 4, 4)" from underarm or where desired:
For placement of darts, see Hints & Tips
(Remember to place them in Front!)

Smallish (Middling, Busty, Wowza!)
Worked over 12 (18, 22, 26) rows, adds approx 3 (4.5, 6, 7) cm / 1.25 (1.75, 2.25, 2.75)".

R1 (RS): Sm, knit to m, sm, knit to 27 (34, 37, 40) sts before Left side m, turn.
R2 (WS): Jsl1, pm, purl to 29 (36, 39, 42) sts before Right side m, turn.
R3 (RS): Jsl1, pm, knit to m, rm, Jk1, k5 (4, 3, 3), turn.
R4: Jsl1, pm, purl to m, rm, Jp1, p5 (4, 3, 3), turn.
Work **Rows 3 & 4** again x 4 (7, 9, 11).
Final Row (RS): Jsl1, pm, knit to m, rm, Jk1, knit to side m. Resume working in the round.
Next Rnd: Sm, TwSl, knit to side m, sm, TwSl, knit to 1 st before m, pass loop behind next st and place loop on LN, rm, k2tog (next st and loop), knit to side m.

AT THE SAME TIME POCKET
Work to 28 (27.5, 28, 28, 27.5) [26.5, 27, 26.5, 26.5, 25.5] cm / 11 (10.75, 11, 11, 10.75) [10.5, 10.75, 10.5, 10.5, 10]" from underarm, make a pocket.

REFER TO POCKET TUTORIAL **2C** FOR INSTRUCTIONS
The Pocket Rounds are worked into the BOX C Rounds with 2-stitch side columns and waist shaping.
Place the pocket welt 22 (24, 26, 26, 30) [30, 36, 36, 40, 40] sts after the Right Side marker.

Make the pocket according to Tutorial instructions and pay attention to waist shaping and the TwSl at each side 'seam'.

Work to 37 (36.5, 37, 37, 36.5) [35.5, 36, 35.5, 35.5, 34.5] cm / 14.5 (14.25, 14.5, 14.5, 14.25) [14, 14.25, 14, 14, 13.5]" from underarm or to 2.5 cm / 1" from desired length.

STEP 11: HEM
Change to smaller (2.75 mm / US 2) circular needle.
Rnd 1: Purl.
Rnd 2: Knit.
Rnd 3: Purl.
Rnd 4: Knit.
Rnds 5 & 6: Purl.
Rnd 7: Knit.
Rnds 8 & 9: Purl.

Bind off in even tension, using Stretchy Bind Off:
K1, *k1, sl2 to LN, k2togtbl*; work from * to end of rnd until all sts are bound off.

STEP 12: SLEEVES
Place 66 (68, 70, 70, 72) [76, 78, 80, 84, 88] Sleeve sts from holder back on larger (3 mm / US 2.5) needle. Join **MC** at right side of gap, p&k6 (6, 7, 8, 9) [8, 9, 9, 8, 9] sts along the first half of the underarm cast on, pm, p&k8 (8, 9, 10, 11) [10, 11, 11, 10, 11] sts more along second half of underarm, knit to m.
80 (82, 86, 88, 92) [94, 98, 100, 102, 108] sts

REFER TO **BOX E** FOR ROUND INSTRUCTIONS
Work **Rnds 1 & 2** to 5 cm / 2" from underarm.

SLEEVE DECREASES
Work **Decrease Rnd & Rnd 2**.
78 (80, 84, 86, 90) [92, 96, 98, 100, 106] sts

Continue with **Rnds 1 & 2**, working **Decrease Rnd** every 12 (12, 10, 10, 10) [8, 8, 8, 8, 8]th round again x 7 (7, 8, 9, 9) [10, 10, 11, 12, 12].
64 (66, 68, 68, 72) [72, 76, 76, 76, 82] sts
Work to 27.5 (27.5, 28.5, 28.5, 28.5) [28.5, 29.5, 29.5, 30.5, 30.5] cm / 10.75 (10.75, 11.25, 11.25, 11.25) [11.25, 11.5, 11.5, 12, 12]" from underarm or 2.5 cm / 1" from desired sleeve length.

BOX E

SLEEVE ROUNDS

Rnd 1: Sm, knit to m.

Rnd 2: Sm, TwSl, knit to m.

Decrease Rnd: Sm, sl1, k2tog, knit to 1 st before m, shift m 1 st right, ssk.

STEP 13: CABLE CUFF

If using CC for the cable detail, work a final round with CC. The cable is worked and attached sideways to Sleeve stitches. Begin by winding on 12 sts perpendicular to the cuff, using the working yarn.

LEFT CUFF

Sl1 to LN, using smaller (2.75 mm / US 2) needle and Provisional Winding Cast On, wind on 12 sts onto LN.
The cable is knitted back and forth; on RS rows ssk the last cable st with 1 or 2 Cuff sts. Attach to approx every 4 of 5 Cuff sts; that is, ssk 3 times, then sssk (using 2 Cuff sts). Alternate the two cable crossings on every 14th row.
R1 (RS): K10, p1, k2tog.
R2 (WS): Sl1wyf, k1, p9, sl1wyf.

REFER TO **BOX F** FOR THE CABLE REPEAT

Work 3 complete cable repeats around cuff, work another half repeat (Rows 1 – 14) or until 1 Cuff st remains, ending with a WS row. If necessary make an additional (or omit one) sssk to accommodate the final cable repeat.

On a RS row, graft sts with provisional sts to close the cable, working a final ssk when grafting the final 2 sts.
Alternatively, close with a 3-Needle Bind Off from WS.

RIGHT CUFF

Work as Left Cuff.

STEP 14: CABLE COLLAR
Notes:
*The cable collar is worked in two halves.
When joining yarn at Centre Front to pick up first half of Neck, use a long yarn end (MC or CC) and leave the main ball at Centre Front for casting on and working the first half of the cable.
Begin by picking up & knitting sts from RS around the neck, starting 1 stitch before Centre Front going clockwise across Right Shoulder and picking up inside an entire selvedge stitch. Then wind on stitches to work and attach a cable (as for Cuff) from Centre Front along Right Front to Centre Back.*

BOX F

CABLE REPEAT AROUND CUFF

R1 (Cable Cross 1, RS): K1, sl3 to CN1, hold to **back**, sl3 to CN2, hold to **front**, k3, k3 from CN2, k3 from CN1, p1, ss(s)k.
R2 (WS): Sl1wyf, k1, p9, sl1wyf.
R3: K10, p1, ss(s)k.
R4: Sl1wyf, k1, p9, sl1wyf.

Work **Rows 3 & 4** again x 5.

R15 (Cable Cross 2): K1, sl3 to CN1, hold to **back**, sl3 to CN2, hold to **back**, k3, k3 from CN2, k3 from CN1, p1, ss(s)k.
R16: Sl1wyf, k1, p9, sl1wyf.

Work **Rows 3 & 4** again x 6.

From Centre Back, pick up sts over Left Shoulder to Centre Front, work cable from the provisional stitches at Centre Front along Left Front to Centre Back. Graft or close with a 3-Needle Bind Off at Centre Back where it will be less obvious if you end up with an incomplete cable repeat – and you will have a perfectly centred cable in Front.

RIGHT HALF

With 2.75 mm (US 2) circular needle and 1 st to the right of Centre Front, from RS attach **MC** or **CC**, p&k approx 36 (37, 40, 41, 42) [43, 43, 43, 45, 46] sts along Right Front to Right Shoulder, approx 28 (29, 31, 32, 33) [35, 36, 37, 37, 39] sts from Shoulder to Centre Back, stop at Centre Back, work Cable from Centre Front as follows.
Approx 64 (66, 71, 73, 75) [78, 79, 80, 82, 85] sts

BOX G

CABLE REPEAT ALONG RIGHT FRONT TO CENTRE BACK

R1 (Cable Cross 1, RS): K1, sl3 to CN1, hold to **back**, sl3 to CN2, hold to **front**, k3, k3 from CN2, k3 from CN1, p1, ss(s)k.
R2 (WS): Sl1wyf, k1, p9, sl1wyf.
R3 (RS): K10, p1, ss(s)k.
R4: Sl1wyf, k1, p9, sl1wyf.

Work **Rows 3 & 4** again x 6.

R17 (Cable Cross 2): K1, sl3 to CN1, hold to **back**, sl3 to CN2, hold to **back**, k3, k3 from CN2, k3 from CN1, p1, ss(s)k.
R18: Sl1wyf, k1, p9, sl1wyf.

Work **Rows 3 & 4** again x 7.

Coucou

The Neck Cable is worked like the Cuff Cable but with 2 additional rows between Cable Crosses. Work and attach the Cable from Centre Front along Right Front to Centre Back.

Provisional Cast On: Sl1 to LN, using the already attached ball of yarn wind on 12 sts onto LN.
R1 (RS): K10, p1, k2tog.
R2 (WS): Sl1wyf, k1, p9, sl1wyf.

Work cable repeats around neck to Centre Back (see BOX G on previous page), stop at Centre Back.

LEFT HALF
From Centre Back, continue with working yarn to pick up sts for Left Half of collar to Centre Front, p&k approx 28 (29, 31, 32, 33) [35, 36, 37, 37, 39] sts to Left Shoulder, approx 34 (35, 38, 39, 40) [41, 41, 41, 43, 44] sts from Shoulder to 1 st before Centre Front.
Approx 62 (64, 69, 71, 73) [76, 77, 78, 80, 83] sts

Slip provisional sts to working needle, remove and discard slip knot, work and attach cable along Left Front to Centre Back as follows.

R1 (RS): Sl1wyb, p1, k9, sl1wyf.
R2 (WS): K1, p9, k1, p2tog.
Work **Rows 1 & 2** again x 5.

Work cable repeats around neck to 1 st before Centre Back (see BOX H).

On a RS row, graft sts with provisional sts to close the cable, working a final ssk when grafting the final 2 sts.
Alternatively close with a 3 Needle Bind Off from WS.

FINISH
Weave in loose ends. Soak and block lightly to measurements, taking care to pin out collar and cuff cables.

BOX H

CABLE REPEAT ALONG LEFT FRONT TO CENTRE BACK
R1 (Cable Cross 1, RS): Sl1wyb, p1, sl3 to CN1, hold to **front**, sl3 to CN2, hold to **back**, k3, k3 from CN2, k3 from CN1, sl1wyf.
R2 (WS): K1, p9, k1, p2(3)tog.
R3 (RS): Sl1wyb, p1, k9, sl1wyf.
R4: K1, p9, k1, p2(3)tog.

Work **Rows 3 & 4** again x 6.

R17 (Cable Cross 2): Sl1wyb, p1, sl3 to CN1, hold to **back**, sl3 to CN2, hold to **front**, k3, k3 from CN2, k3 from CN1, sl1wyf.
R18: K1, p9, k1, p2(3)tog.

Work **Rows 3 & 4** x 7.

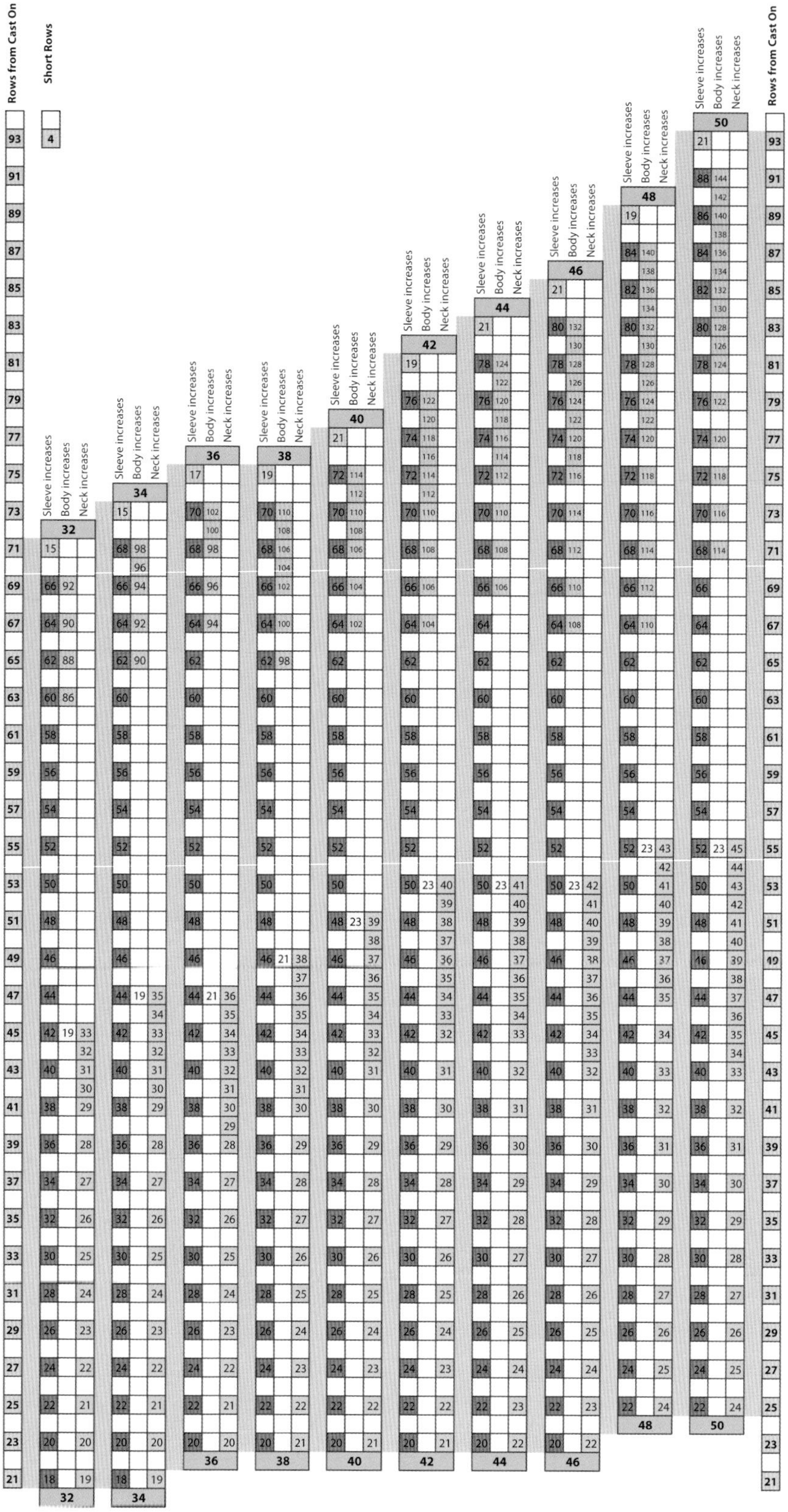

Coucou

Short Rows

Sleeve increases
Body increases
Neck increases

Legend:

- Sleeve increases
- Body increases
- Neck increases
- Front cast on
- Underarm cast on

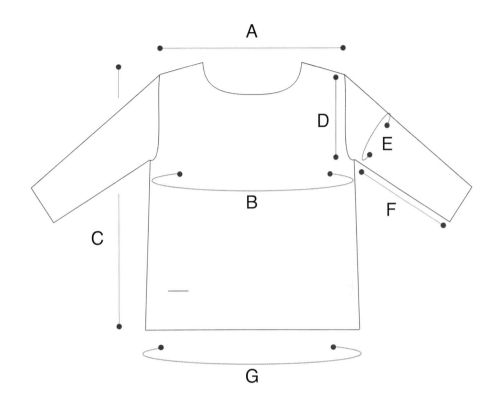

COUCOU TUNIC GARMENT MEASUREMENTS

	32	34	36	38	40	42	44	46	48	50
A – Shoulder width (cm)	32.5	34	35.5	37	38.5	39	40	41	41.5	43
in	12.75	13.5	14	14.5	15.25	15.25	15.75	16.25	16.25	17
B – Bust (cm)	89	94	98.5	106	111	115.5	118.5	124.5	129	134
in	35	37	38.75	41.75	43.75	45.5	46.75	49	50.75	52.75
C – Length (cm)	58	58	59	59	59	59	60	60	61	61
in	22.75	22.75	23.25	23.25	23.25	23.25	23.5	23.5	24	24
D – Armhole depth (cm)	17.5	18	18.5	18.5	19	20	20.5	21	22	23
in	7	7	7.5	7.5	7.5	8	8	8.5	8.5	9
E – Sleeve circumf (cm)	31	31.5	33	34	35.5	36	37.5	38.5	39	41.5
in	12.25	12.5	13	13.5	14	14.25	14.75	15.25	15.25	16.25
F – Sleeve seam (cm)	30	30	31	31	31	31	32	32	33	33
in	11.75	11.75	12.25	12.25	12.25	12.25	12.5	12.5	13	13
G – Hem circumf (cm)	97.5	102.5	107	114.5	119	124	127	133	137.5	142.5
in	38.5	40.25	42.25	45	46.75	48.75	50	52.25	54.25	56

The simple, chic silhouette of this classic cardigan provides a perfect palette for all kinds of colour play. Choose a neutral and highlight it with bright bursts of colour, or keep it all within the same tonal palette. Either way, this modern design with contrasting buttonbands and double knit rectangles of colour on the back will catch the eye both coming and going, and keep your interest as you knit.

Rohrspatz & Wollmeise Blend knitted at a slightly denser gauge than usual provides structure, with rich, subtly shifting shades of hue and the soft halo of cashmere. Like all Wollmeise semi-solids, this yarn has a mere hint of variegation – just the way I like it.

TO FIT SIZE
81 (86, 91, 97, 102) [107, 112, 117, 122, 127] cm
32 (34, 36, 38, 40) [42, 44, 46, 48, 50] inches

ROUND NECK

FIT
Tailored shoulders and waist shaping, no ease

YARN
Rohrspatz & Wollmeise Blend (Fingering, 70% merino, 20%
cashmere, 10% Nylon, 499 m (546 yds) per 150 g)
MC Schwarz (black) x 3 (3, 3, 4, 4) [4, 4, 5, 5, 5] skeins
Small amounts of contrast yarns:
CC1 Q.E.D (grey), **CC2** Grünfink (green)

APPROX YARDAGE
1350 (1400, 1500, 1550, 1650) [1750, 1800, 2000, 2150, 2200] m
1500 (1550, 1600, 1700, 1800) [1900, 2000, 2200, 2350, 2400] yds
Small amounts of contrast colours **CC1** (Q.E.D/grey) and **CC2**
(Grünfink/green) – 100 m / 110 yds

ALTERNATIVE YARN SUGGESTIONS
Malabrigo Sock, Nature's Luxury La Parisienne, Rohrspatz &
Wollmeise Pure

NEEDLES & NOTIONS
3 mm (US 2.5) circular needle, 80 – 100 cm (32 – 40")
or size to obtain gauge
2.5 mm (US 1.5) circular needle, 60 – 100 cm (24 – 40")
Buttons: 9 (9, 9, 9, 9) [9, 9, 10, 10, 10] + 1 if adding bust darts
Stitch holders; stitch markers

BLOCKED GAUGE
26 sts x 36 rows on 3 mm (US 2.5) needle = 10 cm / 4"

SAMPLE SIZE
Sample in size 40 with Middling bust darts weighs 435 g / 15.5 oz,
knitted with just under 3 skeins

STEP 1: CAST ON & RIGHT BACK SHOULDER

WIth **MC**, using longtail cast on and 3 mm (US 2.5) needle, cast on 86 (88, 94, 98, 100) [104, 106, 108, 110, 112] sts.
Setup Row (WS): P17 (18, 19, 20, 21) [22, 23, 24, 25, 26], turn.
R1 (RS): Sl1^, pm, k11 (12, 13, 14, 14) [15, 16, 17, 17, 18], turn.
R2 (WS): Sl1^, purl to m, rm, p1^, p1, turn.
R3: Sl1^, pm, k8 (8, 9, 10, 10) [10, 11, 12, 12, 12], turn.
R4: Sl1^, purl to m, rm, p1^, p1, turn.
R5: Sl1^, pm, k5 (5, 5, 6, 6) [6, 6, 7, 7, 7], turn.
R6: Sl1^, purl to m, rm, p1^, p1, turn.
R7: Sl1^, pm, knit to last 2 sts (working any sl1^ as k1^), sl1wyb, k1.
R8: Purl to m, rm, p1^, p1, turn.
R9: Sl1^, pm, knit to last 2 sts, sl1wyb, k1.
R10: Purl to m, rm, p1^, purl to end.

86 (88, 94, 98, 100) [104, 106, 108, 110, 112] Back sts

STEP 2: LEFT BACK SHOULDER

R1 (RS): K1, sl1wyb, k15 (16, 17, 18, 19) [20, 21, 22, 23, 24], turn.
R2 (WS): Sl1^, pm, p11 (12, 13, 14, 14) [15, 16, 17, 17, 18], turn.
R3: Sl1^, knit to m, rm, k1^, k1, turn.
R4: Sl1^, pm, p8 (8, 9, 10, 10) [10, 11, 12, 12, 12], turn.
R5: Sl1^, knit to m, rm, k1^, k1, turn.
R6: Sl1^, pm, p5 (5, 5, 6, 6) [6, 6, 7, 7, 7], turn.
R7: Sl1^, knit to m, rm, k1^, k1, turn.
R8: Sl1^, pm, purl to end (working any sl1^ as p1^).
R9: K1, sl1wyb, knit to m, rm, k1^, k1, turn.
R10: Sl1^, pm, purl to end.

STEP 3: WORKING ACROSS BACK

R1 (RS): K1, sl1wyb, knit to m, rm, k1^, knit to last 2 sts, sl1wyb, k1.
86 (88, 94, 98, 100) [104, 106, 108, 110, 112] Back sts
R2 (WS): Purl.
R3: K1, sl1wyb, knit to last 2 sts, sl1wyb, k1.
R4: Purl.
Work **Rows 3 & 4** again x 1 (1, 1, 2, 2) [2, 2, 3, 3, 3].
Work **Row 3** once more.
Final Row (WS): Purl to last 2 sts, p2tog, pm, p&p7 (7, 7, 8, 8) [8, 8, 9, 9, 9] sts along edge (for first half of Left Sleeve Cap).

7 (7, 7, 8, 8,) [8, 8, 9. 9, 9] Left Cap sts
85 (87, 93, 97, 99) [103, 105, 107, 109, 111] Back sts

Slide stitches off needle tips to rest on the cable.
Set these stitches aside, continue to next step without turning.

STEP 4: LEFT FRONT SHOULDER

After the shoulder sts have been picked up, add sts for the Buttonband (BB) joining CC1 and using a provisional cast on. After a few rows, these sts can be placed on a holder or safety pin.

Before winding on stitches, wind off but don't cut approx 35g (15 m/ 20 yds) for Left Front Buttonband. Work with this mini-ball, leaving the main CC1 ball at the join.

When switching between MC and CC1, always pick up the new yarn from below and around old yarn.

Note: *For Buttonbands worked with MC, see Buttonband Tutorial.*

Setup Row (WS): Loop cable, p&p16 (17, 18, 19, 20) [21, 22, 23, 24, 25] sts (for Left Front Shoulder) in the cast on of Left Back Shoulder, *and remember to pick up second st in line with faux seam.* Place spare circular parallel to working needle and using Winding Provisional Cast On with **CC1**, wind on 8 sts for BB, pull on spare circular to allow provisional sts to rest on its cable.
16 (17, 18, 19, 20) [21, 22, 23, 24, 25] Left Front sts + 8 BB sts
R1 (RS): With CC1, ksk, k1, ksk, p1, pm, with MC, k12 (12, 13, 14, 15) [15, 16, 17, 18, 18], turn.
This sets the 8 CC1 BB sts for RS rows.
Rows 2, 4, 6 (WS): With MC, sl1^, purl to m, sm, with CC1, [k1, sl1wyf] x 4.
This sets the 8 CC1 BB sts for WS rows.
R3: BB, sm, k8 (8, 8, 9, 10) [10, 10, 11, 12, 12], turn.
R5: BB, sm, k4 (4, 4, 4, 5) [5, 5, 5, 6, 6], turn.
R7: BB, sm, knit to 2 sts before loop (working any sl1^ as k1^), sl1wyb, k1, turn.
R8: Purl to m, sm, BB.
R9: BB, sm, knit to 2 sts before loop, sl1wyb, k1, turn.

R10: Purl to m, sm, BB.

Work **Rows 9 & 10** again x 4 (4, 4, 5, 5) [5, 5, 6, 6, 6].

Final Row (RS): BB, sm, knit to 2 sts before loop, ssk, pm, p&k7 (7, 7, 8, 8) [8, 8, 9, 9, 9] sts (for second half of Left Sleeve Cap), knit to m, sm, sl1wyb, knit to last 2 sts, ssk, pm, p&k7 (7, 7, 8, 8) [8, 8, 9, 9, 9] sts (for first half of Right Sleeve Cap).

14 (14, 14, 16, 16) [16, 16, 18, 18, 18] Left Cap sts
7 (7, 7, 8, 8) [8, 8, 9, 9, 9] Right Cap sts
15 (16, 17, 18, 19) [20, 21, 22, 23, 24] Left Front sts + 8 BB sts
84 (86, 92, 96, 98) [102, 104, 106, 108, 110] Back sts

Slide stitches off needle tips to rest on the cable.
Set these stitches aside.

WORKING BUTTONBAND AROUND BACK NECK

Slide provisional buttonband/collar (BB) sts to 3 mm (US 2.5) needle. With attached **CC1**, work BB and attach it along the neck as follows:

R1 (RS): Slide off and discard slipknot, k2tog, sl1wyf, k2, ksk. *7 sts*
R2 (WS): Sl1wyf, (k1, sl1wyf) x 3.
R3: P&k1 st in neck edge, place on LN, k2tog, sl1wyf, k2, ksk.
Continue to work **Rows 2 & 3** while picking up sts along Back Neck up to the Right Shoulder until all but one st is picked up. Pick up approx 3 sts for every 4, and end with a **Row 2** (WS).

STEP 5: RIGHT FRONT SHOULDER

Continue at Right Shoulder where you stopped in Step 4.

R1 (RS): Loop cable, p&k16 (17, 18, 19, 20) [21, 22, 23, 24, 25] sts (for Right Front Shoulder) in the cast on of Right Back Shoulder, *and remember to pick up second st in line with faux seam*, pm (before BB), with **CC1**, p&k1, ksk, k1, ksk.
16 (17, 18, 19, 20) [21, 22, 23, 24, 25] Right Front sts + 8 BB sts
R2 (WS): With **CC1**, (sl1wyf, k1) x 4, sm, with **MC**, p12 (12, 13, 14, 15) [15, 16, 17, 18, 18], turn.
This sets the 8 CC1 BB sts for WS rows.
Rows 3, 5, 7: Sl1^, knit to m, sm, with **CC1**, p1, ksk, k1, ksk.
This sets the 8 CC1 BB sts for RS rows.
R4: BB, sm, p8 (8, 8, 9, 10) [10, 10, 11, 12, 12], turn.
R6: BB, sm, p4 (4, 4, 4, 5) [5, 5, 5, 6, 6], turn.
R8: BB, sm, purl to loop (working any sl1^ as p1^), turn.
R9: K1, sl1wyb, knit to m, sm, BB.
R10: BB, sm, purl to loop, turn.
Work **Rows 9 & 10** again x 4 (4, 4, 5, 5) [5, 5, 6, 6, 6].
Work **Row 9** once more.
Final Row (WS): BB, sm, purl to 2 sts before loop, p2tog, pm, p&p7 (7, 7, 8, 8) [8, 9, 9, 9] sts (for second half of Right Sleeve Cap), purl to last m, sm, BB.

BOX A

REFER TO BOX A FOR ROW INSTRUCTIONS (see Step 6)

sM1 = sleeve increase   nM1 = neck increase

RS ROW

R1: With **CC1**, ksk, k1, ksk, p1, sm, with **MC**, k2, nM1R, (knit to 1 st before m, sl1wyb, sm, sM1L, knit to m, sM1R, sm, sl1wyb) twice, knit to 2 sts before m, nM1L, k2, sm, with **CC1**, p1, ksk, k1, ksk.
This sets the Left & Right CC1 BB sts for RS rows.

WS ROWS

R2: With **CC1**, (sl1wyf, k1) x 4, sm, with **MC**, purl to BB, sm, with **CC1**, (k1, sl1wyf) x 4.
This sets the Right & Left CC1 BB sts for WS rows.

R4: BB, sm, p2, nM1Lp, purl to 2 sts before m, nM1Rp, p2, sm, BB.

14 (14, 14, 16, 16) [16, 16, 18, 18, 18] sts for each Sleeve Cap
15 (16, 17, 18, 19) [20, 21, 22, 23, 24] sts + 8 BB sts for each Front
84 (86, 92, 96, 98) [102, 104, 106, 108, 110] Back sts

STEP 6: SLEEVE CAPS & BODY

You will now increase for the sleeve and neck (and later also body) simultaneously. Continue to work Buttonband (BB) with **CC1** as set. (See Helpful Table for an overview of all increases.)

DOUBLE-KNITTED DETAIL AT CENTRE BACK

If desired, at 18 cm / 7" from Shoulder (approx just before the next buttonhole) place a double knitted motif over 16 stitches and 11 rows at Centre Back. See Tutorial section.

REFER TO **BOX A** FOR ROW INSTRUCTIONS

Work **Rows 1 & 2** x 10 (10, 10, 9, 9) [10, 11, 11, 11, 13].
34 (34, 34, 34, 34) [36, 38, 40, 40, 44] Sleeve sts
25 (26, 27, 27, 28) [30, 32, 33, 34, 37] sts + 8 BB sts for each Front

Work **Rows 1 & 4** x 2 (2, 2, 3, 3) [3, 3, 3, 3, 2].
38 (38, 38, 40, 40) [42, 44, 46, 46, 48] Sleeve sts
29 (30, 31, 33, 34) [36, 38, 39, 40, 41] sts + 8 BB sts for each Front

Work **Row 1**.
40 (40, 40, 42, 42) [44, 46, 48, 48, 50] Sleeve sts
30 (31, 32, 34, 35) [37, 39, 40, 41, 42] sts + 8 BB sts for each Front

STEP 7: BUTTONBANDS & CENTRE FRONT CAST ONS

Setup Row (WS): BB, sm, p2, nM1Lp, purl to 2 sts before BB, nM1Rp, p2, sm, BB.

31 (32, 33, 35, 36) [38, 40, 41, 42, 43] sts + 8 BB sts for each Front

LEFT FRONT BUTTONBAND

Work only the 8 **CC1** BB sts of the Left Front Buttonband:

R1 (RS): Ksk, k1, ksk, sl1wyf.
R2 (WS): (K1, sl1wyf) x 4.
Work **Rows 1 & 2** again x 13 (13, 15, 15, 15) [15, 14, 14, 14, 14].
Final Row (RS): Ssk, k1, pso to bind off, bind off 3 sts kwise, cut **CC1**.

With working **MC** at edge of Front and going *from left to right*, p&k9 (9, 11, 11, 11) [11, 10, 10, 10, 10] sts onto LN along the slipped stitch edge of the Buttonband, pm, join **CC2**, p&k 5 sts, proceed to the 3 remaining BB sts on N2, with N2 and **CC2**, ssk the final 2 sts, pass the final **CC1**-stitch over to bind off, place resulting **CC2**-st on N1 RN, with **CC2**, k5, sm, with **MC**, *knit to 1 st before m, sl1wyb, sm, **sM1L**, knit to m, **sM1R**, sm, sl1wyb*, work from * to * once more, knit to m, sm, with **CC1**, p1, ksk, k1, ksk.

42 (42, 42, 44, 44) [46, 48, 50, 50, 52] Sleeve sts
40 (41, 44, 46, 47) [49, 50, 51, 52, 53] Left Front sts + 6 BB sts
31 (32, 33, 35, 36) [38, 40, 41, 42, 43] Right Front sts + 8 BB sts

RIGHT FRONT BUTTONBAND

Set body sts aside and work only the 8 **CC1** BB sts of the Right Front.
Mirror the Left Front but make a buttonhole 5 rows before binding off as follows.

Setup Row (WS): [Sl1wyf, k1] x 4.
R1 (RS): Sl1wyf, ksk, k1, ksk.
R2 (WS): [Sl1wyf, k1] x 4.
Work Rows 1 & 2 again x 10 (10, 12, 12, 12) [12, 11, 11, 11, 11].
Make buttonhole over next 3 rows:

BR1 (RS): Sl1wyf, k1, bind off 2 sts, ksk.
BR2 (WS): Sks, k1, *turn work over so RS is facing, borrow last st for cast on loop,* crochet cast on 3 sts, *replace loop onto LN (make a final chain st but not around the needle), turn work over so WS is facing*, sl1wyf, k1.
BR3: Sl1wyf, sl1 kwise, pick up a twisted loop in bar before cast on, pass 2 sts back to LN (twisted loop and sl st), ssk, sl1wyf, k2, k2tog, sl1wyf, k1.
Work **Row 2** once more.
Work **Row 1** once more.

BOX B

sM1 = sleeve increase   bM1 = body increase

RS ROWS

R1: With CC2, k1, sl1wyf, k3, sl1wyf, k1, p1, sm, with MC, (knit to 1 st before m, sl1wyb, sm, sM1L, knit to m, sM1R, sm, sl1wyb) twice, knit to m, sm, with CC1, p1, k1, sl1wyf, k3, sl1wyf, k1.
This sets the Left & Right BB sts for RS rows.

R3: BB, sm, (knit to 1 st before m, **bM1L**, sl1wyb, sm, sM1L, knit to m, sM1R, sm, sl1wyb, **bM1R**) twice, knit to m, sm, BB.

WS ROWS

R2: With CC1, (sl1wyf, k1) x 4, sm, purl to m, sm, with CC2, (k1, sl1wyf) x 4.
This sets the Right and Left BB sts for WS rows.

R4: BB, sm, (purl to m, sm, sM1Rp, purl to m, sM1Lp, sm) twice, purl to m, sm, BB.

R6: BB, sm, (purl to 1 st1 before m, **bM1Rp**, p1, sm, purl to m, sm, p1, **bM1Rp**) twice, purl to m, sm, BB.

BUTTONHOLE ROWS

BR1 (RS): BB, sm, (knit to 1 st before m, **bM1L**, sl1wyb, sm, sM1L, knit to m, sM1R, sm, sl1wyb, **bM1R**) twice, knit to m, sm, p1, k1, bind off 2 sts, k1, sl1wyf, k1.

BR2 (WS): (Sl1wyf, k1) twice, (turn work over so RS is facing) borrow last st for cast on loop, crochet cast on 3 sts, replace loop onto LN, turn work over so WS is facing, sl1wyf, k1, sm, purl to m, sm, BB.

BR3: BB, sm, (knit to 1 st before m, **bM1L**, sl1wyb, sm, sM1L, knit to m, sM1R, sm, sl1wyb, **bM1R**) twice, knit to m, sm, p1, sl1 kwise, pick up a twisted loop in bar before cast on, pass 2 sts back to LN (twisted loop and sl st), ssk, sl1wyf, k2, k2tog, sl1wyf, k1.

Next Row (WS): P2tog, p1, pso to bind off, bind off 2 sts pwise, p2togtbl, pso to bind off, bind off final BB st pwise (*1 st remains on needle*), p&p5 sts in the slipped-stitch edge of the Buttonband. *6 BB sts*

Turn work over so RS is facing, set the BB sts aside for now

Next Row (RS): With working **MC** at Right Front, p&k9 (9, 11, 11, 11) [11, 10, 10, 10, 10] sts in the slipped-stitch edge of BB, pm, with **CC1**, M1L, ksk, k2, M1L, k1. *8 BB sts*

40 (41, 44, 46, 47) [49, 50, 51, 52, 53] Left Front sts + 6 BB sts
40 (41, 44, 46, 47) [49, 50, 51, 52, 53] Right Front sts + 8 BB sts

WORKING ACROSS ALL STITCHES

Next Row (WS): With **CC1**, (sl1wyf, k1) x 4, sm, with **MC**, purl to to BB, sm, with **CC2**, k1, sl1wyf, M1L, sks, M1L, sl1wyf.
40 (41, 44, 46, 47) [49, 50, 51, 52, 53] Left Front sts + 8 BB sts
40 (41, 44, 46, 47) [49, 50, 51, 52, 53] Right Front sts + 8 BB sts

STEP 8: SLEEVE & BODY INCREASES

Continue to work sleeve increases, buttonholes, and later also introduce body increases.

REFER TO BOX B FOR ROW INSTRUCTIONS

Work **Rows 1 & 2** x 7 (6, 7, 7, 7) [6, 5, 4, 4, 4].
56 (54, 56, 58, 58) [58, 58, 58, 58, 60] Sleeve sts
Work **Rows 3 & 2** x 0 (1, 0, 0, 0) [1, 2, 3, 3, 3].
56 (56, 56, 58, 58) [60, 62, 64, 64, 66] Sleeve sts
40 (42, 44, 46, 47) [50, 52, 54, 55, 56] Front sts + BB
84 (88, 92, 96, 98) [104, 108, 112, 114, 116] Back sts

Work Buttonhole Rows BR1 – BR3.
60 (60, 60, 62, 62) [64, 66, 68, 68, 70] Sleeve sts
42 (44, 46, 48, 49) [52, 54, 56, 57, 58] Front sts + BB
88 (92, 96, 100, 102) [108, 112, 116, 118, 120] Back sts

Work **Row 2** x 0 (1, 1, 1, 1) [1, 1, 0, 0, 0].

SIZE 32 ONLY
Work **Row 4**. *62 Sleeve sts*

ALL SIZES
Work **Rows 3 & 2** x 0 (0, 1, 2, 0) [0, 1, 0, 0, 0].
62 (60, 62, 66, 62) [64, 68, 68, 68, 70] Sleeve sts
42 (44, 47, 50, 49) [52, 55, 56, 57, 58] Front sts + BB
88 (92, 98, 104, 102) [108, 114, 116, 118, 120] Back sts

SIZES 34, 36 ONLY
Work **Rows 3 & 4**
64, 66 Sleeve sts
45, 48 Front sts
94, 100 Back sts

SIZES 46, 48, 50 ONLY
Work **Row 6**.
57, 58, 59 Front sts
118, 120, 122 Back sts

ALL SIZES
Work **Rows 3 & 6** x 0 (0, 0, 0, 2) [2, 2, 4, 5].
62 (64, 66, 66, 66) [68, 72, 72, 76, 80] Sleeve sts
42 (45, 48, 50, 53) [56, 59, 61, 66, 69] Front sts + BB
88 (94, 100, 104, 110) [116, 122, 126, 136, 142] Back sts

Work **Rows 3 & 2**.
64 (66, 68, 68, 68) [70, 74, 74, 78, 82] Sleeve sts
43 (46, 49, 51, 54) [57, 60, 62, 67, 70] Front sts + BB
90 (96, 102, 106, 112) [118, 124, 128, 138, 144] Back sts

STEP 9: SEPARATING SLEEVES & BODY

Separation R1 (RS): BB, sm, *knit to 2 sts before m, pm, k2, rm, place all sts to next m on holder, (= sleeve sts) rm, *(turn work over so WS is facing)* borrow last st for cast on loop, crochet cast on 10 (10, 10, 12, 13) [13, 13, 14, 14, 14] sts, pm, cast on 6 (6, 6, 8, 9) [9, 9, 10, 10, 10] sts, *replace loop onto LN (make a final chain st but not around the needle), turn work over so RS is facing*, work from * to * once more, knit to m, sm, BB.

BOX C

BASIC REPEAT & WAIST SHAPING

R1 (RS): BB, sm, knit to BB, sm, BB.

R2 (WS): BB, (purl to m, sm, k1) twice, purl to BB, sm, BB.

Decrease Row (RS): BB, sm, (knit to 3 sts before m, ssk, k1, sm, k2tog) twice, knit to BB, sm, BB.

Increase Row (RS): BB, sm, (knit to 1 st before m, M1R, k1, sm, M1L) twice, knit to BB, sm, BB.

BUTTONHOLE ROWS

BR1 (RS): BB, sm, knit to BB, sm, p1, k1, bind off 2 sts, k1, sl1wyf, k1.

BR2 (WS): Sl1wyf, k1, sl1wyf, k1, (turn work over so RS is facing) borrow last st for cast on loop, crochet cast on 3 sts, replace loop onto LN, turn work over so WS is facing, sl1wyf, k1, sm, (purl to m, sm, k1) twice, purl to BB, sm, BB.

BR3: BB, sm, knit to BB, sm, p1, sl1 kwise, pick up a twisted loop in bar before cast on, pass 2 sts back to LN (twisted loop and sl st), ssk, sl1wyf, k2, k2tog, sl1wyf, k1.

---

52 (55, 58, 62, 66) [69, 72, 75, 80, 83] Left Front sts + BB
50 (53, 56, 60, 64) [67, 70, 73, 78, 81] Right Front sts + BB
106 (112, 118, 126, 134) [140, 146, 152, 162, 168] Back sts

Separation R2 (WS): BB, sm, *purl to 1 st before cast on, sl1 kwise, make twisted loop in cast on bar and place on LN, sl1 to LN, p2tog (loop and sl st), purl to m, sm, k1, purl to 2 sts before m, p2togtbl, rm*, work from * to * once more, purl to m, sm, BB.

51 (54, 57, 61, 65) [68, 71, 74, 79, 82] Left Front sts + BB
50 (53, 56, 60, 64) [67, 70, 73, 78, 81] Right Front sts + BB
105 (111, 117, 125, 133) [139, 145, 151, 161, 167] Back sts

STEP 10: BODY WITH BUTTONHOLES

Note: *A garter st at each side creates a faux side seam (on WS: knit the st after the side marker). This stitch is **not** included in the counts that follow.*

50 (53, 56, 60, 64) [67, 70, 73, 78, 81] Left Front sts + BB
50 (53, 56, 60, 64) [67, 70, 73, 78, 81] Right Front sts + BB
104 (110, 116, 124, 132) [138, 144, 150, 160, 166] Back sts

AT THE SAME TIME
Please read through the entire step before proceeding, as a few things happen at the same time or overlap.

- Optional Bust Darts
- Waist Shaping
- Buttonholes

REFER TO **BOX C** FOR ROW INSTRUCTIONS
Work **Rows 1 & 2** x 6 (5, 4, 4, 4) [4, 3, 4, 2, 1].

AT THE SAME TIME BUTTONHOLES
Work Buttonhole Rows 1 – 3.
You have worked 3 buttonholes.

BOX D

Place your darts at approx 5 (6, 10, 10) cm / 2 (2.25, 4, 4)" from underarm or where desired:

For placement of darts, see Hints & Tips.

Note that an additional buttonhole and button may be required if adding darts.

Smallish (Middling, Busty, Wowza!)

Worked over 12 (18, 24, 28) rows, adds approx 3.5 (5, 6.5, 8) cm / 1.5 (2, 2.5, 3.25)".

Left Front

R1 (RS): BB, sm, knit to 27 (34, 37, 40) sts before m, turn.
R2 (WS): Sl1^, pm, purl to BB, sm, BB.
R3 (RS): BB, sm, knit to m, rm, k1^, k5 (4, 3, 3), turn.
R4: Sl1^, pm, purl to BB, sm, BB.
Work **Rows 3 & 4** again x 4 (7, 10, 12).
Next Row (RS): BB, sm, knit to m, rm, k1^, sm, knit across back to BB, sm, BB (and note buttonhole sequence).

Right Front

R2 (WS): BB, sm, purl to 28 (35, 38, 41) sts before m, turn.
R3 (RS): Sl1^, pm, knit to BB, sm, BB.
R4: BB, sm, purl to m, rm, p1^, p5 (4, 3, 3), turn.
Work **Rows 3 & 4** again x 4 (7, 10, 12).
Work **Row 3** once more.
Next Row (WS): BB, sm, purl to m, rm, p1^, purl to m, sm, k1, purl across back to next side m, sm, k1, purl to BB, sm, BB.

Resume working back and forth as before darts, and with waist shaping, and remember to make buttonholes.

Continue with Basic Repeat **Rows 1 & 2** and make buttonholes, starting on every 20th row (approx every 5.5 cm / 2.25").

AT THE SAME TIME OPTIONAL BUST DARTS
Optional Bust Darts (see BOX D) may be placed at 5 cm / 2" or a bit lower.
   Note: *If you are trying to stretch your skeins, this is a good place to set the body aside and work the sleeves before finishing the body.*

AT THE SAME TIME WAIST SHAPING
Work **Rows 1 & 2** to 5 cm / 2" from underarm.
Work **Decrease Row 3 & Row 2.**
49 (52, 55, 59, 63) [66, 69, 72, 77, 80] Front sts + BB
102 (108, 114, 122, 130) [136, 142, 148, 158, 164] Back sts

Continue to work **Rows 1 & 2** with waist shaping and buttonholes, working **Decrease Row** every 8 (8, 8, 8, 8) [8, 10, 10, 10, 10]th row again x 4.
45 (48, 51, 55, 59) [62, 65, 68, 73, 76] Front sts + BB
94 (100, 106, 114, 122) [128, 134, 140, 150, 156] Back sts

Work **Rows 1 & 2** without decreases for 4 (4, 5, 5, 5) [5, 5, 5, 5, 5] / cm 1.5 (1.5, 2, 2, 2) [2, 2, 2, 2, 2]" – and remember buttonholes.

Work **Increase Row.**
46 (49, 52, 56, 60) [63, 66, 69, 74, 77] Front sts + BB
96 (102, 108, 116, 124) [130, 136, 142, 152, 158] Back sts

OPTIONAL REAR SHAPING
On next **Increase Row** (see below): Make 10 (10, 10, 10, 12) [12, 12, 14, 14, 14] increases (M1L) evenly distributed across Back.
Stitch counts below do not include optional Back increases.

Continue to work **Rows 1 & 2** with waist shaping and buttonholes, working **Increase Row** every 8 (8, 8, 8, 8) [9, 9, 9, 9, 9]th row again x 2.
48 (51, 54, 58, 62) [65, 68, 71, 76, 79] Front sts + BB
100 (106, 112, 120, 128) [134, 140, 146, 156, 162] Back sts

Continue to work **Rows 1 & 2** with waist shaping and buttonholes, working **Increase Row** on next 10th row once, then on next 12th row once.
50 (53, 56, 60, 64) [67, 70, 74, 79, 82] Front sts + BB
104 (110, 116, 124, 132) [138, 144, 152, 162, 168] Back sts

Dusala

WORKING WS ROWS FROM RS
Sl1wyb, p1 backwards (take yarn to front and manoeuvre the yarn so you make a normal p1), then slip the final st wyb.

Work **Rows 1 & 2** as set with increases and buttonholes to 38.5 (38, 37.5, 37.5, 37.5) [37.5, 37, 37.5, 36.5, 35.5] cm /15.25 (15, 14.75, 14.75, 14.75) [14.75, 14.5, 14.75, 14.25, 14]" from underarm or to 2 cm /.75" from desired length.
Consider adding rows as necessary to place final buttonhole directly above the hem.

STEP 11: HEM
Switch to 2.5 mm (US 1.5) needle.
R1 (RS): With CC2, ksk, k2, k2tog, p1, sm, with MC, knit to BB, rm, with CC1, p1, ssk, k2, ksk.
Cut MC, remove side markers.
R2 (WS): With CC1, sks, purl to m, sm, with CC2, k1, p3, sks.
Rows 3, 7, 9: With CC2, ksk, p4, sm, with CC1, purl to last 3 sts, ksk.
Rows 4, 6, 10: With CC1, sks, knit to m, sm, with CC2, k4, sks.
R5: With CC2, ksk, k4, sm, with CC1, knit to last 3 sts, ksk.
R8: With CC1, sks, purl to m, sm, with CC2, k1, p3, sks.

ATTACHED BIND OFF
Borrow final CC2 stitch to crochet cast on 3 sts, make 1 chain st (not around needle), place on LN.
R1 (RS): With CC2, sl1wyb, sl1wyf, ssk (1 edge st with 1 BB st).
R2 (WS): Sks.
R3: K1, sl1wyf, ssk.
R4: Sks.

Tip: Rows 2 & 4 can be worked backwards (from left to right) – this obviates the need to turn work over between rows (see BOX above).

With CC2, work **Rows 3 & 4** again x 2.
With CC1, work **Rows 3 & 4** along the hem until 1 st remains.
Final Row (RS): (Ssk) x 2, pso to bind off final st

STEP 12: SLEEVES
Place 64 (66, 68, 68, 68) [70, 74, 74, 78, 82] Sleeve sts from holder back on larger (3 mm / US 2.5) needle. Attach yarn at right side of gap, p&k7 (7, 7, 9, 10) [10, 10, 11, 11, 11] sts along the first half of the underarm cast on, pm, p&k8 (8, 8, 10, 11) [11, 11, 12, 12, 12] sts more along second half of underarm, knit to m.
79 (81, 83, 87, 89) [91, 95, 97, 101, 105] sts

REFER TO BOX E FOR ROUND INSTRUCTIONS
Work **Rnd 1** to 5 cm / 2" from underarm.

SLEEVE DECREASES
Work **Decrease Rnd**.
77 (79, 81, 85, 87) [89, 93, 95, 99, 103] sts

Continue with **Rnd 1**, working a **Decrease Rnd** every 19 (18, 16, 13, 12) [12, 11, 10, 10, 9]th round again x 7 (8, 9, 11, 12) [12, 13, 14, 14, 16].
63 (63, 63, 63, 63) [65, 67, 67, 71, 71] sts

Work to 43 (43, 44, 44, 45) [45, 45, 45, 45, 45] cm / 17 (17, 17.25, 17.25, 17.75) [17.75, 17.75, 17.75, 17.75, 17.75]" from underarm or to 2 cm /.75" from desired length.
Cut MC.

CUFF
Switch to smaller (2.5 mm / US 1.5) needle, attach CC2.
Rnd 1: Knit.
Rnd 2: Purl.
Rnd 3: Purl.
Work **Rnds 1 – 3** again x 2.

ATTACHED BIND OFF
Work as for Hem but substitute Winding Cast On:
Slip final st back to LN, wind on 3 sts.
Work **Rows 3 & 4** as for Hem around the cuff until all sts are bound off, close the bind off by grafting (or sewing).

FINISH
Weave in loose ends. Soak and block lightly to measurements. Sew on some nice buttons.

BOX E

SLEEVE ROUNDS
Rnd 1: Sm, g1, knit to m.
Decrease Rnd: Sm, g1, k2tog, knit to 2 sts before m, ssk.

Åsa Tricosa Ziggurats :: 16 elegantly seamless knits
34

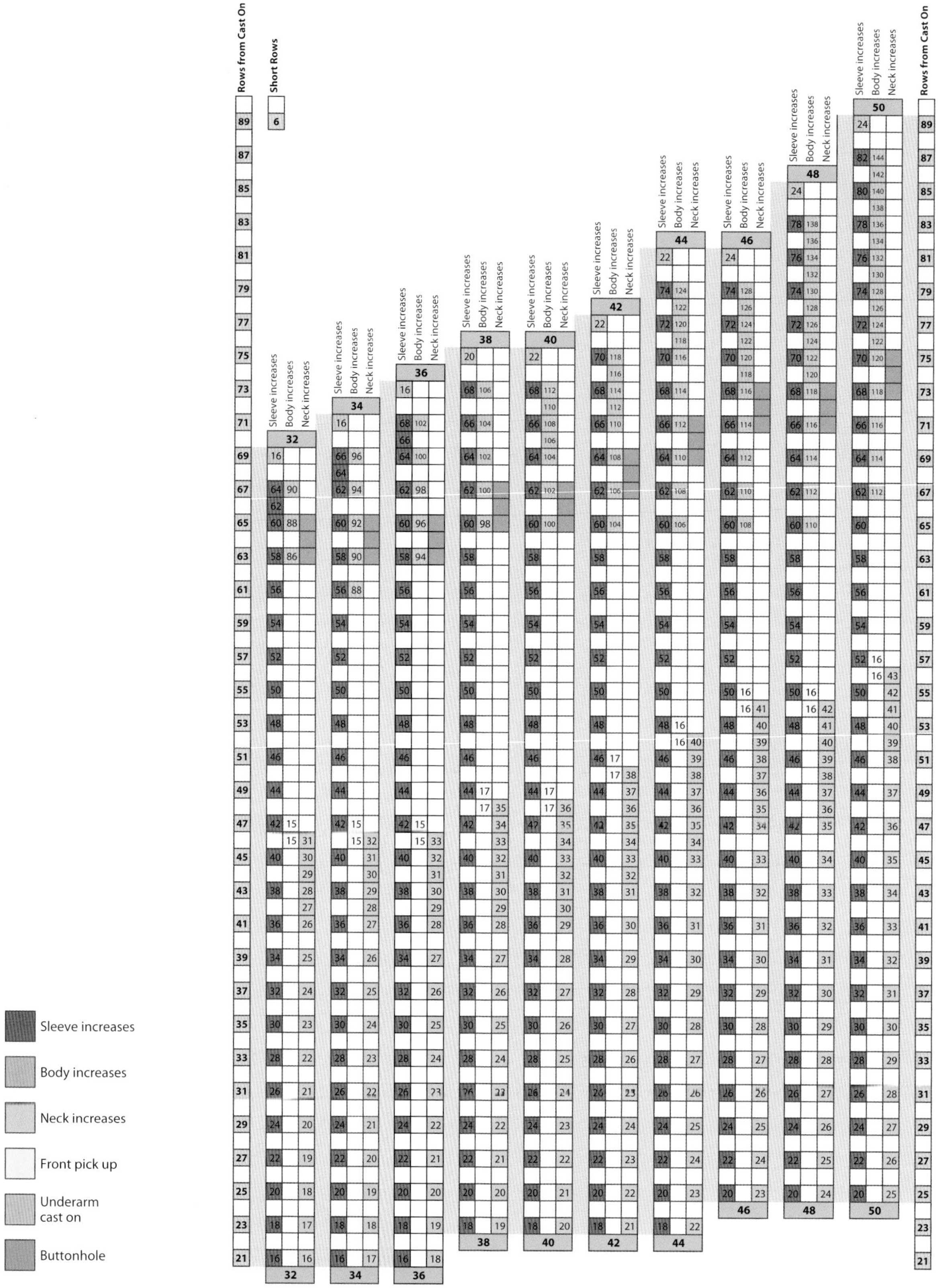

Dusala

Legend:

- Sleeve increases
- Body increases
- Neck increases
- Front pick up
- Underarm cast on
- Buttonhole

Short Rows: 6

(Chart of "Rows from Cast On" numbered 21 through 89 on both left and right margins, with columns of increase values grouped under size labels 32, 34, 36, 38, 40, 42, 44, 46, 48, 50, each with "Sleeve increases", "Body increases", and "Neck increases" subcolumns.)

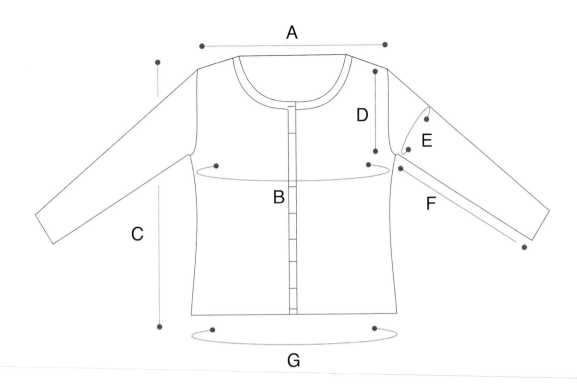

DUSALA GARMENT MEASUREMENTS

	32	34	36	38	40	42	44	46	48	50
A – Shoulder width (cm)	32.5	33	35.5	37	37.5	39	40	41	41.5	42.5
in	12.75	13	14	14.5	14.75	15.25	15.75	16.25	16.25	16.75
B – Bust (cm)	81	85.5	90	96	102.5	107	111.5	116	124	128.5
in	32	33.75	35.5	37.75	40.25	42.25	44	45.75	48.75	50.5
C – Length (cm)	59.5	59.5	59.5	60	60	60.5	61	61.5	61.5	62.5
in	23.5	23.5	23.5	23.5	23.5	23.75	24	24.25	24.25	24.5
D – Armhole depth (cm)	17	17.5	18	19	19	19.5	20.5	20.5	21.5	23
in	6.75	7	7	7.5	7.5	7.75	8	8	8.5	9
E – Sleeve circumf (cm)	29.5	30.5	31	32.5	33.5	34	36	36.5	38	39.5
in	11.5	12	12.25	12.75	13.25	13.5	14.25	14.25	15	15.5
F – Sleeve seam (cm)	45	45	46	46	47	47	47	47	47	47
in	17.75	17.75	18	18	18.5	18.5	18.5	18.5	18.5	18.5
G – Hem circumf (cm)	81.5	86	91	97	103	107.5	112.5	118.5	126	131
in	32	33.75	35.75	38.25	40.5	42.25	44.25	46.75	49.5	51.5
H – Hem with extra sts (cm)	85.5	90	94.5	101	107.5	112.5	117	124	131.5	136
in	33.75	35.5	37.25	39.75	42.25	44.25	46	48.75	51.75	53.5

The ultimate comfortable tunic, Vaudeville winds its way back and forth in the usual Ziggurat manner, and ends with generous side slits and a peekaboo lined hem. Play with your leftovers to create hidden gems at cuff and hem linings.

Vaudeville is, unusually for me, another V-neck. For some unspecified reason I have decided that V-necks do not suit me. Nevertheless, even as a selfish knitter who both designs and knits mostly for herself, I wanted to offer at least one or two V-necks to my knitting friends. Discovery: this V-neck really suits me. Who knew? Maybe it will suit you, too!

The yarn is another favourite from The Uncommon Thread, a single ply merino in a warm, subtly and beautifully shifting grey. The luminous contrast colours are Ripples Crafts Yarns single ply merino, which has such lustre I could swear there is some silk in them. The model is also a favourite.

Vaudeville

TO FIT SIZE
81 (86, 91, 97, 102) [107, 112, 117, 122, 127] cm
32 (34, 36, 38, 40) [42, 44, 46, 48, 50] inches

DEEP V-NECK

FIT
Casual shoulders, relaxed A-line(ish) shaping, approx
14 cm / 5.5" ease

YARN
The Uncommon Thread Everyday Singles (Fingering/single ply,
100% merino, 366 m (400 yds) per 100 g)
MC Olive Leaf x 5 (5, 5, 5, 6) [6, 6, 6, 6, 7] skeins
CC Ripples Crafts Burras Mini Skein (Fingering weight, 1ply, 100%
Merino, 73 m / 20g); A Teal Tale x 1 skein; Slice of Lime x 1 skein,
Damson x 1 skein

APPROX YARDAGE
1500 (1550, 1650, 1800, 1850) [1950, 2000, 2150, 2200, 2300] m
1650 (1700, 1800, 1950, 2050) [2150, 2200, 2350, 2400, 2550] yds

ALTERNATIVE YARN SUGGESTIONS
Outlaw Yarn Bohemia Sport, Ripples Crafts Suilven, Rohrspatz &
Wollmeise Blend

NEEDLES & NOTIONS
3 mm (US 2.5) circular needle, 80 – 100 cm (32 – 40")
or size to obtain gauge
Two 2.5 mm (US 1.5) circular needles, 60 – 100 cm (24 – 40")
Cable or double pointed needles
Stitch holders; stitch markers

BLOCKED GAUGE
27 sts x 38 rows on 3 mm (US 2.5) needle = 10 cm / 4"

SAMPLE SIZE
Sample sweater in size 40 without bust darts weighs 442 g / 15.5 oz

Vaudeville

STEP 1: CAST ON & RIGHT BACK SHOULDER
With **MC**, using longtail cast on and 3 mm (US 2.5) needle, cast on
101 (105, 109, 113, 117) [121, 125, 127, 129, 133] sts.
Setup Row (WS): P22 (23, 25, 27, 29) [29, 30, 31, 31, 32], turn.
R1 (RS): Sl1^, pm, k16 (17, 19, 20, 22) [22, 23, 23, 23, 24], turn.
Rows 2, 4, 6, 8 (WS): Sl1^, purl to m, rm, p1^, p1, turn.
R3: Sl1^, pm, k12 (13, 15, 15, 17) [17, 18, 18, 18, 18], turn.
R5: Sl1^, pm, k9 (9, 11, 11, 12) [12, 13, 13, 13, 13], turn.
R7: Sl1^, pm, k6 (6, 7, 7, 7) [7, 8, 8, 8, 8], turn.
R9: Sl1^, pm, knit to last 2 sts (working any sl1^ as k1^), sl1wyb, k1.
Final Row (WS): Purl to m, rm, p1^, purl to end.

101 (105, 109, 113, 117) [121, 125, 127, 129, 133] Back sts

STEP 2: LEFT BACK SHOULDER
R1 (RS): K1, sl1wyb, k20 (21, 23, 25, 27) [27, 28, 29, 29, 30], turn.
R2 (WS): Sl1^, pm, p16 (17, 19, 20, 22) [22, 23, 23, 23, 24] turn.
Rows 3, 5, 7, 9 (RS): Sl1^, knit to m, rm, k1^, k1, turn.
R4: Sl1^, pm, p12 (13, 15, 15, 17) [17, 18, 18, 18, 18], turn.
R6: Sl1^, pm, p9 (9, 11, 11, 12) [12, 13, 13, 13, 13], turn.
R8: Sl1^, pm, p6 (6, 7, 7, 7) [7, 8, 8, 8, 8], turn.
Final Row (WS): Sl1^, pm, purl to end (working any sl1^ as p1^).

STEP 3: WORKING ACROSS BACK
R1 (RS): K1, sl1wyb, knit to m, rm, k1^, knit to last 2 sts, sl1wyb, k1.
101 (105, 109, 113, 117) [121, 125, 127, 129, 133] Back sts
R2 (WS): Purl.
R3: K1, sl1wyb, knit to last 2 sts, sl1wyb, k1.
R4: Purl.
Work **Rows 3 & 4** again x 5 (5, 5, 7, 7) [7, 9, 9, 9, 9].
Work **Row 3** once more.
Final Row (WS): Purl to last 2 sts, p2tog, pm, p&p13 (13, 13, 16, 16)
[16, 18, 18, 18, 18] sts along edge (for first half of Left Sleeve Cap).

13 (13, 13, 16, 16) [16, 18, 18, 18, 18] Left Cap sts
100 (104, 108, 112, 116) [120, 124, 126, 128, 132] Back sts

Slide stitches off needle tips to rest on the cable.
Set these stitches aside, continue to next step without turning.

STEP 4: LEFT FRONT SHOULDER
*After the shoulder stitches have been picked up, add sts for the Neck
Band (NB). After a few rows, the provisional sts can be placed on a
holder or safety pin. For shoulder pick up – the shoulder sts are picked
up so that the cast on chain is exposed on Right Side (see photo for
Chatoyant Collar).*
Refer to Buttonband Tutorial for Neck Band guidance.
Setup Row (WS): Loop cable, p&p21 (22, 24, 26, 28) [28, 29, 30, 30,
31] sts (for Left Front Shoulder) in the cast on of Left Back Shoulder,
and remember to pick up second stitch in line with faux seam. Place
spare circular parallel to working needle and using Winding
Provisional Cast On and working yarn, wind on 6 sts for NB, pull on
spare circular to allow provisional sts to rest on its cable.
21 (22, 24, 26, 28) [28, 29, 30, 30, 31] Left Front sts + 6 NB sts
R1 (RS): Ksk, k2, p1, pm, k16 (17, 19, 20, 22) [22, 23, 24, 24, 24], turn.
R2 (WS): Sl1^, purl to m, sm, k3, sks.
R3: Ksk, k2, p1, sm, k12 (12, 14, 15, 16) [16, 17, 18, 18, 18], turn.
Rows 4, 6, 8: Sl1^, purl to m, sm, k3, sks.
R5: Ksk, k2, p1, sm, k8 (8, 9, 10, 10) [10, 11, 12, 12, 12], turn.
R7: Ksk, k2, p1, sm, k4 (4, 4, 5, 5) [5, 5, 6, 6, 6], turn.
R9: Ksk, k2, p1, sm, knit to 2 sts before loop (working any sl1^ as
k1^), sl1wyb, k1, turn.
R10: Purl to m, sm, k3, sks.
R11: Ksk, k2, p1, sm, knit to 2 sts before loop, sl1wyb, k1, turn.
R12: Purl to m, sm, k3, sks.
Works **Rows 11 & 12** again x 7 (7, 7, 9, 9) [9, 11, 11, 11, 11].
Final Row (RS): Ksk, k2, p1, sm, knit to 2 sts before loop, ssk, pm,
p&k14 (14, 14, 17, 17) [17, 19, 19, 19, 19] sts (for second half of Left
Sleeve Cap), knit to m, sm, sl1wyb, knit to last 2 sts, ssk, pm, p&k13
(13, 13, 16, 16) [16, 18, 18, 18, 18] sts (for first half of Right Sleeve Cap).

27 (27, 27, 33, 33) [33, 37, 37, 37, 37] Left Cap sts
13 (13, 13, 16, 16) [16, 18, 18, 18, 18] Right Cap sts
20 (21, 23, 25, 27) [27, 28, 29, 29, 30] Left Front sts + 6 NB sts
99 (103, 107, 111, 115) [119, 123, 125, 127, 131] Back sts

Slide stitches off needle tips to rest on the cable.
Set these stitches aside, continue to next step without turning.

WORK NECK BAND AROUND BACK NECK TO RIGHT FRONT
Slide provisional Neck Band sts to 3 mm (US 2.5) needle. At outside
edge of Neck Band, join new **MC** to work and attach Neck Band
along the neck as follows (see Buttonband Tutorial).
Setup Row (WS): Sks, k2, sl1wyf, slide off and discard slipknot. *6 sts*
R1 (RS): P&k1, sl1 to LN, k2tog (the picked up st & 1 NB st), k2, ksk.
R2: Sks, k2, sl1wyf.
Continue to work **Rows 1 & 2** while picking up sts along Back Neck
up to the Right Shoulder until all but 1 st is picked up. Pick up
approx 3 sts for every 4.
Cut yarn.

STEP 5: RIGHT FRONT SHOULDER
Continue at Right Shoulder where you stopped in Step 4.
R1 (RS): Loop cable, p&k21 (22, 24, 26, 28) [28, 29, 30, 30, 31] sts
(for Right Front Shoulder) in the cast on of Right Back Shoulder, *and
remember to pick up second stitch in line with faux seam,* pm, k2tog,
M1Lp, k2, ksk.
21 (22, 24, 26, 28) [28, 29, 30, 30, 31] Right Front sts + 6 NB sts
R2 (WS): Sks, k3, pm, p16 (17, 19, 20, 22) [22, 23, 24, 24, 24], turn.
Rows 3, 5, 7, 9: Sl1^, knit to m, sm, p1, k2, ksk.
R4: Sks, k3, sm, p12 (12, 14, 15, 16) [16, 17, 18, 18, 18], turn.
R6: Sks, k3, sm, p8 (8, 9, 10, 10) [10, 11, 12, 12, 12], turn.
R8: Sks, k3, sm, p4 (4, 4, 5, 5) [5, 5, 6, 6, 6], turn.
R10: Sks, k3, sm, purl to loop, working any sl1^ as p1^), turn.
R11: K1, sl1wyb, knit to m, sm, p1, k2, ksk.
R12: Sks, k3, sm, purl to loop, turn.

Work **Rows 11 & 12** again x 7 (7, 7, 9, 9) [9, 11, 11, 11, 11].
Work **Row 11** once more.
Final row (WS): Sks, k3, sm, purl to 2 sts before loop, p2tog, pm,
p&k14 (14, 14, 17, 17) [17, 19, 19, 19, 19] sts (for second half of Right
Sleeve Cap), purl to last m, sm, k3, sks.

27 (27, 27, 33, 33) [33, 37, 37, 37, 37] sts for each Sleeve Cap
20 (21, 23, 25, 27) [27, 28, 29, 29, 30] sts + 6 NB sts for each Front
99 (103, 107, 111, 115) [119, 123, 125, 127, 131] Back sts

BOX A

sM1 = sleeve increase
nM1 = neck increase
bM1 = body increase

R1: Ksk, k2, p1, sm, k1, nM1R, (knit to 1 st before m, sl1wyb, sm,
sM1L, knit to m, sM1R, sm, sl1wyb) twice, knit to 1 st before m,
nM1L, k1, sm, p1, k2, ksk.

R2: Sks, k3, sm, purl to m, sm, k3, sks.

R3: Ksk, k2, p1, sm, (knit to 1 st before m, sl1wyb, sm, sM1L,
knit to m, sM1R, sm, sl1wyb) twice, knit to m, sm, p1, k2, ksk.

R4: Sks, k3, sm, purl to m, sm, k3, sks.

R5: Ksk, k2, p1, sm, k1, nM1R, (knit to 1 st before m, bM1L,
sl1wyb, sm, sM1L, knit to m, sM1R, sm, sl1wyb, bM1R) twice,
knit to 1 st before m, nM1L, k1, sm, p1, k2, ksk.

STEP 6: SLEEVE CAPS & BODY
You will now increase for the sleeves and neck (and later also body)
simultaneously. (See Helpful Table for an overview of all increases.)

REFER TO BOX A FOR ROWS INSTRUCTIONS
Work **Rows 1 – 4** x 7 (7, 7, 6, 6) [6, 3, 5, 4, 5].
55 (55, 55, 57, 57) [57, 49, 57, 53, 57] Sleeve sts
27 (28, 30, 31, 33) [33, 31, 34, 33, 35] sts + 6 NB sts for each Front

Works **Rows 1 & 2** x 0 (0, 0, 0, 0) [1, 4, 0, 1, 1].
55 (55, 55, 57, 57) [59, 57, 57, 55, 59] Sleeve sts
27 (28, 30, 31, 33) [34, 35, 34, 34, 36] sts + 6 NB sts for each Front

INTRODUCE BODY INCREASES
Works **Rows 5 & 2** x 9 (10, 10, 11, 11) [12, 13, 15, 16, 17].

73 (75, 75, 79, 79) [83, 83, 87, 87, 93] Sleeve sts
45 (48, 50, 53, 55) [58, 61, 64, 66, 70] sts + 6 NB sts for each Front
117 (123, 127, 133, 137) [143, 149, 155, 159, 165] Back sts

Vaudeville

STEP 7: SEPARATING SLEEVES & BODY
Separation Row 1 (RS): Ksk, k2, p1, sm, k1, nM1R, *knit to 2 sts before m, pm, k2, rm, place all sts to next m on holder (= sleeve sts), rm, *(turn work over so WS is facing) borrow last st for cast on loop, crochet cast on 8 (8, 9, 11, 12) [12, 13, 13, 15, 15] sts, pm, cast on 4 (4, 5, 7, 8) [8, 9, 9, 11, 11] sts, replace loop onto LN (make a final chain st but not around the needle), turn work over so RS is facing*, work from *to* once more, knit to 1 st before m, nM1L, k1, sm, p1, k2, ksk.*

53 (56, 59, 64, 67) [70, 74, 77, 81, 85] Left Front sts + 6 NB sts
51 (54, 57, 62, 65) [68, 72, 75, 79, 83] Right Front sts + 6 NB sts
129 (135, 141, 151, 157) [163, 171, 177, 185, 191] Back sts

Separation Row 2 (WS): Sks, k3, sm, *purl to 1 st before underarm cast on, sl1, make loop in bar and place on LN, sl1 back to LN, p2tog, purl to m, sm, k1, purl to 2 sts before m, p2tog tbl, rm*, work from* to *once more, purl to m, sm, k3, sks.

52 (55, 58, 63, 66) [69, 73, 76, 80, 84] Left Front sts + 6 NB sts
51 (54, 57, 62, 65) [68, 72, 75, 79, 83] Right Front sts + 6 NB sts
128 (134, 140, 150, 156) [162, 170, 176, 184, 190] Back sts

Note: One stitch under each arm is worked in garter stitch (k1 on both RS and WS). This stitch is not included in stitch counts that follow.

51 (54, 57, 62, 65) [68, 72, 75, 79, 83] Left Front sts + 6 NB sts
51 (54, 57, 62, 65) [68, 72, 75, 79, 83] Right Front sts + 6 NB sts
127 (133, 139, 149, 155) [161, 169, 175, 183, 189] Back sts

STEP 8: BODY & CONTINUED NECK INCREASES

REFER TO **BOX B** FOR ROW INSTRUCTIONS
Work **Rows (1 & 2)** x 9 (9, 9, 9, 9) [9, 9, 9, 9, 8].
60 (63, 66, 71, 74) [77, 81, 84, 88, 91] sts + 6 NB sts for each Front

Work **Row 1**.
61 (64, 67, 72, 75) [78, 82, 85, 89, 92] sts + 6 NB sts for each Front

Next Row (WS): P2tog, sl1wyf, k3, sm, (purl to m, sm, k1) twice, purl to m, sm, k3, sl1wyf, p2tog tbl.
5 NB sts for each Front

STEP 9: JOIN FRONTS TO KNIT IN THE ROUND
MOVE MARKERS 1 stitch forward at underarms, so they are placed before the single garter stitch.

R1(RS): K4, p1, sm, knit to NBm, rm, turn.
R2 (WS): Sl^, (purl to m, sm, k1) twice, purl to m, rm, turn.

JOINING Row-Round 1 (RS): Sl1^, knit to final 6 sts, pm, place remaining 6 sts (1 short-row st + 5 sts) on a double pointed needle and place this on top of LN NB sts; working 1 st from each needle as a k2tog, (k2tog) x 5, twist loop before next st and place on dpn, k3tog (final st and loop on dpn with next st on LN, (knit to m, sm) twice. You are now at Right Underarm.
Joining Round 2: M1L, knit to m, rm, LATERAL BRAID: cable cast on 1 st (insert RN between next 2 sts to fetch yarn and place loop on LN),

BOX B

STEP 8
nM1 = neck increase

Row 1 (RS): Ksk, k2, p1, sm, k1, nM1R, knit to 1 st before NB, nM1L, k1, sm, p1, k2, ksk.

Row 2 (WS): Sks, k3, sm, (purl to m, sm, k1) twice, purl to m, k3, sks.

BOX C

BODY & SHAPING
Rnd 1: (Sm, g1, knit to m) twice.

Increase Rnd: (Sm, g1, M1L, knit to m, M1R)) twice.

BOX D

OPTIONAL BUST DARTS

Place your darts at approx 5 (6, 10, 10) cm / 2 (2.25, 4, 4)" from underarm or where desired:
For placement of darts, see Hints & Tips
(Remember to place them in Front!)

Smallish (Middling, Busty, Wowza!)
Worked over 12 (18, 22, 28) rows, adds approx 3 (4.5, 6, 7.5) cm / 1.25 (1.75, 2.25, 3)".

R1 (RS): Sm, knit to m, sm, knit to 30 (40, 44, 44) sts before Left side m, turn.
R2 (WS): Sl1^, pm, purl to 31 (41, 45, 45) sts before Right side m, turn.
R3 (RS): Sl1^, pm, knit to m, rm, k1^, k5 (4, 4, 3), turn.
R4: Sl1^, pm, purl to m, rm, p1^, p5 (4, 4, 3), turn.
Work **Rows 3 & 4** again x 4 (7, 9, 12).
Final Row (RS): Sl1^, pm, knit to m, rm, k1^, knit to side m. Resume working in the round.
Next Rnd: Sm, g1, knit to side m, sm, g1, knit to 1 st before m, k1^, rm, knit to m.

go behind first st to knit into back leg of 2nd st and leave on needle, knit first st, slip both sts off needle, slip 1 st to LN, work from * to * again x 4, sl final st on RN to dpn and hold in front, k1, sl1 from dpn to LN, k2tog, knit to m.

You are now at Left Underarm.

127 (133, 139, 149, 155) [161, 169, 175, 183, 189] Front sts
127 (133, 139, 149, 155) [161, 169, 175, 183, 189] Back sts

STEP 10: BODY & SHAPING

Continue in stocking stitch over body stitches only.
The round begins under Left Sleeve.
Note: *One stitch under each arm is worked in garter st (g1) which creates a faux side seam.*

AT THE SAME TIME
Please read through the entire step before proceeding, as a few things happen at the same time or overlap.

- Optional Bust Darts
- Slight A-line Waist Shaping

AT THE SAME TIME OPTIONAL BUST DARTS
Optional Bust Darts may be placed here or a bit lower. See BOX D.
Note: *If you are trying to stretch your skeins, this is a good place to set the body aside to work the sleeves before finishing the body.*

REFER TO **BOX C** FOR ROUND INSTRUCTIONS

AT THE SAME TIME WAIST SHAPING INCREASES
Work **Increase Rnd**.
129 (135, 141, 151, 157) [163, 171, 177, 185, 191] Front/Back sts

Continue with **Rnd 1**, working **Increase Rnd** every 20th rnd x 4.
137 (143, 149, 159, 165) [171, 179, 185, 193, 199] Front/Back sts

Work to 29 cm / 11.5" from underarm.

STEP 11: POCKET & SIDE SLITS

REFER TO POCKET TUTORIAL **3C** FOR INITIAL INSTRUCTIONS
For a simpler pocket consider Pocket 1A, 1B, 2A or 2C.
Prepare an **MC** and **CC1** (lime) pocket welt according to Tutorial instructions.
ATTACH WELT 22 (22, 25, 24, 24) [24, 26, 26, 28, 28] sts from side marker.
Follow Tutorial instructions until directed to return to main pattern.

SET UP SIDE SLITS & DOUBLE KNITTED POCKET
N1: Body sts (becomes holder for Back sts)
N2 (3 mm / US2.5): New needle for Front sts
N3 (2.5 mm / US 1.5): Needle briefly used for Lining sts

Vaudeville

*The first row is worked with **MC** only. Front and Lining stitches are interlaced as stitches on N1 & N3 are worked onto N2.*

R1 (RS): With N2 and working **MC** yarn, start 3 sts before m, p&k7 sts in bars between sts, knit to RPm1, sm, (k1 from N1, sl1wyf from N3) x 24 (to 1 st before RPm2), cross yarns, k1, sm, knit to 3 sts before side m, sl3 to LN (N1), slide sts off N1 onto cable, with N2 and from RS, p&k7 sts in bars between sts, turn.
145 (151, 157, 167, 173) [179, 187, 193, 201, 207] Front sts

No sts remain on N3, set aside N1 (Back sts) for now.

R2 (WS): Sl1wyf, BL1, sl1wyf, k3, sl1wyf, BL1, sl1wyf, pm, purl to RPm2, sm, p1MC, cross yarns, (p1CC, p1MC) x 23, p1CC, cross yarns, p1MC, sm, with **MC** purl to m, sm, sl1wyf, BL1, sl1wyf, k3, sl1wyf, BL1, sl1wyf, turn.
149 (155, 161, 171, 177) [183, 191, 197, 205, 211] Front sts

R3: Ksk, k3, ksk, sm, knit to RPm1, sm, k1MC, cross yarns, (k1CC, k1MC) x 23, k1CC, cross yarns, k1MC, sm, with **MC** knit to m, sm, ksk, k3, ksk.

R4: Sks, k3, sks, sm, purl to RPm2, sm, p1MC, cross yarns, (p1CC, p1MC) x 23, p1CC, cross yarns, p1MC, sm, with **MC** purl to m, sm, sks, k3, sks.

Work **Rows 3 & 4** again x 8 (or to desired depth), cut CC.

CLOSE POCKET
R1 (RS): Ksk, k3, ksk, sm, knit to RPm, rm, k1, k2tog (1 **MC** st with 1 **CC** st) x 24, rm, knit to m, ksk, k3, ksk.

FINISH FRONT
R2 (WS): Sks, k3, sks, purl to m, sks, k3, sks.
R3: Ksk, k3, ksk, sm, knit to m, sm, ksk, k3, ksk.

Work **Rows 2 & 3** to 10 cm / 4" from bottom of pocket or to 3 cm / 1.25" from desired length, ending with a Row 3.

LINED HEM
The lined hem is worked back and forth in double knitting.
If preferred, the hem and lining can be knit separately after the lining stitches have been picked up, and the open sides can then be seamed together with a few stitches.

N2 (3 mm / US 2.5): Front sts/**MC**
N3 (2.5 mm / US 1.5): Lining needle/**CC1** (lime)

Hem lining stitches are picked up on WS (see Tutorial section).
Slide sts off needle tips to rest on the cable (N2).
Working from WS, take **MC** to WS, using a second smaller 2.5 mm (US 1.5) circular needle (N3) p&k1 st in every bar between sts.
148 (154, 160, 170, 176) [182, 190, 196, 204, 210] Lining sts

SET UP DOUBLE KNITTING
*Interlace sts from N2 & N3 onto N3 (smaller needle). Keep working the 9 edge sts for the **MC** layer as set. Slip markers as they appear.*
Note: *It may be easier to transfer Front sts on N3 to a smaller needle before working the first row.*

With the exception of the 2 first and 2 last sts on every row:
RS: Knit all MC sts and work the 9 edging stitches as set.
RS: Purl all CC sts.
WS: Purl all MC sts but work the 9 edging stitches as set.
WS: Knit all CC sts.

Slipped stitches are slipped with yarn in front.

R1 (RS): K1MC, yfMC, p1CC, both yb, CC over MC, yfMC, sl1MC, p1CC, (k1, CCp1) x 5, sl1MC, p1CC, k1MC, sm, CCp1, (k1MC, CCp1) to m, sm, k1MC, p1CC, sl1MC, (p1CC, k1MC) x 5, p1CC, sl1MC, 2 sts remain, sl1CC, k1MC.

R2 (WS): (Both yarns in front) sl1MC, lay CC over MC, ybMC, k1CC, k1MC, k1CC, sl1MC, (k1CC, k1MC) x 3, k1CC, sl1MC, k1CC, k1MC, k1CC, sl1MC, sm, k1CC, (p1MC, k1CC) to m, sm, sl1MC, k1CC, k1MC, k1CC, sl1MC, (k1CC, k1MC) x 3, k1CC, sl1MC, k1CC, k1MC, k1CC, sl1MC, (k1CC, k1MC) x 3, k1CC, sl1MC, k1CC, k1MC, 2 sts remain, k1CC, CCyb, MC under CC, sl1MC, turn.

R3: (MC is in back, CC in front), k1MC, yfMC, MC over CC, CCyb, p1CC, sl1MC, (p1CC, k1MC) x 5, p1CC, sl1MC, p1CC, k1MC, sm, p1CC, (k1MC, p1CC) to m, sm, k1MC, p1CC, sl1MC, (p1CC, k1MC) x 5, p1CC, sl1MC, 2 sts remain, sl1CC, k1MC.

R4: As Row 2.

Work **Rows 3 & 4** again x 4.
Cut **CC**.

*On next Row work only **MC** sts (slip all **CC** sts wyf) as follows:*
Next Row (RS): K1, sl1CC, switch places of next 2 sts, sl1CC, k2togMC, (sl1CC, k1MC) x 4, sl1CC, switch places of next 2 sts (cross CC behind MC), sl1CC, k2togMC, sm, sl1CC, (k1MC, sl1CC) to m, sm, k1MC, sl1CC, switch places of next 2 sts (cross CC behind MC), sl1CC, k2togMC, sl1CC, (k1MC, slCC) x 3, k1MC, sl1CC, switch places of next 2 sts (cross CC behind MC), sl1CC, k2togMC.

*On next Row work only **CC** sts (slip all **MC** sts wyf) as follows:*
Next Row (WS): Sl1MC, sskCC, (sl1MC, k1CC) x 4, sl1MC, sskCC, sl1MC, rm, k1CC, (sl1MC, k1CC) to m, rm, sl1MC, sskCC, (sl1MC, k1CC) x 4, sl1MC, sskCC, sl1MC.

BIND OFF
Each ssk is worked with 1 body st and 1 lining st, then bound off with the previous ssk.
Bind off (RS): Ssk, *ssk, pso to bind off; work from * to last 3 sts, bind off 1, k2tog, pso.
Cut **MC**.

DOUBLE KNITTING (DK)

Work stitches alternately from RS & WS layer.
It is important to keep the layers separate and to only cross yarns/layers at the beginning and end of the pocket.
For this pocket the DK section always begins and ends with CC (WS layer).

RS
MC is held to front (toward you) and is used for RS layer, CC is held to back and used for WS layer.

WS
MC is held to back (RS), CC is held to front (WS).

CROSSING MC/CC:
Both yarns to WS, CC over MC, take MC to RS.

FINISH BACK

Work stitches on N1.

R1 (RS): At Left Side of sweater, join **MC**, k1, BL1, k5, BL1, k1, pm, knit to 3 sts before m, pm, k1, BL1, k2, rm, k3, BL1, k1.
149 (155, 161, 171, 177) [183, 191, 197, 205, 211] Back sts
R2 (WS): Sks, k3, sks, sm, purl to m, sm, sks, k3, sks.
R3: Ksk, k3, ksk, sm, knit to m, sm, ksk, k3, ksk.

Work **Rows 2 & 3** until Back matches Front.

BACK LINED HEM

Lining: Use **CC3** (Damson)
Work as for Front.

STEP 12: SLEEVES

Place 73 (75, 75, 79, 79) [83, 83, 87, 87, 93] Sleeve sts from holder back on larger (3 mm / US 2.5) needle. Join **MC** at right side of gap, p&k5 (5, 6, 8, 9) [9, 10, 10, 12, 12] sts along the first half of the underarm cast on, pm, p&k6 (6, 7, 9, 10) [10, 11, 11, 13, 13] sts more along second half of underarm, knit to m.

84 (86, 88, 96, 98) [102, 104, 108, 112, 118] sts

REFER TO BOX E FOR ROUND INSTRUCTIONS

Work **Rnd 1** to 5 cm / 2" from underarm.

SLEEVE DECREASES

Work **Decrease Rnd**.
82 (84, 86, 94, 96) [100, 102, 106, 110, 116] sts

Continue with **Rnd 1**, working **Decrease Rnd** every 14 (13, 14, 13, 13) [10, 10, 11, 9, 8]th round again x 9 (10, 9, 11, 10) [12, 13, 13, 15, 18].

64 (64, 68, 72, 76) [76, 76, 80, 80, 80] sts

Work to 43 (43, 44, 46, 46) [46, 46, 47, 47, 47] cm / 17 (17, 17.25, 18, 18) [18, 18, 18.5, 18.5, 18.5]" from underarm or 2.5 cm / 1" from desired sleeve length.

BOX E

SLEEVE ROUNDS
Rnd 1: Sm, g1, knit to m.
Decrease Rnd: Sm, g1, k2tog, knit to 2 sts before m, ssk.

STEP 13: LINED CUFF

Sleeve and lining sts are worked separately. Sleeve sts need to be a multiple of 4.

LEFT CUFF

Lining is worked with **CC2** (Teal) and **CC3** (Damson).
Cuff lining stitches are picked up on WS (see Tutorial section).
Slide all sts off needle tips to rest on the cable.
Working from WS, take **MC** to WS, using a smaller 2.5 mm (US 1.5) circular needle (N2) and going counterclockwise, p&k1 st in every bar between sts, take **MC** to RS.
Knit lining on inside of Sleeve going counterclockwise and downwards.
Rnds 1 – 6: (With **CC2** k2, with **CC3** k2) to end of round.

Cuff is worked with **MC** from RS.
With an additional smaller 2.5 mm (US 1.5) circular needle, knit 7 rounds or to slightly longer than lining, take MC to inside.

With **MC** knit 1 round on N2 (Lining sts), take **MC** to RS.

3-NEEDLE BIND OFF

With **MC** and from RS, bind off Cuff sts and Lining sts together using 3-Needle Bind Off and keeping an even tension:
K2tog (1st from N3 & 1 st from N2) to end of round.

RIGHT SLEEVE & CUFF

Work as Left Sleeve using **CC1** (Lime) and **CC3** (Damson) for lining.

FINISH

Tighten any loose stitches at bottom of V-neck, weave in loose ends.
Soak and block to measurements.

Vaudeville

Legend

- Sleeve increases
- Body increases
- Neck increases
- Underarm cast on

Column axes: **Rows from Cast On** · **Short Rows** (value **8** at row 93)

Each size column is divided into three sub-columns: *Sleeve increases* · *Body increases* · *Neck increases*.

Size 32

Row	Sleeve	Body	Neck
75	12		46
73	73	117	45
71	71	115	43
69	69	113	41
67	67	111	39
65	65	109	37
63	63	107	35
61	61	105	33
59	59	103	31
57	57	101	29
55	55		
53	53		27
51	51		
49	49		26
47	47		
45	45		25
43	43		
41	41		24
39	39		
37	37		23
35	35		
33	33		22
31	31		
29	29		21

Size 34

Row	Sleeve	Body	Neck
77	12		49
75	75	123	48
73	73	121	46
71	71	119	44
69	69	117	42
67	67	115	40
65	65	113	38
63	63	111	36
61	61	109	34
59	59	107	32
57	57	105	30
55	55		
53	53		28
51	51		
49	49		27
47	47		
45	45		26
43	43		
41	41		25
39	39		
37	37		24
35	35		
33	33		23
31	31		
29	29		22

Size 36

Row	Sleeve	Body	Neck
77	14		51
75	75	127	50
73	73	125	48
71	71	123	46
69	69	121	44
67	67	119	42
65	65	117	40
63	63	115	38
61	61	113	36
59	59	111	34
57	57	109	32
55	55		
53	53		30
51	51		
49	49		29
47	47		
45	45		28
43	43		
41	41		27
39	39		
37	37		26
35	35		
33	33		25
31	31		
29	29		24

Size 38

Row	Sleeve	Body	Neck
79	18		54
77	79	133	53
75	77	131	51
73	75	129	49
71	73	127	47
69	71	125	45
67	69	123	43
65	67	121	41
63	65	119	39
61	63	117	37
59	61	115	35
57	59	113	33
55	57		
53	55		31
51	53		
49	51		30
47	49		
45	47		29
43	45		
41	43		28
39	41		
37	39		27
35	37		
33	35		26

Size 40

Row	Sleeve	Body	Neck
79	20		56
77	79	137	55
75	77	135	53
73	75	133	51
71	73	131	49
69	71	129	47
67	69	127	45
65	67	125	43
63	65	123	41
61	63	121	39
59	61	119	37
57	59	117	35
55	57		
53	55		33
51	53		
49	51		32
47	49		
45	47		31
43	45		
41	43		30
39	41		
37	39		29
35	37		
33	35		28

Size 42

Row	Sleeve	Body	Neck
83	20		59
81	83	143	58
79	81	141	56
77	79	139	54
75	77	137	52
73	75	135	50
71	73	133	48
69	71	131	46
67	69	129	44
65	67	127	42
63	65	125	40
61	63	123	38
59	61	121	37
57	59		34
55	57		
53	55		33
51	53		
49	51		32
47	49		
45	47		31
43	45		30
41	43		
39	41		
37	39		29
35	37		28

Size 44

Row	Sleeve	Body	Neck
85	22		62
83	85	149	61
81	83	147	59
79	81	145	57
77	79	143	55
75	77	141	54
73	75	139	52
71	73	137	50
69	71	135	48
67	69	133	46
65	67	131	44
63	65	129	42
61	63	127	40
59	61	125	38
57	59		34
55	57		
53	55		34
51	53		33
49	51		33
45	47		32
41	43		31
37	39		30

Size 46

Row	Sleeve	Body	Neck
87	22		65
85	87	155	64
83	85	153	62
81	83	151	60
79	81	149	58
77	79	147	56
75	77	145	54
73	75	143	52
71	73	141	50
69	71	139	48
67	69	135	46
65	67	133	44
63	65	131	42
61	63	129	40
59	61	127	38
57	59	125	36
53	55		34
49	51		33
45	47		32
41	43		31
39	41		30
37	39		30

Size 48

Row	Sleeve	Body	Neck
87	26		67
85	87	159	66
83	85	157	64
81	83	155	62
79	81	153	60
77	79	151	58
75	77	149	56
73	75	147	54
71	73	145	52
69	71	143	50
67	69	141	48
65	67	139	46
63	65	137	44
61	63	135	42
59	61	133	40
57	59	131	38
53	55		34
49	51		33
45	47		32
41	43		31
39	41		30
37	39		30

Size 50

Row	Sleeve	Body	Neck
93	26		71
91	93	165	70
89	91	163	68
87	89	161	66
85	87	159	64
83	85	157	62
81	83	155	60
79	81	153	58
77	79	151	56
75	77	149	54
73	75	147	52
71	73	145	50
69	71	143	48
67	69	141	46
65	67	139	44
63	65	137	42
61	63	135	40
59	61	133	38
57	59		36
55	57		
53	55		35
49	51		34
45	47		33
43	45		22
39	41		31

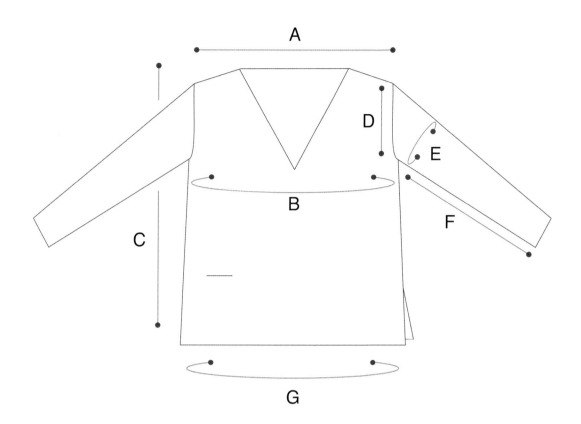

VAUDEVILLE GARMENT MEASUREMENTS

	32	34	36	38	40	42	44	46	48	50
A – Shoulder width (cm)	36.5	38	39.5	41	42.5	44	45.5	46.5	47	48.5
in	14.25	15	15.5	16.25	16.75	17.25	18	18.25	18.5	19
B – Bust (cm)	95.5	100	104.5	112	116.5	120.5	126.5	131	137	141.5
in	37.5	39.25	41.25	44	45.75	47.5	49.75	51.5	54	55.75
C – Length (cm)	65.5	66	66	66.5	66.5	67.5	67.5	68.5	68.5	70
in	25.75	26	26	26.25	26.25	26.5	26.5	27	27	27.5
D – Armhole depth (cm)	17.5	18	18	18.5	18.5	19.5	19.5	20.5	20.5	22
in	6.75	7	7	7.25	7.25	7.75	7.75	8	8	8.75
E – Sleeve circumf (cm)	31	32	32.5	35.5	36.5	38	38.5	40	41.5	43.5
in	12.25	12.5	12.75	14	14.25	15	15.25	15.75	16.25	17.25
F – Sleeve seam (cm)	45	45	46	48	48	48	48	49	49	49
in	17.75	17.75	18	19	19	19	19	19.25	19.25	19.25
G – Hem circumf (cm)	101.5	106	110.5	118	122	126.5	132.5	137	143	147.5
in	40	41.75	43.5	46.5	48	49.75	52.25	54	56.25	58

Rabalder features a lush oversized brioche cowl. With matching folded cuffs it is a warm hug of a jumper. Outlaw Bohemia Worsted is a luxurious natural fibre blend, which provides just the right drape and a dreamy halo, especially when, as here, it is knit at an aran gauge. With a two-colour cowl and cuffs, the relaxed shaping and optional bust darts give this pullover an elegantly casual silhouette, and features a small pocket for tiny treasures.

As a knitting experience, Rabalder is the perfect balance of meditative stocking stitch and thoughtful detail. For blustery days, the green Rabalder has been knit in no-nonsense Pirkkalanka wool on larger needles. For a more understated look, the cowl and cuffs are knit with just one colour in a structured textured rib. This slightly shorter pullover also has plain sleeve caps without the usual slipped-stitch faux seam. The small coin pocket makes yet another appearance here, as does a contrasting lined hem.

TO FIT SIZE
81 (86, 91, 97, 102) [107, 112, 117, 122, 127] cm
32 (34, 36, 38, 40) [42, 44, 46, 48, 50] inches

COWL NECK
Brioche or textured rib cowl

FIT
Relaxed fit with approx 14 – 15 cm / 5.5 – 6″ ease

YARN
Outlaw Bohemia Worsted (45% Polwarth, 45% Alpaca, 10% Possum,
200 m / 219 yds per 100 g)
MC Royal, 6 (6, 7, 7, 7) [7, 8, 8, 9, 9] skeins
CC Fingering or Heavy Lace, Manos del Uruguay Fino (Light
Fingering, 70% Merino, 30% Silk, 448 m / 490 yds per 100 g);
Silver Teaset, 1 skein

APPROX YARDAGE
MC
1100 (1150, 1250, 1300, 1350) [1400, 1500, 1550, 1650, 1700] m
1200 (1250, 1350, 1400, 1450) [1500, 1600, 1700, 1800, 1850] yds
CC 200 m (250 yds)

ALTERNATIVE YARN SUGGESTIONS
Little Grey Sheep Gotland Aran or Hampshire DK,
Vahva (Paksu) Pirkkalanka

NEEDLES & NOTIONS
4.5 mm (US 7) circular needle, 80 – 100 cm (32 – 40″)
or size to obtain gauge
4 mm (US 6) circular needle, 80 – 100 cm (32 – 40″)
Stitch holders; stitch markers

BLOCKED GAUGE
19 sts x 26 rows on 4.5 mm (US 7) needle = 10 cm / 4″

SAMPLE SIZES
Purple (Bohemia Worsted): Size 40 with Middling bust darts weighs
583 g / 20.5 oz, with approx 35 g / 1 oz (150 m / 200 yds) of **CC**
Green (Pirkkakanka): Size 38, with textured rib cowl and contrasting
lining, knitted with 5 mm (US 8) needles weighs 560 g / 19.75 oz
(Variant collar and cuff were knitted with rib stitch pattern
from Aranaranja)

Rabalder

STEP 1: CAST ON & RIGHT BACK SHOULDER

With **MC**, using longtail cast on and 4.5 mm (US 7) needle, cast on 77 (79, 83, 85, 87) [89, 91, 93, 95, 97] sts.

Setup Row (WS): P22 (23, 24, 25, 26) [27, 28, 29, 30, 31], turn.
R1 (RS): Sl1^, pm, k13 (14, 15, 15, 16) [17, 17, 18, 19, 19], turn.
R2 (WS): Sl1^, purl to m, rm, p1^, p1, turn.
R3: Sl1^, pm, k7 (7, 8, 8, 8) [9, 9, 9, 10, 10], turn.
R4: Sl1^, purl to m, rm, p1^, p1, turn.
R5: Sl1^, pm, knit to last 2 sts (working any sl1^ as k1^), sl1wyb, k1.
R6: Purl to m, rm, p1^, p1, turn.
R7: Sl1^, pm, knit to to last 2 sts, sl1wyb, k1.
R8: Purl to m, rm, p1^, purl to end.

77 (79, 83, 85, 87) [89, 91, 93, 95, 97] Back sts

STEP 2: LEFT BACK SHOULDER

R1 (RS): K1, sl1wyb, k20 (21, 22, 23, 24) [25, 26, 27, 28, 29], turn.
R2 (WS): Sl1^, pm, p13 (14, 15, 15, 16) [17, 17, 18, 19, 19], turn.
R3: Sl1^, knit to m, rm, k1^, k1, turn.
R4: Sl1^, pm, p7 (7, 8, 8, 8) [9, 9, 9, 10, 10], turn.
R5: Sl1^, knit to m, rm, k1^, k1, turn.
R6: Sl1^, pm, purl to end (working any sl1^ as p1^).
R7: K1, sl1wyb, knit to m, rm, k1^, k1, turn.
R8: Sl1^, pm, purl to end.

STEP 3: WORKING ACROSS BACK

R1 (RS): K1, sl1wyb, knit to m, rm, k1^, knit to last 2 sts, sl1wyb, k1.
77 (79, 83, 85, 87) [89, 91, 93, 95, 97] Back sts
R2 (WS): Purl.
R3: K1, sl1wyb, knit to last 2 sts, sl1wyb, k1.
R4: Purl.
Work **Rows 3 & 4** again x 1 (1, 1, 2, 2) [2, 2, 3, 3, 3].
Work **Row 3** once more.
Final Row (WS): Purl to last 2 sts, p2tog, pm, p&p7 (7, 7, 8, 8) [8, 8, 9, 9, 9] sts for first half of Left Sleeve Cap.

7 (7, 7, 8, 8) [8, 8, 9, 9, 9] Left Cap sts
76 (78, 82, 84, 86) [88, 90, 92, 94, 96] Back sts

Slide stitches off needle tips to rest on the cable.
Set these stitches aside, continue to next step without turning.

STEP 4: LEFT FRONT SHOULDER

nM1 = neck increase
Setup Row (WS): Loop cable, p&p21 (22, 23, 24, 25) [26, 27, 28, 29, 30] sts along edge (for Left Front Shoulder) in the cast on of Left Back Shoulder, and remember to pick up second stitch in line with faux seam.

21 (22, 23, 24, 25) [26, 27, 28, 29, 30] Left Front sts
R1 (RS): K14 (14, 15, 16, 16) [17, 18, 18, 19, 20], turn.
R2 (WS): Sl1^, purl to end.
R3: K7 (7, 7, 8, 8) [8, 9, 9, 9, 10], turn.
R4: Sl1^, purl to end.
R5: Knit to 2 sts before loop (working any sl1^ as k1^), sl1wyb, k1, turn.
R6: Purl.
R7: Knit to 2 sts before loop, sl1wyb, k1, turn.
R8: Purl.
R9: K2, nM1R, knit to 2 sts before loop, sl1wyb, k1, turn.
22 (23, 24, 25, 26) [27, 28, 29, 30, 31] Left Front sts
R10: Purl.
Work **Rows 9 & 10** again x 3 (3, 3, 4, 4) [4, 4, 5, 5, 5].
25 (26, 27, 29, 30) [31, 32, 34, 35, 36] Left Front sts
Final Row (RS): K2, nM1R, knit to 2 sts before loop, ssk, pm, p&k7 (7, 7, 8, 8) [8, 8, 9, 9, 9] sts (for second half of Left Sleeve Cap), knit to m, sm, sl1wyb, knit to last 2 sts, ssk, pm, p&k7 (7, 7, 8, 8) [8, 8, 9, 9, 9] sts (for first half of Right Sleeve Cap).

14 (14, 14, 16, 16) [16, 16, 18, 18, 18] Left Cap sts
7 (7, 7, 8, 8) [8, 8, 9, 9, 9] Right Cap sts
25 (26, 27, 29, 30) [31, 32, 34, 35, 36] Left Front sts
75 (77, 81, 83, 85) [87, 89, 91, 93, 95] Back sts

Slide stitches off needle tips to rest on the cable.
Set these stitches aside, continue to next step without turning.

BOX A

sM1 = sleeve increase   nM1 = neck increase

RS ROW
R1: K2, nM1R, (knit to 1 st before m, sl1wyb, sm, sM1L, knit to m, sM1R, sm, sl1wyb) twice, knit to last 2 sts, nM1L, k2.

WS ROWS
R2: Purl.

R4: P2, nM1Lp, purl to last 2 sts, nM1Rp, p2.

STEP 6: SLEEVE CAPS & BODY
You will now increase for the sleeves and neck.
(See Helpful Table for an overview of all increases.)

REFER TO **BOX A** FOR ROW INSTRUCTIONS

Work **Rows 1 & 2** x 1 (1, 2, 1, 1) [1, 1, 1, 1, 1].
16 (16, 18, 18, 18) [18, 18, 20, 20, 20] Sleeve sts
26 (27, 29, 30, 31) [32, 33, 35, 36, 37] sts for each Front

Work **Rows 1 & 4**.
18 (18, 20, 20, 20) [20, 20, 22, 22, 22] Sleeve sts
28 (29, 31, 32, 33) [34, 35, 37, 38, 39] sts for each Front

STEP 7: JOIN FRONTS TO KNIT IN THE ROUND
Joining Row/Round 1 (RS): K2, nM1R, (knit to 1 st before m, sl1wyb, sm, sM1L, knit to m, sM1R, sm, sl1wyb) twice, knit to last 2 sts, nM1L, pm (=Nm), k2, *(turn work over so WS is facing)* borrow last st for cast on loop, crochet cast on 18 (18, 18, 18, 18) [18, 18, 16, 16, 16] sts, replace loop onto LN *(make a final chain st but not around the needle)*, turn work over so RS is facing, join to Left Front, knit to m, sm.

You are now at Left Front Sleeve.

20 (20, 22, 22, 22) [22, 22, 24, 24, 24] Sleeve sts
76 (78, 82, 84, 86) [88, 90, 92, 94, 96] Front sts
75 (77, 81, 83, 85) [87, 89, 91, 93, 95] Back sts

Joining Round 2: Knit to Nm, rm, ssk, knit to end of cast on, make loop in bar and place on LN, k2tog (the first st of Left Front and the loop), knit to 1 st before m.

20 (20, 22, 22, 22) [22, 22, 24, 24, 24] Sleeve sts
75 (77, 81, 83, 85) [87, 89, 91, 93, 95] Front sts
75 (77, 81, 83, 85) [87, 89, 91, 93, 95] Back sts

STEP 5: RIGHT FRONT SHOULDER
nM1 = neck increase
R1 (RS): Loop cable, p&k21 (22, 23, 24, 25) [26, 27, 28, 29, 30] sts (for Right Front Shoulder) in the cast on of Right Back Shoulder, and remember to pick up second st in line with faux seam.
21 (22, 23, 24, 25) [26, 27, 28, 29, 30] Right Front sts
R2 (WS): P14 (14, 15, 16, 16) [17, 18, 18, 19, 20], turn.
R3: Sl1^, knit to end.
R4: P7 (7, 7, 8, 8) [8, 9, 9, 9, 10], turn.
R5: Sl1^, knit to end.
R6: Purl to loop, (working any sl1^ as p1^), turn.
R7: K1, sl1wyb, knit to end.
R8: Purl to loop, turn.
R9: K1, sl1wyb, knit to last 2 sts, nM1L, k2.
22 (23, 24, 25, 26) [27, 28, 29, 30, 31] Right Front sts
Row 10: Purl to loop, turn.
Work **Rows 9 & 10** again x 3 (3, 3, 4, 4) [4, 4, 5, 5, 5].
25 (26, 27, 29, 30) [31, 32, 34, 35, 36] Right Front sts
Work **Row 9** once more.
26 (27, 28, 30, 31) [32, 33, 35, 36, 37] Right Front sts
Final Row (WS): Purl to 2 sts before loop, p2tog, pm, p&p7 (7, 7, 8, 8) [8, 8, 9, 9, 9] sts (for second half of Right Sleeve Cap), purl to m, sm, purl to end.

14 (14, 14, 16, 16) [16, 16, 18, 18, 18] sts for each Sleeve Cap
25 (26, 27, 29, 30) [31, 32, 34, 35, 36] sts for each Front
75 (77, 81, 83, 85) [87, 89, 91, 93, 95] Back sts

STEP 8: SLEEVE & BODY INCREASES

Continue to work sleeve increases and also introduce body increases.

The round begins 1 stitch before Left Front Sleeve marker.

REFER TO **BOX B** FOR ROUND INSTRUCTIONS
Work **Rnds 1 & 2** x 10 (11, 9, 10, 9) [9, 10, 8, 8, 8].
40 (42, 40, 42, 40) [40, 42, 40, 40, 40] Sleeve sts

Work **Rnds 1 & 4** x 1 (0, 0, 0, 0) [0, 0, 0, 0, 0].
44 (42, 40, 42, 40) [40, 42, 40, 40, 40] Sleeve sts

INTRODUCE BODY INCREASES
Work **Rnds 3 & 2** x 0 (1, 1, 2, 2) [4, 4, 5, 4, 4].
44 (44, 42, 46, 44) [48, 50, 50, 48, 48] Sleeve sts
75 (79, 83, 87, 89) [95, 97, 101, 101, 103] Front sts
75 (79, 83, 87, 89) [95, 97, 101, 101, 103] Back sts

Work **Rnds 3 & 4** x 2 (2, 3, 2, 3) [2, 2, 2, 4, 3].
52 (52, 54, 54, 56) [56, 58, 58, 64, 60] Sleeve sts
79 (83, 89, 91, 95) [99, 101, 105, 109, 109] Front sts
79 (83, 89, 91, 95) [99, 101, 105, 109, 109] Back sts

Work **Rnds 3 & 6** x 0 (0, 0, 0, 0) [0, 0, 0, 0, 1].
52 (52, 54, 54, 56) [56, 58, 58, 64, 64] Sleeve sts
79 (83, 89, 91, 95) [99, 101, 105, 109, 113] Front sts
79 (83, 89, 91, 95) [99, 101, 105, 109, 113] Back sts

Photo © Emanuel Borsboom

BOX B

sM1 = sleeve increase   **bM1** = body increase

ODD (SLIP-STITCH) ROUNDS
Rnd 1: (Sl1wyb, sm, **sM1L**, knit to m, **sM1R**, sm, sl1wyb, knit to 1 st before m) twice.

Rnd 3: (**bM1L**, sl1wyb, sm, **sM1L**, knit to m, **sM1R**, sm, sl1wyb, **bM1R**, knit to 1 st before m) twice.

EVEN (PLAIN) ROUNDS
Rnd 2: Knit.

Rnd 4: (K1, sm, **SM1L**, knit to m, **SM1R**, sm, knit to 1 st before m) twice.

Rnd 6: (**bM1L**, k1, sm, **sM1L**, knit to m, **sM1R**, sm, k1, **bM1R**, knit to 1 st before m) twice.

Work **Rnd 3**.
54 (54, 56, 56, 58) [58, 60, 60, 66, 66] Sleeve sts
81 (85, 91, 93, 97) [101, 103, 107, 111, 115] Front sts
81 (85, 91, 93, 97) [101, 103, 107, 111, 115] Back sts

Final Rnd: Knit to 2 sts before Left Front Sleeve m.

STEP 9: SEPARATING SLEEVES & BODY

Separation Rnd 1: *Pm, k2, rm, place all sts to next m on holder (= sleeve sts), rm, (turn work over so WS is facing) borrow last st for cast on loop, crochet cast on 6 (6, 6, 7, 8) [8, 9, 10, 11, 11] sts, pm, cast on 4 (4, 4, 5, 6) [6, 7, 8, 9, 9] sts, replace loop onto LN (make a final chain st but not around the needle), turn work over so RS is facing*, knit to 2 sts before m, work from * to * once more, knit to m.

You are now at Left Front Sleeve.

91 (95, 101, 105, 111) [115, 119, 125, 131, 135] Front sts
91 (95, 101, 105, 111) [115, 119, 125, 131, 135] Back sts

BOX C

BODY & SHAPING

Rnd 1: (Sm, g1, knit to marker) twice.

Decrease Rnd: (Sm, g1, k2tog, knit to 2 sts before side m, ssk) twice.

Separation Rnd 2: *Rm, ssk, knit to m, sm, p1, knit to end of underarm cast on, make loop in bar and place on LN, k2tog (next st and loop), knit to m*, work from * to * once more.

90 (94, 100, 104, 110) [114, 118, 124, 130, 134] Front sts
90 (94, 100, 104, 110) [114, 118, 124, 130, 134] Back sts

STEP 10: BODY & SHAPING

Continue in stocking stitch over body stitches only.
The round begins under Left Sleeve.
Note: *One stitch under each arm is worked in garter st (g1), which creates a faux side seam.*

AT THE SAME TIME

Please read through the entire step before proceeding, as a few things happen at the same time or overlap.

- Optional Bust Darts
- Slight Body Shaping (begins before or just after the darts, depending on where you place them)
- Pocket

REFER TO BOX C FOR ROUND INSTRUCTIONS

Work **Rnd 1** to 5 cm/ 2" from underarm.

AT THE SAME TIME BUST DARTS

Optional Bust Darts may be placed here or a bit lower, see BOX D.

Note: *If you are trying to stretch your skeins, this is a good place to set the body aside to work the sleeves before finishing the body.*

AT THE SAME TIME BODY SHAPING

At 5 cm / 2" from underarm, begin decreases.

DECREASES

Work **Decrease Rnd**.
88 (92, 98, 102, 108) [112, 116, 122, 128, 132] Front/Back sts

Continue with **Rnd 1**, working **Decrease Rnd** every 18 (18, 20, 20, 20) [20, 20, 20, 20, 20]]th rnd again x 3.
82 (86, 92, 96, 102) [106, 110, 116, 122, 126] Front/Back sts

AT THE SAME TIME OPTIONAL MINI POCKET

(worked before final decrease round)
At 25.5 (26, 26, 26, 26) [25, 24.5, 25.5, 24.5, 24.5] cm / 10 (10.25, 10.25, 10.25, 10.25) [9.75, 9.75, 10, 9.75, 9.75]" from underarm, set up pocket.

BOX D

OPTIONAL BUST DARTS

Place your darts at approx 5 (6, 10, 10) cm / 2 (2.25, 4, 4)" from underarm or where desired:
For placement of darts, see Hints & Tips
(Remember to place them in Front!)

Smallish (Middling, Busty, Wowza!)
Worked over 8 (12, 16, 20) rows, adds approx 3 (4.5, 6, 7.5) cm / 1.25 (1.75, 2.25, 3)".

R1 (RS): Sm, g1, knit across back to m, sm, g1, knit to 26 (30, 32, 32) sts before left underarm m, turn.
R2 (WS): Sl1^, pm, purl to 27 (31, 33, 33) sts before right underarm m, turn.
R3 (RS): Sl1^, pm, knit to m, rm, k1^, k7 (5, 4, 3), turn.
R4: Sl1^, pm, purl to m, rm, p1^, p7 (5, 4, 3), turn.
Work **Rows 3 & 4** again x 2 (4, 6, 8).
Final Row (RS): Sl1^, pm, knit to m, rm, k1^, knit to m.

Resume working in the round.
Next Rnd: Sm, g1, knit to m, sm, g1, knit to 1 st before m, k1^, rm, knit to m.

REFER TO POCKET TUTORIAL **2A** FOR INSTRUCTIONS
While making the pocket, don't forget the g1 at the side 'seam'.

Continue with BOX C **Rnd 1** (and pay attention to any remaining decreases) to 33 (33, 33, 33.5, 33.5) [32.5, 32, 33, 32, 32] cm / 13 (13, 13, 13.25, 13.25) [12.75, 12.5, 13, 12.5, 12.5]" from underarm or to 3 cm / 1.25" from desired length.
Do not cut the yarn.
82 (86, 92, 96, 102) [106, 110, 116, 122, 126] Front/Back sts

STEP 11: LINED HEM

Change to smaller (4 mm / US 6) needle.
Next Rnd: Purl.

LINING

Hem lining stitches are picked up on WS (see Tutorial section).
Slide stitches off needle tips to rest on the cable.
Take working **MC** to WS. With 4 mm (US 6) needle on WS and going counterclockwise on inside of sweater, p&k sts in every bar between all sts, take **MC** to RS.
82 (86, 92, 96, 102) [106, 110, 116, 122, 126] Front/Back Lining sts

Join Fingering or Heavy Lace **CC**, and knit 8 rounds (approx 2.5 cm / 1") on WS (along inside of sweater, working counterclockwise and downwards).
Cut **CC**.
Slide sts off needle tips to rest on cable, set Lining sts aside.

HEM

With **MC** and smaller (4 mm / US 6) needle, knit 8 rounds (approx 2.5 cm / 1.25") or to slightly longer than lining.
Next Round: Purl, take **MC** to WS.

LINING

With **MC**, knit one round, take **MC** to RS.

Note: If necessary, work an additional hem-round to make hem slightly longer before binding off.

BIND OFF

Weave in any loose ends at hem before binding off.
From RS, bind off hem sts together with lining sts using 3-Needle Bind Off and keeping an even tension.

STEP 12: SLEEVES

Place 54 (54, 56, 56, 58) [58, 60, 60, 66, 66] Sleeve sts from holder back on larger (4.5 mm / US 7) needle. Join **MC** at right side of gap, p&k4 (4, 4, 5, 6) [6, 7, 8, 9, 9] sts along the first half of the underarm cast on, pm, p&k5 (5, 5, 6, 7) [7, 8, 9, 10, 10] sts more along second half of underarm, knit to m.

63 (63, 65, 67, 71) [71, 75, 77, 85, 85] sts

REFER TO **BOX E** FOR ROUND INSTRUCTIONS
Work **Rnd 1** to 5 cm / 2" from underarm.

SLEEVE DECREASES

Work **Decrease Rnd**.
61 (61, 63, 65, 69) [69, 73, 75, 83, 83] sts

Continue with **Rnd 1**, working **Decrease Rnd** every 14 (14, 14, 12, 10) [10, 11, 10, 7, 7]th round again x 6 (6, 6, 7, 9) [9, 8, 9, 13, 13].
49 (49, 51, 51, 51) [51, 57, 57, 57, 57] sts

Work to 44 (44, 45, 45, 46) [46, 46, 46, 47, 47] cm / 17.25 (17.25, 17.75, 17.75, 18) [18, 18, 18, 18.5, 18.5]" from underarm or to desired sleeve length.

BOX E

SLEEVE ROUNDS
Rnd 1: Sm, g1, knit to m.
Decrease Rnd: Sm, g1, k2tog, knit to 2 sts before m, ssk.

BRIOCHE ABBREVIATIONS

brk/p   Knit/purl the stitch that was slipped in the previous round together with its yarn over

brkYObrk   2-stitch increase: brk1 and leave st on LN, yo (yf under needle, then over needle to back), brk1 again into same st

sl1yo   Yf, slip 1 stitch and also make a yarn over – this slipped stitch with its yarn-over "shawl" is counted as one stitch

These now standard brioche abbreviations were invented by brioche conjurer, Nancy Marchant. For more information on Brioche knitting see Links & Resources (page 241).

STEP 13: FOLDED-UP BRIOCHE CUFF
Note: The brioche pattern is worked over an even number of stitches and with one colour at a time.

Change to smaller (4 mm / US 6) needle, join **CC**.
Rnd 1: With **CC**, (sl1yo, k1), to last 3 sts, sl1yo, k2tog.
48 (48, 50, 50, 50) [50, 56, 56, 56, 56] sts
Rnd 2: With **MC**, (brp1, sl1yo) to end of round.
Rnd 3: With **CC**, (sl1yo, brk1) to end of round.
62 (62, 64, 66, 70) [70, 74, 76, 84, 84] sts

Work **Rounds 2 & 3** to 7 cm /2.75" from beginning of brioche.

ATTACHED I-CORD BIND OFF
With **MC** and using Provisional Winding Cast on, on LN wind on 3 sts.
R1: K2, k2tog (1 i-cord st with 1 sleeve st).
R2: Slip 3 sts to LN, k2, ssk (1 i-cord st with 1 sleeve st).

Work **Row 2** until 1 Sleeve st remains.
Graft the i-cord ends together, making a final ssk with the final grafted st.

STEP 14: TWO-COLOUR BRIOCHE COWL COLLAR
The cowl is knitted to double length along the inside (WS) of the Neck and folds outwards. P&k in approx 1 of every 2 rows in the slanting parts and in approx every stitch in the straight parts as follows:

Join **MC** at Left Shoulder and with **MC** and smaller (4 mm / US 6) needles, from WS and working counterclockwise, p&k approx 36 (36, 38, 38, 38) [38, 38, 38, 38, 38] sts along inside of Back Neck, and approx 52 (52, 54, 54, 54) [54, 54, 54, 54, 54] sts along inside of Front Neck.
Approx 88 (88, 92, 92, 92) [92, 92, 92, 92, 92] sts

Rnd 1: (K1, sl1yo) to end of round.
Join **CC**.
Rnd 2: With **CC** (sl1yo, brp1) to end of round.
Rnd 3: With **MC** (brk1, sl1yo) to end of round.
Work **Rnds 2 & 3** to 15 cm / 6" from beg of brioche.
Work **Rnd 2** once more.

INCREASE ROUND
Rnd 4: With **MC** (brk1, sl1yo, brkYObrk, sl1yo) to end of round.
132 (132, 138, 138, 138) [138, 138, 138, 138, 138] sts
Rnd 5: With **CC** (sl1yo, brp1, sl1yo, p1, sl1yo, brp1) to end of round.
Rnd 6: With **MC** (brk1, sl1yo) to end of round.
Rnd 7: With **CC** (sl1yo, brp1) to end of round.

Work **Rnds 6 & 7** to 30 cm / 12" from beginning of brioche.

ATTACHED I-CORD BIND OFF
With **MC** and using Provisional Winding Cast On, on LN wind on 3 sts
R1: K2, ssk (1 i-cord st with 1 Sleeve st).
R2: Slip 3 sts to LN, k2, ssk (1 i-cord st with 1 Collar st).

Work **Row 2** until 1 Collar st remains.
Graft the i-cord ends together, making a final ssk with the final grafted st.

FINISH
Weave in loose ends. Soak and block to measurements.

Rabalder

Size 32

Rows from Cast On	Sleeve increases	Body increases	Neck increases
63			
61			
59			
57			
55			
53	10		
51	54	81	
51	52		
49	50	79	
49	48		
47	46	77	
47	44		
45	42		
43	40		
41	38		
39	36		
37	34		
35	32		
33	30		
31	28		
29	26		
27	24		
25	22		
23	20	18	29
23			28
21	18		27
19	16		26

Size 34

Sleeve increases	Body increases	Neck increases
10		
54	85	
52		
50	83	
48		
46	81	
44	79	
42		
40		
38		
36		
34		
32		
30		
28		
26		
24		
22		
20	18	30
		29
18		28
16		27

Size 36

Sleeve increases	Body increases	Neck increases
10		
56	91	
54		
52	89	
50		
48	87	
46		
44	85	
42	83	
40		
38		
36		
34		
32		
30		
28		
26		
24		
22		30
20		30
18		29
16		28

Size 38

Sleeve increases	Body increases	Neck increases
12		
56	93	
54		
52	91	
50		
48	89	
46	87	
44	85	
42		
40		
38		
36		
34		
32		
30		
28		
26		
24		
22	18	33
		32
20		31
18		30

Size 40

Sleeve increases	Body increases	Neck increases
14		
58	97	
56		
54	95	
52		
50	93	
48		
46	91	
44	89	
42	87	
40		
38		
36		
34		
32		
30		
28		
26		
24		
22	18	34
		33
20		32
18		31

Size 42

Sleeve increases	Body increases	Neck increases
14		
58	101	
56		
54	99	
52		
50	97	
48	95	
46	93	
44	91	
42	89	
40		
38		
36		
34		
32		
30		
28		
26		
24		
22	18	35
		34
20		33
18		32

Size 44

Sleeve increases	Body increases	Neck increases
16		
60	103	
58		
56	101	
54		
52	99	
50	97	
48	95	
46	93	
44	91	
42		
40		
38		
36		
34		
32		
30		
28		
26		
24		
22	18	36
		35
20		34
18		33

Size 46

Sleeve increases	Body increases	Neck increases
18		
60	107	
58		
56	105	
54		
52	103	
50	101	
48	99	
46	97	
44	95	
42	93	
40		
38		
36		
34		
32		
30		
28		
26		
24	16	38
		37
22		36
20		35

Size 48

Sleeve increases	Body increases	Neck increases
20		
66	111	
64		
62	109	
60		
58	107	
56		
54	105	
52		
50	103	
48	101	
46	99	
44	97	
42	95	
40		
38		
36		
34		
32		
30		
28		
26		
24	16	39
		38
22		37
20		36

Size 50

Sleeve increases	Body increases	Neck increases	Rows from Cast On
20			63
66	115		61
64	113		
62	111		59
60			57
58	109		57
56			55
54	107		55
52			53
50	105		53
48	103		51
46	101		49
44	99		47
42	97		45
40			43
38			41
36			39
34			37
32			35
30			33
28			31
26			29
24	16	40	27
		39	
22		38	25
20		37	23
			21
			19

Short Rows: 4

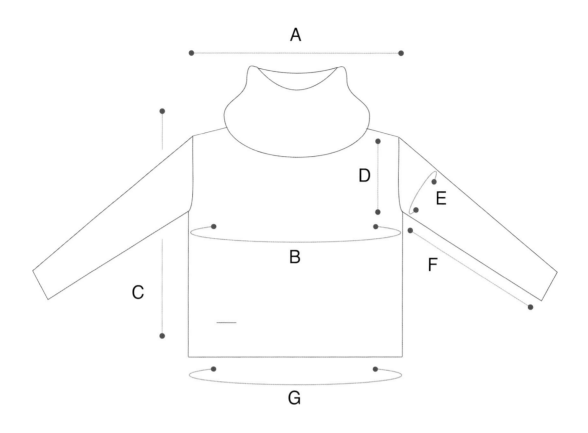

RABALDER GARMENT MEASUREMENTS

	32	34	36	38	40	42	44	46	48	50
A – Shoulder width (cm)	39.5	40.5	42.5	43.5	44.5	46	47	48	49	50
in	15.5	16	16.75	17.25	17.5	18	18.5	19	19.25	19.75
B – Bust (cm)	94.5	99	105.5	109.5	116	120	124	130.5	137	141
in	37.25	39	41.5	43	45.75	47.25	48.75	51.5	54	55.5
C – Length (cm)	56	57	57	58	58	58	58	59	59	59
in	22	22.5	22.5	22.75	22.75	22.75	22.75	23.25	23.25	23.25
D – Armhole depth (cm)	18.5	19	19	20	20	21	21.5	21.5	22.5	22.5
in	7.25	7.5	7.5	8	8	8	8.5	8.5	9	9
E – Sleeve circumf (cm)	33	33	34	35.5	37.5	37.5	39.5	40.5	44.5	44.5
in	13	13	13.5	14	14.75	14.75	15.5	16	17.5	17.5
F – Sleeve seam (cm)	44	44	45	45	46	46	46	46	47	47
in	17.25	17.25	17.75	17.75	18	18	18	18	18.5	18.5
G – Hem circumf (cm)	86.5	90.5	97	101	107.5	111.5	116	122	128.5	132.5
in	34	35.75	38.25	39.75	42.25	44	45.75	48	50.5	52.25

This simple, figure-skimming V-neck cardigan is the perfect layer of graceful warmth and comfort for Stadtbummeln on a late summer evening. The buttonband is a variant of the standard Ziggurat version. The generous pockets are double knitted, with i-cord edging to give a classically finished touch. Sweet Laurel is knitted in a summery, subtly variegated shade of SweetGeorgia DK, a yarn that is pleasingly soft to knit with yet keeps its shape with a gentle drape.

Sweet Laurel

tailored cardigan

TO FIT SIZE

81 (86, 91, 97, 102) [107, 112, 117, 122, 127] cm
32 (34, 36, 38, 40) [42, 44, 46, 48, 50] inches

V-NECK

FIT

Tailored shoulders and gentle waist shaping, no ease

YARN

SweetGeorgia Superwash DK (8ply, 100% merino, 234 m (256 yds)
per 115 g); Laurel 4 (4, 5, 5, 5) [5, 6, 6, 6, 6] skeins

APPROX YARDAGE

850 (900, 1000, 1050, 1100) [1100, 1150, 1200, 1300, 1300] m
950 (1000, 1050, 1100, 1200) [1250, 1300, 1350, 1400, 1450] yds

ALTERNATIVE YARN SUGGESTIONS
Rohrspatz & Wollmeise Merino DK, Cascade 220

NEEDLES & NOTIONS

4 mm (US 6) circular needle, 80 – 100 cm (32 – 40") x 3
or size to obtain gauge
3 mm (US 2.5) circular needle, 60 – 100 cm (24 – 40")
2 shorter circulars 3 mm (US 2.5)
1 double pointed needle 3 mm (US 2.5)
Stitch holders; stitch markers; 6 buttons (7 if adding bust darts)

BLOCKED GAUGE

20 sts x 28 rows on 4 mm (US 6) needles = 10 cm / 4"

SAMPLE SIZE

Size 40 with Middling bust darts weighs 460 g / 16 oz, knitted with
just under 5 skeins

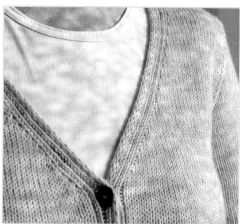

STEP 1: CAST ON & RIGHT BACK SHOULDER

Using longtail cast on and 4 mm (US 6) needle, cast on 66 (68, 72, 76, 78) [80, 82, 84, 86, 88] sts.
Setup Row (WS): P16 (17, 18, 18, 19) [20, 21, 21, 22, 23], turn.
R1 (RS): Sl1^, pm, k10 (10, 11, 11, 12) [12, 13, 13, 14, 14], turn.
R2 (WS): Sl1^, purl to m, rm, p1^, p1, turn.
R3: Sl1^, pm, k6 (6, 6, 6, 7) [7, 7, 7, 8, 8], turn.
R4: Sl1^, purl to m, rm, p1^, p1, turn.
R5: Sl1^, pm, knit to last 2 sts (working any sl1^ as k1^), sl1wyb, k1.
R6: Purl to m, rm, p1^, p1, turn.
R7: Sl1^, pm, knit to last 2 sts, sl1wyb, k1.
Work Rows 6 & 7 once more.
Final Row (WS): Purl to m, rm, p1^, purl to end.

66 (68, 72, 76, 78) [80, 82, 84, 86, 88] Back sts

STEP 2: LEFT BACK SHOULDER

R1 (RS): K1, sl1wyb, k14 (15, 16, 16, 17) [18, 19, 19, 20, 21], turn.
R2 (WS): Sl1^, pm, p10 (10, 11, 11, 12) [12, 13, 13, 14, 14], turn.
R3: Sl1^, knit to m, rm, k1^, k1, turn.
R4: Sl1^, pm, p6 (6, 6, 6, 7) [7, 7, 7, 8, 8], turn.
R5: Sl1^, knit to m, rm, k1^, k1, turn.
R6: Sl1^, pm, purl to end (working any sl1^ as p1^).
R7: K1, sl1wyb, knit to m, rm, k1^, k1, turn.
R8: Sl1^, pm, purl to end.
Work Rows 7 & 8 once more.

STEP 3: WORKING ACROSS BACK

R1 (RS): K1, sl1wyb, knit to m, rm, k1^, knit to last 2 sts, sl1wyb, k1.
66 (68, 72, 76, 78) [80, 82, 84, 86, 88] Back sts
R2 (WS): Purl.
R3: K1, sl1wyb, knit to last 2 sts, sl1wyb, k1.
R4: Purl.
Work **Rows 3 & 4** again x 1 (1, 2, 2, 2) [2, 2, 2, 3, 3].
Work **Row 3** once more.
Final Row (WS): Purl to last 2 sts, p2tog, pm, p&p8 (8, 9, 9, 9) [9, 9, 9, 10, 10] sts along edge (for first half of Left Sleeve Cap).

8 (8, 9, 9, 9) [9, 9, 9, 10, 10] Left Cap sts
65 (67, 71, 75, 77) [79, 81, 83, 85, 87] Back sts
Slide stitches off needle tips to rest on the cable.
Set these stitches aside, continue to next step without turning.

STEP 4: LEFT FRONT SHOULDER

After the shoulder sts have been picked up, add sts for the Buttonband (BB) using the working yarn and a provisional cast on. After a few rows, these sts can be placed on a holder or safety pin.

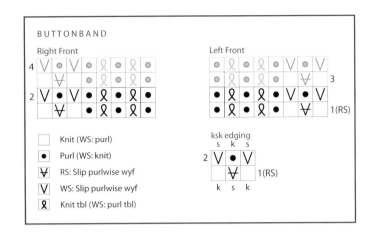

BUTTONBAND

| Knit (WS: purl) |
| Purl (WS: knit) |
| RS: Slip purlwise wyf |
| WS: Slip purlwise wyf |
| Knit tbl (WS: purl tbl) |

ksk edging

Setup Row (WS): Loop cable, p&p15 (16, 17, 17, 18) [19, 20, 20, 21, 22] sts (for Left Front Shoulder) in the cast on of Left Back Shoulder, *and remember to pick up second st in line with faux seam.* Place spare circular parallel to working needle and using Winding Provisional Cast On and working yarn, wind on 8 sts for BB, pull on spare circular to allow provisional sts to rest on its cable.
15 (16, 17, 17, 18) [19, 20, 20, 21, 22] Left Front sts + 8 BB sts
R1 (RS): Ksk, (p1, k1 tbl) twice, p1, pm, k10 (10, 11, 11, 12) [12, 13, 13, 14, 14], turn.
This sets the 8 BB sts for RS rows.
R2 (WS): Sl1^, purl to m, sm, (k1, p1 tbl) x 2, k1, sks.
This sets the 8 BB sts for WS rows.
R3: BB, sm, k5 (5, 5, 5, 6) [6, 6, 6, 7, 7], turn.
R4: Sl1^, purl to m, sm, BB.
R5: BB, sm, knit to 2 sts before loop (working any sl1^ as k1^), sl1wyb, k1, turn.
R6: Purl to m, sm, BB.
R7: BB, sm, knit to 2 sts before loop, sl1wyb, k1, turn.

R8: Purl to m, sm, BB.
Work **Rows 7 & 8** again x 5 (5, 6, 6, 6) [6, 6, 6, 7, 7].
Final Row (RS): BB, sm, knit to 2 sts before loop, ssk, pm, p&k8 (8, 9, 9, 9) [9, 9, 9, 10, 10] sts (for second half of Left Sleeve Cap), knit to m, sm, k1, sl1wyb, knit to last 2 sts, ssk, pm, p&k8 (8, 9, 9, 9) [9, 9, 9, 10, 10] sts (for first half of Right Sleeve Cap).

16 (16, 18, 18, 18) [18, 18, 18, 20, 20] Left Cap sts
8 (8, 9, 9, 9) [9, 9, 9, 10, 10] Right Cap sts
14 (15, 16, 16, 17) [18, 19, 19, 20, 21] Left Front sts + 8 BB sts
64 (66, 70, 74, 76) [78, 80, 82, 84, 86] Back sts

Slide stitches off needle tips to rest on the cable.
Set these stitches aside.

WORKING BUTTONBAND AROUND BACK NECK
Slide provisional buttonband/collar (BB) sts to 4 mm (US 6) needle. With RS facing, at inside edge of BB, join a new yarn to work and attach BB along the neck as follows.

R1 (RS): With new **MC**, p&k1 st in neck edge and place on LN, k2tog, (k1 tbl, p1) twice, ksk. *8 sts*
R2 (WS): Sks, (k1, p1 tbl) twice, sl1wyf.
Continue to work **Rows 1 & 2** while picking up sts along Back Neck up to the Right Shoulder until all sts are picked up. Pick up approx 3 sts for every 4, and end with a Row 2 (**WS**).
Cut yarn.

STEP 5: RIGHT FRONT SHOULDER
Continue from where you stopped in Step 4 at Right Shoulder.
R1 (RS): Loop cable, p&k15 (16, 17, 17, 18) [19, 20, 20, 21, 22] sts (for Right Front Shoulder) in the cast on of Right Back Shoulder, *and remember to pick up second st in line with faux seam,* pm (before BB), p1, (k1 tbl, p1) twice, ksk.
This sets the 8 BB sts for RS rows.
15 (16, 17, 17, 18) [19, 20, 20, 21, 22] Right Front sts + 8 BB sts
R2 (WS): Sks, (k1, p1 tbl) twice, k1, sm, p10 (10, 11, 11, 12) [12, 13, 13, 14, 14], turn.
This sets the 8 BB sts for WS rows.
R3: Sl1^, knit to m, sm, BB.
R4: BB, sm, p5 (5, 5, 5, 6) [6, 6, 6, 7, 7], turn.
R5: Sl1^, knit to m, sm, BB.
R6: BB, sm, purl to loop (working any sl1^ as p1^), turn.
R7: K1, sl1wyb, knit to m, sm, BB.
R8: BB, sm, purl to loop, turn.
Work **Rows 7 & 8** again x 5 (5, 6, 6, 6) [6, 6, 6, 7, 7].
Work **Row 7** once more.
Final Row (WS): BB, sm, purl to 2 sts before loop, p2tog, pm, p&p8

(8, 9, 9, 9) [9, 9, 9, 10, 10] sts (for second half of Right Sleeve Cap), purl to last m, sm, (k1, p1 tbl) x 2, k1, sks.

16 (16, 18, 18, 18) [18, 18, 18, 20, 20] sts for each Sleeve Cap
14 (15, 16, 16, 17) [18, 19, 19, 20, 21] sts + 8 BB sts for each Front
64 (66, 70, 74, 76) [78, 80, 82, 84, 86] Back sts

STEP 6: SLEEVE CAPS & BODY
You will now increase for the sleeve and neck (and later also body) simultaneously. Continue to work Buttonbands (BB) as set. (See Helpful Table for an overview of all increases.)

REFER TO **BOX A** FOR ROW INSTRUCTIONS
Work **Rows 1 – 4** x 8 (7, 7, 8, 7) [8, 7, 7, 7, 7].
48 (44, 46, 50, 46) [50, 46, 46, 48, 48] Sleeve sts
22 (22, 23, 24, 24) [26, 26, 26, 27, 28] sts + 8 BB sts for each Front

Work **Rows 1 & 2** x 0 (1, 1, 0, 1) [0, 1, 2, 1, 2].
48 (46, 48, 50, 48) [50, 48, 50, 50, 52] Sleeve sts
22 (23, 24, 24, 25) [26, 27, 28, 28, 30] sts + 8 BB sts for each Front

Continue to work sleeve and neck increases, and also introduce body increases.

Work **Rows 5 & 2** x 0 (1, 1, 0, 1) [0, 1, 0, 0, 0].
48 (48, 50, 50, 50) [50, 50, 50, 50, 52] Sleeve sts
22 (24, 25, 24, 26) [26, 28, 28, 28, 30] sts + 8 BB sts for each Front
64 (68, 72, 74, 78) [78, 82, 82, 84, 86] Back sts

BOX A

sM1= sleeve increase
nLLI/RLI = neck increase
bM1 = body increase

R1: Ksk, (p1, k1 tbl) twice, p1, sm, k1, nRLI, (knit to 1 st before m, sl1wyb, sm, sM1L, knit to m, sM1R, sm, sl1wyb) twice, knit to 1 st before m, nLLI, k1, sm, p1, (k1 tbl, p1) twice, ksk.
This sets the Left and Right BB sts for RS rows.

Rows 2 & 4: Sks, (k1, p1 tbl) twice, k1, sm, purl to m, sm, k1, (p1 tbl, k1) twice, sks.
This sets the Right and Left BB sts for WS rows.

R3: BB, sm, (knit to 1 st before m, sl1wyb, sm, sM1L, knit to m, sM1R, sm, sl1wyb) twice, knit to m, sm, BB.

ADDITIONAL RS ROWS
R5: BB, sm, (knit to 1 st before m, bM1L, sl1wyb, sm, sM1L, knit to m, sM1R, sm, sl1wyb, bM1R) twice, knit to m, sm, BB.

R7: BB, sm, k1, nRLI, (knit to 1 st before m, bM1L, sl1wyb, sm, sM1L, knit to m, sM1R, sm, sl1wyb, bM1R) twice, knit to 1 st before m, nLLI, k1, sm, BB.

ADDITIONAL WS ROWS
R6: BB, sm, (purl to 1 st before m, bM1Rp, p1, sm, purl to m, sm, p1, bM1Lp) twice, purl to m, sm, BB.

R8: BB, sm, (purl to 1 st before m, bM1Rp, p1, sm, sM1Rp, purl to m, sM1Lp, sm, p1, bM1Lp) twice, purl to m, sm, BB.

Work **Rows 7 & 2** x 0 (0, 0, 1, 0) [1, 1, 1, 3, 2].
48 (48, 50, 52, 50) [52, 52, 52, 56, 56] Sleeve sts
22 (24, 25, 26, 26) [28, 30, 30, 34, 34] sts + 8 BB sts for each Front
64 (68, 72, 76, 78) [80, 84, 84, 90, 90] Back sts

Work **Rows 7 & 6** x 0 (0, 0, 0, 1) [1, 1, 3, 3, 4].
48 (48, 50, 52, 52) [54, 54, 58, 62, 64] Sleeve sts
22 (24, 25, 26, 29) [31, 33, 39, 43, 46] sts + 8 BB sts for each Front
64 (68, 72, 76, 82) [84, 88, 96, 102, 106] Back sts

Work **Rows 7 & 8** x 1 (1, 1, 1, 1) [1, 1, 0, 0, 0].
52 (52, 54, 56, 56) [58, 58, 58, 62, 64] Sleeve sts
25 (27, 28, 29, 32) [34, 36, 39, 43, 46] sts + 8 BB sts for each Front
68 (72, 76, 80, 86) [88, 92, 96, 102, 106] Back sts

Work **Row 5 (5, 5, 7, 7) [7, 7, 7, 7, 7]** once.
54 (54, 56, 58, 58) [60, 60, 60, 64, 66] Sleeve sts
26 (28, 29, 31, 34) [36, 38, 41, 45, 48] sts + 8 BB sts for each Front
70 (74, 78, 82, 88) [90, 94, 98, 104, 108] Back sts

Work **Row 2**.

STEP 7: SEPARATING SLEEVES & BODY

Separation Row 1 (RS): BB, sm, k1, nRLI, *knit to 2 sts before m, pm, k2, rm, place all sts to next m on holder, (= sleeve sts) rm, *(turn work over so WS is facing) borrow last st for cast on loop, crochet cast on 6 (7, 8, 8, 8) [9, 10, 10, 10, 10] sts, pm, cast on 5 (6, 7, 7, 7) [8, 9, 9, 9, 9] sts, replace loop onto LN (make a final chain st but not around the needle), turn work over so RS is facing*, work from * to * once more, knit to 1 st before m, nLLI, k1, sm, BB.

32 (35, 37, 39, 42) [45, 48, 51, 55, 58] Left Front sts + BB
33 (36, 38, 40, 43) [46, 49, 52, 56, 59] Right Front sts + BB
81 (87, 93, 97, 103) [107, 113, 117, 123, 127] Back sts

Separation Row 2 (WS): BB, sm, *purl to 1 st before cast on, sl1 kwise, make twisted loop in cast on bar and place on LN, sl1 to LN, p2tog (loop and sl st), purl to m, sm, purl to 2 sts before m, p2togtbl, rm*, work from *to* once more, purl to m, sm, BB.

31 (34, 36, 38, 41) [44, 47, 50, 54, 57] Left Front sts + BB
33 (36, 38, 40, 43) [46, 49, 52, 56, 59] Right Front sts + BB
80 (86, 92, 96, 102) [106, 112, 116, 122, 126] Back sts

Note: *Two stitches under each arm are worked in a cord pattern that creates a faux side seam.*
These stitches are not included in stitch counts that follow.

31 (34, 36, 38, 41) [44, 47, 50, 54, 57] Left Front sts + BB
31 (34, 36, 38, 41) [44, 47, 50, 54, 57] Right Front sts + BB
78 (84, 90, 94, 100) [104, 110, 114, 120, 124] Back sts

STEP 8: BODY

AT THE SAME TIME
Please read through the entire step before proceeding, as a few things happen at the same time or overlap.

- Waist Shaping
- Buttonholes
- Optional Bust Darts
- Optional Rear Shaping
- Pockets – worked before waist shaping is complete

REFER TO **BOX B** FOR ROW INSTRUCTIONS
Work **Rows 1 & 2** x 6 (6, 7, 7, 7) [6, 6, 5, 4, 3].
37 (40, 43, 45, 48) [50, 53, 55, 58, 60] sts for each Front + BB
Work **Row 3**.

WAIST SHAPING BEGINS FOR SOME SIZES
Work **Row 4 (4, 4, 4, 4) [4, 4, 2, 2, 2]** once.
36 (39, 42, 44, 47) [49, 52, 55, 58, 60] sts for each Front + BB
76 (82, 88, 92, 98) [102, 108, 114, 120, 124] Back sts

Work Buttonhole Rows 1 – 3.
Work **Row 2.**

AT THE SAME TIME BUTTONHOLES
Make further 3-row buttonholes as set, starting on every 18th row (approx every 6.5 cm / 2.5").

Work **Rows 3 & 2** to 5 cm / 2" from underarm, where waist shaping starts for the three largest sizes, and the optional bust darts can be placed.

BOX B

nLLI/RLI = neck increase
RS ROWS
R1: BB, sm, k1, nRLI, (knit to m, sm, TwSl) twice, knit to 1 st before m, nLLI, k1, sm, BB.

R3: BB, sm, (knit to m, sm, TwSl) twice, knit to m, sm, BB.
WS ROWS
R2: BB, sm, purl to BB, sm, BB.

Decrease R4: BB, sm, (purl to 4 sts before m, p2tog, p2, sm, p2tog tbl) twice, purl to m, sm, BB.

Increase R6: BB, sm, (purl to 2 sts before m, LLIp, p2, sm, RLIp) twice, purl to m, sm, BB.

BUTTONHOLE ROWS
BR1 **(RS):** BB, sm, (knit to m, sm, TwSl) twice, knit to BB, sm, p1, k1 tbl, bind off 2 sts, ksk.

BR2 **(WS):** Sks, k1, *(turn work over so RS is facing) borrow last st for cast on loop*, crochet cast on 3 sts, *replace loop onto LN, turn work over so WS is facing*, p1 tbl, k1, sm, purl to BB, sm, BB.

BR3: BB, sm, (knit to m, sm, TwSl) twice, knit to BB, sm, p1, sl1 purlwise, pick up a twisted loop in bar before cast on, pass 2 sts back to LN (twisted loop and sl st), ssk, p1, k1 tbl, p1, k2tog, sl1wyf, k1.

AT THE SAME TIME OPTIONAL BUST DARTS
Optional Bust Darts (see BOX C) may be placed here or a bit lower.
    Note: If you are trying to stretch your skeins, this is a good place to set the body aside to work the sleeves before finishing the body.

AT THE SAME TIME WAIST SHAPING DECREASES
At 5 cm / 2" from underarm, work BOX B **Row 4**.
(For sizes 32 (34, 36, 38, 40) [42, 44] this first decrease has already been worked.)
Continue to work **Rows 3 & 2**, working **Decrease Row 4** every 8th row again x 3 (3, 3, 4, 4) [4, 4, 4, 4, 4].
Work **Rows 3 & 2** without decreases for an additional 5 cm / 2" – and remember buttonholes.

AT THE SAME TIME WAIST SHAPING INCREASES

Work BOX B **Rows 3 & 6**.

34 (37, 40, 41, 44) [46, 49, 52, 55, 57] Front sts + BB

72 (78, 84, 86, 92) [96, 102, 108, 114, 118] Back sts

Work **Rows 3 & 2** as established, working **Increase Row 6** every 8th row again x 2 (2, 2, 3, 3) [3, 3, 3, 3, 3], then on next 10th row once, then on next 12th row once.

38 (41, 44, 46, 49) [51, 54, 57, 60, 62] Front sts + BB

80 (86, 92, 96, 102) [106, 112, 118, 124, 128] Back sts

AT THE SAME TIME OPTIONAL REAR SHAPING & POCKETS

Work to 23.5 (23.5, 24, 24, 24) [23.5, 23.5, 22.5, 22, 21] cm / 9.25 (9.25, 9.5, 9.5, 9.5) [9.25, 9.25, 8.75, 8.75, 8.25]" from underarm or to 16 cm / 6.25" from desired total length.

REAR SHAPING

For a little extra room in the rear, make increases across the back (see BOX C).

BOX C

OPTIONAL BUST DARTS

Place your darts at approx at approx 5 (5, 10, 10) cm / 2 (2, 4, 4)" from underarm or where desired:

For placement of darts, see Hints & Tips.

Note that an additional buttonhole and button may be required if adding darts.

Smallish (Middling, Busty, Wowza!)

Worked over 10 (14, 20, 24) rows, adds approx 3.5 (5, 7, 8.5) cm / 1.5 (2, 2.75, 3.25)".

LEFT FRONT

R1 (RS): BB, sm, knit to 26 (28, 32, 36) sts before m, turn.

R2 (WS): Sl1^, pm, purl to BB, sm, BB.

R3 (RS): BB, sm, knit to m, rm, k1^, k5 (4, 3, 3), turn.

R4: Sl1^, pm, purl to BB, sm, BB.

Work **Rows 3 & 4** again x 3 (5, 8, 10).

Next Row (RS): BB, sm, knit to m, rm, k1^, (knit to m, sm, TwSl) twice, knit to BB, sm, BB (and note buttonhole sequence).

RIGHT FRONT

R2 (WS): BB, sm, purl to 28 (30, 34, 38) sts before m, turn.

R3 (RS): Sl1^, pm, knit to BB, sm, BB.

R4: BB, sm, purl to m, rm, p1^, p5 (4, 3, 3), turn.

Work **Rows 3 & 4** again x 3 (5, 8, 10).

Work **Row 3** once more.

Next Row (WS): BB, sm, purl to m, rm, p1^, purl to m, sm, k1, purl across back to BB, sm, BB.

Resume working back and forth as before darts and remember to make buttonholes.

OPTIONAL REAR SHAPING

Increase (M1L) x 6 (6, 6, 8, 8) [8, 10, 10, 10, 10] evenly distributed across the Back.

POCKET

DOUBLE-KNITTED POCKET WITH SLANTING I-CORD EDGE

This pocket adds approx 12.5 cm / 5".

At 23.5 (23.5, 24, 24, 24) [23.5, 23.5, 22.5, 22, 21] cm / 9.25 (9.25, 9.5, 9.5, 9.5) [9.25, 9.25, 8.75, 8.75, 8.25]" from underarm, make pockets.

REFER TO POCKET TUTORIAL **3B** FOR INSTRUCTIONS

For a simpler pocket consider Pocket 1A or 1B.

Don't forget buttonhole placement and the TwSl detail at each side 'seam'. After the Pockets are finished, work additional rows (BOX B **Rows 3 & 2**) as required to place final buttonhole or to approx 38 (38, 38.5, 38.5, 38.5) [38, 38, 37, 36.5, 35.5] cm / 15 (15, 15.25, 15.25, 15.25) [15, 15, 14.5, 14.25, 14]" from underarm.

STEP 9: HEM WITH ATTACHED BIND OFF
TwSsk = Sl1 tb (as if to p1tbl)l, sl1 kwise, sl2 back to LN, k2tog tbl

Switch to smaller (3 mm / US 2.5) needle.
R1 (RS): K1, k2tog, k1, k1tbl, k2tog, p1, rm, (knit to m, rm, TwSl) twice, knit to m, rm, p1, TwSsk, k1tbl, k1, ssk, k1.
Rows 2 – 4: Sl1wyf, knit to end.

BIND OFF
Borrow final stitch to crochet cast on 2 sts, make 1 chain st (not around needle), place on LN.
R1 (RS): Sl1wyb, sl1wyf, ssk (1 edge st with 1 body st).
R2 (WS): Sks.
R3: K1, sl1wyf, ssk.
R4: Sks.

Tip: Row 4 can be worked backwards (from left to right) – this obviates the need to turn work over between rows (see BOX opposite).

Work **Rows 3 & 4** all the way around the hem until 1 st remains.
Final Row (RS): (Ssk) twice, bind off final st.

STEP 10: SLEEVES
The 2-stitch cord at the side seam continues down the sleeve – adjust marker placement as necessary. Decreases are made on plain rounds.

Place 54 (52, 54, 56, 56) [58, 58, 60, 64, 66] Sleeve sts from holder back on larger (4 mm / US 6) needle. Attach yarn at right side of gap, p&k5 (6, 7, 7, 7) [8, 9, 9, 9, 9] sts along the first half of the underarm cast on, pm, p&k6 (7, 8, 8, 8) [9, 10, 10, 10, 10] sts more along second half of underarm, knit to m.

65 (65, 69, 71, 71) [75, 77, 79, 83, 85] sts

REFER TO **BOX D** FOR ROUND INSTRUCTIONS
Work **Rnds 1 & 2** to 5 cm / 2" from underarm.

SLEEVE DECREASES
Work **Decrease Rnd & Rnd 2**.
63 (63, 67, 69, 69) [73, 75, 77, 81, 83] sts
Continue with **Rnds 1 & 2**, working **Decrease Rnd** every 12 (12, 10,

BOX D

Rnd 1: Sm, TwSl, knit to m.

Rnd 2: Sm, knit to m.

Decrease Rnd: Sm, sl1, k2tog, knit to 1 st before m, shift m 1 st right, ssk.

10, 10) [10, 10, 10, 10, 10]th round again x 8 (8, 10, 10, 10) [11, 8, 7, 7, 6], then every 6th round x 0 (0, 0, 0, 0) [0, 4, 6, 7, 9].
47 (47, 47, 49, 49) [51, 51, 51, 53, 53] sts

Work to 45 (45, 46, 46, 47) [47, 47, 48, 48, 48] cm / 17.75 (17.75, 18, 18, 18.5) [18.5, 18.5, 19, 19, 19]" from underarm or to 1 cm / 0.5" from desired length.

I-CORD BIND OFF
Using Provisional Winding Cast On and working yarn, wind on 3 sts.
Rows 1 – 3 (RS): K2, ssk (last i-cord st together with 1 sleeve st), sl 3 sts onto to LN.
R4 (RS): K2, sssk (last i-cord st together with 2 sleeve sts), sl 3 sts onto to LN.
Work **Rows 1 – 4** around the cuff until all sts are bound off.
Graft or sew the i-cord sts to the provisional sts.

FINISH
Weave in loose ends. Soak and block to measurements. Sew on some nice buttons.

Sweet Laurel

Legend:

- ▓ Sleeve increases
- ▒ Body increases
- ░ Neck increases
- ▥ Underarm cast on

Sizes: 32, 34, 36, 38, 40, 42, 44, 46, 48, 50. Each size has three columns: Sleeve increases (S) · Body increases (B) · Neck increases (N).

Rows from Cast On	Short Rows	32 S	32 B	32 N	34 S	34 B	34 N	36 S	36 B	36 N	38 S	38 B	38 N	40 S	40 B	40 N	42 S	42 B	42 N	44 S	44 B	44 N	46 S	46 B	46 N	48 S	48 B	48 N	50 S	50 B	50 N	Rows from Cast On
71	4																												19		49	71
69																										19		46	66	108	48	69
68																														106		
67																										64	104	45	64	104	45	67
66																														102		
65																							19		42	62	100	42	62	100	42	65
64																											98			98		
63																	17		37	19		39	60	98	41	60	96	39	60	96	39	63
62																								96			94			94		
61											15		32	15		35	60	90	36	60	94	38	56	94	38	58	92	36	58	92	36	61
60																	58	88		58	92			92								
59								15		30	58	82	31	58	88	34	56	86	33	56	90	35	56	90	35	56	90	35	56	90	34	59
58											56	80		56	86									88			88					
57		11		27	13		29	56	78		54	78	28	54	84	31	54	82	30	54	86	32	54	86	32	54	88	32	54	88	32	57
55		54	70		54	74		52	74	27	52	76	26	52	80	28	52	80	28	52	84	30	52	84	30	52	86	30	52		30	55
54		52	68		52	72		54	76																							
53		50	66	24	50	70	26	50	72		50	72		50	78		50			50	82		50		28	50		28	50		29	53
51		48			48	68		48		24	48		24	48		25	48		26	48		27	48		27	48			48			51
49		46		22	46		23	46			46			46			46			46			46			46		27	46		28	49
47		44			44			44		23	44		23	44		24	44		25	44		26	44		26	44			44			47
45		42		21	42		22	42			42			42			42			42			42			42		26	42		27	45
43		40			40			40		22	40		22	40		23	40		24	40		25	40		25	40			40			43
41		38		20	38		21	38			38			38			38			38			38			38		25	38		26	41
39		36			36			36		21	36		21	36		22	36		23	36		24	36		24	36			36			39
37		34		19	34		20	34			34			34			34			34			34			34		24	34		25	37
35		32			32			32		20	32		20	32		21	32		22	32		23	32		23	32			32			35
33		30		18	30		19	30			30			30			30			30			30			30		23	30		24	33
31		28			28			28		19	28		19	28		20	28		21	28		22	28		22	28			28			31
29		26		17	26		18	26			26			26			26			26			26			26		22	26		23	29
27		24			24			24		18	24		18	24		19	24		20	24		21	24		21	24			24			27
25		22		16	22		17	22			22			22			22			22			22			22		21	22		22	25
23		20			20			20		17	20		17	20		18	20		19	20		20	20		20							23
21		18		15	18		16																									21

Size labels (bold): **32**, **34** (bottom, rows 21–23); **36**, **38**, **40**, **42**, **44**, **46** (bottom, row 23); **48**, **50** (bottom, row 25). Top size labels: **32**, **34** (row 57); **36** (row 59); **38**, **40** (row 61); **42**, **44** (row 63); **46** (row 67); **48** (row 69); **50** (row 71).

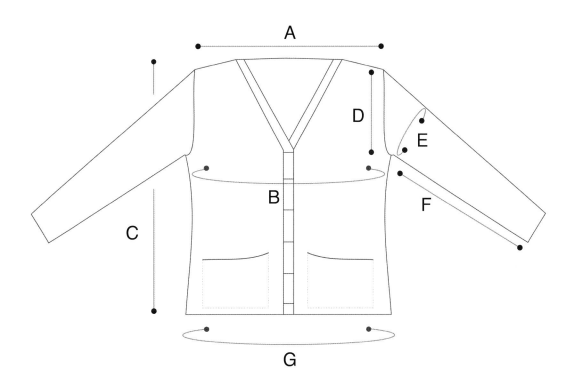

SWEET LAUREL GARMENT MEASUREMENTS

	32	34	36	38	40	42	44	46	48	50
A – Shoulder width (cm)	32	33	35	37	38	39	40	41	42	43
in	12.5	13	13.75	14.5	15	15.25	15.75	16.25	16.5	17
B – Bust (cm)	80	86	92	96	102	106	112	116	122	126
in	31.5	33.75	36.25	37.75	40.25	41.75	44	45.75	48	49.5
C – Length (cm)	59.5	59.5	61	61.5	61.5	61.5	61.5	61.5	62	62
in	23.5	23.5	24	24.25	24.25	24.25	24.25	24.25	24.5	24.5
D – Armhole depth (cm)	18.5	18.5	19.5	20	20	20.5	20.5	21.5	23	23.5
in	7.25	7.5	7.5	8	8	8	8	8.5	9	9.5
E – Sleeve circumf (cm)	32.5	33.5	35.5	36.5	36.5	38.5	39.5	39.5	41.5	42.5
in	12.75	13.25	14	14.25	14.25	15.25	15.5	15.5	16.25	16.75
F – Sleeve seam (cm)	46	46	47	47	48	48	48	49	49	49
in	18	18	18.5	18.5	19	19	19	19.25	19.25	19.25
G – Hem circumf (cm)	82	88	94	98	104	108	114	120	126	130
in	32.25	34.75	37	38.5	41	42.5	45	47.25	49.5	51.25
H – Hem with extra sts (cm)	85	91	97	102	108	112	119	125	131	135
in	33.5	35.75	38.25	40.25	42.5	44	46.75	49.25	51.5	53.25

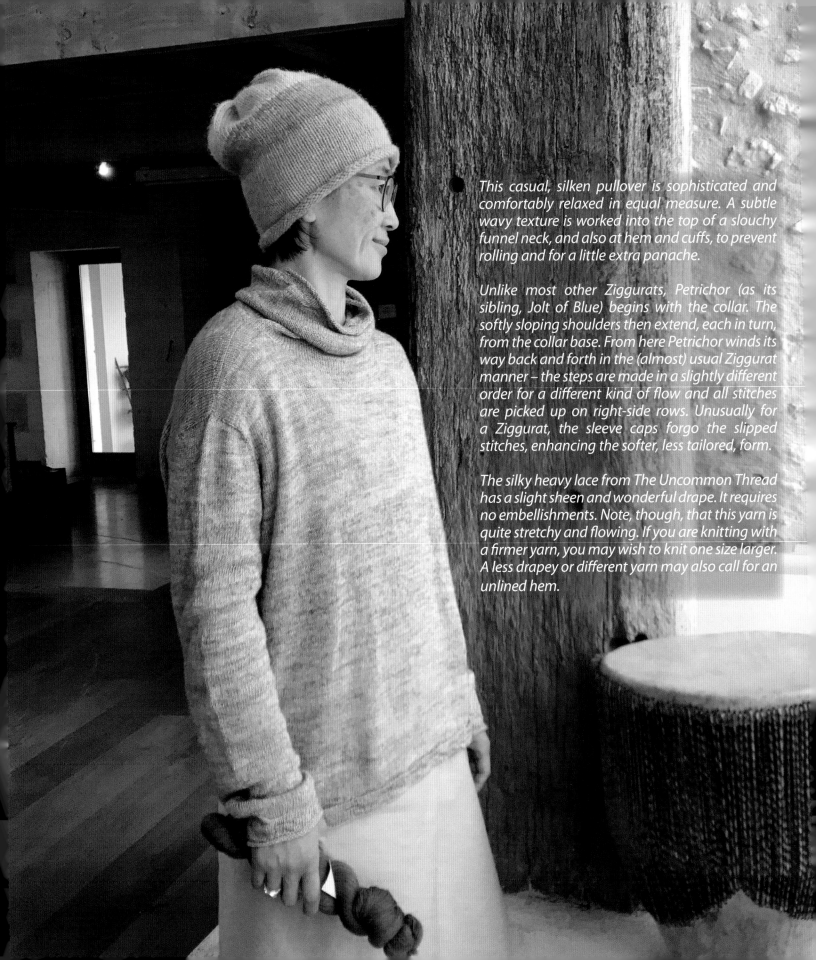

This casual, silken pullover is sophisticated and comfortably relaxed in equal measure. A subtle wavy texture is worked into the top of a slouchy funnel neck, and also at hem and cuffs, to prevent rolling and for a little extra panache.

Unlike most other Ziggurats, Petrichor (as its sibling, Jolt of Blue) begins with the collar. The softly sloping shoulders then extend, each in turn, from the collar base. From here Petrichor winds its way back and forth in the (almost) usual Ziggurat manner – the steps are made in a slightly different order for a different kind of flow and all stitches are picked up on right-side rows. Unusually for a Ziggurat, the sleeve caps forgo the slipped stitches, enhancing the softer, less tailored, form.

The silky heavy lace from The Uncommon Thread has a slight sheen and wonderful drape. It requires no embellishments. Note, though, that this yarn is quite stretchy and flowing. If you are knitting with a firmer yarn, you may wish to knit one size larger. A less drapey or different yarn may also call for an unlined hem.

Petrichor
casual laceweight funnel neck

TO FIT SIZE
81 (86, 91, 97, 102) [107, 112, 117, 122, 127] cm
32 (34, 36, 38, 40) [42, 44, 46, 48, 50] inches

FUNNEL NECK
Slouchy funnel collar

FIT
Relaxed fit with approx 15 cm / 6" ease

YARN
The Uncommon Thread Silky Merino Lace (Heavy Lace, 70% merino, 30% silk, 600 m (656 yds) per 100 g)
Olive Leaf x 3 (3, 3, 4, 4) [4, 4, 4, 4, 5] skeins

APPROX YARDAGE
1550 (1650, 1750, 1850, 1950) [2000, 2150, 2250, 2350, 2450] m
1700 (1800, 1900, 2000, 2100) [2200, 2350, 2450, 2550, 2650] yds

ALTERNATIVE YARN SUGGESTIONS
Nature's Luxury Sheep en Soie, Rohrspatz & Wollmeise Lace-Garn, Walk Collection Delicate Silk

NEEDLES & NOTIONS
2.75 mm (US 2) circular needle, 80 – 100 cm (32 – 40")
or size to obtain gauge
2.5 mm (US 1.5) circular needle, 60 – 100 cm (24 – 40")
Stitch holders; stitch markers

BLOCKED GAUGE
31 sts x 40 rows on 2.75 mm (US 2) needle = 10 cm / 4"

SAMPLE SIZES
Grey: Size 40 weighs 280 g / 10 oz
Rose: Size 38 knitted in Wollmeise Lace Garn (Gloire de Dijon), with 2 cm added length weighs 315 g / 11 oz

It should be possible to knit up to size 40 with 3 skeins of Silky Merino Lace, but you may prefer to finish the sleeves before completing the body, to make sure you have enough yarn. The approximate yardage is calculated with an ample margin of security. If you are knitting Petrichor with Rohrspatz & Wollmeise Lace-Garn, another thing to consider is that Wollmeise skeins are, as a rule, generously overweight.

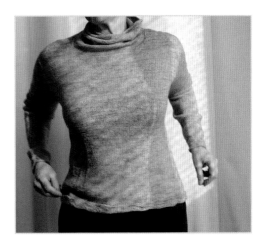

Petrichor

COLLAR

Using longtail cast on and 2.75 mm (US 2) needle, cast on 144 (144, 144, 144, 144) [144, 160, 160, 160, 160] sts.
R1: Knit.
R2: Purl.
Pm, join to knit in the round.
Rnds 3 – 6: Knit.
Rnds 7 – 13: *Sl1 wyf, (k1, sl1 wyf) x 3, k9; work from * to end of rnd.
Rnd 14: Knit.

Continue to knit in the round to 20 cm (8") from cast on.

The shoulders are cast on as extensions, each shoulder in turn, from the base of the collar. At the end of each WS row, work one or two collar stitches as directed below.

STEP 1: RIGHT BACK SHOULDER

R1 (RS): With working yarn, k62 (62, 62, 62, 62) [62, 66, 66, 66, 66] collar sts, *(turn work over so WS is facing)* borrow last st for cast on loop, crochet cast on 32 (33, 35, 37, 38) [40, 41, 43, 44, 46] sts, replace loop onto LN *(make a final chain st but not around the needle)*.
R2 (WS): P32 (33, 35, 37, 38) [40, 41, 43, 44, 46], p2tog tbl (1 cast on st with 1 collar st), p1, turn.
R3: Sl1^, pm, k28 (29, 31, 32, 33) [35, 36, 37, 38, 40], turn.
R4: Sl1^, purl to m, rm, p1^, p1, turn.
R5: Sl1^, pm, k24 (25, 27, 27, 28) [30, 31, 32, 32, 34], turn.
R6: Sl1^, purl to m, rm, p1^, p1, turn.
R7: Sl1^, pm, k20 (21, 23, 23, 23) [25, 26, 27, 27, 28], turn.
Rows 8, 10, 12: Sl1^, purl to m, rm, p1^, p2, turn.
R9: Sl1^, pm, k17 (18, 20, 20, 20) [21, 22, 23, 23, 23], turn.
R11: Sl1^, pm, k14 (15, 17, 17, 17) [17, 18, 19, 19, 19], turn.
R13: Sl1^, pm, k12 (12, 13, 13, 13) [13, 13, 14, 14, 14], turn.
R14: Sl1^, purl to m, rm, p1^, purl to m, rm.

93 (94, 96, 98, 99) [101, 106, 108, 109, 111] Right Back Shoulder & Back Collar sts

Continue to next step without turning.

STEP 2: LEFT BACK SHOULDER

Setup Row (WS): *(Turn work over so WS is facing)* borrow last st for cast on loop, crochet cast on 32 (33, 35, 37, 38) [40, 41, 43, 44, 46] sts, replace loop onto LN *(make a final chain st but not around the needle)*.
R1 (RS): K32 (33, 35, 37, 38) [40, 41, 43, 44, 46], k2tog (1 cast on st with 1 collar st), k1, turn.
R2: Sl1^, pm, p28 (29, 31, 32, 33) [35, 36, 37, 38, 40], turn.
Rows 3 & 5: Sl1^, knit to m, rm, k1^, k1, turn.
R4: Sl1^, pm, p24 (25, 27, 27, 28) [30, 31, 32, 32, 34], turn.

Photo © Sabine Bach

R6: Sl1^, pm, p20 (21, 23, 23, 23) [25, 26, 27, 27, 28], turn.
Rows 7, 9, 11 & 13: Sl1^, knit to m, rm, k1^, k2, turn.
R8: Sl1^, pm, p17 (18, 20, 20, 20) [21, 22, 23, 23, 23], turn.
R10: Sl1^, pm, p14 (15, 17, 17, 17) [17, 18, 19, 19, 19], turn.
R12: Sl1^, pm, p12 (12, 13, 13, 13) [13, 13, 14, 14, 14], turn.
R14: Sl1^, pm, purl to end (working any sl1^ as p1^).
124 (126, 130, 134, 136) [140, 146, 150, 152, 156] Back sts

STEP 3: WORKING ACROSS BACK

R1 (RS): Knit to m, rm, k1^, knit to end, working (working any sl1^ as k1^).
R2 (WS): Purl.
R3: Knit.
R4: Purl.
Work **Rows 3 & 4** again x 6 (6, 6, 7, 7) [7, 9, 9, 9, 9].
Pick up cap stitches in approx 2 of every 3 rows and pick up inside the complete outermost stitch.
Final Row (RS): Knit to last 2 sts, ssk, p&k12 (12, 12, 14, 14) [14, 16, 16, 16, 16] sts along edge for first half of Right Sleeve Cap.

12 (12, 12, 14, 14) [14, 16, 16, 16, 16] Right Cap sts
123 (125, 129, 133, 135) [139, 145, 149, 151, 155] Back sts

Slide stitches off needle tips to rest on the cable.
Set these stitches aside, continue to next step without turning.

STEP 4: RIGHT FRONT SHOULDER

Note: Some short rows begin with sl1wyf instead of sl1^.
The decreases use stitches from the collar to shape the neckline.
R1 (RS): Loop cable, p&k31 (32, 34, 36, 37) [39, 40, 42, 43, 45] sts (for Right Front Shoulder) in the cast on of Right Back Shoulder, *and remember to pick up second stitch in line with second stitch in from edge*, pick up in gap (but don't knit) and place on LN, k2tog (picked up loop with 1 Collar st), turn.
32 (33, 35, 37, 38) [40, 41, 43, 44, 46] Right Front sts
81 (81, 81, 81, 81) [81, 93, 93, 93, 93] Front Collar sts
R2 (WS): Sl1wyf, pm, p26 (27, 29, 30, 31) [33, 34, 35, 36, 38], turn.
R3: Sl1^, knit to m, rm, ssk, turn.
R4: Sl1wyf, pm, p21 (22, 24, 24, 25) [27, 28, 29, 29, 31], turn.
R5: Sl1^, knit to m, rm, ssk, turn.
R6: Sl1wyf, pm, p16 (17, 19, 19, 19) [21, 22, 23, 23, 24], turn.
On the next row ssk or sssk as directed.
R7: Sl1^, knit to m, rm, ssk (ssk, ssk, ssk, ssk) [ssk, sssk, sssk, sssk, sssk], turn.
R8: Sl1wyf, pm, p11 (12, 14, 14, 14) [15, 16, 17, 17, 17], turn.
R9: Sl1^, knit to m, rm, ssk (ssk, ssk, ssk, ssk) [ssk, sssk, sssk, sssk, sssk], turn.
R10: Sl1wyf, pm, p7 (7, 9, 9, 9) [9, 10, 11, 11, 11], turn.
R11: Sl1^, knit to m, rm, sssk, turn.
R12: Sl1wyf, pm, p3 (3, 4, 4, 4) [4, 4, 5, 5, 5], turn.
R13: Sl1^, knit to m, rm, sssk, turn.
R14: Sl1wyf, pm, purl to loop (working any sl1^ as p1^), turn.

SIZES 44, 46, 48, 50 ONLY
R15: Knit to m, rm, sssk, turn.
R16: Sl1wyf, pm, purl to loop, turn.

ALL SIZES
R17: Knit to m, rm, sssk, k1, turn.
33 (34, 36, 38, 39) [41, 42, 44, 45, 47] Right Front sts
R18: Sl1^, pm, purl to loop, turn.
R19: Knit to m, rm, k1^, k1, turn.
34 (35, 37, 39, 40) [42, 43, 45, 46, 48] Right Front sts
R20: Sl1^, pm, purl to loop, turn.
Work **Rows 19 & 20** again x 3 (3, 3, 4, 4) [4, 5, 5, 5, 5].
37 (38, 40, 43, 44) [46, 48, 50, 51, 53] Right Front sts
R21: Knit to m, rm, k1^, k2, turn.
39 (40, 42, 45, 46) [48, 50, 52, 53, 55] Right Front sts
R22: Sl1^, pm, purl to loop, turn.
Work **Rows 21 & 22** again x 2.
43 (44, 46, 49, 50) [52, 54, 56, 57, 59] Right Front sts
Final Row (RS): Knit to m, rm, k1^, knit across collar to last st.

Continue to next step without turning.

STEP 5: LEFT FRONT SHOULDER

Note: Some short rows begin with sl1wyb instead of sl1^.
R1 (RS): Pm, sl1 (last collar st), pick up in gap (but don't knit) and place on LN, sl1 to LN, ssk (picked up loop with 1 Collar st), p&k31 (32, 34, 36, 37) [39, 40, 42, 43, 45] sts (for Left Front Shoulder) in the cast on of Left Back Shoulder, taking care to line up the last 2 sts properly.
32 (33, 35, 37, 38) [40, 41, 43, 44, 46] Left Front sts
80 (80, 80, 80, 80) [80, 92, 92, 92, 92] Front Collar sts
R2 (WS): Purl to 1 st before m, rm, p2tog, turn.
R3: Sl1wyb, pm, k26 (27, 29, 30, 31) [33, 34, 35, 36, 38], turn.
Rows 4, 6, 8: Sl1^, purl to m, rm, p2tog, turn.
R5: Sl1wyb, pm, k21 (22, 24, 24, 25) [27, 28, 29, 29, 31], turn.
R7: Sl1wyb, pm, k16 (17, 19, 19, 19) [21, 22, 23, 23, 24], turn.
R9: Sl1wyb, pm, k11 (12, 14, 14, 14) [15, 16, 17, 17, 17] sts, turn.
On the next row p2tog or p3tog as directed.
R10: Sl1^, purl to m, rm, p2tog (p2tog, p2tog, p2tog, p2tog) [p2tog, p3tog, p3tog, p3tog, p3tog], turn.
R11: Sl1wyb, pm, k7 (7, 9, 9, 9) [9, 10, 11, 11, 11] sts, turn.
R12: Sl1^, purl to m, rm, p3tog, turn.
R13: Sl1wyb, pm, k3 (3, 4, 4, 4) [4, 4, 5, 5, 5] sts, turn.
R14: Sl1^, purl to m, rm, p3tog, turn.
R15: Sl1wyb, pm, knit to loop (working any sl1^ as k1^), turn.

SIZES 44, 46, 48, 50 ONLY
R16: Purl to m, rm, p3tog, turn.
R17: Sl1wyb, pm, knit to loop, turn.

Petrichor

ALL SIZES

R18: Purl to m, rm, p3tog, p1, turn.
33 (34, 36, 38, 39) [41, 42, 44, 45, 47] Left Front sts
R19: Sl1^, pm, knit to loop, turn.
R20: Purl to m, rm, p1^, p1, turn.
34 (35, 37, 39, 40) [42, 43, 45, 46, 48] Left Front sts
Work **Rows 19 & 20** again x 3 (3, 3, 4, 4) [4, 5, 5, 5, 5].
37 (38, 40, 43, 44) [46, 48, 50, 51, 53] Left Front sts
R21: Sl1^, pm, knit to loop, turn.
R22: Purl to m, rm, p1^, p2, turn.
39 (40, 42, 45, 46) [48, 50, 52, 53, 55] Left Front sts
Work **Rows 21 & 22** again x 2.
43 (44, 46, 49, 50) [52, 54, 56, 57, 59] Left Front sts

Note: The next row becomes the first round; Petrichor is knitted in the round from this point.

Final Row/Round(RS): Sl1^, pm, knit to 2 sts before loop, ssk, pm, p&k24 (24, 24, 28, 28) [28, 32, 32, 32, 32] sts along edge for entire Left Sleeve Cap, pm, k2tog, knit to m, sm, k12 (12, 12, 14, 14) [14, 16, 16, 16, 16] Right Sleeve Cap sts, p&k12 (12, 12, 14, 14) [14, 16, 16, 16, 16] sts along edge (for second half of Right Sleeve Cap), pm, k2tog, knit to 1 st before m.

You are now at Left Front Sleeve Cap.

24 (24, 24, 28, 28) [28, 32, 32, 32, 32] sts for each Sleeve Cap
122 (124, 128, 132, 134) [138, 144, 148, 150, 154] Front sts
122 (124, 128, 132, 134) [138, 144, 148, 150, 154] Back sts

STEP 6: SLEEVE CAPS & BODY

You will now increase for the sleeves and and later also the body simultaneously. (See Helpful Table for an overview of all increases.)
The round begins 1 st before the Left Front Sleeve marker.

REFER TO **BOX A** FOR ROUND INSTRUCTIONS
Work **Rnds 1 & 2** x 17 (16, 14, 13, 11) [12, 9, 9, 8, 9].
58 (56, 52, 54, 50) [52, 50, 50, 48, 50] Sleeve sts

INTRODUCE BODY INCREASES
Work **Rnds 3 & 2** x 1 (3, 5, 5, 7) [10, 9, 12, 12, 15].
60 (62, 62, 64, 64) [72, 68, 74, 72, 80] Sleeve sts
124 (130, 138, 142, 148) [158, 162, 172, 174, 184] Front/Back sts

Work **Rnds 3 & 1** x 5 (5, 5, 6, 6) [4, 6, 5, 6, 5].
80 (82, 82, 88, 88) [88, 92, 94, 96, 100] Sleeve sts
134 (140, 148, 154, 160) [166, 174, 182, 186, 194] Front/Back sts

Work **Rnd 3**.
82 (84, 84, 90, 90) [90, 94, 96, 98, 102] Sleeve sts
136 (142, 150, 156, 162) [168, 176, 184, 188, 196] Front/Back sts

Final Rnd: Knit to 2 sts before final m.

STEP 7: SEPARATING SLEEVES & BODY

Separation Rnd 1: *Pm, k2, rm, put all sts to next m on holder (= sleeve sts), rm, *(turn work over so WS is facing) borrow last st for cast on loop*, crochet cast on 8 (9, 9, 10, 11) [12, 12, 12, 14, 14] sts, pm, cast on 6 (7, 7, 8, 9) [10, 10, 10, 12, 12] sts, *replace loop onto LN (make a final chain st but not around the needle), turn work over so RS is facing*, knit to 2 sts before m, work from * to * once more, knit to m.

You are now at Left Front Sleeve.

150 (158, 166, 174, 182) [190, 198, 206, 214, 222] Front/Back sts

Separation Rnd 2: *Rm, ssk, knit to m, sm, p1, knit to end of underarm cast on, make loop in bar and place on LN, k2tog (next st and loop), knit to m*, work from * to * once more.

149 (157, 165, 173, 181) [189, 197, 205, 213, 221] Front/Back sts

STEP 8: BODY TO HEM

Continue in stocking st over body stitches only.
The round begins under Left Sleeve.
One stitch under each arm is worked in garter st (g1), which creates a faux side seam.

BOX A

sM1 = sleeve increase   bLLI/RLI = body increase

Note: *Body increases are made 1 st before and 1 st after each Sleeve. The stitch that is usually sl1wyb in other Ziggurats is here a plain k1.*

Rnd 1: (K1, sm, sM1L, knit to m, sM1R, sm, knit to 1 st before m) twice.

Rnd 2: Knit to 1 st before final m.

Rnd 3: (bLLI, k1, sm, sM1L, knit to m, sM1R, sm, k1, bRLI, knit to 1 st before m) twice.

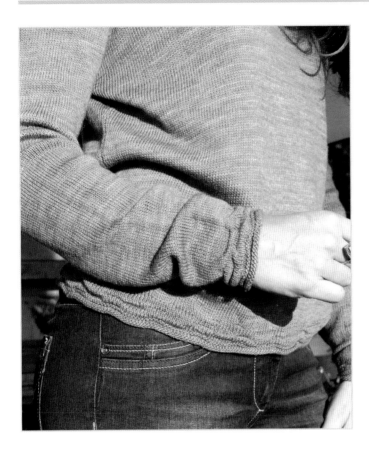

REFER TO **BOX B** FOR ROUND INSTRUCTIONS
Work **Rnd 1** to 5 cm/ 2" from underarm.

Note: If you are trying to stretch your skeins, this is a good place to set the body aside to work the sleeves before finishing the body.

BODY DECREASES
Work **Decrease Rnd**.
147 (155, 163, 171, 179) [187, 195, 203, 211, 219] Front/Back sts

Continue with **Rnd 1**, working **Decrease Rnd** every 26 (26, 28, 28, 28) [28, 28, 28, 28, 28]th round again x 4.
139 (147, 155, 163, 171) [179, 187, 195, 203, 211] Front/Back sts

Work to 32 (32.5, 33.5, 34, 35) [35, 36, 35, 36, 35.5] cm / 12.5 (12.75, 13.25, 13.5, 13.75) [13.75, 14.25, 13.75, 14.25, 14]" from underarm or to 2.5 cm / 1" from desired length.

Next Rnd: Decrease (k2tog) 6 sts evenly over the round.
272 (288, 304, 320, 336) [352, 368, 384, 400, 416] sts

STEP 9: LINED HEM
The lining and hem are knitted separately. Lining sts are picked up on the inside of the sweater, then set aside while the outer layer of the hem is finished.

Option: For a simpler, unlined hem, skip lining, knit hem as directed, then knit a rolled edge as for Cuff.

LINING
Hem lining stitches are picked up on WS (see Tutorial section).
Slide sts off needle tips to rest on the cable.
Take working yarn to WS. With smaller (2.5 mm / US 1.5) needle (N2) and going counterclockwise on inside of sweater, p&k221 (234, 247, 260, 273) [286, 299, 312, 325, 338] sts in the bars *between* sts (approx in 4 for every 5).
221 (234, 247, 260, 273) [286, 299, 312, 325, 338] Lining sts
Take yarn to RS.
Slide sts off needle tips to rest on cable, set Lining sts aside.

HEM
Continue with working yarn and 2.75 mm (US 2) needle.
Rnds 1 – 7: *K9, sl1wyf, (k1, sl1wyf) x 3; work from * to end of rnd.
Rnd 8: Knit.
Work **Rnds 1 – 7** once more.
Next Rnd: *K8, ssk, k2, (ssk) twice; work from * to end of rnd.
Slide sts off needle tips to rest on cable, set Hem sts aside.

221 (234, 247, 260, 273) [286, 299, 312, 325, 338] Hem sts

BOX B

BODY TO HEM
Rnd 1: (Sm, g1, knit to marker) twice..

Decrease Rnd: (Sm, g1, k2tog, knit to 2 sts before side m, ssk) twice.

Photo © Sabine Bach

LINING

Join new yarn.
With N2 and on WS (along inside of Hem and downwards), knit 11 rounds or to slightly shorter than Hem.
Cut Lining yarn.
Slide sts off needle tips to rest on cable, set Lining sts aside.

BIND OFF

Weave in any loose ends at hem before binding off.
With 2.75 mm / US 2 needle and from RS, bind off hem sts together with lining sts, using 3-Needle Bind Off and keeping an even tension.

STEP 10: SLEEVES

Place 82 (84, 84, 90, 90) [90, 94, 96, 98, 102] Sleeve sts from holder back on larger (2.75 mm / US 2) needle. Join yarn at right side of gap, p&k6 (7, 7, 8, 9) [10, 10, 10, 12, 12] sts along the first half of the underarm cast on, pm, p&k7 (8, 8, 9, 10) [11, 11, 11, 13, 13] sts more along second half of underarm, knit to m.
95 (99, 99, 107, 109) [111, 115, 117, 123, 127] sts

REFER TO **BOX C** FOR ROUND INSTRUCTIONS
Work **Rnd 1** to 5 cm / 2" from underarm.

SLEEVE DECREASES

Work **Decrease Rnd**.
93 (97, 97, 105, 107) [109, 113, 115, 121, 125] sts

Continue with **Rnd 1**, working **Decrease Rnd** every 18 (15, 14, 13, 11) [11, 10, 16, 12, 10]th round again x 8 (9, 10, 12, 13) [14, 16, 10, 13, 16].
77 (79, 77, 81, 81) [81, 81, 95, 95, 93] sts

Work to 41.5 (41.5, 42.5, 44.5, 44.5) [44.5, 44.5, 45.5, 45.5, 45.5] cm /16.25 (16.25, 16.75, 17.5, 17.5) [17.5, 17.5, 18, 18, 18]" from underarm or to 3.5 cm / 1.5" from desired sleeve length.

STEP 11: CUFF

Setup Round: Knit and increase 3 (1, 3, 0, 0) [0, 0, 1, 1, 3] sts evenly distributed over the round.
80 (80, 80, 81, 81) [81, 81, 96, 96, 96] sts
Note: For sizes **38, 40, 42, 44** begin next round with (k2tog, k8) instead of k9.
Rnds 1 – 7: *K9, sl1wyf, (k1, sl1wyf) x 3; work from * to end of rnd.
80 (80, 80, 80, 80) [80, 80, 96, 96, 96] sts
Rnd 8: Knit.
Work **Rnds 1 – 7** once more.
Next Rnd: *K8, ssk, k2, (ssk) twice; work from * to end of rnd.
65 (65, 65, 65, 65) [65, 65, 78, 78, 78] sts

Change to smaller (2.5 mm / US 1.5) needle.
Rnd 1: Purl.
Rnds 2 – 7: Knit.
Bind off in even tension.

FINISH

Weave in loose ends. Soak and block to measurements.

BOX C

SLEEVE ROUNDS
Rnd 1: Sm, g1, knit to m.
Decrease Rnd: Sm, g1, k2tog, knit to 2 sts before m, ssk.

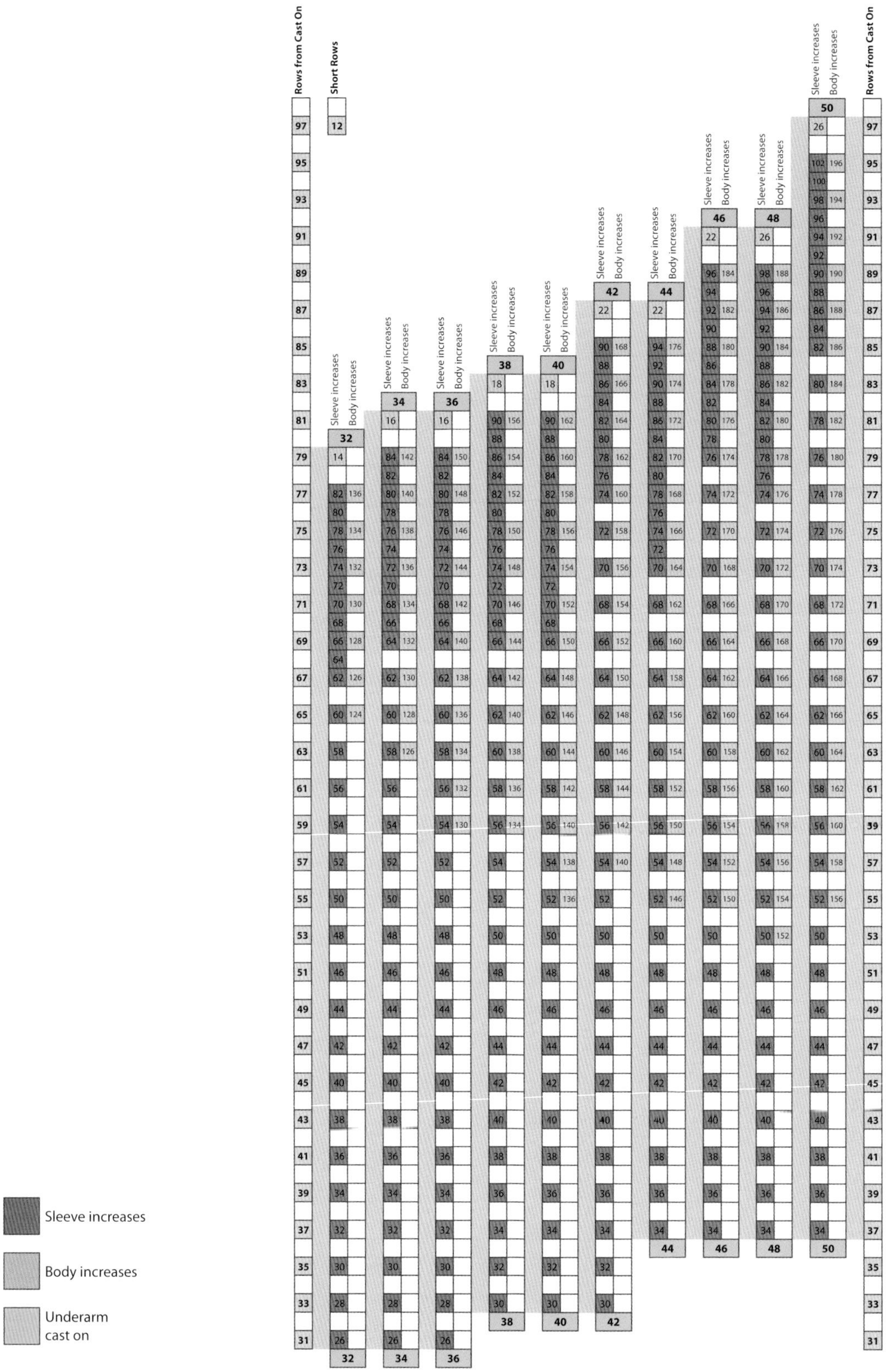

Petrichor — Chart

This page is a full-page knitting chart consisting of a series of size rows. Each size (50, 48, 46, 44, 42, 40, 38, 36, 34, 32) has a "Body increases" row and a "Sleeve increases" row. The chart is bounded at top and bottom by "Rows from Cast On" number strips and includes a "Short Rows" label (value 12).

Rows from Cast On (top strip):

97	95	93	91	89	87	85	83	81	79	77	75	73	71	69	67	65	63	61	59	57	55	53	51	49	47	45	43	41	39	37	35	33	31

Size 50 — Body increases: 50, 196, 194, 192, 190, 188, 186, 184, 182, 180, 178, 176, 174, 172, 170, 168, 166, 164, 162, 160, 158, 156, 50

Size 50 — Sleeve increases: 26, 102, 100, 98, 96, 94, 92, 90, 88, 86, 84, 82, 80, 78, 76, 74, 72, 70, 68, 66, 64, 62, 60, 58, 56, 54, 52, 50, 48, 46, 44, 42, 40, 38, 36, 34

Size 48 — Body increases: 48, 188, 186, 184, 182, 180, 178, 176, 174, 172, 170, 168, 166, 164, 162, 160, 158, 156, 154, 152, 48

Size 48 — Sleeve increases: 26, 98, 96, 94, 92, 90, 88, 86, 84, 82, 80, 78, 76, 74, 72, 70, 68, 66, 64, 62, 60, 58, 56, 54, 52, 50, 48, 46, 44, 42, 40, 38, 36, 34

Size 46 — Body increases: 46, 184, 182, 180, 178, 176, 174, 172, 170, 168, 166, 164, 162, 160, 158, 156, 154, 152, 150, 46

Size 46 — Sleeve increases: 22, 96, 94, 92, 90, 88, 86, 84, 82, 80, 78, 74, 72, 70, 68, 66, 64, 62, 60, 58, 56, 54, 52, 50, 48, 46, 44, 42, 40, 38, 36, 34

Size 44 — Body increases: 44, 176, 174, 172, 170, 168, 166, 164, 162, 160, 158, 156, 154, 152, 150, 148, 146, 44

Size 44 — Sleeve increases: 22, 94, 92, 90, 88, 84, 82, 80, 78, 76, 74, 72, 70, 68, 66, 64, 62, 60, 58, 56, 54, 52, 50, 48, 46, 44, 42, 40, 38, 36, 34

Size 42 — Body increases: 42, 168, 166, 164, 162, 160, 158, 156, 154, 152, 150, 148, 146, 144, 142, 140, 42

Size 42 — Sleeve increases: 22, 90, 88, 86, 84, 82, 80, 78, 76, 74, 72, 70, 68, 66, 64, 62, 60, 58, 56, 54, 52, 50, 48, 46, 44, 42, 40, 38, 36, 34, 32, 30

Size 40 — Body increases: 40, 162, 160, 158, 156, 154, 152, 150, 148, 146, 144, 142, 140, 138, 136, 40

Size 40 — Sleeve increases: 18, 90, 88, 86, 84, 82, 80, 78, 76, 74, 72, 70, 68, 66, 64, 62, 60, 58, 56, 54, 52, 50, 48, 46, 44, 42, 40, 38, 36, 34, 32, 30

Size 38 — Body increases: 38, 156, 154, 152, 150, 148, 146, 144, 142, 140, 138, 136, 134, 38

Size 38 — Sleeve increases: 18, 90, 88, 86, 84, 82, 80, 78, 76, 74, 72, 70, 68, 66, 64, 62, 60, 58, 56, 54, 52, 50, 48, 46, 44, 42, 40, 38, 36, 34, 32, 30

Size 36 — Body increases: 36, 150, 148, 146, 144, 142, 140, 138, 136, 134, 132, 130, 36

Size 36 — Sleeve increases: 16, 84, 82, 80, 78, 76, 74, 72, 70, 68, 66, 64, 62, 60, 58, 56, 54, 52, 50, 48, 46, 44, 42, 40, 38, 36, 34, 32, 30, 28, 26

Size 34 — Body increases: 34, 142, 140, 138, 136, 134, 132, 130, 128, 126, 34

Size 34 — Sleeve increases: 16, 84, 82, 80, 78, 76, 74, 72, 70, 68, 66, 64, 62, 60, 58, 56, 54, 52, 50, 48, 46, 44, 42, 40, 38, 36, 34, 32, 30, 28, 26

Short Rows: 12

Size 32 — Body increases: 32, 136, 134, 132, 130, 128, 126, 124, 32

Size 32 — Sleeve increases: 14, 82, 80, 78, 76, 74, 72, 70, 68, 66, 64, 62, 60, 58, 56, 54, 52, 50, 48, 46, 44, 42, 40, 38, 36, 34, 32, 30, 28, 26

Rows from Cast On (bottom strip):

97	95	93	91	89	87	85	83	81	79	77	75	73	71	69	67	65	63	61	59	57	55	53	51	49	47	45	43	41	39	37	35	33	31

Legend:
- Sleeve increases
- Body increases
- Underarm cast on

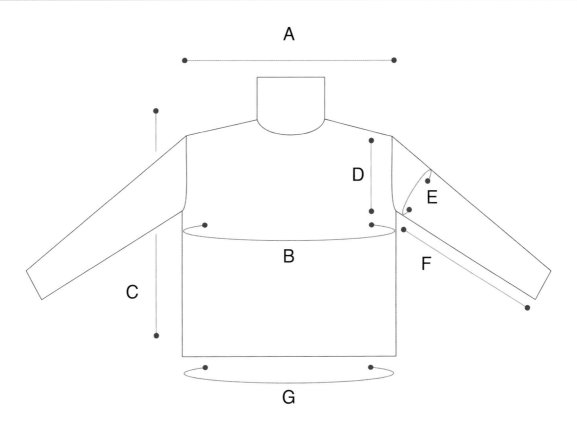

PETRICHOR GARMENT MEASUREMENTS

	32	34	36	38	40	42	44	46	48	50
A – Shoulder width (cm)	39.5	40	41.5	42.5	43	44.5	46.5	47.5	48.5	49.5
in	15.5	15.75	16.25	16.75	17	17.5	18.25	18.75	19	19.5
B – Bust (cm)	96	101.5	106.5	111.5	117	122	127	132.5	137.5	142.5
in	37.75	40	42	44	46	48	50	52.25	54.25	56
C – Length (cm)	54	55	56	57	58	59	60	60	61	62
in	21.25	21.75	22	22.5	22.75	23.25	23.5	23.5	24	24.5
D – Armhole depth (cm)	16.5	17	17	17.5	17.5	18.5	18.5	19.5	19.5	21
in	6.5	6.5	6.5	7	7	7.5	7.5	7.5	7.5	8.5
E – Sleeve circumf (cm)	30.5	32	32	34.5	35	36	37	37.5	39.5	41
in	12	12.5	12.5	13.5	13.75	14.25	14.5	14.75	15.5	16.25
F – Sleeve seam (cm)	45	45	46	48	48	48	48	49	49	49
in	17.75	17.75	18	19	19	19	19	19.25	19.25	19.25
G – Hem circumf (cm)	87.5	93	98	103	108.5	113.5	118.5	124	129	134
in	34.5	36.5	38.5	40.5	42.75	44.75	46.75	48.75	50.75	52.75

Discreet shirring at the edge of the drapey funnel neck, hem and cuffs creates gentle waves, providing a relaxed and coherent structure. With generous ease, this is a three-season wardrobe staple suitable for layering.

Jolt of Blue, like its lace sister, Petrichor, features a variation on the usual Ziggurat construction. Starting with the collar knitted in the round, the softly sloping shoulders extend, each in turn, from the collar base, and the stitches are picked up on right-side rows, going counterclockwise. Less zigging, in other words. But no less exciting.

The intense colour of Walk Collection's single ply Cozy Merino really glows in simple and smooth stocking stitch.

TO FIT SIZE

81 (86, 91, 97, 102) [107, 112, 117, 122, 127] cm
32 (34, 36, 38, 40) [42, 44, 46, 48, 50] inches

FUNNEL NECK

Slouchy funnel collar

FIT

Relaxed fit with approx 15 cm / 6" ease

YARN

WalkCollection Cozy Merino (Fingering/single ply, 100% merino,
366 m (400 yds) per 100 g); Royal x 4 (4, 4, 4) [5, 5, 5, 6, 6] skeins

APPROX YARDAGE

1200 (1350, 1400, 1500, 1600) [1650, 1750, 1850, 1950, 2000] m
1350 (1450, 1550, 1650, 1750) [1800, 1900, 2000, 2100, 2200] yds

ALTERNATIVE YARN SUGGESTIONS

Outlaw Yarn Bohemia Sport, DyeForYarn Sport Merino, The
Uncommon Thread Everyday Singles, Rohrspatz & Wollmeise Blend

NEEDLES & NOTIONS

3 mm (US 2.5) circular needle, 80 – 100 cm (32 – 40")
or size to obtain gauge
2.5 mm (US 1.5) circular needle, 60 – 100 cm (24 – 40")
Stitch holders; stitch markers

BLOCKED GAUGE

25 sts x 36 rows on 3 mm (US 2.5) needle = 10 cm / 4"

SAMPLE SIZE

Size 40 without bust darts weighs 375 g / 13.25 oz

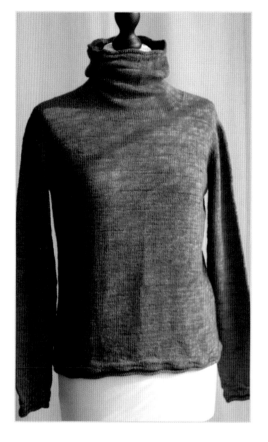

Jolt of Blue

COLLAR

Using longtail cast on and 3 mm (US 2.5) needle, cast on 128 (128, 128, 128, 128) [128, 144, 144, 144, 144] sts.
R1: Knit.
R2: Purl.
Pm, join to knit in the round.
Rnds 3 – 6: Knit.
Rnds 7 – 13: *Sl1 wyf, (k1, sl1 wyf) x 3, k9; work from * to end of rnd.
Rnd 14: Knit.

Continue to knit in the round to 15 cm (6") from cast on.

The shoulders are cast on as extensions, each shoulder in turn, from the base of the collar. At the end of each WS row, work one or two collar stitches as directed below.

STEP 1: RIGHT BACK SHOULDER

R1 (RS): With working yarn, k54 (54, 54, 54, 54) [54, 62, 62, 62, 62] collar sts, *(turn work over so WS is facing) borrow last st for cast on loop*, crochet cast on 23 (24, 26, 28, 29) [31, 29, 30, 31, 32] sts, replace loop onto LN *(make a final chain st but not around the needle)*.
R2 (WS): P23 (24, 26, 28, 29) [31, 29, 30, 31, 32], p2tog tbl (1 cast on st with 1 collar st), p1, turn.
R3: Sl1^, pm, k20 (20, 22, 24, 25) [26, 25, 25, 26, 27], turn.
R4: Sl1^, purl to m, rm, p1^, p1, turn.
R5: Sl1^, pm, k17 (17, 18, 20, 21) [21, 21, 21, 21, 22], turn.

DyeForYarn Sport Merino in Dried brown algae

R6: Sl1^, purl to m, rm, p1^, p1, turn.
R7: Sl1^, pm, k14 (14, 14, 16, 17) [17, 17, 17, 17, 17], turn.
R8: Sl1^, purl to m, rm, p1^, p2, turn.
R9: Sl1^, pm, k12 (12, 12, 13, 14) [14, 14, 14, 14, 14], turn.
R10: Sl1^, purl to m, rm, p1^, p2, turn.
R11: Sl1^, pm, k10 (10, 10, 10, 11) [11, 11, 11, 11, 11], turn.
R12: Sl1^, purl to m, rm, p1^, purl to m, rm.

76 (77, 79, 81, 82) [84, 90, 91, 92, 93] Right Back Shoulder & Back Collar sts.

STEP 2: LEFT BACK SHOULDER

Setup Row (WS): *(Turn work over so WS is facing) borrow last st for cast on loop*, crochet cast on 23 (24, 26, 28, 29) [31, 29, 30, 31, 32] sts, replace loop onto LN *(make a final chain st but not around the needle)*.
R1 (RS): K23 (24, 26, 28, 29) [31, 29, 30, 31, 32], k2tog (1 cast on st with 1 collar st), k1, turn.
R2 (WS): Sl1^, pm, p20 (20, 22, 24, 25) [26, 25, 25, 26, 27], turn.
Rows 3, 5, 7, 9: Sl1^, knit to m, rm, k1^, k1, turn.
R4: Sl1^, pm, p17 (17, 18, 20, 21) [21, 21, 21, 21, 22], turn.
R6: Sl1^, pm, p14 (14, 14, 16, 17) [17, 17, 17, 17, 17], turn.
R8: Sl1^, pm, p12 (12, 12, 13, 14) [14, 14, 14, 14, 14], turn.
R10: Sl1^, pm, p10 (10, 10, 10, 11) [11, 11, 11, 11, 11], turn.
R11: Sl1^, knit to m, rm, k1^, k2, turn.
R12: Sl1^, pm, purl to end (working any sl1^ as p1^).

98 (100, 104, 108, 110) [114, 118, 120, 122, 124] Back sts

STEP 3: WORKING ACROSS BACK

R1 (RS): Knit to m, rm, k1^, knit to end, (working any sl1^ as k1^).
R2 (WS): Purl.
R3: Knit.
R4: Purl.
Work **Rows 3 & 4** again x 6 (6, 6, 7, 7) [7, 9, 9, 9, 9].
Pick up cap stitches in approx 2 of every 3 rows and pick up inside the complete outermost stitch.
Final Row (RS): Knit to last 2 sts, ssk, pm, p&k12 (12, 12, 14, 14) [14, 16, 16, 16, 16] sts along edge for first half of Right Sleeve Cap.

12 (12, 12, 14, 14) [14, 16, 16, 16, 16] Right Cap sts
97 (99, 103, 107, 109) [113, 117, 119, 121, 123] Back sts

Slide stitches off needle tips to rest on the cable.
Set these stitches aside, continue to next step without turning.

STEP 4: RIGHT FRONT SHOULDER

Note: Some short rows begin with sl1wyf instead of sl1^.
The decreases use stitches from the collar to shape the neckline.

R1 (RS): Loop cable, p&k22 (23, 25, 27, 28) [30, 28, 29, 30, 31] sts (for Right Front Shoulder) in the cast on of Right Back Shoulder, *and remember to pick up second stitch in line with second stitch in from edge*, pick up in gap (but don't knit) and place on LN, k2tog (picked up loop with 1 Collar st), turn.

23 (24, 26, 28, 29) [31, 29, 30, 31, 32] Right Front sts
73 (73, 73, 73, 73) [73, 81, 81, 81, 81] Front Collar sts

R2 (WS): Sl1wyf, pm, p18 (19, 20, 22, 23) [24, 23, 24, 24, 25], turn.
Rows 3, 5, 7, 9: Sl1^, knit to m, rm, ssk, turn.
R4: Sl1wyf, pm, p14 (15, 15, 17, 18) [19, 18, 19, 19, 19], turn.
R6: Sl1wyf, pm, p10 (11, 11, 12, 13) [14, 13, 14, 14, 14], turn.
R8: Sl1wyf, pm, p6 (7, 7, 7, 8) [9, 8, 9, 9, 9], turn.
R10: Sl1wyf, pm, p2 (3, 3, 3, 3) [4, 3, 4, 4, 4], turn.
R11: Sl1^, knit to m, rm, sssk, turn.
R12: Sl1wyf, pm, purl to loop (working any sl1^ as p1^), turn.
R13: Knit to m, rm, sssk, turn.
R14: Sl1wyf, pm, purl to loop, turn.
R15: Knit to m, rm, sssk, k1, turn.
24 (25, 27, 29, 30) [32, 30, 31, 32, 33] Right Front sts
R16: Sl1^, pm, purl to loop, turn.
R17: Knit to m, rm, k1^, k1, turn.
25 (26, 28, 30, 31) [33, 31, 32, 33, 34] Right Front sts
R18: Sl1^, pm, purl to loop, turn.
Work **Rows 17 & 18** again x 2 (2, 2, 3, 3) [3, 5, 5, 5, 5].
27 (28, 30, 33, 34) [36, 36, 37, 38, 39] Right Front sts
R19: Knit to m, rm, k1^, k2, turn.
29 (30, 32, 35, 36) [38, 38, 39, 40, 41] Right Front sts
R20: Sl1^, pm, purl to loop, turn.
Work **Rows 19 & 20** again x 2.
33 (34, 36, 39, 40) [42, 42, 43, 44, 45] Right Front sts
Final Row (RS): Knit to m, rm, k1^, knit across collar to last st.

Continue to next step without turning.

STEP 5: LEFT FRONT SHOULDER

Note: Some short rows begin with sl1wyb instead of sl1^.

R1 (RS): Pm, sl1 (last collar st), pick up in gap (but don't knit) and place on LN, sl1 to LN, ssk (picked up loop with 1 Collar st), p&k22 (23, 25, 27, 28) [30, 28, 29, 30, 31] sts (for Left Front Shoulder) in the cast on of Left Back Shoulder, *taking care to line up the last 2 sts properly.*
23 (24, 26, 28, 29) [31, 29, 30, 31, 32] Left Front sts
72 (72, 72, 72, 72) [72, 80, 80, 80, 80] Front Collar sts
R2 (WS): Purl to 1 st before m, rm, p2tog, turn.
R3: Sl1wyb, pm, k18 (19, 20, 22, 23) [24, 23, 24, 24, 25], turn.
Rows 4, 6, 8, 10, 12: Sl1^, purl to m, rm, p2tog, turn.

R5: Sl1wyb, pm, k14 (15, 15, 17, 18) [19, 18, 19, 19, 19], turn.
R7: Sl1wyb, pm, k10 (11, 11, 12, 13) [14, 13, 14, 14, 14], turn.
R9: Sl1wyb, pm, k6 (7, 7, 7, 8) [9, 8, 9, 9, 9] sts, turn.
R11: Sl1wyb, pm, k2 (3, 3, 3, 3) [4, 3, 4, 4, 4] sts, turn.
R13: Sl1wyb, pm, knit to loop (working any sl1^ as k1^), turn.
R14: Purl to m, rm, p3tog, turn.
R15: Sl1wyb, pm, knit to loop, turn.
R16: Purl to m, rm, p3tog, p1, turn.
24 (25, 27, 29, 30) [32, 30, 31, 32, 33] Left Front sts
R17: Sl1^ pm, knit to loop, turn.
R18: Purl to m, rm, p1^, p1, turn.
25 (26, 28, 30, 31) [33, 31, 32, 33, 34] Left Front sts
Work **Rows 17 & 18** again x 2 (2, 2, 3, 3) [3, 5, 5, 5, 5].
27 (28, 30, 33, 34) [36, 36, 37, 38, 39] Left Front sts
R19: Sl1^ pm, knit to loop, turn.
R20: Purl to m, rm, p1^, p2, turn.
29 (30, 32, 35, 36) [38, 38, 39, 40, 41] Left Front sts
Work **Rows 19 & 20** again x 2.
33 (34, 36, 39, 40) [42, 42, 43, 44, 45] Left Front sts

Note: The next row becomes the first round. Jolt of Blue is knitted in the round from this point.

Final Row/First Round(RS): Sl1^, pm, knit to 2 sts before loop, ssk, pm, p&k24 (24, 24, 28, 28) [28, 32, 32, 32, 32] sts along edge for entire Left Sleeve Cap, pm, k2tog, knit to m, sm, k12 (12, 12, 14, 14) [14, 16, 16, 16, 16] Right Sleeve Cap sts, p&k12 (12, 12, 14, 14) [14, 16, 16, 16, 16] sts along edge (for second half of Right Sleeve Cap), pm, k2tog, knit to 1 st before m.
You are now at Left Front Sleeve Cap.

24 (24, 24, 28, 28) [28, 32, 32, 32, 32] sts for each Sleeve Cap
96 (98, 102, 106, 108) [112, 116, 118, 120, 122] Front sts
96 (98, 102, 106, 108) [112, 116, 118, 120, 122] Back sts

STEP 6: SLEEVE CAPS & BODY

You will now increase for the sleeves and and later also the body simultaneously. (See Helpful Table for an overview of all increases.)
The round begins 1 st before Left Front Sleeve marker.

REFER TO **BOX A** FOR ROUND INSTRUCTIONS

Work **Rnds 1 & 2** x 16 (15, 15, 13, 11) [12, 10, 10, 10, 10].
56 (54, 54, 54, 50) [52, 52, 52, 52, 52] Sleeve sts

INTRODUCE BODY INCREASES

Work **Rnds 3 & 2** x 4 (6, 6, 8, 10) [11, 11, 13, 13, 15].
64 (66, 66, 70, 70) [74, 74, 78, 78, 82] Sleeve sts
104 (110, 114, 122, 128) [134, 138, 144, 146, 152] Front/Back sts

Work **Rnd 3**.
66 (68, 68, 72, 72) [76, 76, 80, 80, 84] Sleeve sts
106 (112, 116, 124, 130) [136, 140, 146, 148, 154] Front/Back sts

Final Round: Knit to 2 sts before final m.

STEP 7: SEPARATING SLEEVES & BODY

Separation Rnd 1: *Pm, k2, rm, place all sts to next m on holder (= sleeve sts), rm, *(turn work over so WS is facing) borrow last st for cast on loop*, crochet cast on 8 (8, 9, 9, 9) [9, 10, 10, 13, 13] sts, pm, cast on 6 (6, 7, 7, 7) [7, 8, 8, 11, 11] sts, *replace loop onto LN (make a final chain st but not around the needle), turn work over so RS is facing*, knit to 2 sts before m, work from * to * once more, knit to m.
You are now at Left Front Sleeve.

120 (126, 132, 140, 146) [152, 158, 164, 172, 178] Front/Back sts

BOX A

sM1L/R = sleeve increase   bLLI/RLI = body increase

Note: *Body increases are made 1 st before and 1 st after each Sleeve. The stitch that is usually sl1wyb in other Ziggurats is here a plain k1.=*

Rnd 1: (K1, sm, sM1L, knit to m, sM1R, sm, knit to 1 st before m) twice.

Rnd 2: Knit to 1 st before final m.

Rnd 3: (bLLI, k1, sm, sM1L, knit to m, sM1R, sm, k1, bRLI, knit to 1 st before m) twice.

Separation Rnd 2: *Rm, ssk, knit to m, sm, p1, knit to end of underarm cast on, make loop in bar and place on LN, k2tog (next st and loop), knit to m*, work from *to* once more.

119 (125, 131, 139, 145) [151, 157, 163, 171, 177] Front/Back sts

STEP 8: BODY TO HEM

Continue in stocking stitch over body stitches only.
The round begins under Left Sleeve.
One stitch under each arm is worked in garter st (g1), which creates a faux side seam.

BOX B

BODY TO HEM

Rnd 1: (Sm, g1, knit to marker) twice.

Decrease Rnd: (Sm, g1, k2tog, knit to 2 sts before side m, ssk) twice.

REFER TO **BOX B** FOR ROUND INSTRUCTIONS

Work **Rnd 1** to 5 cm/ 2" from underarm.

Note: If you are trying to stretch your skeins, this is a good place to set the body aside to work the sleeves before finishing the body.

BODY DECREASES

Work **Decrease Rnd**.
117 (123, 129, 137, 143) [149, 155, 161, 169, 175] Front/Back sts

Continue with **Rnd 1**, working **Decrease Rnd** every 28 (18, 22, 18, 30) [32, 20, 20, 24, 34]th round again x 3 (5, 4, 5, 3) [3, 5, 5, 4, 3].
111 (113, 121, 127, 137) [143, 145, 151, 161, 169] Front/Back sts

Work to 31 (31, 32, 32.5, 33.5) [33.5, 34.5, 33.5, 34.5, 34.5] cm / 12.25 (12.25, 12.5, 12.75, 13.25) [13.25, 13.5, 13.25, 13.5, 13.5]" from underarm or to 3.5 cm / 1.5" from desired length.

STEP 9: HEM

SIZES – (34, 36, –, 40) [–, 44, –, 48, 50]
On Rnd 1, decrease 1 st (k2tog) on the first and last repeat.
2 sts decreased

SIZES 32 (–, –, 38, –) [42, –, 46, –, –]
On Rnd 1, increase 1 st (M1L) on the first and last repeat.
2 sts increased

Rnds 1 – 7: *K9, sl1wyf, (k1, sl1wyf) x 3; work from * to end of rnd.
224 (224, 240, 256, 272) [288, 288, 304, 320, 336] sts
Rnd 8: Knit.
Work **Rnds 1 – 7** once more.
Next Rnd: *K8, ssk, k4, ssk; work from * to end of rnd.
196 (196, 210, 224, 238) [252, 252, 266, 280, 294] sts

Change to 2.5 mm / US 1.5 needle.
Rnd 1: Purl
Rnds 2 – 7: Knit.

BIND OFF
Bind off keeping an even tension (or use Stretchy Bind Off).

BOX C

STEP 10: SLEEVES

Place 66 (68, 68, 72, 72) [76, 76, 80, 80, 84] Sleeve sts from holder
back on larger (3 mm / US 2.5) needle. Join yarn at right side of
gap, p&k6 (6, 7, 7, 7) [7, 8, 8, 11, 11] sts along the first half of the
underarm cast on, pm, p&k7 (7, 8, 8, 8) [8, 9, 9, 12, 12] sts more along
second half of underarm, knit to m.
79 (81, 83, 87, 87) [91, 93, 97, 103, 107] sts

REFER TO **BOX C** FOR ROUND INSTRUCTIONS
Work **Rnd 1** to 5 cm / 2" from underarm.

SLEEVE DECREASES
Work **Decrease Rnd**.
77 (79, 81, 85, 85) [89, 91, 95, 101, 105] sts

Continue with **Rnd 1**, working **Decrease Rnd** every 18 (15, 14, 12, 12)
[10, 10, 16, 12, 10]th round again x 7 (8, 9, 11, 11) [13, 14, 8, 11, 13].
63 (63, 63, 63, 63) [63, 63, 79, 79, 79] sts

Work to 41.5 (41.5, 42.5, 44.5, 44.5) [44.5, 44.5, 45.5, 45.5, 45.5]
cm / 16.25 (16.25, 16.75, 17.5, 17.5) [17.5, 17.5, 18, 18, 18]" from
underarm or to 3.5 cm / 1.5" from desired sleeve length.

STEP 11: CUFF
Note: On the first round make 1 increase (M1L) to get 64 (64, 64, 64,
64) [64, 64, 80, 80, 80] sts.
Rnds 1 – 7: *K9, sl1wyf, (k1, sl1wyf) x 3; work from * to end of rnd.
Rnd 8: Knit.
Work **Rnds 1 – 7** once more.
Next Rnd: *K8, ssk, k4, ssk; work from * to end of rnd.
56 (56, 56, 56, 56) [56, 56, 70, 70, 70] sts

Change to smaller (2.5 mm / US 1.5) needle.
Rnd 1: Purl.
Rnds 2 – 7: Knit.
Bind off in even tension.

FINISH
Weave in loose ends. Soak and block to measurements.

Jolt of Blue

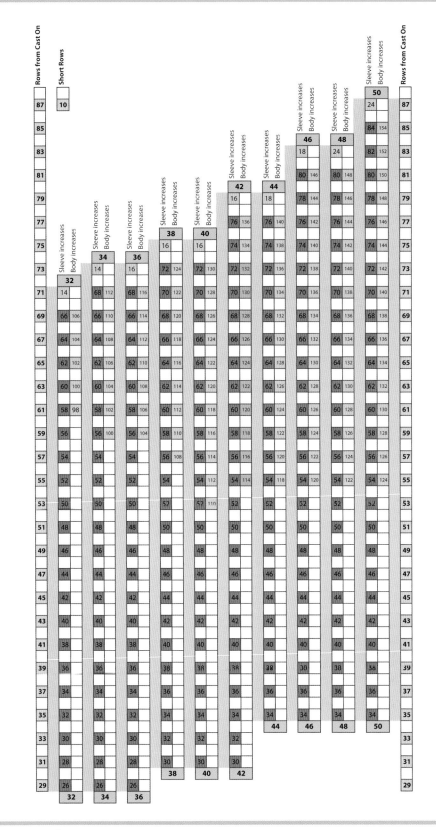

▨	Sleeve increases
▨	Body increases
▨	Underarm cast on

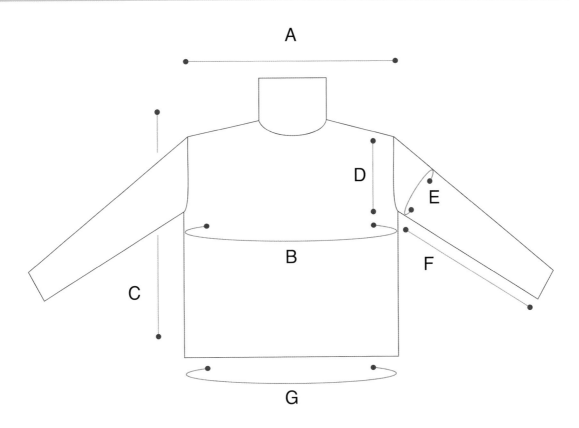

JOLT OF BLUE GARMENT MEASUREMENTS

	32	34	36	38	40	42	44	46	48	50
A – Shoulder width (cm)	38.5	39	41	42.5	43	45	46.5	47	48	49
in	15.25	15.25	16.25	16.75	17	17.75	18.25	18.5	19	19.25
B – Bust (cm)	96	101	105.5	112	117	121.5	126.5	131	137.5	142.5
in	37.75	39.75	41.5	44	46	47.75	49.75	51.5	54.25	56
C – Length (cm)	54	55	56	57	58	59	60	60	61	62
in	21.25	21.75	22	22.5	22.75	23.25	23.5	23.5	24	24.5
D – Armhole depth (cm)	17	17.5	17.5	18	18	19	19	20.5	20.5	21.5
in	6.75	7	7	7	7	7.5	7.5	8	8	8.5
E – Sleeve circumf (cm)	31.5	32.5	33	35	35	36.5	37	39	41	43
in	12.5	12.75	13	13.75	13.75	14.25	14.5	15.25	16.25	17
F – Sleeve seam (cm)	45	45	46	48	48	48	48	49	49	49
in	17.75	17.75	18	19	19	19	19	19.25	19.25	19.25
G – Hem circumf (cm)	89.5	89.5	96	102.5	109	115	115	121.5	128	134.5
in	35.25	35.25	37.75	40.25	43	45.25	45.25	47.75	50.5	53

This is a sleek and luxurious Ziggurat with subtle detailing – an underarm gusset, and decorative slip-stitch cords along the sides and around the lower half of body. The simple plain collar is picked up inside the crochet cast on and inside a slipped edge stitch for an elegant finish. Sleeves are full length and finished with a triangular motif that mirrors the underarm gusset. Both cuff and hem are accented by a contrasting lining. The sample in size 40 just skims the hips, but could be made longer if you prefer. The yarn, Luxe DK from Walk Collection, is both creamy and supple, and makes this little piece a special treat both to knit and to wear.

TO FIT SIZE
81 (86, 91, 97, 102) [107, 112, 117, 122, 127] cm
32 (34, 36, 38, 40) [42, 44, 46, 48, 50] inches

ROUND NECK
Narrow simple collar

FIT
Tailored shoulders and waist shaping, no ease

YARN
Walk Collection Luxe DK (8ply, 70% alpaca, 20% silk, 10% cashmere, 225 m (246 yds) per 100 g); Cement, 4 (4, 4, 5, 5) [5, 5, 5, 6, 6] skeins
Scrap (approx 30m / 35yds) of **CC** in Sport, Fingering or Heavy Lace
Sample: Walk Collection Delicate Lace, Arsenic

APPROX YARDAGE
850 (850, 900, 1000, 1000) [1050, 1100, 1150, 1200, 1250] m
900 (950, 1000, 1100, 1100) [1150, 1200, 1250, 1300, 1350] yds

ALTERNATIVE YARN SUGGESTIONS
Nature's Luxury On Stage

NEEDLES & NOTIONS
3.75 mm (US 5) circular needle, 80 – 100 cm (32 – 40")
or size to obtain gauge
3.5 mm (US 4) circular needle, 60 – 100 cm (24 – 40")
3 mm (US 2.5) circular needle, 60 – 100 cm (24 – 40")
Stitch holders; stitch markers

BLOCKED GAUGE
22 sts x 30 rows on 3.75 mm (US 5) needle = 10 cm / 4"

SAMPLE SIZE
Size 40 with Middling bust darts weighs 385 g / 13.5 oz (including tiny amount of **CC**)
Sizes 32 – 44 can most likely be knit with 4 skeins if you finish the sleeves before the body. Also note that the pattern is written for quite a short pullover. If you plan to make it longer, you will need the larger amounts suggested or an additional skein.

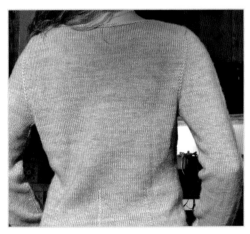

STEP 1: CAST ON & RIGHT BACK SHOULDER

With **MC**, using long tail cast on and 3.75 mm (US 5) needle, cast on 73 (75, 79, 81, 83) [87, 91, 93, 95, 97] sts.
Setup row (WS): P17 (17, 18, 18, 18) [19, 19, 20, 20, 21], turn.
R1 (RS): Sl1^, pm, k10 (10, 11, 11, 11) [11, 11, 12, 12, 13], turn.
R2 (WS): Sl1^, purl to m, rm, p1^, p1, turn.
R3: Sl1^, pm, k5 (5, 6, 6, 6) [6, 6, 6, 6, 7], turn.
R4: Sl1^, purl to m, rm, p1^, p1, turn.
R5: Sl1^, pm, knit to last 2 sts (working any sl1^ as k1^), sl1wyb, k1.
R6: Purl to m, rm, p1^, p1, turn.
R7: Sl1^, pm, knit to last 2 sts, sl1wyb, k1.
R8: Purl to m, rm, p1^, purl to end.

73 (75, 79, 81, 83) [87, 91, 93, 95, 97] Back sts

STEP 2: LEFT BACK SHOULDER

R1 (RS): K1, sl1wyb, k15 (15, 16, 16, 16) [17, 17, 18, 18, 19], turn.
R2 (WS): Sl1^, pm, p10 (10, 11, 11, 11) [11, 11, 12, 12, 13], turn.
R3: Sl1^, knit to m, rm, k1^, k1, turn.
R4: Sl1^, pm, p5 (5, 6, 6, 6) [6, 6, 6, 6, 7], turn.
R5: Sl1^, knit to m, rm, k1^, k1, turn.
R6: Sl1^, pm, purl to end (working any sl1^ as p1^).
R7: K1, sl1wyb, knit to m, rm, k1^, k1, turn.
R8: Sl1^, pm, purl to end.

STEP 3: WORKING ACROSS BACK

R1 (RS): K1, sl1wyb, knit to m, rm, k1^, knit to last 2 sts, sl1wyb, k1.
73 (75, 79, 81, 83) [87, 91, 93, 95, 97] Back sts
R2 (WS): Purl.
R3: K1, sl1wyb, knit to last 2 sts, sl1wyb, k1.
R4: Purl.
Work **Rows 3 & 4** again x 0 (0, 1, 1, 1) [1, 1, 1, 2, 2].
Work **Row 3** once more.
Final Row (WS): Purl to last 2 sts, p2tog, pm, p&p5 (5, 6, 6, 6) [6, 6, 6, 7, 7] sts along edge (for first half of Left Sleeve Cap).

5 (5, 6, 6, 6) [6, 6, 6, 7, 7] Left Cap sts
72 (74, 78, 80, 82) [86, 90, 92, 94, 96] Back sts

Slide stitches off needle tips to rest on the cable.
Set these stitches aside, continue to next step without turning.

STEP 4: LEFT FRONT SHOULDER

Setup Row (WS): Loop cable, p&p16 (16, 17, 17, 17) [18, 18, 19, 19, 20] sts (for Left Front Shoulder) in the cast on of Left Back Shoulder, *and remember to pick up second st in line with faux seam.*
16 (16, 17, 17, 17) [18, 18, 19, 19, 20] Left Front sts
R1 (RS): K1, sl1wyb, k8 (8, 9, 9, 9) [10, 10, 10, 10, 11], turn.

R2 (WS): Sl1^, purl to end.
R3: K1, sl1wyb, k5 (5, 5, 5, 5) [6, 6, 6, 6, 6], turn.
R4: Sl1^, purl to end.
R5: K1, sl1wyb, knit to 2 sts before loop (working any sl1^ as k1^), sl1wyb, k1, turn.
R6: Purl.
R7: K1, sl1wyb, knit to 2 sts before loop, sl1wyb, k1, turn.
R8: Purl.
Works **Rows 7 & 8** again x 3 (3, 4, 4, 4) [4, 4, 4, 5, 5].
Final Row (RS): K1, sl1wyb, knit to 2 sts before loop, ssk, pm, p&k5 (5, 6, 6, 6) [6, 6, 6, 7, 7] sts (for second half of Left Sleeve Cap), knit to m, sm, sl1wyb, knit to last 2 sts, ssk, pm, p&k5 (5, 6, 6, 6) [6, 6, 6, 7, 7] sts (for first half of Right Sleeve Cap).

10 (10, 12, 12, 12) [12, 12, 12, 14] Left Cap sts
5 (5, 6, 6, 6) [6, 6, 6, 7, 7] Right Cap sts
15 (15, 16, 16, 16) [17, 17, 18, 18, 19] Left Front sts
71 (73, 77, 79, 81) [85, 89, 91, 93, 95] Back sts

Slide stitches off needle tips to rest on the cable.
Set these stitches aside, continue to next step without turning.

STEP 5: RIGHT FRONT SHOULDER

R1 (RS): Loop cable, p&k16 (16, 17, 17, 17) [18, 18, 19, 19, 20] sts (for Right Front Shoulder) in the cast on of Right Back Shoulder, *and remember to pick up second st in line with faux seam.*
16 (16, 17, 17, 17) [18, 18, 19, 19, 20] Right Front sts
R2 (WS): P10 (10, 11, 11, 11) [12, 12, 12, 12, 13], turn.
R3: Sl1^, knit to last 2 sts, sl1wyb, k1.
R4: P7 (7, 7, 7, 7) [8, 8, 8, 8, 8], turn.
R5: Sl1^, knit to last 2 sts, sl1wyb, k1.

R6: Purl to loop, working any sl1^ as p1^, turn.
R7: K1, sl1wyb, knit to last 2 sts, sl1wyb, k1.
R8: Purl to loop, turn.
Work **Rows 7 & 8** again x 3 (3, 4, 4, 4) [4, 4, 4, 5, 5].
Work **Row 7** once more.
Final row (WS): Purl to 2 sts before loop, p2tog, pm, p&p5 (5, 6, 6, 6) [6, 6, 6, 7, 7] sts (for second half of Right Sleeve Cap), purl to end.

10 (10, 12, 12, 12) [12, 12, 12, 14, 14] sts for each Sleeve Cap
15 (15, 16, 16, 16) [17, 17, 18, 18, 19] sts for each Front
71 (73, 77, 79, 81) [85, 89, 91, 93, 95] Back sts

STEP 6: SLEEVE CAPS & BODY

You will now increase for the sleeves and neck (and later also body) simultaneously. (See Helpful Table for an overview of all increases.)

REFER TO **BOX A** FOR ROW INSTRUCTIONS
Work **Rows 1 & 2**.
12 (12, 14, 14, 14) [14, 14, 14, 16, 16] Sleeve sts
16 (16, 17, 17, 17) [18, 18, 19, 19, 20] sts for each Front

Work **Rows 3 & 2**.
14 (14, 16, 16, 16) [16, 16, 16, 18, 18] Sleeve sts
16 (16, 17, 17, 17) [18, 18, 19, 19, 20] sts for each Front

Work **Rows 1 & 2** x 6 (6, 6, 5, 6) [8, 7, 7, 6, 6].
26 (26, 28, 26, 28) [32, 30, 30, 30, 30] Sleeve sts
22 (22, 23, 22, 23) [26, 25, 26, 25, 26] sts for each Front

Works **Rows 1 & 4** x 2 (2, 2, 3, 3) [2, 3, 3, 4, 4].
30 (30, 32, 32, 34) [36, 36, 36, 38, 38] Sleeve sts
26 (26, 27, 28, 29) [30, 31, 32, 33, 34] sts for each Front

STEP 7: JOIN FRONTS TO KNIT IN THE ROUND

Joining Row-Round 1 (RS): K1, sl1wyb, k1, nM1R, (knit to 1 st before m, sl1wyb, sm, **sM1L**, knit to m, **sM1R**, sm, sl1wyb) twice, knit to 3 sts before m, nM1L, k1, pm (=Nm), sl1wyb, k1, *(turn work over so WS is facing) borrow last st for cast on loop*, crochet cast on 18 (20, 22, 22, 22) [24, 26, 26, 26, 26] sts, *replace loop onto LN (make a final chain st but not around the needle), turn work over so RS is facing*, join to Left Front, knit to m, sm.

You are now at Left Front Sleeve.

32 (32, 34, 34, 36) [38, 38, 38, 40, 40] Sleeve sts
72 (74, 78, 80, 82) [86, 90, 92, 94, 96] Front sts
71 (73, 77, 79, 81) [85, 89, 91, 93, 95] Back sts

BOX A

sM1L/R = sleeve increase   nM1L/R = neck increase

RS ROWS
R1: K1, sl1wyb, k1, nM1R, (knit to 1 st before m, sl1wyb, sm, **sM1L**, knit to m, **sM1R**, sm, sl1wyb) twice, knit to last 3 sts, nM1L, k1, sl1wyb, k1.

R3: K1, sl1wyb, (knit to 1 st before m, sl1wyb, sm, **sM1L**, knit to m, **sM1R**, sm, sl1wyb) twice, knit to last 2 sts, sl1wyb, k1.

WS ROWS
R2: Purl.

R4: P3, nM1Lp, purl to last 3 sts, nM1Rp, p3.

Joining Round 2: Knit to Nm, rm, ssk, knit to end of cast on, make loop in bar and place on LN, k2tog (the first st of Left Front and the loop), knit to 1 st before m.

32 (32, 34, 34, 36) [38, 38, 38, 40, 40] Sleeve sts
71 (73, 77, 79, 81) [85, 89, 91, 93, 95] Front sts
71 (73, 77, 79, 81) [85, 89, 91, 93, 95] Back sts

STEP 8: SLEEVE & BODY INCREASES
Continue to work sleeve increases and also introduce body increases. *The round begins 1 stitch before the Front Left Sleeve marker.*

REFER TO **BOX B** FOR ROUND INSTRUCTIONS
Work **Rnds 1 & 2** x 8 (8, 8, 8, 6) [6, 6, 6, 7, 7].
48 (48, 50, 50, 48) [50, 50, 50, 54, 54] Sleeve sts

INTRODUCE BODY INCREASES
Work **Rnds 3 & 2** x 2 (1, 1, 2, 2) [2, 2, 2, 1, 1].
52 (50, 52, 54, 52) [54, 54, 54, 56, 56] Sleeve sts
75 (75, 79, 83, 85) [89, 93, 95, 95, 97] Front/Back sts

Work **Rnds 3 & 4** x 0 (1, 1, 1, 2) [2, 2, 3, 4, 5].
52 (52, 54, 56, 56) [58, 58, 60, 64, 66] Sleeve sts
75 (79, 83, 87, 93) [97, 101, 107, 111, 117] Front/Back sts

Work **Rnd 3**.
54 (54, 56, 58, 58) [60, 60, 62, 66, 68] Sleeve sts
77 (81, 85, 89, 95) [99, 103, 109, 113, 119] Front/Back sts

Final Rnd: Knit to 3 sts before Left Front Sleeve m.

BOX B

sM1 = sleeve increase   bM1 = body increase

ODD (SLIP-STITCH) ROUNDS
Rnd 1: (Sl1wyb, sm, **sM1L**, knit to m, **sM1R**, sm, sl1wyb, knit to 1 st before m) twice.

Rnd 3: (**bM1L**, sl1wyb, sm, **sM1L**, knit to m, **sM1R**, sm, sl1wyb, **bM1R**, knit to 1 st before m) twice.

EVEN (PLAIN NO-SLIP) ROUNDS
Rnd 2: Knit.

Rnd 4: (**bM1L**, k1, sm, knit to m, sm, k1, **bM1R**, knit to 1 st before m) twice.

STEP 9: SEPARATING SLEEVES & BODY
Separation Rnd 1: *Pm, k3, rm, place all sts to next m on holder (= sleeve sts), rm, *(turn work over so WS is facing) borrow last st for cast on loop,* crochet cast on 14 (14, 16, 20, 20) [20, 20, 22, 22, 22] sts, *replace loop onto LN (make a final chain st but not around the needle), turn work over so RS is facing*, knit to 3 sts before m, work from * to * once more, knit to m.
You are now at beginning of Left Underarm cast on.
91 (95, 101, 109, 115) [119, 123, 131, 135, 141] Front/Back sts

Separation Rnd 2: *Sm, ssk, **purl** to end of cast on, make loop in bar and place on LN, k2tog (next st and loop)*, knit to m, work from * to * once more, knit to m.
90 (94, 100, 108, 114) [118, 122, 130, 134, 140] Front/Back sts

AT THE SAME TIME OPTIONAL BUST DARTS
Optional Bust Darts may be worked before the gusset is complete, depending on where you choose to place your darts, see BOX D.

AT THE SAME TIME UNDERARM GUSSET
See Abbreviations for TwL marker placement.
Gusset Rnd 1: (TwL, purl all purl sts, TwR, knit to m) twice.
Gusset Rnd 2: (Sm, sl1wyb, k1, purl to 1 st before last purl st, k1, sl1wyb, knit to m) twice.

Work **Gusset Rnds 1 & 2** until 2 purl sts remain.
Next Rnd: (Sm, ssk, k2, k2tog, knit to m) twice.
88 (92, 98, 106, 112) [116, 120, 128, 132, 138] Front/Back sts

Final Gusset Rnd: (TwL, TwR, sm, knit to m) twice.
   Note: If you are trying to stretch your skeins, this is a good place to set the body aside to work the sleeves before finishing the body.

STEP 10: BODY & SHAPING
Continue in stocking stitch over body stitches only.
The round now begins under Left Sleeve.
Note: *Two stitches under each arm are worked in a cord pattern that creates a faux side seam (TwSl on alternate rounds).*

AT THE SAME TIME
Please read through the entire step before proceeding, as a few things happen at the same time or overlap.

- Optional Bust Darts (worked during **or** after gusset)
- Waist Shaping
- Decorative cords on lower body

Chatoyant

BOX C

BODY & SHAPING

Rnd 1: Knit.

Rnd 2: (Sm, TwSl, knit to m) twice.

Pairs of decreases are made at sides on a plain knit round.
Decrease Rnd: Sm, (k2, k2tog, knit to 2 sts before m, ssk) twice.

Pairs of increases are made at sides and at centre back/front cords on a plain knit round.
Increase Rnd: Sm, k2, RLI, knit to Centre Back m, LLI, sm, k2, RLI, knit to side m, LLI, sm, k2, RLI, knit to Centre Front m, LLI, sm, k2, RLI, knit to side m, LLI. *8 sts increased*

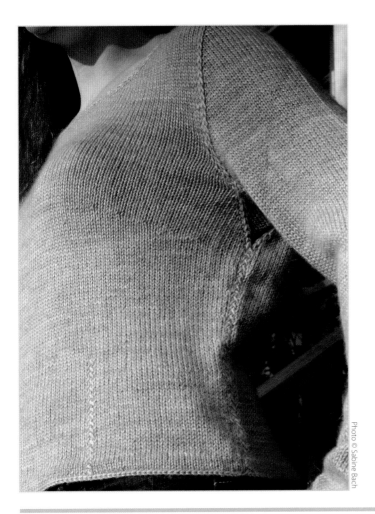

REFER TO **BOX C** FOR ROUND INSTRUCTIONS

AT THE SAME TIME OPTIONAL BUST DARTS (SEE **BOX D**)
If you have not already added the Optional Bust Darts, they may be placed here or a bit lower.

AT THE SAME TIME WAIST SHAPING
When Underam Gusset is complete, continue as follows:
Work **Rnd 2**.
Work **Rnds 1 & 2** x 3.

WAIST DECREASES
Note: Work Decrease Rnd on plain knit rounds to keep in pattern.

Work **Decrease Rnd** & **Rnd 2**.
86 (90, 96, 104, 110) [114, 118, 126, 130, 136] Front/Back sts

Continue with **Rnds 1 & 2**, working **Decrease Rnd** every 8th rnd again x 3.
80 (84, 90, 98, 104) [108, 112, 120, 124, 130] Front/Back sts

Work **Rnds 1 & 2** x 2.
Work **Rnd 1** once.

BOX D

OPTIONAL BUST DARTS

Place your darts at approx 5 (6, 10, 10) cm / 2 (2.25, 4, 4)" from underarm or where desired:
For placement of darts, see Hints & Tips
(Remember to place them in Front!)

Smallish (Middling, Busty, Wowza!)
Worked over 10 (16, 20, 24) rows, adds approx 3.5 (5.5, 6.5, 8) cm / 1.5 (2.25, 2.5, 3.25)".

R1 (RS): Sm, knit to m, sm, knit to 26 (30, 32, 36) sts before Left side m, turn.
R2 (WS): Jsl1, pm, purl to 28 (32, 34, 38) sts before Right side m, turn.
R3: Jsl1, pm, knit to m, rm, Jk1, k5 (4, 3, 3), turn.
R4: Jsl1, pm, purl to m, rm, Jp1, p5 (4, 3, 3), turn.
Work **Rows 3 & 4** again x 3 (6, 8, 10).
Final Row (RS): Jsl1, pm, knit to m, rm, Jk1, knit to side m.
Resume working in the round.
Next Rnd: Sm, TwSl, knit to side m, sm, TwSl, knit to 1 st before m, pass loop behind next st and place loop on LN, rm, k2tog (next stitch and loop), knit to side m.

Photo © Sabine Bach

INTRODUCE CORDS ON FRONT & BACK

On the next round, add 3 cords in Front and 3 in Back evenly spaced along the round, for a total of 8. One cord each is at centre Front and Back.

Next Rnd: Sm, TwSl, k18 (19, 21, 23, 24) [25, 26, 28, 29, 31], {pm, TwSl, k18 (19, 20, 22, 24) [25, 26, 28, 29, 30]} x 2, pm, TwSl, k18 (19, 21, 23, 24) [25, 26, 28, 29, 31], sm, TwSl, k18 (19, 21, 23, 24) [25, 26, 28, 29, 31], {pm, TwSl, k18 (19, 20, 22, 24) [25, 26, 28, 29, 30]} x 2. pm, TwSl, k18 (19, 21, 23, 24) [25, 26, 28, 29, 31].

WORK STRAIGHT

Work **Rnds 1 & 2** x 4.

WAIST INCREASES

Note: Work Increase Rnds on plain knit rounds to keep in pattern.

Work **Increase Rnd** & **Rnd 2**.
84 (88, 94, 102, 108) [112, 116, 124, 128, 134] Front/Back sts

Continue with **Rnds 1 & 2**, working **Increase Rnd** on the next 8 (8, 8, 10, 10) [10, 10, 10, 10, 10]th rnd once, then every 12th rnd x 1 (1, 1, 1, 1) [1, 1, 1, 2, 2].
92 (96, 102, 110, 116) [120, 124, 132, 140, 146] Front/Back sts

Work to 31 (31, 31.5, 30.5, 30.5) [30, 32, 31.5, 30, 29.5] / 12.25 (12.25, 12.5, 12, 12) [11.75, 12.5, 12.5, 11.75, 11.5]" from underarm or to 2 cm / .75" from desired length, ending with a **Rnd 1**.
Do not cut the yarn.

Note: If you are adding length, you may wish to include one more round of increases.

STEP 11: LINED HEM

LINING

Hem lining stitches are picked up on WS (see Tutorial section).
Slide stitches off needle tips to rest on the cable.
With **CC** and 3 mm (US 2.5) needle on WS and going counterclockwise, p&k sts in every bar *between* all sts.
92 (96, 102, 110, 116) [120, 124, 132, 140, 146] Front/Back Lining sts

Knit 6 rounds on WS (along inside of sweater and downwards).
Cut **CC**.
Slide sts off needle tips to rest on cable, set Lining sts aside.

HEM

With **MC** and smaller (3.5 mm / US 4) needle), work 5 rounds as set (with cords), or to *slightly* longer than Lining.

LINING

Unlike the other pullovers in this book, for this sweater the Lining is not finished with a round of **MC**.

Note: If the hem is not slightly longer than lining, work an additional hem-round before binding off.

BIND OFF

Weave in any loose ends at hem.
From RS, bind off hem sts together with lining sts using 3-Needle Bind Off and keeping an even tension.

STEP 12: SLEEVES

Place 54 (54, 56, 58, 58) [60, 60, 62, 66, 68] Sleeve sts from holder back on larger (3.75 mm / US 5) needle. Join **MC** at right side of gap, pm, p&k14 (14, 16, 20, 20) [20, 20, 22, 22, 22] sts, knit to 1 st before m.
68 (68, 72, 78, 78) [80, 80, 84, 88, 90] sts

SLEEVE GUSSET

See Special Abbreviations for TwL moving marker placement.
Gusset Rnd 1: TwL, p12 (12, 14, 18, 18) [18, 18, 20, 20, 20], TwR, knit to m.
Gusset Rnd 2: Sm, sl1wyb, k1, purl to 1 st before last purl st, k1, sl1wyb, knit to m.

Gusset Rnd 3: TwL, purl all purl sts, TwR, knit to m.
Gusset Rnd 4: Sm, sl1wyb, k1, purl to 1 st before last purl st, k1, sl1wyb, knit to m.

Work **Gusset Rnds 3 & 4** until 2 purl sts remain.
Next Rnd: Sm, ssk, k2, k2tog, sm, knit to m.
66 (66, 70, 76, 76) [78, 78, 82, 86, 88] sts

Final Gusset Rnd: TwL, TwR, sm, knit to m.

REFER TO **BOX E** FOR ROUND INSTRUCTIONS

Work **Rnd 2**.

SLEEVE DECREASES
Note: Work Decrease Rnd on plain knit rounds to keep in pattern.

Work repeats of **Rnds 1 & 2**, working **Decrease Rnd** every 14 (14, 14, 12, 10) [10, 10, 10, 10, 10]th round x 7 (7, 4, 9, 9) [10, 10, 8, 6, 5], then every 0 (0, 12, 0, 0) [0, 0, 6, 6, 6]th round x 0 (0, 3, 0, 0) [0, 0, 4, 8, 10].
52 (52, 56, 58, 58) [58, 58, 58, 58, 58] sts

Work to 40 (40, 41, 41, 41) [41, 41, 41, 42, 42] cm / 15.75 (15.75, 16.25, 16.25, 16.25) [16.25, 16.25, 16.25, 16.5, 16.5]" from underarm or to 5 cm / 2" less than desired sleeve length.

STEP 13: CUFF TRIANGLE & LINING
See Special Abbreviations for TwRp moving marker placement.
Rnd 1: Knit.
Rnd 2: Sm, TwSl, knit to 1 st before m, shift m 1 st right.
Rnd 3: TwRp, TwLp, knit to m. *2 purl sts*
Rnd 4: Sm, sl1wyb, purl all purl sts, sl1wyb, knit to 1 st before m, shift m 1 st right.
Rnd 5: TwRp, purl all purl sts, TwLp, knit to m. *4 purl sts*

Work **Rnds 4 & 5** again x 3. *10 purl sts*

CUFF LINING
Cuff lining sts are picked up on WS as for lined hem.
Slide sts off needle tips to rest on the cable. With **CC** and 3 mm (US 2.5) needle, p&k sts in every bar *between* all sts.
Knit 6 rounds on WS (along inside of cuff and downwards).
K3 more sts.
Cut **CC**.
Slide sts off needle tips to rest on cable, set Lining sts aside.

FINISH OUTER CUFF LAYER
With **MC** and 3.5 mm (US 4) needle, continue to knit cuff in the round as follows.
Work **Rnds 4 & 5** again x 3. *16 purl sts*

BIND OFF
Weave in any loose ends at cuff before binding off.
Bind off from RS using 3-Needle Bind Off and keeping an even tension.

STEP 14: SIMPLE COLLAR
*Collar stitches are picked up next to the slipped stitches along Left Front Neck, then **behind** the chained cast on edge along centre front (easier to do with the help of a crochet hook and from WS, then next to the slipped stitches along Right Front, and finally along Back Neck.*
With **MC**, 3.5 mm (US 4) circular needle and starting at Left Shoulder, p&k approx 19 (19, 20, 20, 21) [22, 22, 22, 23, 23] sts along Left Front Neck to Front Cast On, 18 (20, 22, 22, 22) [24, 26, 26, 26, 26] sts behind and inside the chained cast on, approx 19 (19, 20, 20, 21) [22, 22, 22, 23, 23] sts along Right Front Neck to Right Shoulder, and approx 39 (41, 43, 45, 47) [49, 53, 53, 55, 55] along Back Neck.
Approx 95 (99, 105, 107, 111) [117, 123, 123, 127, 127] sts

Purl 1 round.
Bind off keeping an even tension.

FINISH
Weave in loose ends. Soak and block to measurements.

BOX E

SLEEVE ROUNDS
Rnd 1: Knit.
Rnd 2: Sm, TwSl, knit to m.

Decrease Rnd: Sm, k2, k2tog, knit to 2 sts before m, ssk.

Chatoyant

Legend:

- Sleeve increases
- Body increases
- Neck increases
- Front cast on
- Underarm cast on

Column headers (repeated for each size group):
- Rows from Cast On
- Short Rows
- Sleeve increases
- Body increases
- Neck increases

Size groups: 32, 34, 36, 38, 40, 42, 44, 46, 48, 50

(Chart of increase sequences by row for sizes 32–50)

Rows	Short Rows	32 (Sl)	32 (Bd)	34 (Sl)	34 (Bd)	36 (Sl)	36 (Bd)	38 (Sl)	38 (Bd)	40 (Sl)	40 (Bd)	42 (Sl)	42 (Bd)	44 (Sl)	44 (Bd)	46 (Sl)	46 (Bd)	48 (Sl)	48 (Bd)	50 (Sl)	50 (Bd)	Neck	Rows
77	4																22			22			77
73												22		22		22			68	119		117	73
71																	66	113	66	115	111/113		71
69															46		64	109	64	111	107/109		69
67											20		20	20		62	109	62	105	62	107	103/105	67
65						36		38		40	20	60	99	60	103	60	105	60	101	60	103	99/101	65
63		32		34		16		58	89	58	95	58	97	58	99	58	101	58	97	58	99	99	63
61		14		14		56	85	56	85	56	91	56	91	56	95	56	97	56	95	56	97	89	61
59		54	77	54	81	54	81	54	83	54	87	54	89	54	93	54	95	54		54		79	59
57		52	75	52	77	52	79	52	81	52	85	52	87	52	91	52	93	52		52			57
55		50	73	50	75	50		50		50	83	50		50		50		50		50			55
53		48		48		48		48		48		48		48		48		48		48			53
51		46		46		46		46		46		46		46		46		46		46			51
49		44		44		44		44		44		44		44		44		44		44			49
47		42		42		42		42		42		42		42		42		42		42			47
45		40		40		40		40		40		40		40		40		40	26	34	40	26	35	45
43		38		38		38		38		38		38	24	31	38	26	32	38	26	33	38	32	33	43
41		36		36		36		36		36	22	30	36		30	36		30	36	31	36	30	31	41
39		34		34		34	22	28	34	22	29	34	28	34	27	34	28	34	29	34	29	30	39
37		32	18	32	20	32	26	32	26	32	26	32	26	32	26	32	27	32	27	32	27	28	37
35		30	25	30	25	30	24	30	25	30	24	30	25	30	25	30	26	30	25	30	26		35
33		28	23	28	23	28	23	28	23	28	23	28	24	28	24	28	25	28	24	28	25		33
31		26	22	26	22	26	22	26	22	26	22	26	22	26	23	26	24	26	23	26	24		31
29		24	21	24	21	24	21	24	21	24	21	24	22	24	22	24	23	24	22	24	23		29
27		22	20	22	20	22	20	22	20	22	20	22	21	22	21	22	22	22	21	22	22		27
25		20	19	20	19	20	19	20	19	20	19	20	20	20	20	20	21	20	20	20	21		25
23		18	18	18	18	18	18	18	18	18	18	18	19	18	19	18	20	18	19	18	20		23
21		16	17	16	17	16		16		16		16		16		16		16	19	16	20		21
19		14		14		14	17	14	17	14	17	14	18	14	18	14	19						19
17		12	16	12	16	36		38		40		42		44		46		48		50			17
		32		34																			

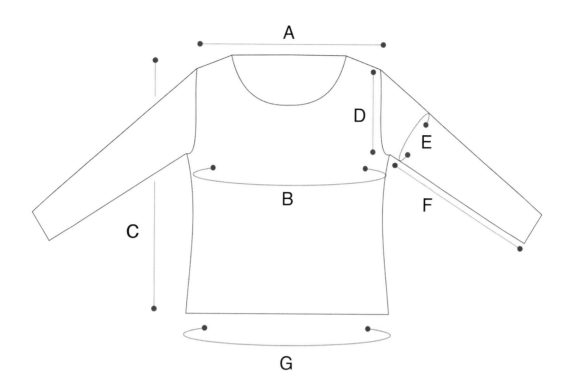

CHATOYANT GARMENT MEASUREMENTS

	32	34	36	38	40	42	44	46	48	50
A – Shoulder width (cm)	32.5	33	35	36	37	38.5	40.5	41.5	42.5	43
in	12.75	13	13.75	14.25	14.5	15.25	16	16.25	16.75	17
B – Bust (cm)	82	85.5	91	98	103.5	107.5	111	118	122	127.5
in	32.25	33.75	35.75	38.5	40.75	42.25	43.75	46.5	48	50.25
C – Length (cm)	53	53	54	54	54	54	56	56	56	56
in	20.75	20.75	21.25	21.25	21.25	21.25	22	22	22	22
D – Armhole depth (cm)	18.5	18.5	19.5	20	20	20.5	20.5	21.5	22.5	23.5
in	7.25	7.5	7.5	8	8	8	8	8.5	9	9
E – Sleeve circumf (cm)	31	31	32.5	35.5	35.5	36.5	36.5	38	40	41
in	12.25	12.25	12.75	14	14	14.25	14.25	15	15.75	16.25
F – Sleeve seam (cm)	45	45	46	46	46	46	46	46	47	47
in	17.75	17.75	18	18	18	18	18	18	18.5	18.5
G – Hem circumf (cm)	83.5	87.5	92.5	100	105.5	109	112.5	120	127.5	132.5
in	32.75	34.5	36.5	39.25	41.5	43	44.25	47.25	50.25	52.25

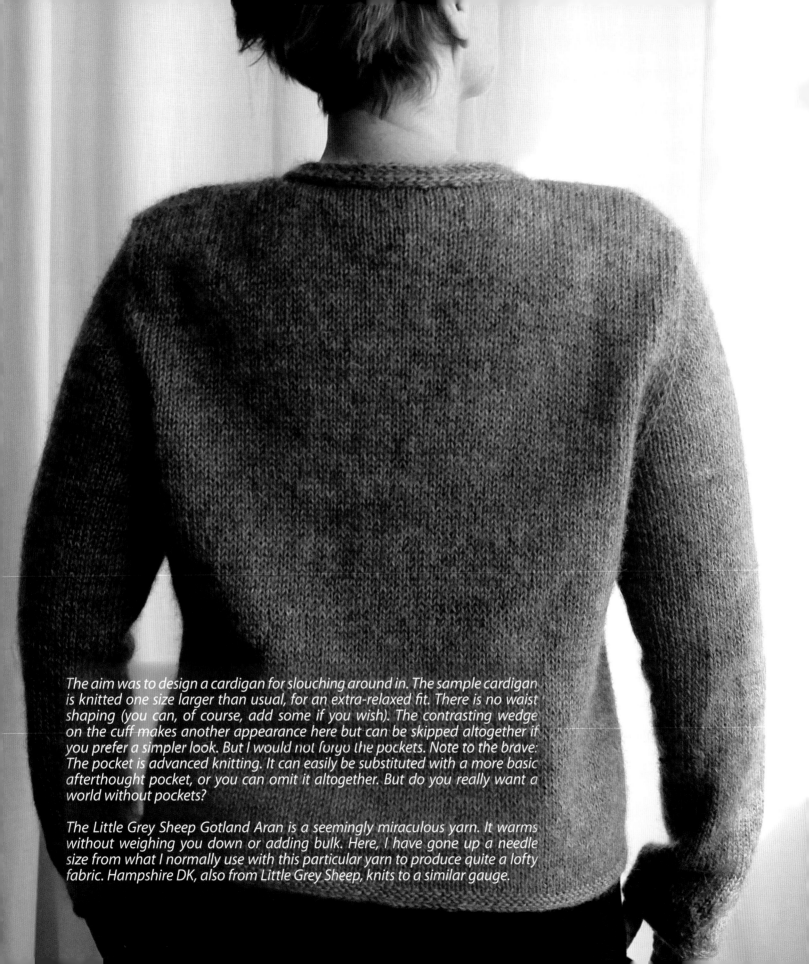

The aim was to design a cardigan for slouching around in. The sample cardigan is knitted one size larger than usual, for an extra-relaxed fit. There is no waist shaping (you can, of course, add some if you wish). The contrasting wedge on the cuff makes another appearance here but can be skipped altogether if you prefer a simpler look. But I would not forgo the pockets. Note to the brave: The pocket is advanced knitting. It can easily be substituted with a more basic afterthought pocket, or you can omit it altogether. But do you really want a world without pockets?

The Little Grey Sheep Gotland Aran is a seemingly miraculous yarn. It warms without weighing you down or adding bulk. Here, I have gone up a needle size from what I normally use with this particular yarn to produce quite a lofty fabric. Hampshire DK, also from Little Grey Sheep, knits to a similar gauge.

Jadeite

TO FIT SIZE

81 (86, 91, 97, 102) [107, 112, 117, 122, 127] cm
32 (34, 36, 38, 40) [42, 44, 46, 48, 50] inches

V-NECK

FIT

Relaxed with approx 14 – 15 cm / 5.5 – 6" ease

YARN

Little Grey Sheep Gotland Aran (10ply, 100% wool, 176 m (192 yds)
per 100 g)
MC Lemoncello x 5 (5, 5, 5, 6) [6, 6, 6, 6, 7]
CC Teal (scrap of Aran or DK)

APPROX YARDAGE

700 (750, 800, 850, 900) [900, 950, 1000, 1050, 1100] m
800 (800, 850, 900, 950) [1000, 1050, 1100, 1150, 1150] yds

ALTERNATIVE YARN SUGGESTION
Little Grey Sheep Hampshire DK (knits to Aran gauge)

NEEDLES & NOTIONS

5.5 mm (US 9) circular needle, 80 – 100 cm (32 – 40") x 3
or size to obtain gauge
4.5 mm (US 7) circular needle, 80 – 100 cm (32 – 40")
2 shorter circulars 4.5 mm (US 7)
Stitch holders; stitch markers; 5 buttons (6 if adding bust darts)

BLOCKED GAUGE

16 sts x 22 rows on 5.5 mm (US 9) needle = 10 cm / 4"

SAMPLE SIZE

Size 42 with Middling bust darts weighs 450 g / 16 oz

Åsa Tricosa Ziggurats :: 16 elegantly seamless knits

99

Jadeite

STEP 1: CAST ON & RIGHT BACK SHOULDER
With **MC**, using longtail cast on and 5.5 mm (US 9) needle, cast on 66 (68, 70, 72, 74) [76, 78, 80, 82, 84] sts.
Setup Row (WS): P17 (19, 20, 20, 21) [21, 22, 22, 23, 23], turn.
R1 (RS): Sl1^, pm, k10 (11, 12, 12, 13) [13, 13, 13, 14, 14], turn.
R2 (WS): Sl1^, purl to m, rm, p1^, p1, turn.
R3: Sl1^, pm, k5 (6, 6, 6, 7) [7, 7, 7, 7, 7], turn.
R4: Sl1^, purl to m, rm, p1^, p1, turn.
R5: Sl1^, pm, knit to last 2 sts (working any sl1^ as k1^), sl1wyb, k1.
R6: Purl to m, rm, p1^, p1, turn.
R7: Sl1^, pm, knit to last 2 sts, sl1wyb, k1.
R8: Purl to m, rm, p1^, purl to end.

66 (68, 70, 72, 74) [76, 78, 80, 82, 84] Back sts

STEP 2: LEFT BACK SHOULDER
R1 (RS): K1, sl1wyb, k15 (17, 18, 18, 19) [19, 20, 20, 21, 21], turn.
R2 (WS): Sl1^, pm, p10 (11, 12, 12, 13) [13, 13, 13, 14, 14], turn.
R3: Sl1^, knit to m, rm, k1^, k1, turn.
R4: Sl1^, pm, p5 (6, 6, 6, 7) [7, 7, 7, 7, 7], turn.
R5: Sl1^, knit to m, rm, k1^, k1, turn.
R6: Sl1^, pm, purl to end (working any sl1^ as p1^).
R7: K1, sl1wyb, knit to m, rm, k1^, k1, turn.
R8: Sl1^, pm, purl to end.

STEP 3: WORKING ACROSS BACK
R1 (RS): K1, sl1wyb, knit to m, rm, k1^, knit to last 2 sts, sl1wyb, k1.
66 (68, 70, 72, 74) [76, 78, 80, 82, 84] Back sts
R2 (WS): Purl.
R3: K1, sl1wyb, knit to last 2 sts, sl1wyb, k1.
R4: Purl.
Work **Rows 3 & 4** again x 2 (2, 2, 2, 2) [3, 3, 3, 3, 3].
Work **Row 3** once more.
Final Row (WS): Purl to last 2 sts, p2tog, pm, p&p7 (7, 7, 7, 7) [8, 8, 8, 8, 8] sts along edge (for first half of Left Sleeve Cap).

7 (7, 7, 7, 7) [8, 8, 8, 8, 8] Left Cap sts
65 (67, 69, 71, 73) [75, 77, 79, 81, 83] Back sts

Slide stitches off needle tips to rest on the cable.
Set these stitches aside, continue to next step without turning.

STEP 4: LEFT FRONT SHOULDER
After the shoulder sts have been picked up, add sts for the Buttonband (BB) using the working yarn and a provisional cast on. After a few rows, these sts can be placed on a holder or safety pin.

Setup Row (WS): Loop cable, p&p16 (18, 19, 19, 20) [20, 21, 21, 22,

22] sts (for Left Front Shoulder) in the cast on of Left Back Shoulder, *and remember to pick up second st in line with faux seam.* Place spare circular parallel to working needle and using Winding Provisional Cast On and working yarn, wind on 8 sts for BB, pull on spare circular to allow provisional sts to rest on its cable.
16 (18, 19, 19, 20) [20, 21, 21, 22, 22] Left Front sts + 8 BB sts
R1 (RS): Ksk, k1, ksk, p1, pm, k10 (12, 12, 12, 13) [13, 14, 14, 14, 14], turn.
This sets the 8 BB sts for RS rows.
R2 (WS): Sl1^, purl to m, sm, (k1, sl1wyf) x 4.
This sets the 8 BB sts for WS rows.
R3: BB, sm, k5 (6, 6, 6, 6) [6, 7, 7, 7, 7], turn.
R4: Sl1^, purl to m, sm, BB.
R5: BB, sm, knit to 2 sts before loop (working any sl1^ as k1^), sl1wyb, k1, turn.
R6: Purl to m, sm, BB.
R7: BB, sm, knit to 2 sts before loop, sl1wyb, k1, turn.
R8: Purl to m, sm, BB.
Work **Rows 7 & 8** again x 0 (0, 0, 0, 0) [1, 1, 1, 1, 1].

nM1 = neck increase
R9: BB, sm, k2, nM1R, knit to 2 sts before loop, sl1wyb, k1, turn.
17 (19, 20, 20, 21) [21, 22, 22, 23, 23] Left Front sts + 8 BB sts
R10: Purl to m, sm, BB.
R11: BB, sm, knit to 2 sts before loop, sl1wyb, k1, turn.
R12: Purl to 2 sts before m, nM1Rp, p2, sm, BB.
18 (20, 21, 21, 22) [22, 23, 23, 24, 24] Left Front sts + 8 BB sts

R13: BB, sm, knit to 2 sts before loop, sl1wyb, k1, turn.
R14: Purl to m, sm, BB.
Work **Rows 9 – 12** once more.
20 (22, 23, 23, 24) [24, 25, 25, 26, 26] Left Front sts + 8 BB sts

Final Row (RS): BB, sm, knit to 2 sts before loop, ssk, pm, p&k7 (7, 7, 7, 7) [8, 8, 8, 8, 8] sts (for second half of Left Sleeve Cap), knit to m, sm, sl1wyb, knit to last 2 sts, ssk, pm, p&k7 (7, 7, 7, 7) [8, 8, 8, 8, 8] sts (for first half of Right Sleeve Cap).

14 (14, 14, 14, 14) [16, 16, 16, 16, 16] Left Cap sts
7 (7, 7, 7, 7) [8, 8, 8, 8, 8] Right Cap sts
19 (21, 22, 22, 23) [23, 24, 24, 25, 25] Left Front sts + 8 BB sts
65 (67, 69, 71, 73) [75, 77, 79, 81, 83] Back sts

Slide stitches off needle tips to rest on the cable.
Set these stitches aside for now.

WORKING BUTTONBAND AROUND BACK NECK

Slide provisional buttonband/collar (BB) sts to 5.5 mm (US 9) needle. With RS facing, at inside edge of BB, join new **MC** to work and attach BB along the neck as follows (see Buttonband Tutorial):

R1 (RS): Slide off and discard slipknot, k2tog, sl1wyf, k2, ksk. *7 sts*
R2 (WS): Sl1wyf, (k1, sl1wyf) x 3.
R3: P&k1 st in neck edge, place on LN, k2tog, sl1wyf, k2, ksk.
Continue to work **Rows 2 & 3** while picking up sts along Back Neck up to the Right Shoulder until all but 1 st is picked up. Pick up approx 3 sts for every 4, and end with a Row 2 (**WS**).
Next row (RS): P&k1 st in neck sts, ksk, k1, ksk. *8 sts*
Final row (WS): (Sl1wyf, k1) x 4. Cut yarn.

STEP 5: RIGHT FRONT SHOULDER

Continue at Right Shoulder where you stopped in Step 4.
R1 (RS): Loop cable, p&k16 (18, 19, 19, 20) [20, 21, 21, 22, 22] sts (for Right Front Shoulder) in the cast on of Right Back Shoulder, *and remember to pick up second st in line with faux seam*, pm (before BB), p1, ksk, k1, ksk.
This sets the 8 BB sts for RS rows.
16 (18, 19, 19, 20) [20, 21, 21, 22, 22] Right Front sts + 8 BB sts
R2 (WS): (Sl1wyf, k1) x 4, sm, p10 (12, 12, 12, 13) [13, 14, 14, 14, 14], turn.
This sets the 8 BB sts for WS rows.
R3: Sl1^, knit to m, sm, BB.
R4: BB, sm, p5 (6, 6, 6, 6) [6, 7, 7, 7, 7], turn.
R5: Sl1^, knit to m, sm, BB.
R6: BB, sm, purl to loop (working any sl1^ as p1^), turn.
R7: K1, sl1wyb, knit to m, sm, BB.
R8: BB, sm, purl to loop, turn.
Work **Rows 7 & 8** again x 0 (0, 0, 0, 0) [1, 1, 1, 1, 1].

nM1 = neck increase
R9: K1, sl1wyb, knit to 2 sts before m, nM1L, k2, sm, BB.
17 (19, 20, 20, 21) [21, 22, 22, 23, 23] Right Front sts + 8 BB sts
R10: BB, sm, purl to loop, turn.
R11: K1, sl1wyb, knit to m, sm, BB.
R12: BB, sm, p2, nM1Lp, purl to loop, turn.
18 (20, 21, 21, 22) [22, 23, 23, 24, 24] Right Front sts + 8 BB sts
R13: K1, sl1wyb, knit to m, sm, BB.
R14: BB, sm, purl to loop, turn.
Works **Rows 9 – 13** once more.
20 (22, 23, 23, 24) [24, 25, 25, 26, 26] Right Front sts + 8 BB sts
Final Row (WS): (Sl1wyf, k1) x 4, sm, purl to 2 sts before loop, p2tog, pm, p&p7 (7, 7, 7, 7) [8, 8, 8, 8, 8] sts (for second half of Right Sleeve Cap), purl to last m, sm, (k1, sl1wyf) x 4.

14 (14, 14, 14, 14) [16, 16, 16, 16, 16] sts for each Sleeve Cap
19 (21, 22, 22, 23) [23, 24, 24, 25, 25] sts + 8 BB sts for each Front
64 (66, 68, 70, 72) [74, 76, 78, 80, 82] Back sts

Jadeite

STEP 6: SLEEVE CAPS & BODY

You will now increase for the sleeve and neck (and later also body) simultaneously. Continue to work Buttonbands (BB) as set. (See Helpful Table for an overview of all increases.)

REFER TO **BOX A** FOR ROW INSTRUCTIONS
Work **Rows 1 – 6** x 2 (2, 3, 3, 3) [2, 3, 2, 3, 2].
26 (26, 32, 32, 32) [28, 34, 28, 34, 28] Sleeve sts
23 (25, 28, 28, 29) [27, 30, 28, 31, 29] sts + 8 BB sts for each Front

Work **Rows 1 & 2** x 7 (7, 5, 5, 5) [7, 5, 8, 5, 8].
40 (40, 42, 42, 42) [42, 44, 44, 44, 44] Sleeve sts
30 (32, 33, 33, 34) [34, 35, 36, 36, 37] sts + 8 BB sts for each Front

Continue to work sleeve and neck increases, and also introduce body increases.

Work **Rows 7 & 2** x 0 (0, 0, 1, 1) [2, 1, 1, 2, 1].
40 (40, 42, 44, 44) [46, 46, 46, 48, 46] Sleeve sts
30 (32, 33, 35, 36) [38, 37, 38, 40, 39] sts + 8 BB sts for each Front
64 (66, 68, 72, 74) [78, 78, 80, 84, 84] Back sts

Work **Rows 7 & 8** x 0 (0, 0, 0, 0) [0, 1, 1, 1, 2].
40 (40, 42, 44, 44) [46, 48, 48, 50, 50] Sleeve sts
30 (32, 33, 35, 36) [38, 40, 41, 43, 45] sts + 8 BB sts for each Front
64 (66, 68, 72, 74) [78, 82, 84, 88, 92] Back sts

FIRST BUTTONHOLE

BR1 (RS): BB, sm, (knit to 1 st before m, **bM1L**, sl1wyb, sm, sM1L, knit to m, **sM1R**, sm, sl1wyb, **bM1R**) twice, knit to m, sm, p1, k1, bind off 2 sts, k1, sl1wyf, k1.
42 (42, 44, 46, 46) [48, 50, 50, 52, 52] Sleeve sts
31 (33, 34, 36, 37) [39, 41, 42, 44, 46] sts + 8 BB sts for each Front
66 (68, 70, 74, 76) [80, 84, 86, 90, 94] Back sts

BR2 (WS): Sks, k1, (*turn work over so RS is facing) borrow last st for cast on loop,* crochet cast on 3 sts, *replace loop onto LN, turn work over so WS is facing,* sl1wyf, k1, sm, (purl to 1 st before m, **bM1Rp**, p1, sm, **sM1Rp**, purl to m, **sM1Lp**, sm, p1, **bM1Lp**) twice, purl to BB, sm, BB.
44 (44, 46, 48, 48) [50, 52, 52, 54, 54] Sleeve sts
32 (34, 35, 37, 38) [40, 42, 43, 45, 47] sts + 8 BB sts for each Front
68 (70, 72, 76, 78) [82, 86, 88, 92, 96] Back sts

BR3: Ksk, k1, ksk, p1, sm, (knit to 1 st before m, **bM1L**, sl1wyb, sm, **sM1L**, knit to m, **sM1R**, sm, sl1wyb, **bM1R**) twice, knit to m, sm, p1, sl1 kwise, pick up a twisted loop in bar before cast on, pass 2 sts back to LN (twisted loop and sl st), ssk, sl1wyf, k2, k2tog, sl1wyf, k1.

46 (46, 48, 50, 50) [52, 54, 54, 56, 56] Sleeve sts
33 (35, 36, 38, 39) [41, 43, 44, 46, 48] sts + 8 BB sts for each Front
70 (72, 74, 78, 80) [84, 88, 90, 94, 98] Back sts

Work BOX A **Row 2**.

BOX A

sM1= sleeve increase
nM1 = neck increase
bM1 = body increase

R1 (RS): Ksk, k1, ksk, p1, sm, k2, nM1R, (knit to 1 st before m, sl1wyb, sm, sM1L, knit to m, sM1R, sm, sl1wyb) twice, knit to 2 sts before m, nM1L, k2, sm, p1, ksk, k1, ksk.
This sets the Left & Right BB sts for RS rows.

R2 (WS): (Sl1wyf, k1) x 4, sm, purl to BB, sm, (k1, sl1wyf) x 4.
This sets the Right & Left BB sts for WS rows.

Rows 3 & 5: BB, sm, (knit to 1 st before m, sl1wyb, sm, sM1L, knit to m, **sM1R**, sm, sl1wyb) twice, knit to m, sm, BB.

R4: BB, sm, p2, nM1Lp, purl to 2 sts before last m, nM1Rp, p2, sm, BB.

R6: BB, sm, purl to BB, sm, BB.

ADDITIONAL RS ROWS
R7: BB, sm, k2, nM1R, (knit to 1 st before m, **bM1L**, sl1wyb, sm, sM1L, knit to m, sM1R, sm, sl1wyb, **bM1R**) twice, knit to 2 sts before m, nM1L, k2, sm, BB.

R9: BB, sm, (knit to 1 st before m, **bM1L**, sl1wyb, sm, sM1L, knit to m, sM1R, sm, sl1wyb, **bM1R**) twice, knit to m, sm, BB.

ADDITIONAL WS ROW
R8: BB, sm, (purl to 1 st before m, **bM1Rp**, p1, sm, purl to m, sm, p1, **bM1Lp**) twice, purl to BB, sm, BB.

BOX B

BASIC REPEAT

R1 (RS): BB, sm, knit to BB, sm, BB.

R2 (WS): BB, (purl to m, sm, g1) twice, purl to BB, sm, BB.

BUTTONHOLE ROWS

BR1 (RS): BB, sm, knit to BB, sm, p1, k1, bind off 2 sts, ksk.

BR2 (WS): Sks, k1, (turn work over so RS is facing) borrow last st for cast on loop, crochet cast on 3 sts, replace loop onto LN, turn work over so WS is facing, sl1wyf, k1, sm, (purl to m, sm, g1) twice, purl to BB, sm, BB.

BR3: BB, sm, knit to BB, sm, p1, sl1 kwise, pick up a twisted loop in bar before cast on, pass 2 sts back to LN (twisted loop and sl st), ssk, sl1wyf, k2, k2tog, sl1wyf, k1.

STEP 7: SEPARATING SLEEVES & BODY

Separation Row 1 (RS): BB, sm, *knit to 2 sts before m, pm, k2, rm, place all sts to next m on holder, (= sleeve sts) rm, (turn work over so WS is facing) borrow last st for cast on loop, crochet cast on 6 (7, 8, 8, 9) [9, 9, 10, 10, 10] sts, pm, cast on 2 (3, 4, 4, 5) [5, 5, 6, 6, 6] sts, replace loop onto LN (make a final chain st but not around the needle), turn work over so RS is facing*, work from *to* once more, knit to m, sm, BB.

38 (41, 43, 45, 47) [49, 51, 53, 55, 57] Left Front sts + BB
36 (39, 41, 43, 45) [47, 49, 51, 53, 55] Right Front sts + BB
78 (82, 86, 90, 94) [98, 102, 106, 110, 114] Back sts

Separation Row 2 (WS): BB, sm, *purl to 1 st before cast on, sl1 kwise, make twisted loop in cast on bar and place on LN, sl1 to LN, p2tog (loop and sl st), purl to m, sm, purl to 2 sts before m, p2togtbl, rm*, work from *to* once more, purl to m, sm, BB.

37 (40, 42, 44, 46) [48, 50, 52, 54, 56] Left Front sts + BB
36 (39, 41, 43, 45) [47, 49, 51, 53, 55] Right Front sts + BB
77 (81, 85, 89, 93) [97, 101, 105, 109, 113] Back sts

Note: A garter stitch at each side creates a faux side seam (on WS: k1 after the side marker).
This stitch is not included in the stitch counts that follow.

36 (39, 41, 43, 45) [47, 49, 51, 53, 55] Left Front sts + BB
36 (39, 41, 43, 45) [47, 49, 51, 53, 55] Right Front sts + BB
76 (80, 84, 88, 92) [96, 100, 104, 108, 112] Back sts

STEP 8: BODY WITH BUTTONHOLES

REFER TO **BOX B** FOR ROW INSTRUCTIONS
Work **Rows 1 & 2** x 5.

Work Buttonhole Rows 1 – 3.
Work **Row 2**.

Continue with Basic Repeat **Rows 1 & 2** and make buttonholes starting on every 16th row (approx every 7.5 cm / 3").

Work to 5 cm / 2" from underarm.

BOX C

OPTIONAL BUST DARTS
Place your darts at approx 5 (5, 10, 10) cm / 2 (2, 4, 4)" from underarm or where desired.
For placement of darts, see Hints & Tips.
Note that an additional buttonhole and button may be required if adding darts.

Smallish (Middling, Busty, Wowza!)
Worked over 10 (12, 16, 20) rows, adds approx 4.5 (5.5, 7.5, 9) cm / 1.75 (2.25, 3, 3.5)".

LEFT FRONT
R1 (RS): BB, sm, knit to 20 (20, 24, 28) sts before m, turn.
R2 (WS): Sl1^, pm, purl to BB, sm, BB.
R3 (RS): BB, sm, knit to m, rm, k1^, k5 (4, 3, 3), turn.
R4: Sl1^, pm, purl to BB, sm, BB.
Work **Rows 3 & 4** again x 2 (3, 5, 7).
Next Row (RS): BB, sm, knit to BB, sm, BB (and note buttonhole sequence).

RIGHT FRONT
R2 (WS): BB, sm, purl to 19 (19, 23, 27) sts before m, turn.
R3 (RS): Sl1^, pm, knit to BB, sm, BB.
R4: BB, sm, purl to m, rm, p1^, p5 (4, 3, 3), turn.
Work **Rows 3 & 4** again x 2 (3, 5, 7).
Work **Row 3** once more.
Next Row (WS): BB, sm, purl to m, rm, p1^, (purl to m, sm, g1) twice, purl to BB, sm, BB.

Resume working back and forth as before darts and remember to make buttonholes.

OPTIONAL BUST DARTS
Optional Bust Darts (see BOX C) may be placed here or a bit lower.

Note: *you are trying to stretch your skeins, this is a good place to set the body aside to work the sleeves before finishing the body.*

Continue with Basic Repeat **Rows 1 & 2** and buttonholes as set to 17 cm / 6.75" from underarm or to 14 cm / 5.5" from desired length.

WORKING WS ROWS FROM RS
Sl1wyb, p1 backwards (take yarn to front and manoeuvre the yarn so you make a normal p1), then slip the final st wyb.

STEP 9: POCKETS
The double-knitted pocket starts with a band that adds 4 cm / 1.5". If you opt for another pocket, you may wish to place it a bit lower. The entire Pocket adds approx 12 cm / 4.75".

At 17 cm / 6.75" from underarm, make pockets.

REFER TO POCKET TUTORIAL 3D FOR INSTRUCTIONS
For a simpler pocket consider Pocket 1A, 1B or 2C.
Don't forget buttonhole placement and the g1 at each side 'seam'.

Work Pockets to 29 cm or 11.5" from underarm or to 2 cm / .75" from desired length.
Consider adding rows if necessary to place final buttonhole directly above the hem.

STEP 10: HEM
Switch to smaller (4.5 mm / US 7) needle.
Knit three rows.

BIND OFF
Borrow final stitch to crochet cast on 2 sts onto LN, make 1 chain st (not around needle), place on LN.
R1 (RS): Sl1wyb, sl1wyf, ssk (1 edge st with 1 body st).
R2 (WS): Sks.
R3: K1, sl1wyf, ssk.
R4: Sks.

Tip: Rows 2 & 4 can be worked backwards (from left to right) – this obviates the need to turn work over between rows (see BOX).

Work **Rows 3 & 4** all the way around the hem to last 5 sts.
Final Row (RS): Ssk, bind off 1 st, ssk, bind off final st.

STEP 11: SLEEVES
Place 50 (50, 50, 52, 52) [54, 56, 56, 58, 58] Sleeve sts from holder back on larger (5.5 mm / US 9) needle. Join yarn at right side of gap, p&k3 (4, 5, 5, 6) [6, 6, 7, 7, 7] sts along the first half of the underarm cast on, pm, p&k4 (5, 6, 6, 7) [7, 7, 8, 8, 8] sts more along second half of underarm, knit to m.
57 (59, 61, 63, 65) [67, 69, 71, 73, 73] sts

REFER TO BOX D FOR ROUND INSTRUCTIONS
Work **Rnd 1** to 5 cm / 2" from underarm.

SLEEVE DECREASES
Work **Decrease Rnd**.
55 (57, 59, 61, 63) [65, 67, 69, 71, 71] sts

Continue with **Rnd 1**, working **Decrease Rnd** every 8 (8, 8, 8, 7) [7, 7, 7, 7, 7]th round again x 5 (5, 4, 5, 4) [1, 1, 1, 1, 1], then every 6th round x 2 (2, 4, 4, 5) [9, 9, 9, 9, 9].
41 (43, 43, 43, 45) [45, 47, 49, 51, 51] sts

Work to 33 (33, 34, 36, 36) [36, 36, 37, 37, 37] cm / 13 (13, 13.5, 14.25, 14.25) [14.25, 14.25, 14.5, 14.5, 14.5]" from underarm or to approx 12 cm / 4.75" from desired length.

STEP 12: CONTRAST WEDGE

Rnd 1: Rm, k19 (20, 20, 20, 21) [21, 22, 23, 24, 24], pm, sl2 to CN and hold in front, k1, k2 from CN, knit to m.
Rnd 2: Sm, knit to m.
Rnd 3: Sm, k1, sl2 to CN and hold in front, k1, k2 from CN, k2tog, knit to 2 sts before m, ssk, sm, k2, turn.
39 (41, 41, 41, 43) [43, 45, 47, 49, 49] sts
Work back and forth from here.

Setup Row (WS): P2, sm, purl to 2 sts before m, turn.
R1 (RS): Knit to m, rm, k2, turn.
R2: Purl.
R3: K2, k2tog, knit to last 4 sts, ssk, k2.
37 (39, 39, 39, 41) [41, 43, 45, 47, 47] sts
R4: Purl.
R5: Knit.
R6: Purl.
Work **Rows 3 – 6** again x 5 or to 1.5 cm / 0.75" from desired sleeve length.
27 (29, 29, 29, 31) [31, 33, 35, 37, 37] sts

Slide stitches off needle tips to rest on the cable, set sts aside.

WEDGE

*The **CC** wedge is worked back and forth in stocking stitch, starting from the split, and widening toward the cuff as you work the picked up sts at each side at the end of every row. Pick up inside the entire outermost stitch.*

With RS facing, with **CC** and smaller needle (RN), start at the cuff, and p&k15 sts (in every second row) along the split to its beginning, with a second needle (LN) p&k1 st in centre of split (taking care not to create a gap), p&k15 sts along split to cuff, cut yarn.

Join new **CC** at the split point, with an additional 4.5 mm / US 7 needle (N1), work the contrast triangle as follows.
R1 (RS): K1 from LN, turn.
R2 (WS): P1, turn.
R3: Sl1wyb, k1 from LN, turn. *2 sts*

R4: Sl1wyf, p1, p1 from RN, turn. *3 sts*
R5: Sl1wyb, knit to last st, ssk (last st from N1 with first st from LN), turn.
R6: Sl11wyf, purl to last st, p2tog (last st from N1 with first st from RN), turn.
R7: Sl1wyb, knit all sts on N1, k1 from LN, turn.
R8: Sl1wyf, purl all sts on N1, p1 from RN, turn.

Continue to work **Rows 5 – 8** until all sts on LN and RN are used up. All sts are on N1.

I-CORD BIND OFF

Using Provisional Winding Cast On and working **CC** yarn, wind on 3 sts onto LN.
Rows 1 – 3 (RS): K2, ssk (last i-cord st together with 1 sleeve st), sl 3 sts back to LN.
R4 (RS): K2, sssk (last i-cord st together with 2 sleeve sts), sl 3 sts back to LN.
Work **Rows 1 – 4** around the cuff until all sts are bound off, switching to **MC** where **MC** sleeve sts begin.
With Kitchener stitch, graft or sew the i-cord sts to the provisional sts.

FINISH

Weave in loose ends. Soak and block to measurements. Sew on some nice buttons.

BOX D

SLEEVE ROUNDS
Rnd 1: Sm, g1, knit to m.
Decrease Rnd: Sm, g1, k2tog, knit to 2 sts before m, ssk.

Jadeite

Legend:

- ■ Sleeve increases
- ■ Body increases
- □ Neck increases
- ▨ Underarm cast on
- ▦ Buttonhole

The chart plots increases against "Rows from Cast On" (row numbers shown at both left and right margins, odd rows 21–61). Each size (32, 34, 36, 38, 40, 42, 44, 46, 48, 50) has three columns: Sleeve increases, Body increases, Neck increases. A "Short Rows" column at top left shows **4** at row 61.

Size 32

Row	Sleeve	Body	Neck
51	8		
49	46	70	
48	44	68	
47	42	66	
45	40		30
43	38		29
41	36		28
39	34		27
37	32		26
35	30		25
33	28		24
31	26		
30			23
29	24		
27	22		22
25	20		
24			21
23	18		
21	16		20

Size 34

Row	Sleeve	Body	Neck
51	10		
49	46	72	
48	44	70	
47	42	68	
45	40		32
43	38		31
41	36		30
39	34		29
37	32		28
35	30		27
33	28		26
31	26		
30			25
29	24		
27	22		24
25	20		
24			23
23	18		
21	16		22

Size 36

Row	Sleeve	Body	Neck
55		12	
53		12	
51	48	74	
50	46	72	
49	44	70	
47	42		33
45	40		32
43	38		31
41	36		30
39	34		29
37	32		28
35	30		
33	28		27
31	26		
30			26
29	24		
27	22		25
25	20		
24			24
23	18		
21	16		23

Size 38

Row	Sleeve	Body	Neck
55	12		
53	50	78	
52	48	76	
51	46	74	
49	44	72	36
47	42		34
45	40		32
43	38		31
41	36		30
39	34		29
37	32		28
35	30		
33	28		27
31	26		
30			26
29	24		
27	22		25
25	20		
24			24
23	18		
21	16		23

Size 40

Row	Sleeve	Body	Neck
55	14		
53	50	80	
52	48	78	
51	46	76	
49	44	74	36
47	42		34
45	40		33
43	38		32
41	36		31
39	34		30
37	32		29
35	30		
33	28		28
31	26		
30			27
29	24		
27	22		26
25	20		
24			25
23	18		
21	16		24

Size 42

Row	Sleeve	Body	Neck
59		14	
57		14	
55	52	84	
54	50	82	
53	48	80	
51	46	78	38
49	44	76	36
47	42		34
45	40		33
43	38		32
41	36		31
39	34		30
37	32		29
35	30		28
33	28		27
31	26		
29	24		26
27	22		25
25	20		
23	18		24

Size 44

Row	Sleeve	Body	Neck
59		14	
57	54	88	
56	52	86	
55	50	84	
53	48	80	39
51	46	78	37
49	44		35
47	42		34
45	40		33
43	38		32
41	36		31
39	34		30
37	32		
35	30		29
33	28		27
31	26		
29	24		27
27	22		25
25	20		
23	18		25

Size 46

Row	Sleeve	Body	Neck
59		16	
57	54	90	
56	52	88	
55	50	86	
53	48	82	40
51	46	80	38
49	44		36
47	42		35
45	40		34
43	38		33
41	36		32
39	34		31
37	32		30
35	30		29
33	28		28
31	26		
29	24		27
27	22		26
25	20		
23	18		25

Size 48

Row	Sleeve	Body	Neck
61		16	
59	56	94	
57	54	92	
55	52	90	
54		88	
53	50	86	42
52	48	84	40
51	46	82	38
49	44		36
47	42		35
45	40		34
43	38		33
41	36		32
39	34		31
37	32		
35	30		30
33	28		
31			29
29	24		28
27	22		27
25	20		
23	18		26

Size 50

Row	Sleeve	Body	Neck
61		16	
59	56	98	
57	54	96	
55	52	94	
54		92	
53	50	90	44
52		88	
51	48	86	41
49	46	84	39
47	44		37
45	42		36
43	40		35
41	38		34
39	36		33
37	34		32
35	32		31
33	30		30
31	28		
29			29
27	24		28
25	22		27
23	20		
21	18		26

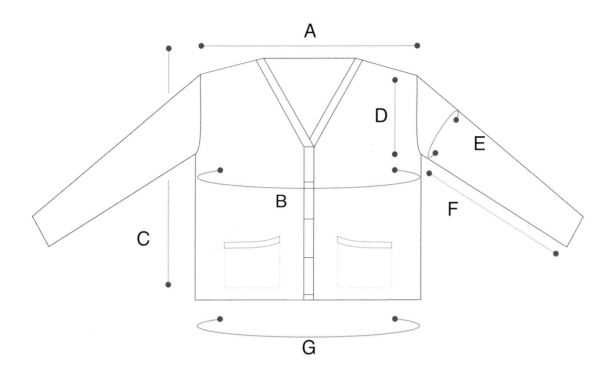

JADEITE GARMENT MEASUREMENTS

	32	34	36	38	40	42	44	46	48	50
A – Shoulder width (cm)	40	41.5	42.5	44	45	46.5	47.5	49	50	51.5
in	15.75	16.25	16.75	17.25	17.75	18.25	18.75	19.25	19.75	20.25
B – Bust (cm)	96.5	101.5	106.5	111.5	116.5	121.5	126.5	131.5	136.5	141.5
in	38	40	42	44	45.75	47.75	49.75	51.75	53.75	55.75
C – Length (cm)	54	54	54.5	55.5	55.5	56.5	57.5	57.5	58.5	58.5
in	21.25	21.25	21.5	21.75	21.75	22.25	22.75	22.75	23	23
D – Armhole depth (cm)	21	21	22	22.5	22.5	23.5	24.5	24.5	25.5	25.5
in	8.25	8	8.5	9	9	9.5	9.5	9.5	10	10
E – Sleeve circumf (cm)	35.5	37	38	39.5	40.5	42	43	44.5	45.5	45.5
in	14	14.5	15	15.5	16	16.5	17	17.5	18	18
F – Sleeve seam (cm)	45	45	46	48	48	48	48	49	49	49
in	17.75	17.75	18	19	19	19	19	19.25	19.25	19.25
G – Hem circumf (cm)	96.5	101.5	106.5	111.5	116.5	121.5	126.5	131.5	136.5	141.5
in	38	40	42	44	45.75	47.75	49.75	51.75	53.75	55.75

This is the original Simple Ziggurat Sweater, knitted in Rohrspatz & Wollmeise Pure, a fingering weight yarn. It is the most basic Ziggurat imaginable. Knit it exactly as written, or use the design and instructions as a canvas for adding your own details. Choose a hem from another design, a pocket from the Tutorial section, or add your own embellishments.

The yellow-green/white pullover has a simple rolled neckline, hem, and cuffs. The brown/black Simple Ziggurat features a contrasting lined hem and cuffs. Instructions for both versions are included here.

TO FIT SIZE

81 (86, 91, 97, 102) [107, 112, 117, 122, 127] cm
32 (34, 36, 38, 40) [42, 44, 46, 48, 50] inches

ROUND NECK

Rolled collar

FIT

Tailored shoulders and waist shaping, no ease

YARN

Rohrspatz & Wollmeise Pure (Fingering, 100% Merino Superwash,
525 m (574 yds) per 150 g)
MC Zarte Knospe (yellow), 2 (2, 2, 2, 2) [3, 3, 3, 3, 3] skeins
CC1 Natur (white), 1 skein
Optional: **CC2** for hem and cuff lining (approx 100 m /150 yds)

APPROX YARDAGE

MC
800 (850, 900, 950, 1000) [1050, 1100, 1150, 1200, 1250] m
850 (900, 950, 1050, 1100) [1150, 1200, 1250, 1350, 1350] yds
CC1
350 (350, 400, 400, 450) [450, 500, 500, 500, 550] m
400 (400, 450, 450, 500) [500, 550, 550, 550, 600] yds

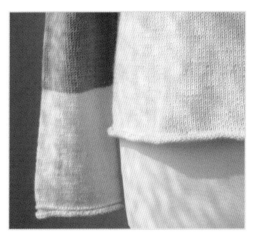

ALTERNATIVE YARN SUGGESTIONS

Dibadu Funnies Twisted Fifties, Nature's Luxury Farouche,
SweetGeorgia Yarn Merino Silk Fine, Rohrspatz & Wollmeise Blend

NEEDLES & NOTIONS

3 mm (US 2.5) circular needle, 80 – 100 cm (32 – 40")
or size to obtain gauge
2.5 mm (US 1.5) circular needle, 60 – 100 cm (24 – 40")
For optional lined hem:
2.75 mm (US 2) circular needle, 60 – 100 cm (24 – 40")
Stitch holders; stitch markers

BLOCKED GAUGE

26 sts x 36 rows on 3 mm (US 2.5) needle = 10 cm / 4"

SAMPLE SIZES

Yellow/white: Size 40 with Middling bust darts, rolled collar, hem,
and cuffs, colours: Rohrspatz & Wollmeise Zarte Knospe (yellow-
green) and Natur weighs 362 g / 12.75 oz
Brown/black: Size 38 with Middling bust darts, rolled collar, lined
hem and cuffs, knitted with Rohrspatz & Wollmeise Pure Gianduia
(brown) and Schwarz (black) weighs 334 g / 11.75 oz

Simple Summer Ziggurat

STEP 1: CAST ON & RIGHT BACK SHOULDER

With **MC**, using longtail cast on and 3 mm (US 2.5) needle, cast on 86 (88, 94, 98, 100) [104, 106, 108, 110, 112] sts.
Setup Row (WS): P17 (18, 19, 20, 21) [22, 23, 24, 25, 26], turn.
R1 (RS): Sl1^, pm, k11 (12, 13, 14, 14) [15, 16, 17, 17, 18], turn.
Rows 2, 4, 6 (WS): Sl1^, purl to m, rm, p1^, p1, turn.
R3: Sl1^, pm, k8 (8, 9, 10, 10) [10, 11, 12, 12, 12], turn.
R5: Sl1^, pm, k5 (5, 5, 6, 6) [6, 6, 7, 7, 7], turn.
R7: Sl1^, pm, knit to last 2 sts (working any sl1^ as k1^), sl1wyb, k1.
R8: Purl to m, rm, p1^, p1, turn.
R9: Sl1^, pm, knit to last 2 sts, sl1wyb, k1.
R10: Purl to m, rm, p1^, purl to end.

86 (88, 94, 98, 100) [104, 106, 108, 110, 112] Back sts

STEP 2: LEFT BACK SHOULDER

R1 (RS): K1, sl1wyb, k15 (16, 17, 18, 19) [20, 21, 22, 23, 24], turn.
R2 (WS): Sl1^, pm, p11 (12, 13, 14, 14) [15, 16, 17, 17, 18], turn.
Rows 3, 5, 7: Sl1^, knit to m, rm, k1^, k1, turn.
R4: Sl1^, pm, p8 (8, 9, 10, 10) [10, 11, 12, 12, 12], turn.
R6: Sl1^, pm, p5 (5, 5, 6, 6) [6, 6, 7, 7, 7], turn.
R8: Sl1^, pm, purl to end (working any sl1^ as p1^).
R9: K1, sl1wyb, knit to m, rm, k1^, k1, turn.
R10: Sl1^, pm, purl to end.

STEP 3: WORKING ACROSS BACK

R1 (RS): K1, sl1wyb, knit to m, rm, k1^, knit to last 2 sts, sl1wyb, k1.
86 (88, 94, 98, 100) [104, 106, 108, 110, 112] Back sts
R2 (WS): Purl.
R3: K1, sl1wyb, knit to last 2 sts, sl1wyb, k1.
R4: Purl.
Work **Rows 3 & 4** again x 1 (1, 1, 2, 2) [2, 2, 3, 3, 3].
Work **Row 3** once more.
Final Row (WS): Purl to last 2 sts, p2tog, pm, p&p7 (7, 7, 8, 8) [8, 8, 9, 9, 9] sts along edge (for first half of Left Sleeve Cap).

7 (7, 7, 8, 8) [8, 8, 9, 9, 9] Left Cap sts
85 (87, 93, 97, 99) [103, 105, 107, 109, 111] Back sts

Slide stitches off needle tips to rest on the cable.
Set these stitches aside, continue to next step without turning.

STEP 4: LEFT FRONT SHOULDER

Setup Row (WS): Loop cable, p&p16 (17, 18, 19, 20) [21, 22, 23, 24, 25] sts (for Left Front Shoulder) in the cast on of Left Back Shoulder, *and remember to pick up second st in line with faux seam.*
16 (17, 18, 19, 20) [21, 22, 23, 24, 25] Left Front sts
R1 (RS): K1, sl1wyb, k10 (10, 11, 12, 13) [13, 14, 15, 16, 16], turn.

Rows 2, 4, 6 (WS): Sl1^, purl to end.
R3: K1, sl1wyb, k6 (6, 6, 7, 8) [8, 8, 9, 10, 10], turn.
R5: K1, sl1wyb, k2 (2, 2, 2, 3) [3, 3, 3, 4, 4], turn.
R7: K1, sl1wyb, knit to 2 sts before loop (working any sl1^ as k1^), sl1wyb, k1, turn.
R8: Purl.
R9: K1, sl1wyb, knit to 2 sts before loop, sl1wyb, k1, turn.
R10: Purl.
Work **Rows 9 & 10** again x 4 (4, 4, 5, 5) [5, 5, 5, 6, 6].
Final Row (RS): K1, sl1wyb, knit to 2 sts before loop, ssk, pm, p&k7 (7, 7, 8, 8) [8, 8, 9, 9, 9] sts (for second half of Left Sleeve Cap), knit to m, sm, sl1wyb, knit to last 2 sts, ssk, pm, p&k7 (7, 7, 8, 8) [8, 8, 9, 9, 9] sts (for first half of Right Sleeve Cap).

14 (14, 14, 16, 16) [16, 16, 18, 18, 18] Left Cap sts
7 (7, 7, 8, 8) [8, 8, 9, 9, 9] Right Cap sts
15 (16, 17, 18, 19) [20, 21, 22, 23, 24] Left Front sts
84 (86, 92, 96, 98) [102, 104, 106, 108, 110] Back sts

Slide stitches off needle tips to rest on the cable.
Set these stitches aside, continue to next step without turning.

STEP 5: RIGHT FRONT SHOULDER

R1 (RS): Loop cable, p&k16 (17, 18, 19, 20) [21, 22, 23, 24, 25] sts (for Right Front Shoulder) in the cast on of Right Back Shoulder, *and remember to pick up second st in line with faux seam.*

16 (17, 18, 19, 20) [21, 22, 23, 24, 25] Right Front sts
R2 (WS): P12 (12, 13, 14, 15) [15, 16, 17, 18, 18], turn.
Rows 3, 5, 7: Sl1^, knit to last 2 sts, sl1wyb, k1.
R4: P8 (8, 8, 9, 10) [10, 10, 11, 12, 12], turn.
R6: P4 (4, 4, 4, 5) [5, 5, 5, 6, 6], turn.
R8: Purl to loop (working any sl1^ as p1^), turn.
R9: K1, sl1wyb, knit to last 2 sts, sl1wyb, k1.
R10: Purl to loop, turn.
Work **Rows 9 & 10** again x 4 (4, 4, 5, 5) [5, 5, 6, 6, 6].
Work **Row 9** once more.
Final Row (WS): Purl to 2 sts before loop, p2tog, pm, p&p7 (7, 7, 8, 8) [8, 8, 9, 9, 9] sts (for second half of Right Sleeve Cap), purl to end.

14 (14, 14, 16, 16) [16, 16, 18, 18, 18] sts for each Sleeve Cap
15 (16, 17, 18, 19) [20, 21, 22, 23, 24] sts for each Front
84 (86, 92, 96, 98) [102, 104, 106, 108, 110] Back sts

STEP 6: SLEEVE CAPS & BODY
You will now increase for the sleeves and neck (and later also body) simultaneously. (See Helpful Table for an overview of all increases.)

REFER TO **BOX A** FOR ROW INSTRUCTIONS
Work **Rows 1 & 2** x 11 (11, 11, 10, 10) [11, 13, 13, 13, 13].
36 (36, 36, 36, 36) [38, 42, 44, 44, 44] Sleeve sts
26 (27, 28, 28, 29) [31, 34, 35, 36, 37] sts for each Front

Work **Rows 1 & 4** x 2 (2, 2, 3, 3) [3, 2, 2, 2, 2].
40 (40, 40, 42, 42) [44, 46, 48, 48, 48] Sleeve sts
30 (31, 32, 34, 35) [37, 38, 39, 40, 41] sts for each Front

BOX A

sM1 = sleeve increase   nM1 = neck increase

RS ROWS
R1: K1, sl1wyb, k1, nM1R, (knit to 1 st before m, sl1wyb, sm, sM1L, knit to m, sM1R, sm, sl1wyb) twice., knit to last 3 sts, nM1L, k1, sl1wyb, k1.

WS ROWS
R2: Purl.

R4: P3, nM1Lp, purl to last 3 sts, nM1Rp, p3.

STEP 7: JOIN FRONTS TO KNIT IN THE ROUND
Joining Row-Round 1 (RS): K1, sl1wyb, nM1R, (knit to 1 st before m, sl1wyb, sm, sM1L, knit to m, sM1R, sm, sl1wyb) twice, knit to last 2 sts, nM1L, pm (=Nm), k2, *(turn work over so WS is facing) borrow last st for cast on loop, crochet cast on 23 (23, 27, 27, 27) [27, 27, 27, 27, 27] sts, replace loop onto LN (make a final chain st but not around the needle), turn work over so RS is facing, join to Left Front, knit to m, sm.*

You are now at Left Front Sleeve.

42 (42, 42, 44, 44) [46, 48, 50, 50, 50] Sleeve sts
85 (87, 93, 97, 99) [103, 105, 107, 109, 111] Front sts
84 (86, 92, 96, 98) [102, 104, 106, 108, 110] Back sts

Joining Round 2: Knit to Nm, rm, ssk, knit to end of cast on, make loop in bar and place on LN, k2tog (the first st of Left Front and the loop), knit to 1 st before m.

42 (42, 42, 44, 44) [46, 48, 50, 50, 50] Sleeve sts
84 (86, 92, 96, 98) [102, 104, 106, 108, 110] Front sts
84 (86, 92, 96, 98) [102, 104, 106, 108, 110] Back sts

Photo © Bob Dietrich

STEP 8: SLEEVE & BODY INCREASES
Continue to work sleeve increases and also introduce body increases. *The round begins 1 stitch before Left Front Sleeve marker.*

REFER TO **BOX B** FOR ROW INSTRUCTIONS
Work **Rnds 1 & 2** x 7 (7, 8, 7, 7) [6, 5, 4, 4, 5].
56 (56, 58, 58, 58) [58, 58, 58, 58, 60] Sleeve sts

INTRODUCE BODY INCREASES
Work **Rnds 3 & 2** x 0 (2, 3, 4, 2) [3, 5, 4, 4, 4].
56 (60, 64, 66, 62) [64, 68, 66, 66, 68] Sleeve sts
84 (90, 98, 104, 102) [108, 114, 114, 116, 118] Front sts
84 (90, 98, 104, 102) [108, 114, 114, 116, 118] Back sts

Work **Rnds 3 & 4** x 0 (0, 0, 0, 2) [2, 2, 3, 5, 6].
56 (60, 64, 66, 66) [68, 72, 72, 76, 80] Sleeve sts
84 (90, 98, 104, 110) [116, 122, 126, 136, 142] Front sts
84 (90, 98, 104, 110) [116, 122, 126, 136, 142] Back sts

Work **Rnds 3 & 6** x 2 (0, 0, 0, 0) [0, 0, 0, 0, 0].
64 (60, 64, 66, 66) [68, 72, 72, 76, 80] Sleeve sts
88 (90, 98, 104, 110) [116, 122, 126, 136, 142] Front sts
88 (90, 98, 104, 110) [116, 122, 126, 136, 142] Back sts

BOX B

sM1 = sleeve increase   **bM1** = body increase

ODD (SLIP-STITCH) ROUNDS
Rnd 1: (Sl1wyb, sm, sM1L, knit to m, sM1R, sm, sl1wyb, knit to 1 st before m) twice.
Rnd 3: (**bM1L**, sl1wyb, sm, sM1L, k to m, sM1R, sm, sl1wyb, **bM1R**, knit to 1 st before m) twice.

EVEN (PLAIN) ROUNDS
Rnd 2: Knit.
Rnd 4: (**bM1L**, k1, sm, knit to m, sm, k1, **bM1R**, knit to 1 st before m) twice.
Rnd 6: (K1, sm, sM1L, k to m, sM1R, sm, knit to 1 st before m) twice.
Rnd 8: (**bM1L**, k1, sm, sM1L, knit to m, sM1R, sm, k1, **bM1R**, knit to 1 st before m) twice.

Work **Rnds 3 & 8** x 0 (1, 0, 0, 0) [0, 0, 0, 0, 0].
64 (64, 64, 66, 66) [68, 72, 72, 76, 80] Sleeve sts
88 (94, 98, 104, 110) [116, 122, 126, 136, 142] Front sts
88 (94, 98, 104, 110) [116, 122, 126, 136, 142] Back sts

Work **Rnd 3.**
66 (66, 66, 68, 68) [70, 74, 74, 78, 82] Sleeve sts
90 (96, 100, 106, 112) [118, 124, 128, 138, 144] Front sts
90 (96, 100, 106, 112) [118, 124, 128, 138, 144] Back sts

Final Rnd: Knit to 2 sts before Left Front Sleeve m.

STEP 9: SEPARATING SLEEVES & BODY
Separation Rnd 1: *Pm, k2, rm, place all sts to next m on holder (= sleeve sts), rm, *(turn work over so WS is facing) borrow last st for cast on loop, crochet cast on 8 (9, 10, 11, 12) [12, 12, 13, 12, 12] sts, pm, cast on 6 (7, 8, 9, 10) [10, 10, 11, 10, 10] sts, *replace loop onto LN (make a final chain st but not around the needle), turn work over so RS is facing*, knit to 2 sts before m, work from * to * once more, knit to m.

You are now at Left Front Sleeve.

104 (112, 118, 126, 134) [140, 146, 152, 160, 166] Front sts
104 (112, 118, 126, 134) [140, 146, 152, 160, 166] Back sts

Separation Rnd 2: *Rm, ssk, knit to m, sm, p1, knit to end of underarm cast on, make loop in bar and place on LN, k2tog (next st and loop), knit to m*, work from * to * once more.

103 (111, 117, 125, 133) [139, 145, 151, 159, 165] Front sts
103 (111, 117, 125, 133) [139, 145, 151, 159, 165] Back sts

STEP 10: BODY & SHAPING
Continue in stocking stitch over body stitches only.
The round begins under Left Sleeve.
Note: *One stitch under each arm is worked in garter st (g1), which creates a faux side seam.*

AT THE SAME TIME
Please read through the entire step before proceeding, as a few things happen at the same time or overlap.

- Optional Bust Darts
- Waist Shaping (begins before or just after the darts, depending on where you place it)
- Optional Rear Shaping
- Change to **CC1**

BOX C

BODY & SHAPING
Rnd 1: (Sm, g1, knit to marker) x 2.

Decrease Rnd: (Sm, g1, k2tog, knit to 2 sts before side m, ssk) twice.

Increase Rnd: (Sm, g1, M1L, knit to m, M1R) twice.

REFER TO **BOX C** FOR ROUND INSTRUCTIONS
Work **Rnd 1** to 5 cm/ 2" from underarm.

AT THE SAME TIME OPTIONAL BUST DARTS
Optional Bust Darts may be placed here or a bit lower, see BOX D.

Note: If you are trying to stretch your skeins, this is a good place to set the body aside to work the sleeves before finishing the body.

AT THE SAME TIME WAIST SHAPING
At 5 cm / 2" from underarm, begin waist shaping.

WAIST DECREASES
Work **Decrease Rnd**.
101 (109, 115, 123, 131) [137, 143, 149, 157, 163] Front/Back sts

Continue with **Rnd 1**, working **Decrease Rnd** every 8 (8, 8, 8, 8) [9, 9, 9, 9, 9]th rnd again x 4.
93 (101, 107, 115, 123) [129, 135, 141, 149, 155] Front/Back sts

WORK STRAIGHT
Work **Rnd 1** for 4 (4, 5, 5, 5) [5, 5, 5, 5, 5] cm / 1.5 (1.5, 2, 2, 2) [2, 2, 2, 2, 2]".
Note: Please read ahead to the end of this step. The change to **CC1** takes place before waist shaping is complete.

WAIST INCREASES
Work **Increase Rnd**.
95 (103, 109, 117, 125) [131, 137, 143, 151, 157] Front/Back sts

Continue with **Rnd 1**, working **Increase Rnd** every 8 (8, 8, 8, 8) [9, 9, 9, 9, 9]th round again x 2, then on next 10th round once, then on every 12th round x 1 (1, 1, 1, 1) [1, 1, 2, 2, 2].
103 (111, 117, 125, 133) [139, 145, 153, 161, 167] Front/Back sts

Work to 24 (24.5, 24.5, 25, 25.5) [26, 25.5, 25.5, 25, 24] cm / 9.5 (9.75, 9.75, 9.75, 10) [10.25, 10, 10, 9.75, 9.5]" from underarm (with waist shaping as instructed).

AT THE SAME TIME OPTIONAL REAR SHAPING (SEE **BOX D**)

BOX D

OPTIONAL BUST DARTS
Place your darts at approx 5 (6, 10, 10) cm / 2 (2.25, 4, 4)" from underarm or where desired:
For placement of darts, see Hints & Tips
(Remember to place them in Front!)

Smallish (Middling, Busty, Wowza!)
Worked over 12 (18, 24, 28) rows, adds approx 3.5 (5, 6.5, 8) cm / 1.5 (2, 2.5, 3.25)".

R1 (RS): Sm, g1, knit across back to m, sm, g1, knit to 27 (34, 37, 40) sts before left underarm m, turn.
R2 (WS): Sl1^, pm, purl to 28 (35, 38, 41) sts before right underarm m, turn.
R3 (RS): Sl1^, pm, knit to m, rm, k1^, k5 (4, 3, 3), turn.
R4: Sl1^, pm, purl to m, rm, p1^, p5 (4, 3, 3), turn.
Work **Rows 3 & 4** again x 4 (7, 10, 12).
Final Row (RS): Sl1^, pm, knit to m, rm, k1^, knit to m.

Resume working in the round.
Next Rnd: Sm, g1, knit to m, sm, g1, knit to 1 st before m, k1^, rm, knit to m.

OPTIONAL REAR SHAPING
If **MC** is darker than **CC1** make increases on final **MC** round.
If **CC1** is darker than **MC**, make increases on second **CC1** round:
Increase (M1L) x 10 (10, 10, 10, 12) [12, 12, 14, 14, 14] evenly distributed across the Back.

Simple Summer Ziggurat

Photo © Bob Dietrich

STEP 11: LINED HEM

This is one of two options for the hem. Instructions for a rolled hem follow further below.

LINING

Hem lining stitches are picked up on WS (see Tutorial section). Slide stitches off needle tips to rest on the cable. Take yarn to WS. With 2.5 mm (US 1.5) needle on WS and going counterclockwise, p&k sts in every bar *between* all sts, take yarn to RS.

103 (111, 117, 125, 133) [139, 145, 153, 161, 167] Front/Back Lining sts
With OPTIONAL REAR SHAPING:
113 (121, 127, 135, 145) [151, 157, 167, 175, 181] Back Lining sts

Join Fingering (or Heavy Lace weight) **CC2**, knit 10 rounds on WS (along inside of sweater, going counterclockwise and downwards). Cut **CC2**.
Slide sts off needle tips to rest on cable, set Lining sts aside.

HEM

With **CC1** and 2.75 mm (US 2) needle, knit 10 rnds (or to *slightly longer than lining*), take **CC1** to WS.

LINING

With **CC1**, knit one round, take **CC1** to RS.

Note: If required, work an additional hem-round to make hem slightly longer before binding off.

BIND OFF

Weave in any loose ends at hem.
From RS, bind off hem sts together with lining sts using 3-Needle Bind Off and keeping an even tension.

ALTERNATIVE ROLLED HEM

Knit an additional 1.5 cm / 0.75" before switching to smaller needles. With 2.5 mm (US 1.5) needle, purl one round.

AT THE SAME TIME CHANGE TO CONTRAST COLOUR

Cut **MC**, join **CC1** and continue with **Rnd 1**, working **Increase Rnd** as instructed to 34.5 (35, 35.5, 36, 37) [37.5, 37.5, 37.5, 37, 36] cm / 13.5 (13.75, 14, 14.25, 14.5) [14.75, 14.75, 14.75, 14.5, 14.25]" from underarm or to 2.5 cm / 1" from desired length.
Do not cut the yarn.

103 (111, 117, 125, 133) [139, 145, 153, 161, 167] Front/Back sts
With Optional Rear Shaping:
113 (121, 127, 135, 145) [151, 157, 167, 175, 181] Back sts

Note: If you are adding length, you may wish to include one or more rounds of increases.

BOX E

Knit 7 rounds.
Bind off in even tension, using Stretchy Bind Off:
K1, *k1, sl2 to LN, k2togtbl*, work from * to * until all sts are bound off.

STEP 12: SLEEVES

Place 66 (66, 66, 68, 68) [70, 74, 74, 78, 82] Sleeve sts from holder back on larger (3 mm / US 2.5) needle. Join **MC** at right side of gap, p&k6 (7, 8, 9, 10) [10, 10, 11, 10, 10] sts along the first half of the underarm cast on, pm, p&k7 (8, 9, 10, 11) [11, 11, 12, 11, 11] sts more along second half of underarm, knit to m.
79 (81, 83, 87, 89) [91, 95, 97, 99, 103] sts

REFER TO **BOX E** FOR ROUND INSTRUCTIONS
Work **Rnd 1** to 5 cm / 2" from underarm.

SLEEVE DECREASES
Work **Decrease Rnd**.
77 (79, 81, 85, 87) [89, 93, 95, 97, 101] sts
Note: Please read ahead to the end of this step. The change to **CC1** takes place before sleeve decreases are complete.

Continue with **Rnd 1**, working **Decrease Rnd** every 20 (18, 18, 13, 12) [12, 12, 11, 11, 10]th round again x 6 (7, 7, 10, 11) [11, 11, 12, 12, 14].
65 (65, 67, 65, 65) [67, 71, 71, 73, 73] sts

Work to 32 (32, 33, 33, 34) [34, 34, 34, 34, 34] cm /12.5 (12.5, 13, 13, 13.5) [13.5, 13.5, 13.5, 13.5, 13.5]" from underarm.

CHANGE TO CONTRAST COLOUR
Contrast colour adds 13 cm / 5" to Sleeve.
Cut **MC**, join **CC1** and continue to work sleeve with decreases to 42.5 (42.5, 43.5, 43.5, 44.5) [44.5, 44.5, 44.5, 44.5, 44.5] cm / 16.75 (16.75, 17.25, 17.25, 17.5) [17.5, 17.5, 17.5, 17.5, 17.5]" from underarm or 2.5 cm / 1" from desired sleeve length.

LINED CUFF
Work cuff lining as for the Hem.

ALTERNATIVE ROLLED CUFF
Knit an additional 1.5 cm / 0.75" before switching to smaller needles and work as for Rolled Hem.

STEP 13: ROLLED COLLAR

Join **MC** at Left Shoulder and with 2.5 mm (US 1.5) needle, p&k approx 64 (64, 68, 70, 70) [72, 74, 76, 76, 76] sts along Front Neck, continue along Back Neck and p&k approx 52 (52, 56, 58, 58) [60, 61, 62, 62, 63] sts (approx 2 for every 3 sts along the straight bits along Back Neck, 4 for every 5 along Front Neck, and 1 for every 2 rows in the slanting bits).
Approx 116 (116, 124, 128, 128) [132, 135, 138, 138, 139] sts
Purl 1 round.
Knit 7 rounds.
Bind off rather loosely, using Stretchy Bind Off as for Rolled Hem.

FINISH

Weave in loose ends. Soak and block to measurements.

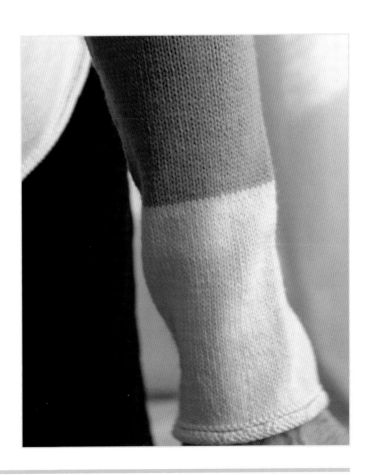

Simple Summer Ziggurat

Legend:
- Sleeve increases
- Body increases
- Neck increases
- Front cast on
- Underarm cast on

Chart axis labels: **Rows from Cast On** (left and right edges), **Short Rows**

Each size group is headed by the three sub-columns: *Sleeve increases*, *Body increases*, *Neck increases*, with size labels **32, 34, 36, 38, 40, 42, 44, 46, 48, 50**.

Simple Summer Ziggurat sizing chart — rows from cast on numbered (odd) from 21 up to 89 on both the left and right margins, with a "Short Rows: 6" note at row 89. Sleeve, body, and neck increase stitch counts are tabulated for sizes 32 through 50.

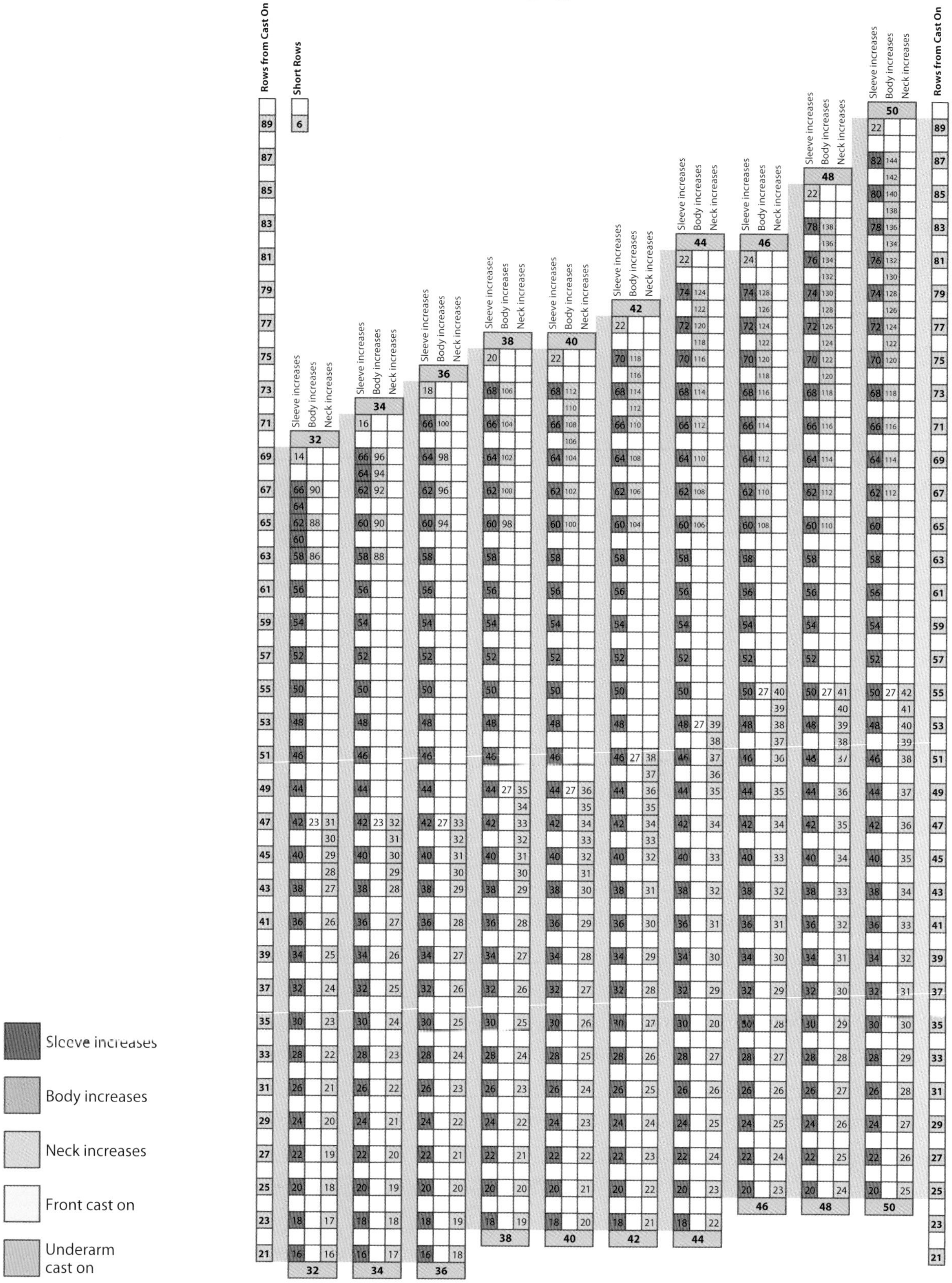

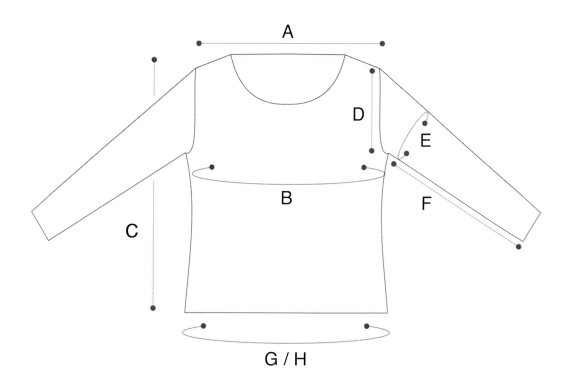

SIMPLE SUMMER ZIGGURAT GARMENT MEASUREMENTS

	32	34	36	38	40	42	44	46	48	50
A – Shoulder width (cm)	32.5	33	35.5	37	37.5	39	40	41	41.5	42.5
in	12.75	13	14	14.5	14.75	15.25	15.75	16.25	16.25	16.75
B – Bust (cm)	81	85.5	90	96	102.5	107	111.5	116	124	128.5
in	32	33.75	35.5	37.75	40.25	42.25	44	45.75	48.75	50.5
C – Length (cm)	59.5	59.5	59.5	60	60	60.5	61	61.5	61.5	62.5
in	23.5	23.5	23.5	23.5	23.5	23.75	24	24.25	24.25	24.5
D – Armhole depth (cm)	17	17.5	18	19	19	19.5	20.5	20.5	21.5	23
in	6.75	7	7	7.5	7.5	7.75	8	8	8.5	9
E – Sleeve circumf (cm)	29.5	30.5	31	32.5	33.5	34	36	36.5	38	39.5
in	11.5	12	12.25	12.75	13.25	13.5	14.25	14.25	15	15.5
F – Sleeve seam (cm)	45	45	46	46	47	47	47	47	47	47
in	17.75	17.75	18	18	18.5	18.5	18.5	18.5	18.5	18.5
G – Hem circumf (cm)	81.5	86	91	97	103	107.5	112.5	118.5	126	131
in	32	33.75	35.75	38.25	40.5	42.25	44.25	46.75	49.5	51.5
H – Hem with extra sts (cm)	85.5	90	94.5	101	107.5	112.5	117	124	131.5	136
in	33.75	35.5	37.25	39.75	42.25	44.25	46	48.75	51.75	53.5

Sammelsurium is a twist on the original Simple Ziggurat Sweater. Knitted in lofty, warm, and wondrously soft Little Grey Sheep Gotland DK this pullover quickly became a favourite to wear at home, going out, everywhere. With its contrasting lined hem, lined collar and cuffs, Sammelsurium has a higher neckline and finer finishing details than other Simple Ziggurats.

In addition, a travelling cable snakes its way down one sleeve. For a plainer look you can omit the travelling cable. Or knit it with a more subtly different yarn. Oh, and I added a small coin pocket as well, for there is always room for a pocket.

TO FIT SIZE
81 (86, 91, 97, 102) [107, 112, 117, 122, 127] cm
32 (34, 36, 38, 40) [42, 44, 46, 48, 50] inches

ROUND NECK
Lined or rolled narrow collar

FIT
Tailored shoulders and waist shaping, no ease

YARN
The Little Grey Sheep Gotland DK (8ply, 100% wool, 237 m (259 yds)
per 100 g); **MC** The Dark Side, 3 (3, 3, 3, 4) [4, 4, 4, 4, 4] skeins
CC1 Naturally, 1 (1, 1, 1, 2) [2, 2, 2, 2, 2] skeins
Scrap (approx 50 m / 60 yds) of **CC2** in Sport or Fingering, such as The
Little Grey Sheep Stein Fine Wool mini skein

APPROX YARDAGE
MC
600 (650, 700, 700, 750) [800, 850, 850, 900, 950] m
650 (700, 750, 800, 800) [850, 900, 950, 1000, 1000] yds
CC1
200 (200, 250, 250, 250) [250, 300, 300, 300, 300] m
250 (250, 250, 300, 300) [300, 350, 350, 350, 350] yds

ALTERNATIVE YARN SUGGESTIONS
Rohrspatz & Wollmeise Merino DK, Malabrigo Silky Merino,
Cascade 220

NEEDLES & NOTIONS
4 mm (US 6) circular needle, 80 – 100 cm (32 – 40")
or size to obtain gauge
Two 3.25 mm (US 3) circular needles, 60 – 100 cm (24 – 40")
Stitch holders; stitch markers

BLOCKED GAUGE
20 sts x 28 rows on 4 mm (US 6) needle = 10 cm / 4"

SAMPLE SIZES
Grey: Size 40 with Middling bust darts, travelling cable, and a coin
pocket, knitted with less than 3 skeins of **MC**, 1 skein of **CC1**
Blue: Size 42 increasing to size 46 with Wowza! bust darts, knitted
with every little scrap of 3 skeins **MC**, 1 skein **CC1**

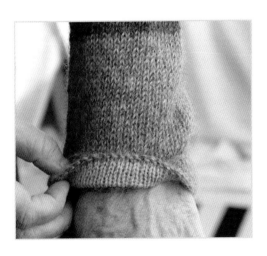

Sammelsurium

STEP 1: CAST ON & RIGHT BACK SHOULDER

With **MC**, using longtail cast on, and 4 mm (US 6) needle, cast on 66 (68, 72, 76, 78) [80, 82, 84, 86, 88] sts.

Setup Row (WS): P14 (15, 16, 16, 17) [18, 18, 18, 19, 20], turn.

R1 (RS): Sl1^, pm, k8 (9, 10, 10, 10) [11, 11, 11, 12, 12], turn.

R2 (WS): Sl1^, purl to m, rm, p1^, p1, turn.

R3: Sl1^, pm, k5 (5, 6, 6, 6) [6, 6, 6, 7, 7], turn.

R4: Sl1^, purl to m, rm, p1^, p1, turn.

R5: Sl1^, pm, knit to last 2 sts (working any sl1^ as k1^), sl1wyb, k1.

R6: Purl to m, rm, p1^, p1, turn.

R7: Sl1^, pm, knit to last 2 sts, sl1wyb, k1.

R8: Purl to m, rm, p1^, purl to end.

66 (68, 72, 76, 78) [80, 82, 84, 86, 88] Back sts

Photo © Kaire Kitse

STEP 2: LEFT BACK SHOULDER

R1 (RS): K1, sl1wyb, k12 (13, 14, 14, 15) [16, 16, 16, 17, 18], turn.

R2 (WS): Sl1^, pm, p8 (9, 10, 10, 10) [11, 11, 11, 12, 12], turn.

R3: Sl1^, knit to m, rm, k1^, k1, turn.

R4: Sl1^, pm, p5 (5, 6, 6, 6) [6, 6, 6, 7, 7], turn.

R5: Sl1^, knit to m, rm, k1^, k1, turn.

R6: Sl1^, pm, purl to end (working any sl1^ as p1^).

R7: K1, sl1wyb, knit to m, rm, k1^, k1, turn.

R8: Sl1^, pm, purl to end.

STEP 3: WORKING ACROSS BACK

R1 (RS): K1, sl1wyb, knit to m, rm, k1^, knit to last 2 sts, sl1wyb, k1.

66 (68, 72, 76, 78) [80, 82, 84, 86, 88] Back sts

R2 (WS): Purl.

R3: K1, sl1wyb, knit to last 2 sts, sl1wyb, k1.

R4: Purl.

Work **Rows 3 & 4** again x 2 (2, 3, 3, 3) [3, 3, 3, 4, 4].

Work **Row 3** once more.

Final Row (WS): Purl to last 2 sts, p2tog, pm, p&p8 (8, 9, 9, 9) [9, 9, 9, 10, 10] sts along edge (for first half of Left Sleeve Cap).

8 (8, 9, 9, 9) [9, 9, 9, 10, 10] Left Cap sts

65 (67, 71, 75, 77) [79, 81, 83, 85, 87] Back sts

Slide stitches off needle tips to rest on the cable.

Set these stitches aside, continue to next step without turning.

STEP 4: LEFT FRONT SHOULDER

nM1 = neck increase

Setup Row (WS): Loop cable, p&p13 (14, 15, 15, 16) [17, 17, 17, 18, 19] sts (for Left Front Shoulder) in the cast on of Left Back Shoulder, *and remember to pick up second st in line with faux seam*

13 (14, 15, 15, 16) [17, 17, 17, 18, 19] Left Front sts

R1 (RS): K1, sl1wyb, k6 (7, 8, 8, 8) [9, 9, 9, 10, 10], turn.

R2 (WS): Sl1^, purl to end.

R3: K1, sl1wyb, k2 (2, 3, 3, 3) [3, 3, 3, 4, 4], turn.

R4: Sl1^, purl to end.

R5: K1, sl1wyb, knit to 2 sts before loop (working any sl1^ as k1^), sl1wyb, k1, turn.

Row 6, 8, 10: Purl.

R7: K1, sl1wyb, knit to 2 sts before loop, sl1wyb, k1, turn.

R9: K1, sl1wyb, nM1R, knit to 2 sts before loop, sl1wyb, k1, turn.

14 (15, 16, 16, 17) [18, 18, 18, 19, 20] Left Front sts

Work **Rows 9 & 10** again x 4 (4, 5, 5, 5) [5, 5, 5, 6, 6].

18 (19, 21, 21, 22) [23, 23, 23, 25, 26] Left Front sts

*Note: For a plain Right Sleeve without the CC2 cable, pick up the total number of Right Cap sts with **MC**.*

Final Row (RS): K1, sl1wyb, nM1R, knit to 2 sts before loop, ssk, pm, p&k8 (8, 9, 9, 9) [9, 9, 9, 10, 10] sts (for second half of Left Sleeve

BOX A

sM1 = sleeve increase   nM1 = neck increase

Shift the 2-stitch CC2 cable on the Right Sleeve Cap according to your fancy – travelling left or right on every or every second row (later: round), or sometimes not at all for several rows/rounds.

RS ROWS

R1: K1, sl1wyb, nM1R, (knit to 1 st before m, sl1wyb, sm, **sM1L**, knit to m, **sM1R**, sm, sl1wyb) twice, knit to last 2 sts, nM1L, sl1wyb, k1.

WS ROWS

R2: Purl.
R4: P2, nM1Lp, purl to last 2 sts, nM1Rp, p2.

Cap), knit to m, sm, sl1wyb, knit to last 2 sts, ssk, pm, p&k3 sts, join **CC2** to p&k2 sts, with **MC**, p&k3 (3, 4, 4, 4) [4, 4, 4, 5, 5] sts (for first half of Right Sleeve Cap).

16 (16, 18, 18, 18) [18, 18, 18, 20, 20] Left Cap sts
8 (8, 9, 9, 9) [9, 9, 9, 10, 10] Right Cap sts
18 (19, 21, 21, 22) [23, 23, 23, 25, 26] Left Front sts
64 (66, 70, 74, 76) [78, 80, 82, 84, 86] Back sts

Slide stitches off needle tips to rest on the cable.
Set these stitches aside, continue to next step without turning.

STEP 5: RIGHT FRONT SHOULDER

nM1 = neck increase
R1 (RS): Loop cable, p&k13 (14, 15, 15, 16) [17, 17, 17, 18, 19] sts (for Right Front Shoulder) in the cast on of Right Back Shoulder, *and remember to pick up second st in line with faux seam.*
13 (14, 15, 15, 16) [17, 17, 17, 18, 19] Right Front sts
R2 (WS): P8 (9, 10, 10, 10) [11, 11, 11, 12, 12], turn.
R3: Sl1^, knit to last 2 sts, sl1wyb, k1.
R4: P4 (4, 5, 5, 5) [5, 5, 5, 6, 6], turn.
R5: Sl1^, knit to last 2 sts, sl1wyb, k1.
R6: Purl to loop (working any sl1^ as p1^), turn.
R7: K1, sl1wyb, knit to last 2 sts, sl1wyb, k1.
R8: Purl to loop, turn.
R9: K1, sl1wyb, knit to last 2 sts, nM1L, sl1wyb, k1.
14 (15, 16, 16, 17) [18, 18, 18, 19, 20] Right Front sts
R10: Purl to loop, turn.
Work **Rows 9 & 10** again x 4 (4, 5, 5, 5) [5, 5, 5, 6, 6].
18 (19, 21, 21, 22) [23, 23, 23, 25, 26] Right Front sts

Work **Row 9** once more.
19 (20, 22, 22, 23) [24, 24, 24, 26, 27] Right Front sts
Final Row (WS): Purl to 2 sts before loop, p2tog, pm, p&p8 (8, 9, 9, 9) [9, 9, 9, 10, 10] sts (for second half of Right Sleeve Cap), purl to end.
16 (16, 18, 18, 18) [18, 18, 18, 20, 20] sts for each Sleeve Cap
18 (19, 21, 21, 22) [23, 23, 23, 25, 26] sts for each Front
64 (66, 70, 74, 76) [78, 80, 82, 84, 86] Back sts

STEP 6: SLEEVE CAPS & BODY

You will now increase for the sleeves and neck (and later also body) simultaneously. (See Helpful Table for an overview of all increases.)

REFER TO BOX A FOR ROW INSTRUCTIONS
Work **Rows 1 & 2** x 1 (1, 1, 1, 3) [3, 4, 3, 4, 4].
18 (18, 20, 20, 24) [24, 26, 24, 28, 28] Sleeve sts
19 (20, 22, 22, 25) [26, 27, 26, 29, 30] sts for each Front

Work **Rows 1 & 4** x 1 (1, 1, 2, 1) [1, 1, 2, 1, 1].
20 (20, 22, 24, 26) [26, 28, 28, 30, 30] Sleeve sts
21 (22, 24, 26, 27) [28, 29, 30, 31, 32] sts for each Front

STEP 7: JOIN FRONTS TO KNIT IN THE ROUND

Joining Row-Round 1 (RS): K1, sl1wyb, nM1R, (knit to 1 st before m, sl1wyb, sm, **sM1L**, knit to m, **sM1R**, sm, sl1wyb) twice, knit to 2 sts before m, nM1L, pm (=Nm), k2, *(turn work over so WS is facing) borrow last st for cast on loop, crochet cast on 21 sts, replace loop onto LN (make a final chain st but not around the needle), turn work over so RS is facing,* join to Left Front, knit to m, sm.
You are now at Left Front Sleeve.

22 (22, 24, 26, 28) [28, 30, 30, 32, 32] Sleeve sts
65 (67, 71, 75, 77) [79, 81, 83, 85, 87] Front sts
64 (66, 70, 74, 76) [78, 80, 82, 84, 86] Back sts

Joining Round 2: Knit to Nm, rm, ssk, knit to end of cast on, make loop in bar and place on LN, k2tog (the first st of Left Front and the loop), knit to 1 st before m.

22 (22, 24, 26, 28) [28, 30, 30, 32, 32] Sleeve sts
64 (66, 70, 74, 76) [78, 80, 82, 84, 86] Front sts
64 (66, 70, 74, 76) [78, 80, 82, 84, 86] Back sts

STEP 8: SLEEVE & BODY INCREASES

Continue to work sleeve increases and also introduce body increases.

The round begins 1 stitch before Left Front Sleeve marker.

REFER TO **BOX B** FOR ROUND INSTRUCTIONS
Work **Rnds 1 & 2** x 13 (12, 12, 12, 10) [11, 9, 10, 9, 10].
48 (46, 48, 50, 48) [50, 48, 50, 50, 52] Sleeve sts

INTRODUCE BODY INCREASES
Work **Rnds 3 & 2** x 0 (1, 1, 1, 1) [1, 2, 1, 3, 2].
48 (48, 50, 52, 50) [52, 52, 52, 56, 56] Sleeve sts
64 (68, 72, 76, 78) [80, 84, 84, 90, 90] Front sts
64 (68, 72, 76, 78) [80, 84, 84, 90, 90] Back sts

Work **Rnds 3 & 4** x 0 (0, 0, 0, 1) [1, 1, 3, 3, 4].
48 (48, 50, 52, 52) [54, 54, 58, 62, 64] Sleeve sts
64 (68, 72, 76, 82) [84, 88, 96, 102, 106] Front sts
64 (68, 72, 76, 82) [84, 88, 96, 102, 106] Back sts

Work **Rnds 3 & 6** x 1 (1, 1, 1, 1) [1, 1, 0, 0, 0].
52 (52, 54, 56, 56) [58, 58, 58, 62, 64] Sleeve sts
68 (72, 76, 80, 86) [88, 92, 96, 102, 106] Front sts
68 (72, 76, 80, 86) [88, 92, 96, 102, 106] Back sts

Work **Rnd 3**.
54 (54, 56, 58, 58) [60, 60, 60, 64, 66] Sleeve sts
70 (74, 78, 82, 88) [90, 94, 98, 104, 108] Front sts
70 (74, 78, 82, 88) [90, 94, 98, 104, 108] Back sts

Final Rnd: Knit to 2 sts before Left Front Sleeve m.

STEP 9: SEPARATING SLEEVES & BODY

Separation Rnd 1: *Pm, k2, rm, place all sts to next m on holder (= sleeve sts), rm, *(turn work over so WS is facing) borrow last st for cast on loop*, crochet cast on 7 (8, 9, 9, 9) [10, 11, 11, 11, 11] sts, pm, cast on 5 (6, 7, 7, 7) [8, 9, 9, 9, 9] sts, *replace loop onto LN (make a final chain st but not around the needle), turn work over so RS is facing*, knit to 2 sts before m, work from *to* once more, knit to m.

You are now at Left Front Sleeve.

82 (88, 94, 98, 104) [108, 114, 118, 124, 128] Front sts
82 (88, 94, 98, 104) [108, 114, 118, 124, 128] Back sts

Separation Rnd 2: *Rm, ssk, knit to m, sm, p1, knit to end of underarm cast on, make loop in bar and place on LN, k2tog (next st and loop), knit to m*, work from *to* once more.

81 (87, 93, 97, 103) [107, 113, 117, 123, 127] Front sts
81 (87, 93, 97, 103) [107, 113, 117, 123, 127] Back sts

BOX B

sM1 = sleeve increase   bM1 = body increase

ODD (SLIP-STITCH) ROUNDS
Rnd 1: (Sl1wyb, sm, sM1L, knit to m, sM1R, sm, sl1wyb, knit to 1 st before m) twice.
Rnd 3: (bM1L, sl1wyb, sm, sM1L, k to m, sM1R, sm, sl1wyb, bM1R, knit to 1 st before m) twice.

EVEN (PLAIN) ROUNDS
Rnd 2: Knit.
Rnd 4: (bM1L, k1, sm, knit to m, sm, k1, **bM1R**, knit to 1 st before m) twice.
Rnd 6: (bM1L, k1, sm, sM1L, knit to m, sM1R, sm, k1, bM1R, knit to 1 st before m) twice.

STEP 10: BODY & SHAPING

Continue in stocking stitch over body stitches only.
The round begins under Left Sleeve.
Note: *One stitch under each arm is worked in garter st (g1), which creates a faux side seam.*

AT THE SAME TIME
Please read through the entire step before proceeding, as a few things happen at the same time or overlap.

- Waist Shaping (begins before or just after the darts, depending on where you place them)
- Optional Bust Darts
- Optional Pocket
- Optional Rear Shaping
- Change to CC1

REFER TO **BOX C** FOR ROUND INSTRUCTIONS

Work **Rnd 1** to 5 cm/ 2" from underarm.

AT THE SAME TIME BUST DARTS
Optional Bust Darts may be placed here or a bit lower, see BOX D.

Note: *If you are trying to stretch your skeins, this is a good place to set the body aside to work the sleeves before finishing the body.*

AT THE SAME TIME WAIST SHAPING
At 5 cm / 2" from underarm, begin waist shaping.

BOX C

BODY & SHAPING

Rnd 1: (Sm, g1, knit to marker) twice.

Decrease Rnd: (Sm, g1, k2tog, knit to 2 sts before side m, ssk) twice.

Increase Rnd: (Sm, g1, M1L, knit to m, M1R) twice.

WAIST DECREASES

Work **Decrease Rnd**.

79 (85, 91, 95, 101) [105, 111, 115, 121, 125] Front/Back sts

Continue to with **Rnd 1**, working **Decrease Rnd** every 6 (6, 8, 8, 8) [8, 8, 8, 10, 10]th rnd again x 3 (3, 3, 4, 4) [4, 4, 4, 4, 4].

73 (79, 85, 87, 93) [97, 103, 107, 113, 117] Front/Back sts

WORK STRAIGHT

Work **Rnd 1** for 5 cm / 2".

Note: Please read ahead to the end of this step. The change to CC1 takes place before waist shaping is complete.

WAIST INCREASES

Work **Increase Rnd**.

75 (81, 87, 89, 95) [99, 105, 109, 115, 119] Front/Back sts

Continue with **Rnd 1**, working **Increase Rnd** every 8th round again x 2 (2, 2, 3, 3) [3, 3, 3, 3, 3], then on next 10th round once, then on next 12th round once.

83 (89, 95, 99, 105) [109, 115, 119, 125, 129] Front/Back sts

AT THE SAME TIME OPTIONAL MINI POCKET

At 25 (25.5, 26, 26, 26.5) [26.5, 27.5, 26.5, 26, 25] cm / 9.75 (10, 10.25, 10.25, 10.5) [10.5, 10.75, 10.5, 10.25, 9.75]" from underarm, or at three rounds before changing to **CC1**, make a pocket.

REFER TO POCKET TUTORIAL **2C** FOR INSTRUCTIONS

The Pocket Rounds are worked into the BOX C Rounds with a g1-stitch at the side 'seams' and waist shaping.

Prepare a welt of 17 sts.

Place pocket welt 15 (15, 15, 20, 20) [20, 25, 25, 25, 25] sts after the Right Side marker.

AT THE SAME TIME OPTIONAL REAR SHAPING (SEE BOX D)

AT THE SAME TIME CHANGE TO CONTRAST COLOUR

At 26 (26.5, 27, 27, 27.5) [27.5, 28.5, 27.5, 27, 26] cm / 10.25 (10.5, 10.75, 10.75, 10.75) [10.75, 11.25, 10.75, 10.75, 10.25]" from underarm, change to **CC1**.

Cut **MC**, join **CC1** and continue with **Rnd 1**, working **Increase Rnd** as instructed to 35 (36, 36, 36.5, 37.5) [38, 39, 37.5, 37.5, 36.5] cm / 13.75 (14.25, 14.25, 14.25, 14.75) [15, 15.25, 14.75, 14.75, 14.25]" from underarm or to 2.5 cm / 1" from desired length.

Do not cut the yarn.

83 (89, 95, 99, 105) [109, 115, 119, 125, 129] Front/Back sts
With Optional Rear Shaping:
89 (95, 101, 107, 113) [117, 125, 129, 135, 139] Back sts
***Note:** If you are adding length, you may wish to include one or more rounds of increases.*

BOX D

OPTIONAL BUST DARTS

Place your darts at approx 5 (6, 10, 10) cm / 2 (2.25, 4, 4)" from underarm or where desired:

For placement of darts, see Hints & Tips

(Remember to place them in Front!)

Smallish (Middling, Busty, Wowza!)
Worked over 10 (14, 20, 24) rows, adds approx 3.5 (5, 7, 8.5) cm / 1.5 (2, 2.75, 3.25)".

R1 (RS): Sm, g1, knit across back to m, sm, g1, knit to 26 (28, 32, 36) sts before left underarm m, turn.
R2 (WS): Sl1^, pm, purl to 27 (29, 33, 37) sts before right underarm m, turn.
R3 (RS): Sl1^, pm, knit to m, rm, k1^, k5 (4, 3, 3), turn.
R4: Sl1^, pm, purl to m, rm, p1^, p5 (4, 3, 3), turn.
Work **Rows 3 & 4** again x 3 (5, 8, 10).
Final Row (RS): Sl1^, pm, knit to m, rm, k1^, knit to m.

Resume working in the round.
Next Rnd: Sm, g1, knit to m, sm, g1, knit to 1 st before m, k1^, rm, knit to m.

OPTIONAL REAR SHAPING

If **MC** is darker than **CC1** make increases on final **MC** round.
If **CC1** is darker than **MC**, make increases on second **CC1** round:
Increase (M1L) x 10 (10, 10, 10, 12) [12, 12, 14, 14, 14] evenly distributed across the Back.

BOX E

BIND OFF
Weave in any loose ends at hem.
From RS, bind off hem sts together with lining sts using 3-Needle Bind Off and keeping an even tension.

STEP 12: SLEEVES
Place 54 (54, 56, 58, 58) [60, 60, 60, 64, 66] Sleeve sts from holder back on larger (4 mm / US 6) needle. Join **MC** at right side of gap, p&k5 (6, 7, 7, 7) [8, 9, 9, 9, 9] sts along the first half of the underarm cast on, pm, p&k6 (7, 8, 8, 8) [9, 10, 10, 10, 10] sts more along second half of underarm, knit to m.
65 (67, 71, 73, 73) [77, 79, 79, 83, 85] sts

RIGHT SLEEVE CC2 CABLE
Shift the **CC2** cable one stitch over on every round, alternating with every other round, and rounds with no travel as desired.

REFER TO BOX E FOR ROUND INSTRUCTIONS
Work **Rnd 1** to 5 cm / 2" from underarm.

SLEEVE DECREASES
Work **Decrease Rnd**.
63 (65, 69, 71, 71) [75, 77, 77, 81, 83] sts

Note: *Please read ahead to the end of this step. The change to CC1 takes place before sleeve decreases are complete.*

Continue with **Rnd 1**, working **Decrease Rnd** every 13 (13, 12, 11, 11) [10, 10, 10, 9, 8]th round again x 7 (7, 8, 9, 9) [10, 10, 10, 11, 12].
49 (51, 53, 53, 53) [55, 57, 57, 59, 59] sts

Work to 32 (32, 33, 33, 34) [34, 34, 34, 34, 34] cm / 12.5 (12.5, 13, 13, 13.5) [13.5, 13.5, 13.5, 13.5, 13.5]" from underarm.

CHANGE TO CONTRAST COLOUR
Contrast colour adds 13 cm / 5" to Sleeve.
Cut **MC**, join **CC1** and continue to work sleeve with decreases to 42.5 (42.5, 43.5, 43.5, 44.5) [44.5, 44.5, 44.5, 44.5, 44.5] cm / 16.75 (16.75, 17.25, 17.25, 17.5) [17.5, 17.5, 17.5, 17.5, 17.5]" from underarm or 2.5 cm / 1" from desired length.

STEP 11: LINED HEM
For a plain rolled hem, see Simple Summer Ziggurat.

LINING
Hem lining sts are picked up on WS (see Tutorial section).
Slide stitches off needle tips to rest on the cable.
Take working **MC** to WS. With 3.25 mm (US 3) needle on WS and going counterclockwise, p&k sts in every bar *between* all sts, take **MC** to RS.
83 (89, 95, 99, 105) [109, 115, 119, 125, 129] Front/Back Lining sts
With Optional Rear Shaping:
89 (95, 101, 107, 113) [117, 125, 129, 135, 139] Front/Back Lining sts

Join Fingering (or Sport weight) **CC2**, knit 7 rounds on WS (along inside of sweater, working counterclockwise and downwards).
Cut **CC2**.
Slide sts off needle tips to rest on cable, set Lining sts aside.

HEM
With **CC1** and 3.25 mm (US 3) needle, knit 6 rnds (or to *slightly* longer than lining), take **CC1** to WS.

LINING
With **CC1**, knit one round, take **CC1** to RS.

Note: *If required, work an additional hem-round to make hem slightly longer before binding off.*

LINED CUFF

Work cuff lining as for the Hem.

*Tip: If you double-knit the cuff, CC2 can be used for both lining and the
CC2 cable continuing on outside of cuff, which creates a corresponding
CC1 cable for the lining layer.*

STEP 13: LINED COLLAR WITH SMALL TRAVELLING CABLE

Join **MC** at Left Shoulder and with 3.25 mm (US 3) needle (N1) p&k
sts along Front Neck, then continue along Back Neck. P&k in approx
every stitch along the straight bits, and 1 for every 2 rows in the
slanting bits.

Approx 93 (93, 97, 103, 105) [105, 109, 111, 113, 113] sts

LINING

See tutorials for tips on picking up stitches for collar lining.

On WS, join **CC1** at Left Shoulder and with 3.25 mm (US 3) needle
(N2) p&k sts in every bar between **MC** sts.

Slide sts off needle tips to rest on cable, set lining sts aside.

COLLAR

Knit outside layer on N1 as follows:

Rnd 1: K16, join **CC2**, with **CC2** k2, with **MC** knit to end of rnd.
Rnds 2 – 5: Knit to 1 st before **CC2**, with **CC2** k2, with **MC** knit to end
of rnd.

Set sts aside.

LINING

Knit lining sts on N2 on the inside (WS) with **CC1** as follows:
Rnds 1 – 4: Knit. Cut yarn.
Rnd 5: Take **MC** to inside, with **MC** knit.

Weave in any loose ends at cuff before binding off.
With N1 and working from the outside, join the two layers with a
3-Needle Bind Off.

FINISH

Weave in loose ends. Soak and block to measurements.

Sammelsurium

Legend
- ■ Sleeve increases
- ▨ Body increases
- ▦ Neck increases
- ☐ Front cast on
- ▧ Underarm cast on

Short Rows (column): Row 71 → 4

Columns for each size read: Sleeve increases | Body increases | Neck increases. "Rows from Cast On" shown on both left and right edges.

Size 32
Row	Sleeve	Body	Neck
57	12		
55	54	70	
54	52	68	
53	50	66	
51	48		
49	46		
47	44		
45	42		
43	40		
41	38		
39	36		
37	34		
35	32		
33	30		
31	28		
29	26		
27	24		
25	22	21	22
24		21	
23	20		20
21	18		19
bottom	**32**		

Size 34
Row	Sleeve	Body	Neck
57	14		
55	54	74	
54	52	72	
53	50	70	
51	48	68	
49	46		
47	44		
45	42		
43	40		
41	38		
39	36		
37	34		
35	32		
33	30		
31	28		
29	26		
27	24		
25	22	21	23
24		21	22
23	20		21
21	18		20
bottom	**34**		

Size 36
Row	Sleeve	Body	Neck
59	16		
57	56	78	
56	54	76	
55	52	74	
53	50	72	
51	48		
49	46		
47	44		
45	42		
43	40		
41	38		
39	36		
37	34		
35	32		
33	30		
31	28		
29	26		
27	24	21	25
26			24
25	22		23
23	20		22
bottom	**36**		

Size 38
Row	Sleeve	Body	Neck
61	16		
59	58	82	
58	56	80	
57	54	78	
55	52	76	
53	50		
51	48		
49	46		
47	44		
45	42		
43	40		
41	38		
39	36		
37	34		
35	32		
33	30		
31	28		
29	26	21	27
28			26
27	24		25
25	22		23
23	20		22
bottom	**38**		

Size 40
Row	Sleeve	Body	Neck
61	16		
59	58	88	
58	56	86	
57	54	84	
56		82	
55	52	80	
53	50	78	
51	48		
49	46		
47	44		
45	42		
43	40		
41	38		
39	36		
37	34		
35	32		
33	30		
31	28	21	28
30			27
29	26		26
27	24		25
25	22		24
23	20		23
bottom	**40**		

Size 42
Row	Sleeve	Body	Neck
63	18		
61	60	90	
59	58	88	
58	56	86	
57	54	82	
55	52	80	
53	50		
51	48		
49	46		
47	44		
45	42		
43	40		
41	38		
39	36		
37	34		
35	32		
33	30		
31	28	21	29
30			28
29	26		27
27	24		26
25	22		25
23	20		24
bottom	**42**		

Size 44
Row	Sleeve	Body	Neck
63	20		
61	60	94	
60	58	92	
59	56	90	
58		88	
57	54	86	
55	52	84	
53	50	82	
51	48		
49	46		
47	44		
45	42		
43	40		
41	38		
39	36		
37	34		
35	32		
33	30	21	31
32			30
31	28		29
29	26		27
27	24		26
25	22		25
23	20		24
bottom	**44**		

Size 46
Row	Sleeve	Body	Neck
65	20		
63	60		
61	58	94	
59	56	90	
57	54	86	
55	52	84	
53	50		
51	48		
49	46		
47	44		
45	42		
43	40		
41	38		
39	36		
37	34		
35	32		
33	30	21	31
32			30
31	28		29
29	26		28
27	24		27
25	22		25
bottom	**46**		

Size 48
Row	Sleeve	Body	Neck
67	20		
65	20		
63	60	98	
61	58	94	
59	56	90	
57	54	86	
55	52		
53	50		
51	48		
49	46		
47	44		
45	42		
43	40		
41	38		
39	36		
37	34		
35	32	21	32
34			31
33	30		30
31	28		29
29	26		28
27	24		27
25	22		26
bottom	**48**		

Size 50
Row	Sleeve	Body	Neck
71	20		
69	66	108	
68		106	
67	64	104	
66		102	
65	62	100	
64		98	
63	60	96	
62		94	
61	58	92	
59	56	90	
57	54	88	
55	52		
53	50		
51	48		
49	46		
47	44		
45	42		
43	40		
41	38		
39	36		
37	34		
35	32	21	33
34			32
33	30		31
31	28		30
29	26		29
27	24		28
25	22		27
bottom	**50**		

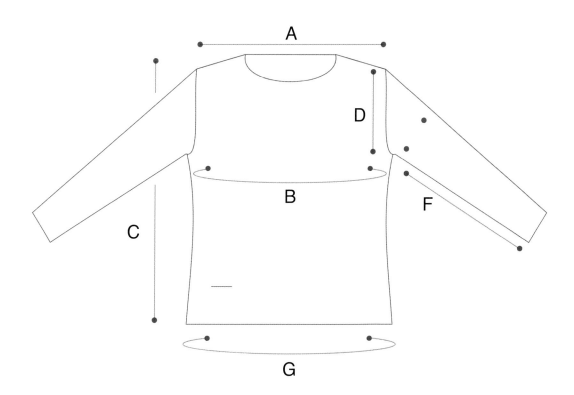

SAMMELSURIUM GARMENT MEASUREMENTS

	32	34	36	38	40	42	44	46	48	50
A – Shoulder width (cm)	32	33	35	37	38	39	40	41	42	43
in	12.5	13	13.75	14.5	15	15.25	15.75	16.25	16.5	17
B – Bust (cm)	81	87	93	97	103	107	113	117	123	127
in	32	34.25	36.5	38.25	40.5	42.25	44.5	46	48.5	50
C – Length (cm)	56	57	58	59	60	61	62	62	63	63
in	22	22.5	22.75	23.25	23.5	24	24.5	24.5	24.75	24.75
D – Armhole depth (cm)	18	18	19	19.5	19.5	20.5	20.5	21.5	23	23.5
in	7.25	7	7.5	7.5	7.5	8	8	8.5	9	9.5
E – Sleeve circumf (cm)	32.5	33.5	35.5	36.5	36.5	38.5	39.5	39.5	41.5	42.5
in	12.75	13.25	14	14.25	14.25	15.25	15.5	15.5	16.25	16.75
F – Sleeve seam (cm)	45	45	46	46	47	47	47	47	47	47
in	17.75	17.75	18	18	18.5	18.5	18.5	18.5	18.5	18.5
G – Hem circumf (cm)	83	89	95	99	105	109	115	119	125	129
in	32.75	35	37.5	39	41.25	43	45.25	46.75	49.25	50.75
H – Hem with extra sts (cm)	86	92	98	103	109	113	120	124	130	134
in	33.75	36.25	38.5	40.5	43	44.5	47.25	48.75	51.25	52.75

Black Basalt is an everyday wardrobe staple, your 'always-reach-for' basic cardigan. With a classic round neck and a relaxed fit, it is neither bulky nor boxy. It goes with everything. An optional contrasting triangle insert/detail on the cuff adds interest without making a big statement. The double-knitted pockets require concentration and commitment. If you follow the step-by-step tutorial you should be fine. You could, if you prefer, opt for a simple pocket, or none at all. The teal sample features a simple afterthought pocket with a contrasting cord edging, which is a good alternative to the double-knitted ones.

Black Basalt

casual aran cardigan

FIT SIZE

6, 91, 97, 102) [107, 112, 117, 122, 127] cm
34, 36, 38, 40) [42, 44, 46, 48, 50] inches

UND NECK

xed with approx 14 – 15 cm / 5.5 – 6" ease

RN

abrigo Yarn Rios (10ply superwash merino,
m (210 yds) per 100 g)
Black x 6 (6, 7, 7, 7) [8, 8, 8, 9, 9] skeins
grey scrap of Fingering or DK

ROX YARDAGE

0 (1100, 1200, 1250, 1300) [1350, 1350, 1450, 1500, 1550] m
0 (1200, 1300, 1350, 1400) [1450, 1500, 1600, 1650, 1700] yds

ERNATIVE YARN SUGGESTIONS

cade Lana d'Oro, Dibadu Alpaka Walk, Little Grey Sheep
mpshire DK (knits to Aran gauge)

EDLES & NOTIONS

mm (US 7) circular needle, 80 – 100 cm (32 – 40") x 3
ize to obtain gauge
mm (US 4) circular needle, 60 – 100 cm (24 – 40")
horter circulars 3.5 mm (US 4)
ch holders; stitch markers; 7 buttons (8 if adding bust darts)

OCKED GAUGE

sts x 26 rows on 4.5 mm (US 7) needles = 10 cm / 4"

MPLE SIZES

ck: Size 38 without bust darts weighs 560 g / 20 oz and was
tted with just under 6 skeins
l: Size 38 without bust darts, alternative Simple Afterthought
cket with **CC** edging weighs 510 g / 18 oz

Black Basalt

STEP 1: CAST ON & RIGHT BACK SHOULDER

With **MC**, using longtail cast on and 4.5 mm (US 7) needle, cast on 74 (76, 78, 80, 82) [84, 86, 90, 92, 94] sts.
Setup Row (WS): P16 (17, 18, 19, 20) [21, 22, 23, 23, 24], turn.
R1 (RS): Sl1^, pm, k9 (10, 11, 11, 12) [13, 13, 14, 14, 15], turn.
R2 (WS): Sl1^, purl to m, rm, p1^, p1, turn.
R3: Sl1^, pm, k5 (5, 6, 6, 6) [7, 7, 7, 7, 8], turn.
R4: Sl1^, purl to m, rm, p1^, p1, turn.
R5: Sl1^, pm, knit to last 2 sts (working any sl1^ as k1^), sl1wyb, k1.
R6: Purl to m, rm, p1^, p1, turn.
R7: Sl1^, pm, knit to last 2 sts, sl1wyb, k1.
R8: Purl to m, rm, p1^, purl to end.

74 (76, 78, 80, 82) [84, 86, 90, 92, 94] Back sts

STEP 2: LEFT BACK SHOULDER

R1 (RS): K1, sl1wyb, k14 (15, 16, 17, 18) [19, 20, 21, 21, 22], turn.
R2 (WS): Sl1^, pm, p9 (10, 11, 11, 12) [13, 13, 14, 14, 15], turn.
R3: Sl1^, knit to m, rm, k1^, k1, turn.
R4: Sl1^, pm, p5 (5, 6, 6, 6) [7, 7, 7, 7, 8], turn.
R5: Sl1^, knit to m, rm, k1^, k1, turn.
R6: Sl1^, pm, purl to end (working any sl1^ as p1^).
R7: K1, sl1wyb, knit to m, rm, k1^, k1, turn.
R8: Sl1^, pm, purl to end.

STEP 3: WORKING ACROSS BACK

R1 (RS): K1, sl1wyb, knit to m, rm, k1^, knit to last 2 sts, sl1wyb, k1.
74 (76, 78, 80, 82) [84, 86, 90, 92, 94] Back sts
R2 (WS): Purl.
R3: K1, sl1wyb, knit to last 2 sts, sl1wyb, k1.
R4: Purl.
Work **Row 3** once more.
Final Row (WS): Purl to last 2 sts, p2tog, pm, p&p7 (7, 8, 8, 8) [8, 8, 9, 9, 9] sts along edge (for first half of Left Sleeve Cap).

7 (7, 8, 8, 8) [8, 8, 9, 9, 9] Left Cap sts
73 (75, 77, 79, 81) [83, 85, 89, 91, 93] Back sts

Slide stitches off needle tips to rest on the cable.
Set these stitches aside, continue to next step without turning.

STEP 4: LEFT FRONT SHOULDER

After the shoulder sts have been picked up, add sts for the Buttonband (BB) using the working yarn and a provisional cast on. After a few rows, these sts can be placed on a holder or safety pin.
Setup Row (WS): Loop cable, p&p15 (16, 17, 18, 19) [20, 21, 22, 22, 23] sts (for Left Front Shoulder) in the cast on of Left Back Shoulder, *and remember to pick up second st in line with faux seam.* Place spare

circular parallel to working needle and using Winding Provisional Cast On and working yarn, wind on 8 sts for BB, pull on spare circular to allow provisional sts to rest on its cable.
15 (16, 17, 18, 19) [20, 21, 22, 22, 23] Left Front sts + 8 BB sts

R1 (RS): Ksk, k1, ksk, p1, pm, k9 (9, 10, 11, 11) [12, 13, 13, 13, 14], turn.
This sets the 8 BB sts for RS rows.
R2 (WS): Sl1^, purl to m, sm, (k1, sl1wyf) x 4.
This sets the 8 BB sts for WS rows.

nM1 = neck increase
R3: BB, sm, k2, nM1R, k3 (3, 3, 4, 4) [4, 5, 5, 5, 5], turn.
16 (17, 18, 19, 20) [21, 22, 23, 23, 24] Left sts + 8 BB sts
R4: Sl1^, purl to m, sm, BB.
R5: BB, sm, knit to 2 sts before loop (working any sl1^ as k1^), sl1wyb, k1, turn.
Rows 6, 8, 10: Purl to m, sm, BB.
R7: BB, sm, k2, nM1R, knit to 2 sts before loop, sl1wyb, k1, turn.
17 (18, 19, 20, 21) [22, 23, 24, 24, 25] Left Front sts + 8 BB sts
R9: BB, sm, knit to 2 sts before loop, sl1wyb, k1, turn.
Work **Rows (7 & 8)** again x 4 (4, 5, 5, 5) [5, 5, 1, 1, 1].
21 (22, 24, 25, 26) [27, 28, 25, 25, 26] Left Front sts + 8 BB sts
Work **Rows (9 & 10)** again x 0 (0, 0, 0, 0) [0, 0, 1, 1, 1].
Work **Rows (7 & 8)** again x 0 (0, 0, 0, 0) [0, 0, 4, 4, 4].
21 (22, 24, 25, 26) [27, 28, 29, 29, 30] Left Front sts + 8 BB sts

Final Row (RS): BB, sm, k2, nM1R, knit to 2 sts before loop, ssk, pm, p&k7 (7, 8, 8, 8) [8, 8, 9, 9, 9] sts (for second half of Left Sleeve Cap), knit to m, sm, k1, sl1wyb, knit to last 2 sts, ssk, pm, p&k7 (7, 8, 8, 8) [8, 8, 9, 9, 9] sts (for first half of Right Sleeve Cap).

14 (14, 16, 16, 16) [16, 16, 18, 18, 18] *Left Cap sts*
7 (7, 8, 8, 8) [8, 8, 9, 9, 9] *Right Cap sts*
21 (22, 24, 25, 26) [27, 28, 29, 29, 30] *Left Front sts + 8 BB sts*
73 (75, 77, 79, 81) [83, 85, 89, 91, 93] *Back sts*

Slide stitches off needle tips to rest on the cable.
Set these stitches aside for now.

WORKING BUTTONBAND AROUND BACK NECK
Slide provisional buttonband/collar (BB) sts to 4.5 mm (US 7) needle.
With RS facing, at inside edge of BB, join new **MC** to work and attach
BB along the neck as follows:

R1 (RS): With new **MC**, k2tog, sl1wyf, k2, ksk. *7 sts*
R2 (WS): Sl1wyf, (k1, sl1wyf) x 3.
R3: P&k1 st in neck edge, place on LN, k2tog, sl1wyf, k2, ksk.
Continue to work **Rows 2 & 3** while picking up sts along Back Neck
up to the Right Shoulder until all but one st is picked up. Pick up
approx 3 sts for every 4, and end with a Row 2 (**WS**).
Next row (RS): P&k1 st in neck sts, ksk, k1, ksk. *8 sts*
Final row (WS): (Sl1wyf, k1) x 4. Cut yarn.

STEP 5: RIGHT FRONT SHOULDER
Continue at Right Shoulder where you stopped in Step 4.
R1 (RS): Loop cable, p&k15 (16, 17, 18, 19) [20, 21, 22, 22, 23] sts
(for Right Front Shoulder) in the cast on of Right Back Shoulder, *and
remember to pick up second st in line with faux seam*, pm (before BB),
p1, ksk, k1, ksk.
This sets the 8 BB sts for RS rows.
15 (16, 17, 18, 19) [20, 21, 22, 22, 23] Right Front sts + 8 BB sts
R2 (WS): (Sl1wyf, k1) x 4, sm, p9 (9, 10, 11, 11) [12, 13, 13, 13, 14],
turn.
This sets the 8 BB sts for WS rows.

nM1 = neck increase
R3: Sl1^, knit to 2 sts before m, nM1L, k2, sm, BB.
16 (17, 18, 19, 20) [21, 22, 23, 23, 24] Right Front sts + 8 BB sts
R4: BB, sm, p5 (5, 5, 6, 6) [6, 7, 7, 7, 7], turn.
R5: Sl1^, knit to m, sm, BB.
R6: BB, sm, purl to loop (working any sl1^ as p1^), turn.
R7: K1, sl1wyb, knit to 2 sts before m, nM1L, k2, sm, BB.
17 (18, 19, 20, 21) [22, 23, 24, 24, 25] Right Front sts + 8 BB sts
R8: BB, sm, purl to loop, turn.
R9: K1, sl1wyb, knit to m, sm, BB.
R10: BB, sm, purl to loop, turn.
Work **Rows 7 & 8** again x 4 (4, 5, 5, 5) [5, 5, 1, 1, 1].
21 (22, 24, 25, 26) [27, 28, 25, 25, 26] Right Front sts + 8 BB sts
Works **Rows 9 & 10** again x 0 (0, 0, 0, 0) [0, 0, 1, 1, 1].

Work **Rows 7 & 8** again x 0 (0, 0, 0, 0) [0, 0, 4, 4, 4].
21 (22, 24, 25, 26) [27, 28, 29, 29, 30] Right Front sts + 8 BB sts
Work **Row 7** once more.
22 (23, 25, 26, 27) [28, 29, 30, 30, 31] Right Front sts + 8 BB sts
Final Row (WS): BB, sm, purl to 2 sts before loop, p2tog, pm, p&p7
(7, 8, 8, 8) [8, 8, 9, 9, 9] sts (for second half of Right Sleeve Cap), purl
to last m, sm, BB.

14 (14, 16, 16, 16) [16, 16, 18, 18, 18] sts for each Sleeve Cap
21 (22, 24, 25, 26) [27, 28, 29, 29, 30] sts + 8 BB sts for each Front
72 (74, 76, 78, 80) [82, 84, 88, 90, 92] Back sts

STEP 6: SLEEVE CAPS & BODY
You will now increase for the **sleeve** and neck (and later also **body**)
simultaneously. Continue to work Buttonbands (BB) as set. (See
Helpful Table for an overview of all increases.)

REFER TO **BOX A** FOR ROW INSTRUCTIONS
Work **Rows 1 & 2** x 2 (2, 3, 3, 3) [3, 3, 4, 4, 4].
18 (18, 22, 22, 22) [22, 22, 26, 26, 26] Sleeve sts
23 (24, 27, 28, 29) [30, 31, 33, 33, 34] sts + 8 BB sts for each Front

Work **Rows 1 & 4** x 1 (1, 0, 0, 0) [0, 0, 0, 0, 0].
20 (20, 22, 22, 22) [22, 22, 26, 26, 26] Sleeve sts
25 (26, 27, 28, 29) [30, 31, 33, 33, 34] sts + 8 BB sts for each Front

Work **Row 1**.
22 (22, 24, 24, 24) [24, 24, 28, 28, 28] Sleeve sts
26 (27, 28, 29, 30) [31, 32, 34, 34, 35] sts + 8 BB sts for each Front

BOX A

sM1L= sleeve increase   nM1 = neck increase

RS ROWS
R1: Ksk, k1, ksk, p1, sm, k2, nM1R, (knit to 1 st before m,
sl1wyb, sm, sM1L, knit to m, sM1R, sm, sl1wyb) twice,
knit to 2 sts before m, nM1L, k2, sm, p1, ksk, k1, ksk.
This sets the Left and Right BB sts for RS rows.

WS ROWS
R2: (Sl1wyf, k1) x 4, sm, purl to m, sm, (k1, sl1wyf) x 4.
This sets the Right and Left BB sts for WS rows.

R4: BB, sm, p2, nM1Lp, purl to 2 sts before m, nM1Lp p2,
sm, BB.

Black Basalt

STEP 7: BUTTONBANDS & FRONTS CAST ON
Setup Row (WS): BB, sm, p2, nM1Lp, purl to 2 sts before BB, nM1Rp, p2, sm, BB.
27 (28, 29, 30, 31) [32, 33, 35, 35, 36] sts + 8 BB sts for each Front

LEFT FRONT BUTTONBAND
Work only the 8 sts of the Left Front Buttonband:
R1 (RS): Ksk, k1, ksk, sl1wyf.
R2 (WS): [K1, sl1wyf] x 4.
Work **Rows 1 & 2** again x 11 (11, 11, 11, 11) [11, 11, 11, 12, 12].
Final Row (RS): Ssk, k1, pass st over to bind off, bind off 3 sts kwise, k2tog, pass st over to bind off (*1 st remains*), p&k5 sts in the slipped stitch edge of the buttonband, pm, p&k7 (7, 7, 7, 7) [7, 7, 7, 8, 8] sts more, (knit to 1 st before m, sl1wyb, sm, **sM1L**, knit to m, **sM1R**, sm, sl1wyb) twice, knit to m, sm, p1, ksk, k1, ksk.

24 (24, 26, 26, 26) [26, 26, 30, 30, 30] Sleeve sts
34 (35, 36, 37, 38) [39, 40, 42, 43, 44] Left Front sts + 6 BB sts
27 (28, 29, 30, 31) [32, 33, 35, 35, 36] Right Front sts + 8 BB sts

RIGHT FRONT BUTTONBAND
Set body sts aside and work only the 8 sts of the Right Front Buttonband.
Mirror the Left Front but make a buttonhole 5 rows before binding off as follows.
Setup Row (WS): [Sl1wyf, k1] x 4.
R1 (RS): Sl1wyf, ksk, k1, ksk.
R2 (WS): [Sl1wyf, k1] x 4.
Work Rows 1 & 2 again x 8 (8, 8, 8, 8) [8, 8, 8, 9, 9].
Make buttonhole over next 3 rows:
Buttonhole R1 (RS): Sl1wyf, k1, bind off 2 sts, ksk.
Buttonhole R2 (WS): Sks, k1, *turn work over so RS is facing, borrow last st for cast on loop*, crochet cast on 3 sts, *replace loop onto LN (make a final chain st but not around the needle, turn work over so WS is facing)*, sl1wyf, k1.
Buttonhole R3: Sl1wyf, sl1 kwise, pick up a twisted loop in bar before cast on, pass 2 sts back to LN (twisted loop and sl st), ssk, sl1wyf, k2, k2tog, sl1wyf, k1.
Work **Row 2** once more.
Work **Row 1** once more.

Next Row (WS): P2tog, p1, pass stitch over to bind off, bind off 3 sts pwise, p2togtbl, pass st over to bind off (*1 st remains*), p&p5 sts in the slipped stitch edge of the Buttonband, pm, p&p7 (7, 7, 7, 7) 7, 7, 7, 8, 8 sts more, purl to Left BB, sm, k1, sl1wyf, M1Lp, sl1wyf, k1, sl1wyf, M1Lp, sl1wyf.

34 (35, 36, 37, 38) [39, 40, 42, 43, 44] Left Front sts + 8 BB sts
34 (35, 36, 37, 38) [39, 40, 42, 43, 44] Right Front sts + 6 BB sts
WORKING ACROSS ALL STITCHES
R1 (RS): Ksk, k1, ksk, p1, sm, (knit to 1 st before m, sl1wyb, sm, **sM1L**, knit to m, **sM1R**, sm, sl1wyb) twice, knit to m, sm, p1, k1, M1L, k3, M1L, k1.

26 (26, 28, 28, 28) [28, 28, 32, 32, 32] Sleeve sts
34 (35, 36, 37, 38) [39, 40, 42, 43, 44] sts + 8 BB sts for each Front
72 (74, 76, 78, 80) [82, 84, 88, 90, 92] Back sts

STEP 8: SLEEVE & BODY INCREASES
Continue to work sleeve increases, buttonholes, and **body increases**.

REFER TO BOX B FOR ROW INSTRUCTIONS
Work **Row 2**.
Work **Rows 1 & 2** x 5.
36 (36, 38, 38, 38) [38, 38, 42, 42, 42] Sleeve sts

BOX B

sM1 = sleeve increase   bM1 = body increase

RS ROWS
R1: Ksk, k1, ksk, p1, sm, (knit to 1 st before m, sl1wyb, sm, sM1L, knit to m, sM1R, sm, sl1wyb) twice, knit to m, sm, p1, ksk, k1, ksk.
This sets the Left and Right BB sts for RS rows.

R3: BB, sm, (knit to 2 sts before m, bM1L, k1, sl1wyb, sm, sM1L, knit to m, sM1R, sm, sl1wyb, k1, bM1R) twice, knit to m, sm, BB.

WS ROWS
R2: (Sl1wyf, k1) x 4), sm, purl to m, sm, (k1, sl1wyf) x4.
This sets the Right and Left BB sts for WS rows.

R4: BB, sm, (purl to m, sm, sM1Rp, purl to m, sM1Lp, sm) twice, purl to m, sm, BB.

R6: BB, sm, (purl to 2 sts before m, bM1Rp, p2, sm, purl to m, sm, p2, bM1Lp) twice, purl to m, sm, BB.

R8: BB, sm, (purl to 2 sts before m, bM1Rp, p2, sm, sM1Rp, purl to m, sM1Lp, sm, p2, bM1Lp) twice, purl to m, sm, BB.

BUTTONHOLE #2

BR1 (RS): BB, sm, (knit to 1 st before m, sl1wyb, sm, **sM1L**, knit to m, **sM1R**, sm, sl1wyb) twice, knit to BB, sm, p1, k1, bind off 2 sts, k1, sl1wyf, k1.
38 (38, 40, 40, 40) [40, 40, 44, 44, 44] Sleeve sts

BR2 (WS): Sks, k1, *turn work over so RS is facing, borrow last st for cast on loop, crochet cast on 3 sts, replace loop onto LN, turn work over so WS is facing,* sl1wyf, k1, sm, purl to m, sm, BB.

BR3: BB, sm, (knit to 1 st before m, sl1wyb, sm, **sM1L**, knit to m, **sM1R**, sm, sl1wyb) twice, knit to BB, sm, p1, sl1 kwise, pick up a twisted loop in bar before cast on, pass 2 sts back to LN (twisted loop and sl st), ssk, sl1wyf, k2, k2tog, sl1wyf, k1.
40 (40, 42, 42, 42) [42, 42, 46, 46, 46] Sleeve sts

Work **Row 2**.

Work **Rows 1 & 2** x 0 (0, 0, 2, 1) [1, 1, 0, 0, 0].
40 (40, 42, 46, 44) [44, 44, 46, 46, 46] Sleeve sts

Work **Rows 1 & 4** x 2 (2, 0, 0, 0) [0, 0, 0, 0, 0].
48 (48, 42, 46, 44) [44, 44, 46, 46, 46] Sleeve sts

Work **Rows 3 & 2** x 0 (0, 0, 0, 0) [2, 1, 1, 2, 1].
48 (48, 42, 46, 44) [48, 46, 48, 50, 48] Sleeve sts
34 (35, 36, 37, 38) [41, 41, 43, 45, 45] Front sts + BB
72 (74, 76, 78, 80) [86, 86, 90, 94, 94] Back sts

Work **Rows 3 & 4** x 0 (0, 2, 0, 1) [0, 0, 0, 0, 0].
48 (48, 50, 46, 48) [48, 46, 48, 50, 48] Sleeve sts
34 (35, 38, 37, 39) [41, 41, 43, 45, 45] Front sts + BB
72 (74, 80, 78, 82) [86, 86, 90, 94, 94] Back sts

Work **Rows 3 & 6** x 0 (0, 0, 0, 0) [0, 1, 1, 1, 2].
48 (48, 50, 46, 48) [48, 48, 50, 52, 52] Sleeve sts
34 (35, 38, 37, 39) [41, 43, 45, 47, 49] Front sts + BB
72 (74, 80, 78, 82) [86, 90, 94, 98, 102] Back sts

Work **Rows 3 & 8** x 1 (1, 1, 2, 2) [2, 2, 2, 2, 2].
52 (52, 54, 54, 56) [56, 56, 58, 60, 60] Sleeve sts
36 (37, 40, 41, 43) [45, 47, 49, 51, 53] Front sts + BB
76 (78, 84, 86, 90) [94, 98, 102, 106, 110] Back sts

Work **Rows 3 & 2** once.
54 (54, 56, 56, 58) [58, 58, 60, 62, 62] Sleeve sts
37 (38, 41, 42, 44) [46, 48, 50, 52, 54] Front sts + BB
78 (80, 86, 88, 92) [96, 100, 104, 108, 112] Back sts

STEP 9: SEPARATING SLEEVES & BODY

Separation Row 1 (RS): BB, sm, *knit to 2 sts before m, pm, k2, rm, place all sts to next m on holder, (= sleeve sts) rm, (turn work over so WS is facing) borrow last st for cast on loop, crochet cast on 6 (7, 7, 8, 8) [9, 9, 9, 9, 10] sts, pm, cast on 2 (3, 3, 4, 4) [5, 5, 5, 5, 6] sts, replace loop onto LN (make a final chain st but not around the needle), turn work over so RS is facing*, work from * to * once more, knit to m, sm, BB.*

42 (44, 47, 49, 51) [54, 56, 58, 60, 63] Left Front sts + BB
40 (42, 45, 47, 49) [52, 54, 56, 58, 61] Right Front sts + BB
86 (90, 96, 100, 104) [110, 114, 118, 122, 128] Back sts

Separation Row 2 (WS): BB, sm, *purl to 1 st before cast on, sl1 kwise, make twisted loop in cast on bar and place on LN, sl1 to LN, p2tog (loop and sl st), purl to m, sm, purl to 2 sts before m, p2togtbl, rm*, work from * to * once more, purl to m, sm, BB.

41 (43, 46, 48, 50) [53, 55, 57, 59, 62] Left Front sts + BB
40 (42, 45, 47, 49) [52, 54, 56, 58, 61] Right Front sts + BB
85 (89, 95, 99, 103) [109, 113, 117, 121, 127] Back sts

***Note:** A garter stitch at each side creates a faux side seam (on WS: k1 after the side marker).*
This stitch is not included in the stitch counts that follow.

40 (42, 45, 47, 49) [52, 54, 56, 58, 61] Left Front sts + BB
40 (42, 45, 47, 49) [52, 54, 56, 58, 61] Right Front sts + BB
84 (88, 94, 98, 102) [108, 112, 116, 120, 126] Back sts

STEP 10: BODY WITH BUTTONHOLES

REFER TO **BOX C** FOR ROW INSTRUCTIONS
Work **Rows 1 & 2** x 2 (2, 2, 1, 1) [0, 0, 1, 0, 0].

Work **Buttonhole Rows 1 – 3**.
Work **Row 2**.

Continue with Basic Repeat **Rows 1 & 2**, and make **buttonholes** starting on every 18th row (approx every 7 cm / 2.75").

Work to 5 cm / 2" from underarm.

OPTIONAL BUST DARTS
Optional Bust Darts (see BOX D) may be placed here or a bit lower.

Note: If you are trying to stretch your skeins, this is a good place to set the body aside to work the sleeves before finishing the body.

Continue with Basic Repeat **Rows 1 & 2** and **buttonholes** as set to 14.5 (15, 15.5, 15.5, 16.5) [17, 18, 17, 17.5, 17.5] cm / 5.75 (6, 6, 6, 6.5) [6.75, 7, 6.75, 7, 7]" from underarm or to 18 cm / 7" from desired length.

BOX C

BASIC REPEAT
R1 (RS): BB, sm, knit to BB, sm, BB.

R2 (WS): BB, (purl to m, sm, g1) twice, purl to BB, sm, BB.

BUTTONHOLE ROWS
BR1 (RS): BB, sm, knit to BB, sm, p1, k1, bind off 2 sts, ksk.

BR2 (WS): Sks, k1, turn work over so RS is facing, borrow last st for cast on loop, crochet cast on 3 sts, replace loop onto LN, turn work over so WS is facing, sl1wyf, k1, sm, (purl to m, sm, g1) twice, purl to BB, sm, BB.

BR3: BB, sm, knit to BB, sm, p1, sl1 kwise, pick up a twisted loop in bar before cast on, pass 2 sts back to LN (twisted loop and sl st), ssk, sl1wyf, k2, k2tog, sl1wyf, k1.

BOX D

OPTIONAL BUST DARTS
Place your darts at approx 5 (5, 10, 10) cm / 2 (2, 4, 4)" from underarm or where desired.
For placement of darts, see Hints & Tips.
Note that an additional buttonhole and button may be required if adding darts.

Smallish (Middling, Busty, Wowza!)
Worked over 10 (12, 16, 18) rows, adds approx 4 (4.5, 6, 7) cm / 1.5 (1.75, 2.25, 2.75)".

LEFT FRONT
R1 (RS): BB, sm, knit to 20 (20, 24, 28) sts before m, turn.
R2 (WS): Sl1^, pm, purl to BB, sm, BB.
R3 (RS): BB, sm, knit to m, rm, k1^, k5 (4, 3, 3), turn.
R4: Sl1^, pm, purl to BB, sm, BB.
Work **Rows 3 & 4** again x 3 (4, 6, 7).
Next Row (RS): BB, sm, knit to BB, sm, BB (and note **buttonhole** sequence).

RIGHT FRONT
R2 (WS): BB, sm, purl to 19 (19, 23, 27) sts before m, turn.
R3 (RS): Sl1^, pm, knit to BB, sm, BB.
R4: BB, sm, purl to m, rm, p1^, p5 (4, 3, 3), turn.
Work **Rows 3 & 4** again x 3 (4, 6, 7).
Work **Row 3** once more.
Next Row (WS): BB, sm, purl to m, rm, p1^, (purl to m, sm, g1) twice, purl to BB, sm, BB.

Resume working back and forth as before darts and remember to make **buttonholes**.

STEP 11: POCKETS
The double-knitted pocket starts with a band that adds 4 cm / 1.5".
If you opt for another pocket, you may wish to place it a bit lower. The entire pocket adds approx 16 cm / 6.25".

At 15 (15, 15, 14.5, 14.5) [13.5, 13.5, 14.5, 13.5, 13.5] cm / 6 (6, 6, 5.75, 5.75) [5.25, 5.25, 5.75, 5.25, 5.25]" from underarm, make pockets.

REFER TO POCKET TUTORIAL **3D** FOR INSTRUCTIONS
For a simpler pocket consider Pocket 1A, 1B or 2C.
Don't forget **buttonhole** placement and the g1 at each side 'seam'.

Work pockets to 31 (32, 32.5, 32.5, 33.5) [34, 34, 34, 34.5, 35.5] cm or 12.25 (12.5, 12.75, 12.75, 13.25) [13.5, 13.5, 13.5, 13.5, 14]" from underarm or to 2 cm /.75" from desired length.

Consider adding rows if necessary to place final buttonhole directly above the hem.

STEP 12: HEM
Switch to smaller (3.5 mm /US 4) needle.
Knit three rows.

BIND OFF
Borrow final stitch to crochet cast on 2 sts onto LN, make 1 chain st (not around needle), place on LN.
R1 (RS): Sl1wyb, sl1wyf, ssk (1 edge st with 1 body st).
R2 (WS): Sks.
R3: K1, sl1wyf, ssk.
R4: Sks.

Tip: Rows 2 & 4 can be worked backwards (from left to right) – this obviates the need to turn work over between rows (see BOX).

Work **Rows 3 & 4** all the way around the hem to last 5 sts.
Final Row (RS): Ssk, bind off 1 st, ssk, bind off final st.

Pocket 1B

Pocket 3D

WORKING WS ROWS FROM RS
Sl1wyb, p1 backwards (take yarn to front and manoeuvre the yarn so you make a normal p1), then slip the final st wyb.

STEP 13: SLEEVES

Place 54 (54, 56, 56, 58) [58, 58, 60, 62, 62] Sleeve sts from holder back on larger (4.5 mm / US 7) needle. Attach yarn at right side of gap, p&k3 (4, 4, 5, 5) [6, 6, 6, 6, 7] sts along the first half of the underarm cast on, pm, p&k4 (5, 5, 6, 6) [7, 7, 7, 7, 8] sts more along second half of underarm, knit to m.
61 (63, 65, 67, 69) [71, 71, 73, 75, 77] sts

REFER TO **BOX E** FOR ROUND INSTRUCTIONS
Work **Rnd 1** to 5 cm / 2" from underarm.

SLEEVE DECREASES
Work **Decrease Rnd**.
59 (61, 63, 65, 67) [69, 69, 71, 73, 75] sts

Continue with **Rnd 1**, working **Decrease Rnd** every 9 (9, 8, 8, 8) [8, 8, 8, 7, 6]th round again x 8 (8, 9, 10, 10) [6, 7, 6, 5, 14], then every 6th round x 0 (0, 0, 0, 0) [5, 4, 6, 8, 0].
43 (45, 45, 45, 47) [47, 47, 47, 47, 47] sts

Work to 36 (36, 37, 39, 39) [39, 39, 40, 40, 40] cm / 14 (14, 14.5, 15.25, 15.25) [15.25, 15.25, 15.75, 15.75, 15.75]" from underarm or to approx 9 cm / 3.75" from desired length.

STEP 14: CONTRAST WEDGE

Rnd 1: Rm, k20 (21, 21, 21, 22) [22, 22, 22, 22, 22], pm, sl2 to CN and hold in front, k1, k2 from CN, knit to m.
Rnd 2: Sm, knit to m.
Rnd 3: Sm, k1, sl2 to CN and hold in front, k1, k2 from CN, k2tog, knit to 2 sts before m, ssk, sm, k2, turn.
41 (43, 43, 43, 45) [45, 45, 45, 45, 45] sts

Work back and forth from here.

Cuff with contrasting wedge.

Setup Row (WS): P2, sm, purl to 2 sts before m, turn.
R1 (RS): Knit to m, rm, k2, turn.
Rows 2, 4, 6: Purl.
R3: K2, k2tog, knit to last 4 sts, ssk, k2.
39 (41, 41, 41, 43) [43, 43, 43, 43, 43] sts
R5: Knit.
Work **Rows 3 – 6** again x 5 or to 1 cm / 0.5" from desired sleeve length.

29 (31, 31, 31, 33) [33, 33, 33, 33, 33] sts

Set sts aside.

WEDGE
The CC wedge is worked back and forth in stocking stitch, starting from the split, and widening toward the cuff as you work the picked up sts at each side at the end of every row. Pick up inside the entire outermost st.

With RS facing, with **CC** and smaller needle (RN), starting at the cuff, p&k15 sts (in every second row) along the split to its beginning, with a second needle (LN) p&k1 st in centre of split (taking care not to create a gap), p&k15 sts along split to cuff, cut yarn.

BOX E

SLEEVE ROUNDS
Rnd 1: Sm, g1, knit to m.
Decrease Rnd: Sm, g1, k2tog, knit to 2 sts before m, ssk.

Join new **CC** at the split point, with an additional 3.5 mm (US 4) needle (N1), work the contrast triangle as follows.

R1 (RS): K1 from LN, turn.

R2 (WS): P1, turn.

R3: Sl1wyb, k1 from LN, turn. *2 sts*

R4: Sl1wyf, p1, p1 from RN, turn. *3 sts*

R5: Sl1wyb, knit to last st, ssk (last st from N1 with first st from LN), turn.

R6: Sl11wyf, purl to last st, p2tog (last st from N1 with first st from RN), turn.

R7: Sl1wyb, knit all sts on N1, k1 from LN, turn.

R8: Sl1wyf, purl all sts on N1, p1 from RN, turn.

Continue to work **Rows 5 – 8** until all sts on LN and RN are used up. All sts are on N1.

I-CORD BIND OFF

Using Provisional Winding Cast On and working **CC** yarn, wind on 3 sts onto LN.

Rows 1 – 3 (RS): K2, ssk (last i-cord st together with 1 sleeve st), sl 3 sts back to LN.

R4 (RS): K2, sssk (last i-cord st together with 2 sleeve sts), sl 3 sts back to LN.

Work **Rows 1 – 4** around the cuff until all sts are bound off, switching to **MC** where **MC** sleeve sts begin.

With Kitchener stitch, graft (or sew) the i-cord sts to the provisional sts.

FINISH

Weave in loose ends. Soak and block to measurements. Sew on some nice buttons.

Pocket 1B

Black Basalt

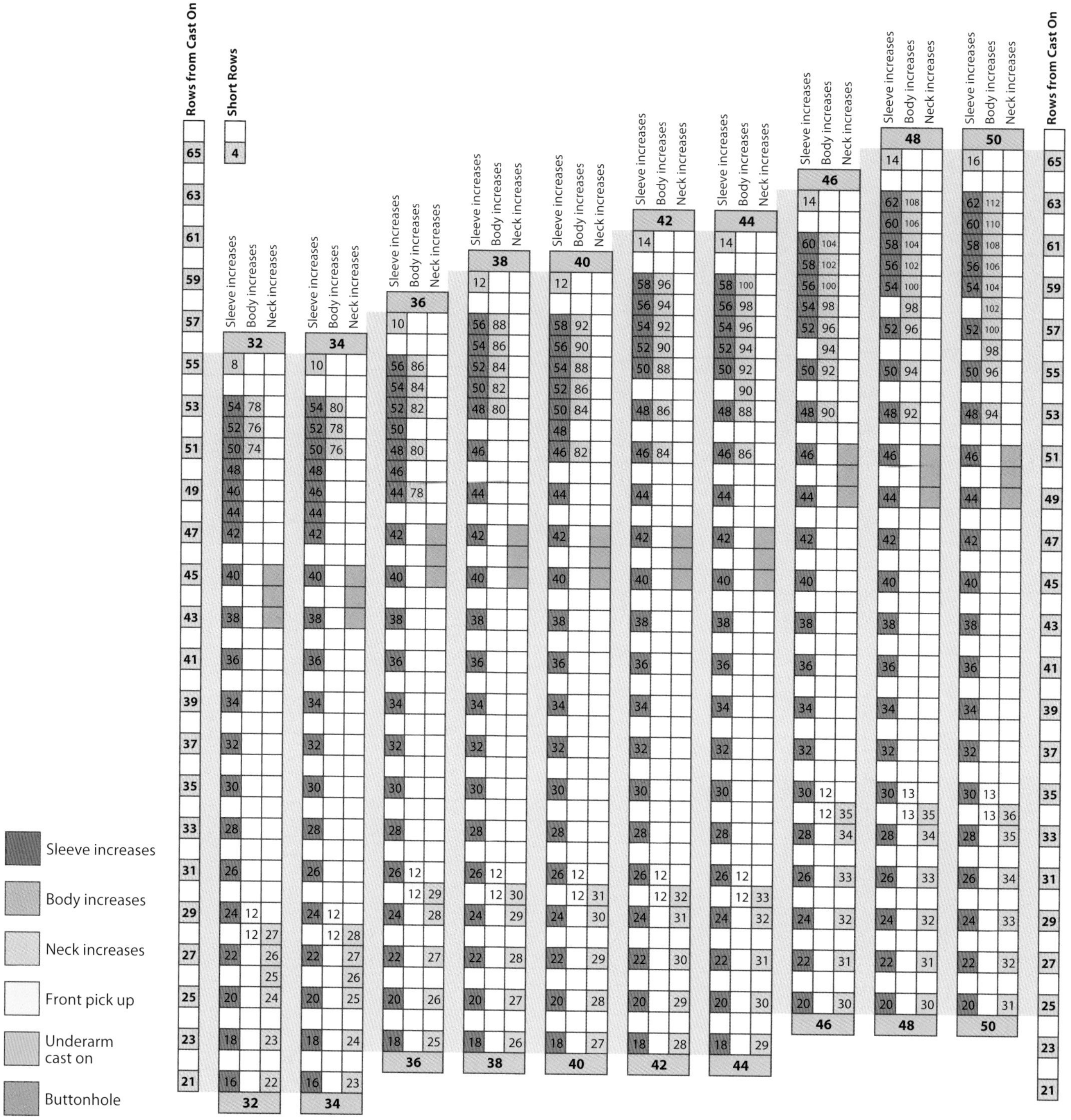

Legend:
- Sleeve increases
- Body increases
- Neck increases
- Front pick up
- Underarm cast on
- Buttonhole

Column headers (left): Rows from Cast On | Short Rows

Size sections: 32, 34, 36, 38, 40, 42, 44, 46, 48, 50

Each size column group: Sleeve increases | Body increases | Neck increases

Rows from Cast On (right): 65, 63, 61, 59, 57, 55, 53, 51, 49, 47, 45, 43, 41, 39, 37, 35, 33, 31, 29, 27, 25, 23, 21

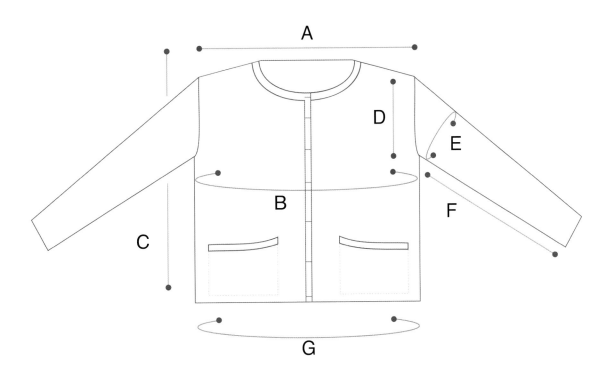

BLACK BASALT GARMENT MEASUREMENTS

	32	34	36	38	40	42	44	46	48	50
A – Shoulder width (cm)	40	41	42	43.5	44.5	45.5	46.5	49	50	51
in	15.75	16.25	16.5	17.25	17.5	18	18.25	19.25	19.75	20
B – Bust (cm)	95.5	100	106.5	111	115.5	122	126.5	131	135.5	142
in	37.5	39.25	42	43.75	45.5	48	49.75	51.5	53.25	56
C – Length (cm)	54.5	54.5	55.5	55.5	55.5	55.5	55.5	57	57	57
in	21.5	21.50	21.75	21.75	21.75	21.75	21.75	22.5	22.5	22.5
D – Armhole depth (cm)	20	20	21	21.5	21.5	22.5	22.5	23	24	24
in	7.75	8	8	8.5	8.5	9	9	9	9.5	9.5
E – Sleeve circumf (cm)	34	35	36	37	38.5	39.5	39.5	40.5	41.5	43
in	13.5	13.75	14.25	14.5	15.25	15.5	15.5	16	16.25	17
F – Sleeve seam (cm)	45	45	46	48	48	48	48	49	49	49
in	17.75	17.75	18	19	19	19	19	19.25	19.25	19.25
G – Hem circumf (cm)	95.5	100	106.5	111	115.5	122	126.5	131	135.5	142
in	37.5	39.25	42	43.75	45.5	48	49.75	51.5	53.25	56

The crisp yet cosy broken rib patterning in this swingy, open-fronted cardigan is beautifully enhanced by the yarn. Choose Ginger's Hand Dyed Masham rare breed blend by Ginger Twist Studio or Outlaw Yarn's opulent Bohemia Worsted in your favourite shade. In either yarn the fronts are light and lofty with a drape that works equally well when worn casually open or elegantly overlapping.

Tailored set-in sleeves and a gather artfully worked into the patterning at centre back enhance the movement of this versatile Ziggurat. The compact pocket is an expert finishing detail.

TO FIT SIZE
81 (86, 91, 97, 102) [107, 112, 117, 122, 127] cm
32 (34, 36, 38, 40) [42, 44, 46, 48, 50] inches

CROSSOVER NECK
Overlapping fronts

FIT
Relaxed with approx 7 - 10 cm / 2.5 – 4" ease

YARN
Ginger Twist Studio Ginger's Hand Dyed Masham Mayhem DK (75%
Bluefaced Leicester, 25% Masham, 240 m / 262 yds per 100 g),
Muddy Sunshine x 4 (4, 5, 5, 5) [6, 6, 6, 6, 7] skeins
Small scrap of DK for contrasting pocket lining
CC scrap of DK or Fingering
(Sample **CC**: Masham Mayhem 4ply, Wine)

APPROX YARDAGE
950 (1000, 1050, 1100, 1150) [1250, 1250, 1350, 1400, 1450] m
1000 (1050, 1150, 1200, 1250) [1300, 1350, 1450, 1500, 1600] yds

ALTERNATIVE YARN SUGGESTION
Little Grey Sheep Gotland DK, Cascade 220, Nature's Luxury On
Stage, Outlaw Yarn Bohemia Vanitas, Rauwerk Heavy DK

NEEDLES & NOTIONS
4.5 mm (US 7) circular needle, 80 – 100 cm (32 – 40")
or size to obtain gauge
3.5 mm (US 4) circular needles, 80 – 100 cm (32 – 40")
3.5 mm (US 4) circular needles, 40 – 100 cm (16 – 40")
Stitch holders; stitch markers

BLOCKED GAUGE
20 sts x 28 rows on 4.5 mm (US 7) needle = 10 cm / 4" in broken rib
stitch pattern

SAMPLE SIZE
Size 40 weighs 415 g /14.75 oz
It should be possible to knit up to size 42 with 5 skeins of yarn, but
you may prefer to finish the sleeves before completing the body, to
make sure you have enough yarn.

Photo © Friederike Winter

Mayhem dk

4-ROW BROKEN RIB

4-ROW BROKEN RIB
R1 (RS): Knit
R2 (WS): Knit
R3: (K1, p1)
R4: (K1, p1)

On **Rows 3 & 4**, line up rib rows with previous rib rows, so that purl stitches line up with purl columns and knit stitches with knit columns.

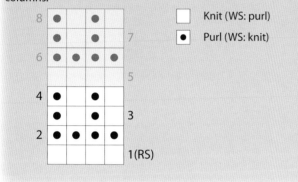

| | Knit (WS: purl) |
| | Purl (WS: knit) |

STEP 1: CAST ON & RIGHT BACK SHOULDER

See chart for an illustration and explanation of the simple broken rib pattern.
With **MC**, using longtail cast on and 4.5 mm (US 7) needle, cast on 61 (65, 69, 73, 77) [81, 85, 87, 89, 93] sts.
Setup Row (WS): K18 (18, 20, 20, 22) [22, 24, 24, 26, 26], turn.
R1 (RS): Sl1^, pm, (p1, k1) x 6 (6, 7, 7, 7) [7, 8, 8, 9, 9], and then (p1) x 0, (0, 0, 0, 1) [1, 1, 1, 0, 0], turn.
R2 (WS): Sl1^, work in set rib (that is, work sts as they appear) to m, rm, p1^, k1, turn.
R3: Sl1^, pm, k8 (8, 10, 10, 10) [10, 12, 12, 12, 12], turn.
R4: Sl1^, knit to m, rm, k1^, k1, turn.
R5: Sl1^, pm, rib 5 (5, 6, 6, 6) [6, 7, 7, 7, 7] sts, turn.
R6: Sl1^, rib to m, rm, p1^, k1, turn.
R7: Sl1^, pm, knit to end (working any sl1^ as k1^).
R8: P1, knit to m, rm, k1^, k1, turn.
R9: Sl1^, pm, rib to last 2 sts, k2.
R10: P2, rib to m, rm, p1^, (k1, p1) to last 18 (18, 20, 20, 22) [22, 24, 24, 26, 26] sts, pm, knit to last st, p1.

61 (65, 69, 73, 77) [81, 85, 87, 89, 93] Back sts

STEP 2: LEFT BACK SHOULDER

R1 (RS): K2, (p1, k1) x 8 (8, 9, 9, 10) [10, 11, 11, 12, 12], rm, turn.
R2 (WS): Sl1^, pm, rib 12 (12, 14, 14, 15) [15, 17, 17, 18, 18] sts, turn.
R3: Sl1^, knit to m, rm, k1^, k1, turn.
R4: Sl1^, pm, k8 (8, 10, 10, 10) [10, 12, 12, 12, 12], turn.
R5: Sl1^, rib to m, rm, p1^, k1, turn.
R6: Sl1^, pm, rib 5 (5, 6, 6, 6) [6, 7, 7, 7, 7] sts, turn.
R7: Sl1^, knit to m, rm, k1^, k1, turn.
R8: Sl1^, pm, knit to last st, (working any sl1^ as k1^), p1.
R9: K2, rib to m, rm, p1^, k1, turn.
R10: Sl1^, rib to last 2 sts, p2.

STEP 3: WORKING ACROSS BACK

R1 (RS): Knit to m, rm, k1^, knit to end.
61 (65, 69, 73, 77) [81, 85, 87, 89, 93] Back sts
R2 (WS): P1, knit to last st, p1.
R3: K2, rib to last 2 sts, k2.
R4: P2, rib to last 2 sts, p2.
R5: Knit.
R6: P1, knit to last st, p1.

Work **Rows 3 – 5** again x 1.
Final Row (WS): P1, knit to last 2 sts, p2tog, pm, p&p8 sts along edge (for first half of Left Sleeve Cap).

8 Left Cap sts
60 (64, 68, 72, 76) [80, 84, 86, 88, 92] Back sts

Slide stitches off needle tips to rest on the cable.
Set these stitches aside, continue to next step without turning.

STEP 4: LEFT FRONT SHOULDER

After the shoulder sts are picked up, with working yarn, crochet cast on stitches for the overlapping front.
Setup Row (WS): Loop cable, p&p17 (17, 19, 19, 21) [21, 23, 23, 25, 25] sts (for Left Front Shoulder) in the cast on of Left Back Shoulder, *borrow last st for cast on loop*, crochet cast on 1 st, pm, crochet cast on 34 (36, 38, 40, 42) [44, 46, 48, 50, 52] sts, *replace loop onto LN (make a final chain st but not around the needle).*
52 (54, 58, 60, 64) [66, 70, 72, 76, 78] Left Front sts
R1 (RS): K1, (k1, p1) to m, sm, k2tog, and then (p1, k1) x 5 (5, 6, 6, 6) [6, 7, 8, 8, 8], and then (p1) x 0 (0, 0, 0, 1) [1, 1, 1, 0, 0], turn.
51 (53, 57, 59, 63) [65, 69, 71, 75, 77] Left Front sts
R2 (WS): Sl1^, rib to last 2 sts, p2.
R3: Knit to m, sm, k7 (7, 8, 8, 9) [9, 10, 10, 11, 11], turn.
R4: Sl1^, knit to last st, p1.
R5: K2, rib to m, rm, rib 3 (3, 3, 3, 4) [4, 4, 4, 5, 5] sts, turn.
R6: Sl1^, rib to last 2 sts, p2.

R7: Knit to loop, working any sl1^ as k1^, turn.
R8: P1, knit to last st, p1.
R9: K2, rib to 2 sts before loop, k2, turn.
R10: P2, rib to last 2 sts, p2.
R11: Knit to loop, turn.
R12: P1, knit to last st, p1.
Work **Rows 9 – 12** again x 2.
Final Row (RS): K2, rib to 2 sts before loop, ssk, pm, p&k9 sts (for second half of Left Sleeve Cap), knit to m, sm, rib to last 2 sts, ssk, pm, p&k8 sts (for first half of Right Sleeve Cap).

17 Left Cap sts
8 Right Cap sts
50 (52, 56, 58, 62) [64, 68, 70, 74, 76] Left Front sts
59 (63, 67, 71, 75) [79, 83, 85, 87, 91] Back sts

Slide stitches off needle tips to rest on the cable.
Set these stitches aside, continue to next step without turning.

STEP 5: RIGHT FRONT SHOULDER
R1 (RS): Loop cable, p&k17 (17, 19, 19, 21) [21, 23, 23, 25, 25] sts (for Right Front Shoulder) in the cast on of Right Back Shoulder, *(turn work over so WS is facing) borrow last st for cast on loop,* crochet cast on 1 st, pm, crochet cast on 34 (36, 38, 40, 42) [44, 46, 48, 50, 52] sts, *replace loop onto LN (make a final chain st but not around the needle).*
52 (54, 58, 60, 64) [66, 70, 72, 76, 78] Right Front sts
R2 (WS): P1, (p1, k1) to m, sm, p2tog tbl, (k1, p1) x 5 (5, 6, 6, 6) [6, 7, 7, 8, 8], (k1) x 0 (0, 0, 0, 1) [1, 1, 1, 0, 0], turn.
51 (53, 57, 59, 63) [65, 69, 71, 75, 77] Right Front sts
R3: Sl1^, knit to end.
R4: P1, knit to m, sm, k7 (7, 8, 8, 9) [9, 10, 10, 11, 11], turn.
R5: Sl1^, rib to last 2 sts, k2.
R6: P2, rib to m, rm, rib 3 (3, 3, 3, 4) [4, 4, 4, 5, 5] sts, turn.
R7: Sl1^, knit to end.
R8: P1, knit to 1 st before loop (working any sl1^ as k1^), p1, turn.
R9: K2, rib to last 2 sts, k2.
R10: P2, rib to 2 sts before loop, p2, turn.
R11: Knit to end.
R12: P1, knit to 1 st before loop, p1, turn.
R13: K2, rib to last 2 sts, k2.
R14: P2, rib to 2 sts before loop, p2, turn.
Work **Rows 11 – 14** again x 1.
Work **Rows 11 – 13** again x 1.
Final Row (WS): P2, rib to 2 sts before loop, p2tog, pm, p&p9 sts (for second half of Right Sleeve Cap), (p1, k1) to m, sm, rib to m, sm, k1, (p1, k1) to m, sm, rib to last 2 sts, p2.

BOX A

17 sts for each Sleeve Cap
50 (52, 56, 58, 62) [64, 68, 70, 74, 76] sts for each Front
59 (63, 67, 71, 75) [79, 83, 85, 87, 91] Back sts

STEP 6: SLEEVE CAPS & BODY
You will now increase for the sleeve (and later also body) simultaneously. (See Helpful Table for an overview of all increases.)

Note: *The stitch on either side of the sleeve cap is always k1 on RS.*

REFER TO **BOX A** FOR ROW INSTRUCTIONS
Work **Rows 1 – 4** x 3 (3, 3, 3, 3) [3, 3, 4, 4, 4].
29 (29, 29, 29, 29) [29, 29, 33, 33, 33] Sleeve sts

Work **Rows 1 & 2** once.
31 (31, 31, 31, 31) [31, 31, 35, 35, 35] Sleeve sts

INCREASES CENTRE BACK
R5 (RS; first part): K2, *rib to m, sm, **sM1R**, rib to m, **sM1L**, sm*, rib 21 (23, 21, 23, 25) [27, 29, 30, 27, 29] sts.
R5 (middle part):
   SIZE 46 only: (M1R, k1, M1L, p1, k1, p1) x 7.
   ALL SIZES except size 46: (M1R, p1, M1L, k1, p1, k1) x 5 (5, 7, 7, 7) [7, 7, –, 9, 9].
R5 (final part): Work from * to * once more, rib to last 2 sts, k2.
33 (33, 33, 33, 33) [33, 33, 37, 37, 37] Sleeve sts
69 (73, 81, 85, 89) [93, 97, 99, 105, 109] Back sts

Work new sts into set rib pattern (the stitches on either side of the increases line up with previous rows as before).

BOX B

sM1= sleeve increase   bM1 = body increase

R1 (RS): (Knit to 1 st before m, **bM1L**, k1, sm, sM1R, knit to m, sM1L, sm, k1, **bM1R**) twice, knit to end.

R2 (WS): P1, knit to last st, p1.

R3: K2, (rib to 1 st before m, **bM1L**, k1, sm, sM1R, rib to m, sM1L, sm, k1, **bM1R**) twice, rib to last 2 sts, k2.

R4: P2, rib to last 2 sts, p2.

R6 (WS): P2, rib to Right Sleeve m, sm, rib as set to m, sm, p1, (k1, p1) to Left Sleeve m, sm, rib to last 2 sts, p2.

Work **Rows 1 – 4** x 3 (3, 3, 3, 3) [4, 4, 3, 2, 2].
45 (45, 45, 45, 45) [49, 49, 49, 45, 45] Sleeve sts

Work **Rows 1 & 2** x 0 (0, 1, 1, 1) [1, 1, 0, 1, 1].
45 (45, 47, 47, 47) [51, 51, 49, 47, 47] Sleeve sts

INTRODUCE BODY INCREASES

REFER TO **BOX B** FOR ROW INSTRUCTIONS
Work **Rows 3 & 4** x 0 (0, 1, 1, 1) [1, 1, 0, 1, 1].
45 (45, 49, 49, 49) [53, 53, 49, 49, 49] Sleeve sts
50 (52, 57, 59, 63) [65, 69, 70, 75, 77] Front sts
69 (73, 83, 87, 91) [95, 99, 99, 107, 111] Back sts

Work **Rows 1 – 4** x 3 (3, 3, 3, 3) [3, 3, 4, 4, 4].
57 (57, 61, 61, 61) [65, 65, 65, 65, 65] Sleeve sts
56 (58, 63, 65, 69) [71, 75, 78, 83, 85] Front sts
81 (85, 95, 99, 103) [107, 111, 115, 123, 127] Back sts

Work **Rows 1 & 2** x 1 (1, 0, 0, 1) [0, 0, 1, 1, 1].
59 (59, 61, 61, 63) [65, 65, 67, 67, 67] Sleeve sts
57 (59, 63, 65, 70) [71, 75, 79, 84, 86] Front sts
83 (87, 95, 99, 105) [107, 111, 117, 125, 129] Back sts

STEP 7: SEPARATING SLEEVES & BODY

SIZES 32, 34, 40, 46, 48, 50

Separation R1 (RS): k2, *rib to 2 sts before m, pm, rib 2, rm, place all sts to next m on holder, (= sleeve sts), rm, *(turn work over so WS is facing) borrow last st for cast on loop*, crochet cast on 6 (7, –, –, 7) [–, –, 9, 9, 10] sts, pm, crochet cast on 4 (5, –, –, 5) [–, –, 7, 7, 8] sts, replace loop onto LN (make a final chain st but not around the needle), turn work over so RS is facing, work from *to* once more, crochet cast on 7 (8, –, –, 8) [–, –, 10, 10, 11] sts, pm, crochet cast on 3 (4, –, –, 4) [–, –, 6, 6, 7] sts, replace loop onto LN (make a final chain st but not around the needle), turn work over so RS is facing, rib to last 2 sts, k2.*
62 (65, –, –, 76) [–, –, 87, 92, 95] Left Front sts
61 (64, –, –, 75) [–, –, 86, 91, 94] Right Front sts
94 (100, –, –, 118) [–, –, 136, 142, 148] Back sts

Separation R2 (WS): p2, *rib to 1 st before cast on, sl1 pwise, make twisted loop in cast on bar and place on LN, sl1 to LN, knit or purl 2 sts tog (loop and sl st), rib to m, sm, rib to 2 sts before m, knit or purl 2 sts tog tbl, rm*, work from *to* once more, rib to last 2 sts, p2.
61 (64, –, –, 75) [–, –, 86, 91, 94] Left Front sts
61 (64, –, –, 75) [–, –, 86, 91, 94] Right Front sts
93 (99, –, –, 117) [–, –, 135, 141, 147] Back sts

BOX C

4-ROW BROKEN RIB REPEAT
R1 (RS): Knit.

R2 (WS): P1, knit to last st, p1.

R3: K2, p1, (k1, p1) to last 2 sts, k2.

R4: P2, k1, (p1, k1) to last 2 sts, p2.

STEP 8: BODY & OPTIONAL POCKET

REFER TO **BOX C** FOR ROW INSTRUCTIONS
Begin the 4-row repeat with **Row** 1 (1, 3, 3, 1) [3, 3, 1, 1, 1].

Note: If you are trying to stretch your skeins, set the body aside after a few 4-row repeats to work the sleeves before finishing the body.

WITHOUT POCKETS
Skip to STEP 9.

OPTIONAL POCKET
Work **Rows 1 – 4** to 18 (18, 18, 19, 19) [19, 19, 20, 20, 20] cm / 7 (7, 7, 7.5, 7.5) [7.5, 7.5, 7.75, 7.75, 7.75]" from underarm.
End with a WS rib row (**Row 4**).

The hidden pocket is worked over 17 sts. The sample has only one (Left) pocket. You may choose to make one, two, or none.

REFER TO POCKET TUTORIAL **2A** FOR INSTRUCTIONS

SIZES 36, 38, 42, 44

Separation R1 (RS): k2, *knit to 2 sts before m, pm, k2, rm, place all sts to next m on holder, (= sleeve sts) rm, *(turn work over so WS is facing) borrow last st for cast on loop*, crochet cast on – (–, 7, 7, –) [8, 9, –, –, –] sts, pm, crochet cast on – (–, 5, 5, –) [6, 7, –, –, –] sts, *replace loop onto LN (make a final chain st but not around the needle), turn work over so RS is facing*, work from * to * once more, crochet cast on – (–, 8, 8, –) [9, 10, –, –, –] sts, pm, – (–, 4, 4, –) [5, 6, –, –, –] sts, *replace loop onto LN (make a final chain st but not around the needle), turn work over so RS is facing*, knit to end.
– (–, 69, 71, –) [78, 83, –, –, –] Left Front sts
– (–, 68, 70, –) [77, 82, –, –, –] Right Front sts
– (–, 108, 112, –) [122, 128, –, –, –] Back sts

Separation R2 (WS): p1, *knit to 1 st before cast on, sl1 pwise, make twisted loop in cast on bar and place on LN, sl1 to LN, k2tog (loop and sl st), knit to m, sm, knit to 2 sts before m, k2tog, rm*, work from * to * once more, knit to last st, p1.
– (–, 68, 70, –) [77, 82, –, –, –] Left Front sts
– (–, 68, 70, –) [77, 82, –, –, –] Right Front sts
– (–, 107, 111, –) [121, 127, –, –, –] Back sts

ALL SIZES
61 (64, 68, 70, 75) [77, 82, 86, 91, 94] Left Front sts
61 (64, 68, 70, 75) [77, 82, 86, 91, 94] Right Front sts
93 (99, 107, 111, 117) [121, 127, 135, 141, 147] Back sts

BOX D

SLEEVE ROUNDS

Rnd 1: Knit.

Rnd 2: Purl.

Rnds 3 & 4: (K1, p1) to end.

Decrease Rnd: Work in set pattern to 2 sts before m, sl2 tog kwise, rm, k1, psso, pm.

STEP 9: HEM

Work **Rows 1 – 4** to 25 (25, 25, 26, 25.5) [25.5, 25.5, 26, 27, 27] cm / 9.75 (9.75, 9.75, 10.25, 10) [10, 10, 10.25, 10.75, 10.75]" from underarm.
End with a WS knit row (**Row 2**).

Change to smaller (3.5 mm / US 4) needle.
Work 4 more rows (**Rows 3 & 4**, then **Rows 1 & 2**), ending with a knit WS row.

BIND OFF

Bind off from RS in even tension.

STEP 10: SLEEVES

On the first rib round (Rnd 3), make sure to line up knits and purls with previous rows from Step 7.

Place 59 (59, 61, 61, 63) [65, 65, 67, 67, 67] Sleeve sts from holder back on larger (4.5 mm / US 7) needle. Join yarn at right side of gap, p&k5 (5, 6, 6, 6) [7, 7, 8, 8, 9] sts along the first half of the underarm cast on, pm, p&k4 (4, 5, 5, 5) [6, 6, 7, 7, 8] sts more along second half of underarm, continue in set pattern to m.
68 (68, 72, 72, 74) [78, 78, 82, 82, 84] sts

REFER TO BOX D FOR ROUND INSTRUCTIONS

Beginning with a round that fits into established rib pattern, work
Rnds 1 – 4, to 5 cm / 2" from underarm.

SLEEVE DECREASES

Work **Decrease Rnd.**
66 (66, 70, 70, 72) [76, 76, 80, 80, 82]
Continue with **Rnds 1 – 4**, working **Decrease Rnd** every 11 (11, 10, 9, 9) [8, 8, 8, 7, 7]th round again x 10 (10, 11, 12, 12) [13, 14, 14, 16, 16].
46 (46, 48, 46, 48) [50, 48, 52, 48, 50] sts

Work to 44.5 (44.5, 45.5, 46, 46) [46.5, 46.5, 47.5, 47.5, 47.5] cm / 17.5 (17.5, 18, 18, 18) [18.25, 18.25, 18.75, 18.75, 18.75]" from underarm. End with a purl round (**Rnd 2**).

BIND OFF

Bind off in even tension, using Stretchy Bind Off:
K1, *k1, sl2 to LN, k2togtbl; work from * to end of rnd until all sts are bound off.

FINISH

Weave in loose ends. Soak and block lightly to measurements.

Rauwerk Heavy DK with lining in Rohrspatz & Wollmeise (Zarte Knospe)

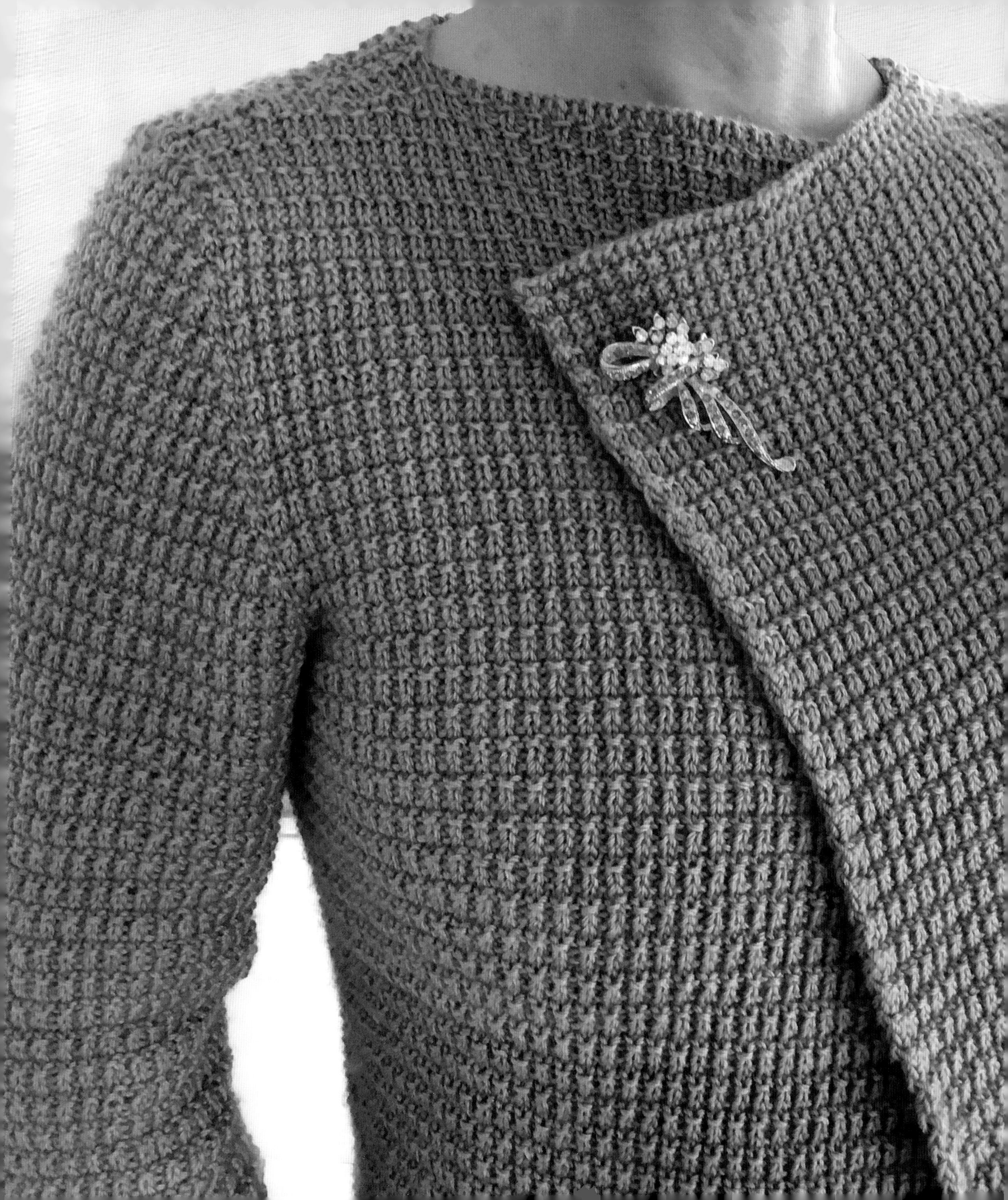

Mayhem dk

Rows from Cast On	Short Rows	32 Sleeve inc.	32 Body inc.	34 Sleeve inc.	34 Body inc.	36 Sleeve inc.	36 Body inc.	38 Sleeve inc.	38 Body inc.	40 Sleeve inc.	40 Body inc.	42 Sleeve inc.	42 Body inc.	44 Sleeve inc.	44 Body inc.	46 Sleeve inc.	46 Body inc.	48 Sleeve inc.	48 Body inc.	50 Sleeve inc.	50 Body inc.	Rows from Cast On
		32		**34**		**36**		**38**		**40**		**42**		**44**		**46**		**48**		**50**		
73	6															16		16		18		73
71												14		16		67	119	67	125	67	129	71
69										12		65	107	65	111	65	117	65	123	65	127	69
67						12		12		63	105	63	105	63	109	63	115	63	121	63	125	67
65		10		12		61	95	61	99	61	103	61	103	61	107	61	113	61	119	61	123	65
63		59	83	59	87	59	93	59	97	59	101	59	101	59	105	59	111	59	117	59	121	63
61		57	81	57	85	57	91	57	95	57	99	57	99	57	103	57	109	57	115	57	119	61
59		55	79	55	83	55	89	55	93	55	97	55	97	55	101	55	107	55	113	55	117	59
57		53	77	53	81	53	87	53	91	53	95	53	95	53	99	53	105	53	111	53	115	57
55		51	75	51	79	51	85	51	89	51	93	51		51		51	103	51	109	51	113	55
53		49	73	49	77	49	83	49	87	49	91	49		49		49		49	107	49	111	53
51		47	71	47	75	47		47		47		47		47		47		47		47		51
49		45		45		45		45		45		45		45		45		45		45		49
47		43		43		43		43		43		43		43		43		43		43		47
45		41		41		41		41		41		41		41		41		41		41		45
43		39		39		39		39		39		39		39		39		39		39		43
41		37		37		37		37		37		37		37		37	101	37	105	37	109	41
39		35		35		35		35		35		35		35		35		35		35		39
37		33	69	33	73	33	81	33	85	33	89	33	93	33	97	33		33		33		37
35		31		31		31		31		31		31		31		31		31		31		35
33		29		29		29		29		29		29		29		29		29		29		33
31		27		27		27		27		27		27		27		27		27		27		31
29		25		25		25		25		25		25		25		25		25		25		29
27		23		23		23		23		23		23		23		23		23		23		27
25		21		21		21		21		21		21		21		21		21		21		25
23		19		19		19		19		19		19		19		19		19		19		23
		32		**34**		**36**		**38**		**40**		**42**		**44**		**46**		**48**		**50**		

Legend:
- Rib rows
- Knit rows
- Sleeve increases
- Body increases
- Gather
- Underarm cast on

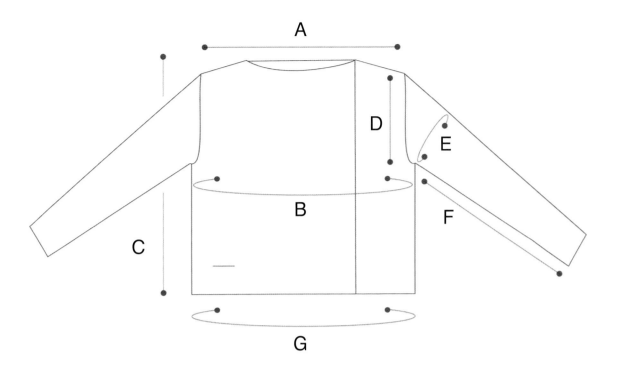

MAYHEM DK TABLE OF MEASUREMENTS

	32	34	36	38	40	42	44	46	48	50
A – Shoulder width (cm)	29.5	31.5	33.5	35.5	37.5	39.5	41.5	43.5	43.5	45.5
in	11.5	12.5	13.25	14	14.75	15.5	16.25	17.25	17.25	18
B – Bust (cm)	88	94	100	104	110	114	120	128	132	138
in	34.75	37	39.25	41	43.25	45	47.25	50.5	52	54.25
C – Length (cm)	50	50	51	52	52	53	53	54	55	55
in	19.75	19.75	20	20.5	20.5	20.75	20.75	21.25	21.75	21.75
D – Armhole depth (cm)	21	21	22	22	22.5	23	23	24	24	24
in	8.25	8.25	8.5	8.5	8.75	9.25	9.25	9.5	9.5	9.5
E – Sleeve circumf (cm)	34	35	36	36	37	39	40	41	41	42
in	13.5	13.75	14.25	14.25	14.5	15.25	15.75	16.25	16.25	16.5
F – Sleeve seam (cm)	45	45	46	46.5	46.5	47	47	48	48	48
in	17.75	17.75	18	18.25	18.25	18.5	18.5	19	19	19
G – Hem circumf (cm)	88	94	100	104	110	114	120	128	132	138
in	34.75	37	39.25	41	43.25	45	47.25	50.5	52	54.25

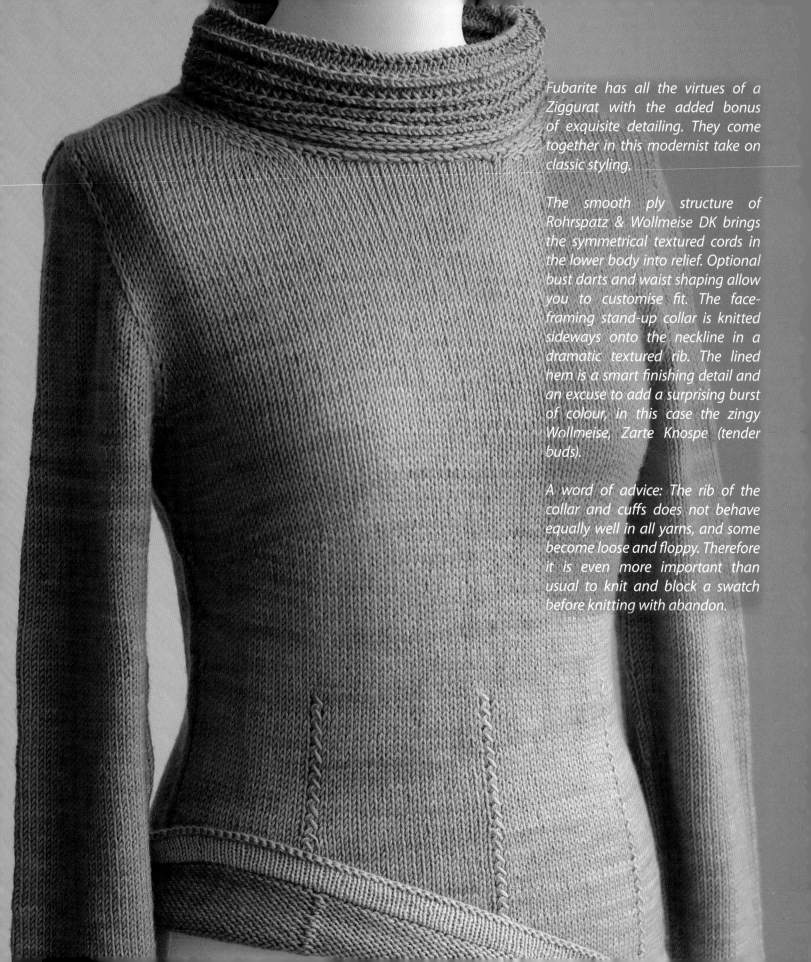

Fubarite has all the virtues of a Ziggurat with the added bonus of exquisite detailing. They come together in this modernist take on classic styling.

The smooth ply structure of Rohrspatz & Wollmeise DK brings the symmetrical textured cords in the lower body into relief. Optional bust darts and waist shaping allow you to customise fit. The face-framing stand-up collar is knitted sideways onto the neckline in a dramatic textured rib. The lined hem is a smart finishing detail and an excuse to add a surprising burst of colour, in this case the zingy Wollmeise, Zarte Knospe (tender buds).

A word of advice: The rib of the collar and cuffs does not behave equally well in all yarns, and some become loose and floppy. Therefore it is even more important than usual to knit and block a swatch before knitting with abandon.

Fubarite

TO FIT SIZE
81 (86, 91, 97, 102) [107, 112, 117, 122, 127] cm
32 (34, 36, 38, 40) [42, 44, 46, 48, 50] inches

TURTLENECK
Folded collar, knitted sideways with textured rib

FIT
Grey: Tailored shoulders and waist shaping with no ease or slight negative ease
Brown: A wider version

YARN
Rohrspatz & Wollmeise Merino DK (8ply, 100% merino, 428 m (468 yds) per 200 g); Q.E.D., 3 (3, 3, 3, 3) [3, 3, 4, 4, 4] skeins
Scrap (approx 30 m / 35 yds) of **CC** in Sport or Fingering
CC used for sample: Rohrspatz & Wollmeise Pure (Fingering), Zarte Knospe (yellow-green)

APPROX YARDAGE
900 (950, 1000, 1100, 1100) [1200, 1200, 1250, 1300, 1350] m
1000 (1050, 1100, 1200, 1250) [1300, 1300, 1400, 1450, 1450] yds

ALTERNATIVE YARN SUGGESTIONS
Cascade Lana d'Oro, SweetGeorgia DK

NEEDLES & NOTIONS
4 mm (US 6) circular needle, 80 – 100 cm (32 – 40")
or size to obtain gauge
3.25 mm (US 3) circular needle, 60 – 100 cm (24 – 40")
Stitch holders; stitch markers

BLOCKED GAUGE
20 sts x 28 rows on 4 mm (US 6) needle = 10 cm / 4"

SAMPLE SIZES
Grey (Q.E.D): Size 38 with Middling bust darts weighs 510 g / 18 oz
Brown (dra di ned um): Size 40 with Middling bust darts and a more relaxed fit with less waist shaping and additional increases weighs 560 g / 19.75 oz
Dark Grey: Size 40 with Middling bust darts knitted with Cascade Lana d'Oro (worsted weight) at DK gauge weighs 590 g / 21 oz

Fubarite

STEP 1: CAST ON & RIGHT BACK SHOULDER

With **MC**, using longtail cast on, and 4 mm (US 6) needle, cast on
66 (68, 72, 74, 78) [80, 82, 84, 86, 88] sts.
Setup Row (WS): P14 (15, 16, 16, 17) [18, 18, 18, 19, 20], turn.
R1 (RS): Sl1^, pm, k8 (9, 10, 10, 10) [11, 11, 11, 12, 12], turn.
R2 (WS): Sl1^, purl to m, rm, p1^, p1, turn.
R3: Sl1^, pm, k5 (5, 6, 6, 6) [6, 6, 6, 7, 7], turn.
R4: Sl1^, purl to m, rm, p1^, p1, turn..
R5: Sl1^, pm, knit to last 2 sts (working any sl1^ as k1^), sl1wyb, k1.
R6: Purl to m, rm, p1^, p1, turn.
R7: Sl1^, pm, knit to last 2 sts, sl1wyb, k1.
R8: Purl to m, rm, p1^, purl to end.

66 (68, 72, 74, 78) [80, 82, 84, 86, 88] Back sts

STEP 2: LEFT BACK SHOULDER

R1 (RS): K1, sl1wyb, k12 (13, 14, 14, 15) [16, 16, 16, 17, 18], turn.
R2 (WS): Sl1^, pm, p8 (9, 10, 10, 10) [11, 11, 11, 12, 12], turn.
R3: Sl1^, knit to m, rm, k1^, k1, turn.
R4: Sl1^, pm, p5 (5, 6, 6, 6) [6, 6, 6, 7, 7], turn.
R5: Sl1^, knit to m, rm, k1^, k1, turn.
R6: Sl1^, pm, purl to end (working any sl1^ as p1^).
R7: K1, sl1wyb, knit to m, rm, k1^, k1, turn.
R8: Sl1^, pm, purl to end.

STEP 3: WORKING ACROSS BACK

R1 (RS): K1, sl1wyb, knit to m, rm, k1^, knit to last 2 sts, sl1wyb, k1.
66 (68, 72, 74, 78) [80, 82, 84, 86, 88] Back sts
R2 (WS): Purl.
R3: K1, sl1wyb, knit to last 2 sts, sl1wyb, k1.
R4: Purl.
Work **Rows 3 & 4** again x 0 (0, 1, 1, 1) [1, 1, 2, 2, 2].
Work **Row 3** once more.
Final Row (WS): Purl to last 2 sts, p2tog, pm, p&p6 (6, 7, 7, 7) [7, 7, 8, 8, 8] sts along edge (for first half of Left Sleeve Cap).

6 (6, 7, 7, 7) [7, 7, 8, 8, 8] Left Cap sts
65 (67, 71, 73, 77) [79, 81, 83, 85, 87] Back sts

Slide stitches off needle tips to rest on the cable.
Set these stitches aside, continue to next step without turning.

STEP 4: LEFT FRONT SHOULDER

nM1 = neck increase
Setup Row (WS): Loop cable, p&p13 (14, 15, 15, 16) [17, 17, 17, 18, 19] sts (for Left Front Shoulder) in the cast on of Left Back Shoulder, *and remember to pick up second st in line with faux seam.*
13 (14, 15, 15, 16) [17, 17, 17, 18, 19] Left Front sts
R1 (RS): K1, sl1wyb, k6 (7, 8, 8, 8) [9, 9, 9, 10, 10], turn.

R2 (WS): Sl1^, purl to end.
R3: K1, sl1wyb, k2 (4, 5, 5, 5) [5, 5, 5, 6, 6], turn.
R4: Sl1^, purl to end.
R5: K1, sl1wyb, knit to 2 sts before loop (working any sl1^ as k1^), sl1wyb, k1, turn.
R6: Purl.
R7: K1, sl1wyb, knit to 2 sts before loop, sl1wyb, k1, turn.
R8: Purl.
R9: K1, sl1wyb, k1, nM1R, knit to 2 sts before loop, sl1wyb, k1, turn.
14 (15, 16, 16, 17) [18, 18, 18, 19, 20] Left Front sts
R10: Purl.
Work **Rows 9 & 10** again x 2 (2, 3, 3, 3) [3, 3, 4, 4, 4].
16 (17, 19, 19, 20) [21, 21, 22, 23, 24] Left Front sts
Final Row (RS): K1, sl1wyb, k1, nM1R, knit to 2 sts before loop, ssk,

BOX A

sM1L = sleeve increase   nM1 = neck increase

RS ROWS
R1: K1, sl1wyb, k1, nM1R, (knit to 1 st before m, sl1wyb, sm, sM1L, knit to m, sM1R, sm, sl1wyb) twice, knit to last 3 sts, nM1L, k1, sl1wyb, k1.

WS ROWS
R2: Purl.

R4: P3, nM1Lp, purl to last 3 sts, nM1Rp, p3.

pm, p&k6 (6, 7, 7, 7) [7, 7, 8, 8, 8] sts (for second half of Left Sleeve Cap), knit to m, sm, k1, sl1wyb, knit to last 2 sts, ssk, pm, p&k6 (6, 7, 7, 7) [7, 7, 8, 8, 8] sts (for first half of Right Sleeve Cap).

12 (12, 14, 14, 14) [14, 14, 16, 16, 16] Left Cap sts
6 (6, 7, 7, 7) [7, 7, 8, 8, 8] Right Cap sts
16 (17, 19, 19, 20) [21, 21, 22, 23, 24] Left Front sts
64 (66, 70, 72, 76) [78, 80, 82, 84, 86] Back sts

Slide stitches off needle tips to rest on the cable.
Set these stitches aside, continue to next step without turning.

STEP 5: RIGHT FRONT SHOULDER
nM1 = neck increase
R1 (RS): Loop cable, p&k13 (14, 15, 15, 16) [17, 17, 17, 18, 19] sts (for Right Front Shoulder) in the cast on of Right Back Shoulder, *and remember to pick up second st in line with faux seam.*
13 (14, 15, 15, 16) [17, 17, 17, 18, 19] Right Front sts
R2 (WS): P8 (9, 10, 10, 10) [11, 11, 11, 12, 12], turn.
R3: Sl1^, knit to last 2 sts, sl1wyb, k1.
R4: P4 (6, 7, 7, 7) [7, 7, 7, 8, 8], turn.
R5: Sl1^, knit to last 2 sts, sl1wyb, k1.
R6: Purl to loop (working any sl1^ as p1^), turn.
R7: K1, sl1wyb, knit to last 2 sts, sl1wyb, k1.
R8: Purl to loop, turn.
R9: K1, sl1wyb, knit to last 3 sts, nM1L, k1, sl1wyb, k1.
14 (15, 16, 16, 17) [18, 18, 18, 19, 20] Right Front sts
R10: Purl to loop, turn.
Work **Rows 9 & 10** again x 2 (2, 3, 3, 3) [3, 3, 4, 4, 4].
16 (17, 19, 19, 20) [21, 21, 22, 23, 24] Right Front sts
Work **Row 9** once more.

17 (18, 20, 20, 21) [22, 22, 23, 24, 25] Right Front sts
Final Row (WS): Purl to 2 sts before loop, p2tog, pm, p&p6 (6, 7, 7, 7) [7, 7, 8, 8, 8] sts (for second half of Right Sleeve Cap), purl to end.

12 (12, 14, 14, 14) [14, 14, 16, 16, 16] sts for each Sleeve Cap
16 (17, 19, 19, 20) [21, 21, 22, 23, 24] sts for each Front
64 (66, 70, 72, 76) [78, 80, 82, 84, 86] Back sts

STEP 6: SLEEVE CAPS & BODY
You will now increase for the sleeves and neck.
(See Helpful Table for an overview of all increases.)

REFER TO **BOX A** FOR ROW INSTRUCTIONS
Work **Rows 1 & 2** x 2 (2, 2, 3, 2) [2, 3, 2, 2, 2].
16 (16, 18, 20, 18) [18, 20, 20, 20, 20] Sleeve sts
18 (19, 21, 22, 22) [23, 24, 24, 25, 26] sts for each Front

Work **Rows 1 & 4** x 1 (1, 1, 1, 2) [2, 2, 2, 2, 2].
18 (18, 20, 22, 22) [22, 24, 24, 24, 24] Sleeve sts
20 (21, 23, 24, 26) [27, 28, 28, 29, 30] sts for each Front

STEP 7: JOIN FRONTS TO KNIT IN THE ROUND
Joining Row-Round 1 (RS): K1, sl1wyb, k1, nM1R, (knit to 1 st before m, sl1wyb, sm, sM1L, knit to m, sM1R, sm, sl1wyb) twice, knit to last 3 sts, nM1L, k1, pm (=Nm), sl1wyb, k1, *(turn work over so WS is facing) borrow last st for cast on loop*, crochet cast on 23 (23, 23, 23, 23) [23, 23, 25, 25, 25] sts, *replace loop onto LN (make a final chain st but not around the needle), turn work over so RS is facing*, join to Left Front, knit to m, sm.

You are now at Left Front Sleeve.

20 (20, 22, 24, 24) [24, 26, 26, 26, 26] Sleeve sts
65 (67, 71, 73, 77) [79, 81, 83, 85, 87] Front sts
64 (66, 70, 72, 76) [78, 80, 82, 84, 86] Back sts

Joining Round 2: Knit to Nm, rm, ssk, knit to end of cast on, make loop in bar and place on LN, k2tog (the first st of Left Front and the loop), knit to 1 st before m.
20 (20, 22, 24, 24) [24, 26, 26, 26, 26] Sleeve sts
64 (66, 70, 72, 76) [78, 80, 82, 84, 86] Front sts
64 (66, 70, 72, 76) [78, 80, 82, 84, 86] Back sts

STEP 8: SLEEVE & BODY INCREASES
Continue to work sleeve increases and also introduce body increases.
The round begins 1 stitch before Left Front Sleeve marker.

Fubarite

REFER TO **BOX B** FOR ROUND INSTRUCTIONS
Work **Rnds 1 & 2** x 13 (12, 12, 11, 11) [12, 10, 11, 12, 13].
46(44, 46, 46, 46) [48, 46, 48, 50, 52] Sleeve sts

INTRODUCE BODY INCREASES
Work **Rnds 3 & 2** x 0 (1, 1, 2, 1) [1, 2, 2, 3, 2].
46 (46, 48, 50, 48) [50, 50, 52, 56, 56] Sleeve sts
64 (68, 72, 76, 78) [80, 84, 86, 90, 90] Front sts
64 (68, 72, 76, 78) [80, 84, 86, 90, 90] Back sts

Work **Rnds 3 & 4** x 1 (1, 1, 0, 1) [2, 2, 3, 3, 4].
48 (48, 50, 50, 50) [54, 54, 58, 62, 64] Sleeve sts
68 (72, 76, 76, 82) [88, 92, 98, 102, 106] Front sts
68 (72, 76, 76, 82) [88, 92, 98, 102, 106] Back sts

Work **Rnds 3 & 6** x 0 (0, 0, 1, 1) [0, 0, 0, 0, 0].
48 (48, 50, 54, 54) [54, 54, 58, 62, 64] Sleeve sts
68 (72, 76, 80, 86) [88, 92, 98, 102, 106] Front sts
68 (72, 76, 80, 86) [88, 92, 98, 102, 106] Back sts

Work **Rnd 3**.
50 (50, 52, 56, 56) [56, 56, 60, 64, 66] Sleeve sts
70 (74, 78, 82, 88) [90, 94, 100, 104, 108] Front sts
70 (74, 78, 82, 88) [90, 94, 100, 104, 108] Back sts

Final Rnd: Knit to 2 sts before Left Front Sleeve m.

BOX B

sM1 = sleeve increase   bM1 = body increase

ODD (SLIP-STITCH) ROUNDS
Rnd 1: (Sl1wyb, sm, sM1L, knit to m, sM1R, sm, sl1wyb, knit to 1 st before m) twice.

Rnd 3: (bM1L, sl1wyb, sm, sM1L, knit to m, sM1R, sm, sl1wyb, bM1R, knit to 1 st before m) twice.

EVEN (PLAIN) ROUNDS
Rnd 2: Knit.

Rnd 4: (bM1L, k1, sm, knit to m, sm, k1, bM1R, knit to 1 st before m) twice.

Rnd 6: (bM1L, k1, sm, sM1L, knit to m, sM1R, sm, k1, bM1R, knit to 1 st before m) twice.

STEP 9: SEPARATING SLEEVES & BODY

Separation Rnd 1: *Pm, k2, rm, place all sts to next m on holder (= sleeve sts), rm, *(turn work over so WS is facing) borrow last st for cast on loop*, crochet cast on 6 (6, 7, 8, 8) [9, 9, 9, 9, 10] sts, pm, cast on 5 (5, 6, 7, 7) [8, 8, 8, 8, 9] sts, *replace loop onto LN (make a final chain st but not around the needle), turn work over so RS is facing*, knit to 2 sts before m, work from * to * once more, knit to m.

You are now at Left Front Sleeve.

81 (85, 91, 97, 103) [107, 111, 117, 121, 127] Front sts
81 (85, 91, 97, 103) [107, 111, 117, 121, 127] Back sts

Separation Rnd 2: *Rm, ssk, knit to m, sm, p1, knit to end of underarm cast on, make loop in bar and place on LN, k2tog (next st and loop), knit to m*, work from * to * once more.

80 (84, 90, 96, 102) [106, 110, 116, 120, 126] Front sts
80 (84, 90, 96, 102) [106, 110, 116, 120, 126] Back sts

STEP 10: BODY & SHAPING

Continue in stocking stitch over body stitches only.
The round begins under Left Sleeve.
Note: *Two stitches under each arm are worked in a cord pattern that creates a faux side seam (TwSl on alternate rounds).*

The instructions below are for the sleek and more fitted grey pullover. Refer to BOX E (page 156) for an alternative more relaxed shaping (brown pullover).

AT THE SAME TIME
Please read through the entire step before proceeding, as a few things happen at the same time or overlap.

- Waist Shaping (begins before or just after the darts, depending on where you place them)
- Optional Bust Darts
- Decorative cords on lower body

REFER TO **BOX C** FOR ROUND INSTRUCTIONS
Work **Rnds 1 & 2** to 5 cm/ 2" from underarm.

AT THE SAME TIME OPTIONAL BUST DARTS
Optional Bust Darts may be placed here or a bit lower. See BOX D.
Note: *If you are trying to stretch your skeins, this is a good place to set the body aside to work the sleeves before finishing the body.*

BOX C

BODY & SHAPING

Rnd 1: Knit.

Rnd 2: (Sm, TwSl, knit to m) to end of round.

Decreases and increases are made on plain knit rounds.
Decrease Rnd 3: Sm, (k2, k2tog, knit to 2 sts before side m, ssk) twice. *4 sts decreased*

Increase Rnd 4: (Sm, k2, RLI, (knit to m, sm, k2, LLI) x 3, knit to m, LLI) twice. *10 sts increased*

Increase Rnd 5: (Sm, k2, RLI, knit to side m, LLI) twice.
4 sts increased

Increase Rnd 7 (for wider body)**:** Sm, k2, RLI, knit to Centre Back m, LLI, sm, k2, RLI, knit to side m, LLI, sm, k2, RLI, knit to Centre Front m, LLI, sm, k2, RLI, knit to side m, LLI.
8 sts increased

AT THE SAME TIME WAIST SHAPING
At 5 cm / 2" from underarm, begin waist shaping.

WAIST DECREASES
Work **Decrease Rnd 3 & Rnd 2**.
78 (82, 88, 94, 100) [104, 108, 114, 118, 124] Front/Back sts

Continue with **Rnds 1 & 2**, working **Decrease Rnd 3** every 6 (6, 8, 8, 8) [8, 8, 8, 8, 8]th rnd again x 2.
74 (78, 84, 90, 96) [100, 104, 110, 114, 120] Front/Back sts

Work **Rnds 2 & 1** x 2 (2, 3, 3, 3) [3, 3, 3, 3, 3].

INTRODUCE CORDS ON FRONT & BACK
On the next round, add 3 cords in Front and 3 in Back evenly spaced along the round, for a total of 8. One cord each is at centre Front and Back.
Next Rnd: Sm, TwSl, k17 (18, 19, 21, 22) [23, 24, 26, 27, 28], {pm, TwSl, k16 (17, 19, 20, 22) [23, 24, 25, 26, 28]} x 2, pm, TwSl, k17 (18, 19, 21, 22) [23, 24, 26, 27, 28], sm, TwSl, k17 (18, 19, 21, 22) [23, 24, 26, 27, 28], {pm, TwSl, k16 (17, 19, 20, 22) [23, 24, 25, 26, 28]} x 2, pm, TwSl, k17 (18, 19, 21, 22) [23, 24, 26, 27, 28].
Work **Decrease Rnd 3 & Rnd 2**.
72 (76, 82, 88, 94) [98, 102, 108, 112, 118] Front/Back sts

WORK STRAIGHT
Work **Rnds 1 & 2** for 4 (4, 5, 5, 5) [5, 5, 5, 5, 5] cm / 1.5 (1.5, 2, 2, 2) [2, 2, 2, 2, 2]".

WAIST INCREASES
Work **Increase Rnd 4**.
77 (81, 87, 93, 99) [103, 107, 113, 117, 123] Front/Back sts

Continue with **Rnds 1 & 2**, working **Increase Rnd 5** every 6 (6, 8, 8, 8) [8, 8, 8, 8, 8]th round X 2.
81 (85, 91, 97, 103) [107, 111, 117, 121, 127] Front/Back sts

Work to 32 (33, 33.5, 34, 35) [35, 36, 34.5, 34, 34.5] cm / 12.5 (13, 13.25, 13.5, 13.75) [13.75, 14.25, 13.5, 13.5, 13.5]" from underarm or to 2.5 cm / 1" from desired length.
Do not cut the yarn.

Note: *If you are adding length, you may wish to include one or more rounds of increases.*

BOX D

OPTIONAL BUST DARTS
Place your darts at approx 5 (6, 10, 10) cm / 2 (2.25, 4, 4)" from underarm or where desired:
For placement of darts, see Hints & Tips
(Remember to place them in Front!)

Smallish (Middling, Busty, Wowza!)
Worked over 10 (14, 18, 22) rows, adds approx 3.5 (5, 6.5, 8) cm / 1.5 (2, 2.5, 3.25)"

R1 (RS): Sm, knit to m, sm, knit to 26 (30, 34, 36) sts before left underarm m, turn.
R2 (WS): Sl1^, pm, purl to 28 (32, 36, 38) sts before right underarm m, turn.
R3 (RS): Sl1^, pm, knit to m, rm, k1^, k5 (4, 4, 3), turn.
R4: Sl1^, pm, purl to m, rm, p1^, p5 (4, 4, 3), turn.
Work **Rows 3 & 4** again x 3 (5, 7, 9).

Final Row (RS): Sl1^, pm, knit to m, rm, knit to m.
Resume working in the round.
Next Rnd: Sm, TwSl, knit to m, sm, TwSl, knit to 1 st before m, k1^, rm, knit to m.

Fubarite

STEP 11: LINED HEM

LINING

Hem lining stitches are picked up on WS (see Tutorial section).
Slide stitches off needle tips to rest on the cable.
With 4-ply or sport weight **CC** and 3.25 mm (US 3) needle on WS and going counterclockwise, p&k sts in every bar *between* all sts.
81 (85, 91, 97, 103) [107, 111, 117, 121, 127] Front/Back Lining sts

Knit 8 rounds on WS (along inside of sweater and downwards).
Cut **CC**.
Slide sts off needle tips to rest on cable, set Lining sts aside.

HEM

With **MC** and 3.25 mm (US 3) needle, work 7 rnds as set (with cords), or to *slightly* longer than Lining, take **MC** to WS

LINING

With **MC**, knit one round, take **MC** to RS.

Note: If necessary, work an additional hem-round to make hem slightly longer before binding off.

BIND OFF

Weave in any loose ends at hem.
From RS, bind off hem sts together with lining sts using 3-Needle Bind Off and keeping an even tension.

BOX E

WIDER BODY

Follow the general instructions and BOX C Rounds but omit Decreases altogether, and also make additional increases.

Work **Rnds 1 & 2** to 5 cm / 2" from underarm.
Work **Increase Rnd 5**.
82 (86, 92, 98, 104) [108, 112, 118, 122, 128] Front/Back sts

Optional Bust Darts may be placed here or a bit lower (see BOX D)

Continue with **Rnds 1 & 2**, working **Increase Rnd 5** on the next 10 (10, 12, 12, 12) [12, 14, 14, 14, 14]th rnd.
86 (90, 96, 102, 108) [112, 116, 122, 126, 132] Front/Back sts

Work to13 (13, 14.5, 14.5, 14.5) [14.5, 15.5, 15.5, 15.5, 15.5] cm / 5 (5, 5.75, 5.75, 5.75) [5.75, 6, 6, 6, 6]" from underarm (approx 10 (10, 12, 12, 12) [12, 14, 14, 14, 14] rnds).

INTRODUCE CORDS ON FRONT & BACK

Next Rnd: Sm, TwSl, k19 (20, 22, 23, 25) [26, 27, 28, 29, 31], {pm, TwSl, k19 (20, 21, 23, 24) [25, 26, 28, 29, 30]} x 2,pm, TwSl, k19 (20, 22, 23, 25) [26, 27, 28, 29, 31],sm, TwSl, k19 (20, 22, 23, 25) [26, 27, 28, 29, 31],{pm, TwSl, k19 (20, 21, 23, 24) [25, 26, 28, 29, 30]} x 2,pm, TwSl, k19 (20, 22, 23, 25) [26, 27, 28, 29, 31].
Increases now take place at each side, at Centre Front, and Centre Back.
Work **Increase Rnd 7**.
88 (92, 98, 104, 110) [114, 118, 124, 128, 134] Front/Back sts

Continue with **Rnds 1 & 2**, working **Increase Rnd 7** on every 18 (18, 20, 20, 20) [20, 20, 20, 20, 20]th rnd x 2.
96 (100, 106, 112, 118) [122, 126, 132, 136, 142] Front/Back sts

Work to Hem as for the fitted pullover.

BOX F

STEP 12: SLEEVES

Place 50 (50, 52, 56, 56) [56, 56, 60, 64, 66] Sleeve sts from holder back on larger (4 mm / US 6) needle. Join **MC** at right side of gap, p&k5 (5, 6, 7, 7) [8, 8, 8, 8, 9] sts along the first half of the underarm cast on, pm, p&k6 (6, 7, 8, 8) [9, 9, 9, 9, 10] sts more along second half of underarm, knit to m.
61 (61, 65, 71, 71) [73, 73, 77, 81, 85] sts

REFER TO **BOX F** FOR ROUND INSTRUCTIONS
See BOX G for a wider Sleeve (brown pullover).
Work **Rnd 1** to 5 cm / 2" from underarm.

SLEEVE DECREASES
Work **Decrease Rnd**.
59 (59, 63, 69, 69) [71, 71, 75, 79, 83] sts

Continue with **Rnd 1**, working **Decrease Rnd** every 12 (12, 11, 11, 10) [9, 9, 9, 9, 8]th round again x 7 (7, 8, 8, 9) [10, 10, 10, 10, 12].
45 (45, 47, 53, 51) [51, 51, 55, 59, 59] sts
Work to 37 (37, 38, 39, 39) [39, 39, 40, 40, 40] cm /14.5 (14.5, 15, 15.25, 15.25) [15.25, 15.25, 15.75, 15.75, 15.75]" from underarm or 10 cm / 4" from desired sleeve length.

SIDEWAYS RIB CUFF
The cuff is worked sideways and attached clockwise on every RS row. Attach to approx 3 of every 4 sleeve sts (attach into 1st, 2nd, then into 3rd & 4th together with an sssk).
After the winding cast on, begin with a RS.

Sl1 from RN to LN. Onto LN, provisionally wind on 26 sts.
R1 (RS): Ksk, (p2, yo, p1, yo) x 7, p1, ssk (last cuff st with one sleeve st).
Rows 2, 4, 6 (WS): Sl1wyf, k1, (p3tog, k2) x 7, sks.
R3: Ksk, (p2, yo, p1, yo) x 7, p1, ssk (last cuff st with one sleeve st).
R5: Ksk, (p2, yo, p1, yo) x 7, p1, sssk (last cuff st with 2 sleeve sts).
Keep working **Rows 1 – 6** until 1 sleeve st remains, ending with a RS row.
Final Row (WS): Sl1wyf, k1, (p3tog, k2) x 7, sl1wyf, p2togtbl.

Join the cuff with a 3-Needle Bind Off from RS, working the final bind off together with the final sleeve st.

STEP 13: SIDEWAYS RIB COLLAR

The folded collar is worked inside out (RS of rib is on inside) and attached at the end of every RS row, going counterclockwise. Beginning at Left Shoulder, pick up and attach collar on WS, around the back, then along front (see Tutorials section).
Along Back, attach to every second row in the slanting parts, and approx 4 of every 5 stitches along the straight parts. Along Front, attach to 2 of every 3 rows in the slanting parts and every stitch along the cast on.
Approx 77 (77, 81, 84, 86) [86, 89, 93, 93, 93] sts

With **MC** and 3.25 mm (US 3) needle, provisionally wind on 33 sts.
R1 (RS): Ksk, (p2, yo, p1, yo) x 9, p2, sl1wyf, yb, p&k1, sl2 to LN, ssk.
R2 (WS): Sl1wyb, (k2, p3tog) to last 5 sts, k2, sks.
Keep working **Rows 1 & 2** until 1 collar pick up remains, ending with a RS row.
Final Row (WS): Sl1wyb, (k2, p3tog) to last 5 sts, k2, sl1wyf, p2togtbl.

Join the collar from its RS (inside of collar) with a 3-Needle Bind Off, working the final bind off together with the final picked up collar st.

FINISH

Weave in loose ends. Soak and block lightly to measurements, taking care not to stretch the collar and cuff ribbing.

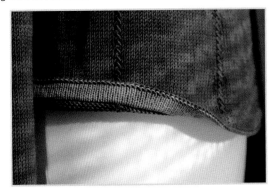

BOX G

Legend:
- Sleeve increases
- Body increases
- Neck increases
- Front cast on
- Underarm cast on

Rows from Cast On (both left and right margins): 71, 69, 67, 65, 63, 61, 59, 57, 55, 53, 51, 49, 47, 45, 43, 41, 39, 37, 35, 33, 31, 29, 27, 25, 23, 21, 19, 17

Short Rows: 4 (at row 71)

Each size block has three sub-columns: Sleeve increases | Body increases | Neck increases

Size 32

Row	Sleeve	Body	Neck
55	11		
53	50	70	
52		68	
51	48	66	
49	46		
47	44		
45	42		
43	40		
41	38		
39	36		
37	34		
35	32		
33	30		
31	28		
29	26		
27	24		
25	22		
23	20	23	21
22			20
21	18		19
19	16		18
17	14		17

Size 34

Row	Sleeve	Body	Neck
55	11		
53	50	74	
52		72	
51	48	70	
49	46	68	
47–25	44 … 22		
23	20	23	22
22			21
21	18		20
19	16		19
17	14		18

Size 36

Row	Sleeve	Body	Neck
57	12		
55	52	78	
54		76	
53	50	74	
51	48	72	
49–27	46 … 24		
25	22	23	24
24			23
23	20		22
21	18		21
19	16		20

Size 38

Row	Sleeve	Body	Neck
59	14		
57	54	80	
55	52	78	
53	50	76	
51	48	74	
49–29	46 … 26		
27	24	23	25
26			24
25	22		23
23	20		22
21	18		21
19	16		20

Size 40

Row	Sleeve	Body	Neck
59	14		
57	56	88	
56	54	86	
55	52	84	
54		82	
53	50	80	
51	48	78	
49–29	46 … 26		
27	24	23	27
26			26
25	22		25
24			24
23	20		23
21	18		22
19	16		21

Size 42

Row	Sleeve	Body	Neck
61	16		
59	56	90	
58		88	
57	54	86	
56		84	
55	52	82	
53	50	80	
51–31	48 … 28		
29	26	23	29
28			28
27	24	23	28
26			27
25	22		25
23	20		24
21	18		23
19	16		22

Size 44

Row	Sleeve	Body	Neck
61	16		
59	56	94	
58		92	
57	54	90	
56		88	
55	52	86	
53	50	84	
51	48	82	
49–29	46 … 26		
27	24	23	28
26			27
25	22		26
24			25
23	20		24
21	18		23
19	16		22

Size 46

Row	Sleeve	Body	Neck
65	16		
61	58	96	
60		94	
59	56	92	
58		88	
57	54	86	
55	52	84	
53	50	82	
51–31	48 … 28		
29	26	25	29
28			28
27	24		27
26			26
25	22		25
23	20		24
21	18		23
19	16		

Size 48

Row	Sleeve	Body	Neck
69	16		
67	64	104	
66		102	
65	62	100	
64		98	
63	60	96	
61	58	92	
59	56	90	
57	54	88	
55	52	86	
53–31	50 … 28		
29	26	25	30
28			29
27	24		28
26			27
25	22		26
23	20		25
21	18		24

Size 50

Row	Sleeve	Body	Neck
71	18		
69	66	108	
68		106	
67	64	104	
66		102	
65	62	100	
64		98	
63	60	96	
62		94	
61	58	92	
59	56	90	
57	54	88	
55	52		
53–31	50 … 28		
29	26	25	31
28			30
27	24		29
26			28
25	22		27
23	20		26
21	18		25

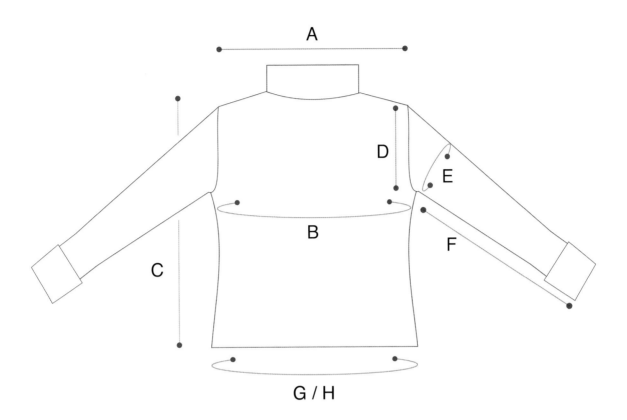

FUBARITE GARMENT MEASUREMENTS

	32	34	36	38	40	42	44	46	48	50
A – Shoulder width (cm)	32	33	35	36	38	39	40	41	42	43
in	12.5	13	13.75	14.25	15	15.25	15.75	16.25	16.5	17
B – Bust (cm)	80	84	90	96	102	106	110	116	120	126
in	31.5	33	35.5	37.75	40.25	41.75	43.25	45.75	47.25	49.5
C – Length (cm)	54	55	56	57	58	59	60	60	61	62
in	21.25	21.75	22	22.5	22.75	23.25	23.5	23.5	24	24.5
D – Armhole depth (cm)	18	18	18.5	19.5	19.5	20	20	21.5	23	23.5
in	7	7	7.5	7.5	7.5	8	8	8.5	9	9.5
E – Sleeve circumf (cm)	30.5	30.5	32.5	35.5	35.5	36.5	36.5	38.5	40.5	42.5
in	12	12	12.75	14	14	14.25	14.25	15.25	16	16.75
F – Sleeve seam (cm)	47	47	48	49	49	49	49	50	50	50
in	18.5	18.5	19	19.25	19.25	19.25	19.25	19.75	19.75	19.75
G – Hem circumf (cm)	81	85	91	97	103	107	111	117	121	127
in	32	33.5	35.75	38.25	40.5	42.25	43.75	46	47.75	50
H – Hem with extra sts (cm)	96	100	106	112	118	122	126	132	136	142
in	37.75	39.25	41.75	44	46.5	48	49.5	52	53.5	56

Verdite is an elegant tunic with a small gather at centre back for added ease and freedom of movement, finished by a split hem, lined with a splash of colour. An undulating cable adorns both the ballerina neckline and the cuffs at the end of the bracelet-length sleeves. The hem is, but need not be, double knitted.

This yarn, Funnies Curly Silk by Dibadu, seems to glow from within. It is the same luxuriant base that was (and still is!) one of my first favourite indie dyer yarns, Faery Wings, from back when I fell out of philosophy and into obsessive knitting. The original Simple Ziggurat was indeed designed for and knitted with this yarn base. Here, I have chosen to knit it into a slightly tighter fabric that drapes gorgeously and will keep its shape well.

TO FIT SIZE
81 (86, 91, 97, 102) [107, 112, 117, 122, 127] cm
32 (34, 36, 38, 40) [42, 44, 46, 48, 50] inches

BALLERINA NECK
Wide cable collar

FIT
Tailored shoulders and relaxed fit with approx 12 cm / 4.75" ease

YARN
Dibadu Funnies Curly Silk (sport weight, 67% Silk, 23% Mohair, 10% Nylon, 350 m (383 yds) per 100 g),
MC Grün ja grün (green) x 4 (4, 4, 4, 5) [5, 5, 5, 5, 6] skeins
CC Ripples Crafts Burras Mini Skein (fingering weight, 1ply, 100% Merino, 73 m / 20 g); A Teal Tale x 1 skein

APPROX YARDAGE
1150 (1200, 1250, 1350, 1450) [1500, 1550, 1600, 1700, 1750] m
1250 (1300, 1350, 1450, 1600) [1600, 1700, 1750, 1900, 1950] yds

ALTERNATIVE YARN SUGGESTIONS
Fyberspates Faery Wings

NEEDLES & NOTIONS
3 mm (US 2.5) circular needle, 80 – 100 cm (32 – 40")
or size to obtain gauge
Two 2.75 mm (US 2) circular needles, 60 – 100 cm (24 – 40")
Two cable or double pointed needles
Stitch holders; stitch markers

BLOCKED GAUGE
24 sts x 31 rows on 3 mm (US 2.5) needle = 10 cm / 4"

SAMPLE SIZES
Size 40 with Middling bust darts weighs 359 g / 12.75 oz
It *should* be possible to knit up to size 44 or even 46 with 4 skeins, but you may prefer to finish the sleeves before completing the body, to make sure you have enough yarn

Verdite

STEP 1: CAST ON & RIGHT BACK SHOULDER

With **MC**, using longtail cast on and 3 mm (US 2.5) needle, cast on 79 (81, 85, 89, 91) [95, 99, 101, 105, 109] sts.

Setup Row (WS): P12 (12, 12, 13, 13) [13, 14, 14, 16, 16], turn.

R1 (RS): Sl1^, pm, k7 (7, 7, 7, 7) [7, 8, 8, 9, 9], turn.

R2 (WS): Sl1^, purl to m, rm, p1^, p1, turn.

R3: Sl1^, pm, k4 (4, 4, 4, 4) [4, 4, 4, 5, 5], turn.

R4: Sl1^, purl to m, rm, p1^, p1, turn.

R5: Sl1^, pm, knit to last 2 sts (working any sl1^ as k1^), sl1wyb, k1.

R6: Purl to m, rm, p1^, p1, turn.

R7: Sl1^, pm, knit to last 2 sts, sl1wyb, k1.

Work **Rows 6 & 7** once more.

Final Row (WS): Purl to m, rm, p1^, purl to end.

79 (81, 85, 89, 91) [95, 99, 101, 105, 109] Back sts

STEP 2: LEFT BACK SHOULDER

R1 (RS): K1, sl1wyb, k10 (10, 10, 11, 11) [11, 12, 12, 14, 14], turn.

R2 (WS): Sl1^, pm, p7 (7, 7, 7, 7) [7, 8, 8, 9, 9] turn.

R3: Sl1^, knit to m, rm, k1^, k1, turn.

R4: Sl1^, pm, p4 (4, 4, 4, 4) [4, 4, 4, 5, 5], turn.

R5: Sl1^, knit to m, rm, k1^, k1, turn.

R6: Sl1^, pm, purl to end (working any sl1^ as p1^).

R7: K1, sl1wyb, knit to m, rm, k1^, k1, turn.

R8: Sl1^, pm, purl to end.

Work **Rows 7 & 8** once more.

STEP 3: WORKING ACROSS BACK

R1 (RS): K1, sl1wyb, knit to m, rm, k1^, knit to last 2 sts, sl1wyb, k1.

79 (81, 85, 89, 91) [95, 99, 101, 105, 109] Back sts

R2 (WS): Purl.

R3: K1, sl1wyb, knit to last 2 sts, sl1wyb, k1.

R4: Purl.

Work **Rows 3 & 4** again x 1 (1, 2, 2, 2) [2, 2, 2, 3, 3].

Work **Row 3** once more.

Final Row (WS): Purl to last 2 sts, p2tog, pm, p&p7 (7, 8, 8, 8) [8, 8, 8, 9, 9] sts along edge (for first half of Left Sleeve Cap).

7 (7, 8, 8, 8) [8, 8, 8, 9, 9] Left Cap sts
78 (80, 84, 88, 90) [94, 98, 100, 104, 108] Back sts

Slide stitches off needle tips to rest on the cable.
Set these stitches aside, continue to next step without turning.

STEP 4: LEFT FRONT SHOULDER

nM1 = neck increase

Setup Row (WS): Loop cable, p&p11 (11, 11, 12, 12) [12, 13, 13, 15, 15] sts (for Left Front Shoulder) in the cast on of Left Back Shoulder,

and remember to pick up second st in line with faux seam.

11 (11, 11, 12, 12) [12, 13, 13, 15, 15] Left Front sts

R1 (RS): K7 (7, 7, 8, 8) [8, 8, 8, 10, 10], turn.

R2: Sl1^, purl to end.

R3: K3 (3, 3, 4, 4) [4, 4, 4, 5, 5], turn.

R4: Sl1^, purl to end.

R5: Knit to 2 sts before loop (working any sl1^ as k1^), sl1wyb, k1, turn.

R6: Purl.

R7: K2, **nM1R**, knit to 2 sts before loop, sl1wyb, k1, turn.

12 (12, 12, 13, 13) [13, 14, 14, 16, 16] Left Front sts

R8: Purl.

Works **Rows 7 & 8** again x 5 (5, 6, 6, 6) [6, 6, 6, 7, 7].

17 (17, 18, 19, 19) [19, 20, 20, 23, 23] Left Front sts

BOX A

sM1 = sleeve increase   nM1 = neck increase

RS ROW
R1: K2, nM1R, (knit to 1 st before m, sl1wyb, sm, **sM1L**, knit to m, **sM1R**, sm, sl1wyb) twice, knit to last 2 sts, nM1L, k2.

WS ROWS
R2: Purl.

R4: P2, nM1Lp, purl to last 2 sts, nM1Rp, p2.

Final Row (RS): K2, nM1R, knit to 2 sts before loop, ssk, pm, p&k8 (8, 9, 9, 9) [9, 9, 9, 10, 10] sts (for second half of Left Sleeve Cap), knit to m, sm, sl1wyb, knit to last 2 sts, ssk, pm, p&k7 (7, 8, 8, 8) [8, 8, 8, 9, 9] sts (for first half of Right Sleeve Cap).

15 (15, 17, 17, 17) [17, 17, 17, 19, 19] Left Cap sts
7 (7, 8, 8, 8) [8, 8, 8, 9, 9] Right Cap sts
17 (17, 18, 19, 19) [19, 20, 20, 23, 23] Left Front sts
77 (79, 83, 87, 89) [93, 97, 99, 103, 107] Back sts

Slide stitches off needle tips to rest on the cable.
Set these stitches aside, continue to next step without turning.

STEP 5: RIGHT FRONT SHOULDER
nM1 = neck increase
R1 (RS): Loop cable, p&k11 (11, 11, 12, 12) [12, 13, 13, 15, 15] sts (for Right Front Shoulder) in the cast on of Right Back Shoulder, *and remember to pick up second st in line with faux seam.*
11 (11, 11, 12, 12) [12, 13, 13, 15, 15] Right Front sts
R2 (WS): P7 (7, 7, 8, 8) [8, 8, 8, 10, 10], turn.
R3: Sl1^, knit to end.
R4: P3 (3, 3, 4, 4) [4, 4, 4, 5, 5], turn.
R5: Sl1^, knit to end.
R6: Purl to loop, working any sl1^ as p1^, turn.
R7: K1, sl1wyb, knit to last 2 sts, nM1L, k2.
12 (12, 12, 13, 13) [13, 14, 14, 16, 16] Right Front sts
R8: Purl to loop, turn.
Work **Rows 7 & 8** again x 5 (5, 6, 6, 6) [6, 6, 6, 7, 7].
17 (17, 18, 19, 19) [19, 20, 20, 23, 23] Right Front sts
Work **Row 7** once more.
18 (18, 19, 20, 20) [20, 21, 21, 24, 24] Right Front sts

Final row (WS): Purl to 2 sts before loop, p2tog, pm, p&p8 (8, 9, 9, 9) [9, 9, 9, 10, 10] sts (for second half of Right Sleeve Cap), purl to end.

15 (15, 17, 17, 17) [17, 17, 17, 19, 19] sts for each Sleeve Cap
17 (17, 18, 19, 19) [19, 20, 20, 23, 23] sts for each Front
77 (79, 83, 87, 89) [93, 97, 99, 103, 107] Back sts

STEP 6: SLEEVE CAPS & BODY
You will now increase for the sleeves and neck.
(See Helpful Table for an overview of all increases.)

REFER TO **BOX A** FOR ROW INSTRUCTIONS
Work **Rows 1 & 2** x 5 (5, 5, 5, 5) [4, 5, 6, 7, 6].
25 (25, 27, 27, 27) [25, 27, 29, 33, 31] Sleeve sts
22 (22, 23, 24, 24) [23, 25, 26, 30, 29] sts for each Front

Works **Rows 1 & 4** x 1 (1, 1, 1, 1) [2, 2, 2, 1, 2].
27 (27, 29, 29, 29) [29, 31, 33, 35, 35] Sleeve sts
24 (24, 25, 26, 26) [27, 29, 30, 32, 33] sts for each Front

BOX B

sML = sleeve increase   bM1 = body increase

ODD (SLIP-STITCH) ROUNDS

Rnd 1: (Sl1wyb, sm, sM1L, knit to m, sM1R, sm, sl1wyb, knit to 1 st before m) twice.

Rnd 3: (bM1L, sl1wyb, sm, sM1L, knit to m, sM1R, sm, sl1wyb, bM1R, knit to 1 st before m) twice.

EVEN (PLAIN) ROUNDS

Rnd 2: Knit.

Rnd 4: (bM1L, k1, sm, knit to m, sm, k1, bM1R, knit to 1 st before m) twice.

Rnd 6: (bM1L, k1, sm, sM1L, knit to m, sM1R, sm, k1, bM1R, knit to 1 st before m) twice.

STEP 7: JOIN FRONTS TO KNIT IN THE ROUND

Joining Row-Round 1 (RS): K2, nM1R, (knit to 1 st before m, sl1wyb, sm, **sM1L**, knit to m, **sM1R**, sm, sl1wyb) twice, knit to last 2 sts, nM1L, pm (=Nm), k2, *(turn work over so WS is facing) borrow last st for cast on loop*, crochet cast on 28 (30, 32, 34, 36) [38, 38, 38, 38, 40] sts, *replace loop onto LN (make a final chain st but not around the needle), turn work over so RS is facing*, join to Left Front, knit to m, sm.

You are now at Left Front Sleeve.

29 (29, 31, 31, 31) [31, 33, 35, 37, 37] Sleeve sts
78 (80, 84, 88, 90) [94, 98, 100, 104, 108] Front sts
77 (79, 83, 87, 89) [93, 97, 99, 103, 107] Back sts

Joining Round 2: Knit to Nm, rm, ssk, knit to end of cast on, make loop in bar and place on LN, k2tog (the first st of Left Front and the loop), knit to 1 st before m.

29 (29, 31, 31, 31) [31, 33, 35, 37, 37] Sleeve sts
77 (79, 83, 87, 89) [93, 97, 99, 103, 107] Front sts
77 (79, 83, 87, 89) [93, 97, 99, 103, 107] Back sts

STEP 8: SLEEVE & BODY INCREASES

Continue to work sleeve increases and also introduce body increases.
The round begins 1 stitch before Left Front Sleeve marker.

REFER TO **BOX B** FOR ROUND INSTRUCTIONS
Work **Rnds 1 & 2** x 3 (3, 3, 3, 3) [3, 2, 1, 1, 1].
35 (35, 37, 37, 37) [37, 37, 37, 39, 39] Sleeve sts
Work **Rnd 1**.
37 (37, 39, 39, 39) [39, 39, 39, 41, 41] Sleeve sts

CREATE A GATHER OF STITCHES CENTRE BACK
Increase Rnd: (Knit to m, sm) twice, k27 (28, 30, 32, 30) [32, 34, 35, 37, 39], (k2, M1R, k1, M1L) x 7 (7, 7, 7, 9) [9, 9, 9, 9, 9], knit to end of round.
91 (93, 97, 101, 107) [111, 115, 117, 121, 125] Back sts

Work **Rnds 1 & 2** x 5 (5, 5, 4, 4) [4, 5, 5, 6, 5].
47 (47, 49, 47, 47) [47, 49, 49, 53, 51] Sleeve sts

INTRODUCE BODY INCREASES
Work **Rnds 3 & 2** x 3 (3, 2, 4, 3) [3, 4, 4, 4, 5].

53 (53, 53, 55, 53) [53, 57, 57, 61, 61] Sleeve sts
83 (85, 87, 95, 95) [99, 105, 107, 111, 117] Front sts
97 (99, 101, 109, 113) [117, 123, 125, 129, 135] Back sts

Work **Rnds 3 & 4** x 2 (2, 3, 3, 3) [3, 4, 4, 3, 3].
57 (57, 59, 61, 59) [59, 65, 65, 67, 67] Sleeve sts
91 (93, 99, 107, 107) [111, 121, 123, 123, 129] Front sts
105 (107, 113, 121, 125) [129, 139, 141, 141, 147] Back sts

BOX C

BODY & SHAPING

Rnd 1: (Sm, g1, knit to m) twice.

Decrease Rnd: (Sm, g1, k2tog, knit to 2 sts before side m, ssk) twice.

Increase Rnd: (Sm, g1, M1L, knit to m, M1R) twice.

Work **Rnds 3 & 6** x 0 (0, 0, 0, 1) [1, 0, 0, 1, 1].
57 (57, 59, 61, 63) [63, 65, 65, 71, 71] Sleeve sts
91 (93, 99, 107, 111) [115, 121, 123, 127, 133] Front sts
105 (107, 113, 121, 129) [133, 139, 141, 145, 151] Back sts

Work **Rnd 3**.
59 (59, 61, 63, 65) [65, 67, 67, 73, 73] Sleeve sts
93 (95, 101, 109, 113) [117, 123, 125, 129, 135] Front sts
107 (109, 115, 123, 131) [135, 141, 143, 147, 153] Back sts

Final Rnd: Knit to 2 sts before Left Front Sleeve m.

STEP 9: SEPARATING SLEEVES & BODY

Separation Rnd 1: *Pm, k2, rm, place all sts to next m on holder (= sleeve sts), rm, *(turn work over so WS is facing) borrow last st for cast on loop,* crochet cast on 7 (8, 8, 8, 10) [10, 10, 12, 13, 13] sts, pm, cast on 5 (6, 6, 6, 8) [8, 8, 10, 11, 11] sts, *replace loop onto LN (make a final chain st but not around the needle), turn work over so RS is facing*, knit to 2 sts before m, work from * to * once more, knit to m.

You are now at Left Front Sleeve.

105 (109, 115, 123, 131) [135, 141, 147, 153, 159] Front sts
119 (123, 129, 137, 149) [153, 159, 165, 171, 177] Back sts

Separation Rnd 2: *Rm, ssk, knit to m, sm, p1, knit to end of underarm cast on, make loop in bar and place on LN, k2tog (next st and loop), knit to m*, work from * to * once more.

104 (108, 114, 122, 130) [134, 140, 146, 152, 158] Front sts
118 (122, 128, 136, 148) [152, 158, 164, 170, 176] Back sts

STEP 10: BODY & SHAPING

Continue in stocking stitch over body stitches only.
The round begins under Left Sleeve.
Note: *One stitch under each arm is worked in garter st (g1), which creates a faux side seam.*

AT THE SAME TIME

Please read through the entire step before proceeding, as a few things happen at the same time or overlap.

- Optional Bust Darts
- Waist Shaping (begins before or just after the darts, depending on where you place them)

REFER TO **BOX C** FOR ROUND INSTRUCTIONS
Work **Rnd 1** to 5 cm/ 2" from underarm.

AT THE SAME TIME OPTIONAL BUST DARTS
Optional Bust Darts may be placed here or a bit lower. See BOX D.

Note: If you are trying to stretch your skeins, this is a good place to set the body aside to work the sleeves before finishing the body.

AT THE SAME TIME WAIST SHAPING
At 5 cm / 2" from underarm, begin waist shaping.

BOX D

OPTIONAL BUST DARTS

Place your darts at approx 5 (6, 10, 10) cm / 2 (2.25, 4, 4)" from underarm or where desired:
For placement of darts, see Hints & Tips
(Remember to place them in Front!)

Smallish (Middling, Busty, Wowza!)
Worked over 10 (16, 18, 22) rows, adds approx 3 (5, 6.5, 7.5) cm / 1.25 (2, 2.5, 3)".

R1 (RS): Sm, g1, knit to m, sm, g1, knit to 26 (34, 34, 36) sts before Left Underarm m, turn.
R2 (WS): Sl1^, pm, purl to 27 (35, 35, 37) sts before Right Underarm m, turn.
R3 (RS): Sl1^, pm, knit to m, rm, k1^, k5 (4, 3, 3), turn.
R4: Sl1^, pm, purl to m, rm, p1^, p5 (4, 3, 3), turn.
Work **Rows 3 & 4** again x 3 (6, 8, 10).
Final Row (RS): Sl1^, pm, knit to m, rm, k1^, knit to m.
Resume working in the round.
Next Rnd: Sm, g1, knit to m, sm, g1, knit to 1 st before m, k1^, rm, knit to m.

WAIST DECREASES

Work **Decrease Rnd**.

102 (106, 112, 120, 128) [132, 138, 144, 150, 156] Front sts
116 (120, 126, 134, 146) [150, 156, 162, 168, 174] Back sts

Continue with **Rnd 1**, working **Decrease Rnd** every 6 (6, 8, 8, 8) [8, 8, 8, 8, 8]th rnd again x 3.
96 (100, 106, 114, 122) [126, 132, 138, 144, 150] Front sts
110 (114, 120, 128, 140) [144, 150, 156, 162, 168] Back sts

WORK STRAIGHT

Work **Rnd 1** for 4 (4, 4, 4, 4) [4, 4, 5, 5, 5] cm / 1.5 (1.5, 1.5, 1.5, 1.5) [1.5, 1.5, 2, 2, 2]".

WAIST INCREASES

Work **Increase Rnd**.
98 (102, 108, 116, 124) [128, 134, 140, 146, 152] Front sts
112 (116, 122, 130, 142) [146, 152, 158, 164, 170] Back sts

Continue with **Rnd 1**, working **Increase Rnd** every 8th round twice, then on next 16 (16, 16, 12, 12) [12, 12, 12, 12, 12]th x 1 (1, 1, 1, 2, 2) [2, 2, 2, 2, 2], then on the next 30 (30, 20, 25, 25) [25, 25, 25, 25, 25]th rnd once.
106 (110, 116, 126, 134) [138, 144, 150, 156, 162] Front sts
120 (124, 130, 140, 152) [156, 162, 168, 174, 180] Back sts

Work to 41 (41, 40.5, 42, 42) [42, 40.5, 41.5, 40.5, 40.5] cm / 16.25 (16.25, 16, 16.5, 16.5) [16.5, 16, 16.25, 16, 16]" from underarm or to 3.5 cm / 1.5" from desired length.
Do not cut the yarn.

Note: *If you are adding length, you may wish to include one or more rounds of increases.*

STEP 11: SPLIT LINED HEM

The lined Front and Back hems are finished separately and worked back and forth in double knitting.
If preferred, the hem and lining can be knit one at a time after the lining stitches have been picked up, and the open sides can then be seamed together with a few stitches.

N1 (3 mm / US 2.5): Outer layer/**MC**
N2 (2.75 mm / US 2): Lining needle/**CC**
N3 (2.75 mm / US 2): New working needle

BOX E

SLEEVE ROUNDS
Rnd 1: Sm, g1, knit to m.
Decrease Rnd: Sm, g1, k2tog, knit to 2 sts before m, ssk.

LINING

Hem lining stitches are picked up on WS (see Tutorial section).
Working from WS, sl1^, take **MC** to WS, slide stitches off needle tips to rest on the circular cable (N1).
With N2, p&k1 st in every bar between sts all the way around.

On RS **MC** is kept to front (toward you), **CC** to back.
On WS **CC** is kept to front, **MC** to back.

BACK HEM

Set up Double Knitting.
Take **MC** to RS.
With N3, work sts alternately from N1 and N2:
R1 (RS): K1**MC** from N1, p1**CC** from N2 to 1 st before m, take both yarns to back, take **CC** to front (taking care not to catch **MC**), sl1wyb from N1, sl1wyf from N2.

BOX F

CABLE REPEAT AROUND CUFF
R1 (Cable Cross 1, RS): K1, sl3 to CN1, hold to **back**, sl3 to CN2, hold to **front**, k3, k3 from CN2, k3 from CN1, p1, ss(s)k.

R2 (WS): Sl1wyf, k1, p9, sl1wyf.

R3 (RS): K10, p1, ss(s)k.

R4: Sl1wyf, k1, p9, sl1wyf.

Work **Rows 3 & 4** again x 5.

R15 (Cable Cross 2): K1, sl3 to CN1, hold to **back**, sl3 to CN2, hold to **back**, k3, k3 from CN2, k3 from CN1, p1, ss(s)k.

R16: Sl1wyf, k1, p9, sl1wyf.

Work **Rows 3 & 4** again x 6.

N1: Front Hem sts, set aside for now.
N2: Front Lining sts, set aside for now.
N3: Back Hem sts

R2 (WS): K1CC, p1MC, take **MC** to back, double knit to last 2 sts, take both yarns to back, take **MC** to front (take care not to catch **CC**), sl1wyb, sl1wyf.
R3: K1MC, p1CC, take **CC** to back, double knit to last 2 sts, take both yarns to back, take **CC** to front, sl1wyb, sl1wyf.
R4: As Row 2.

Work **Rows 3 & 4** again x 4, cut **CC**.
*On the next row **MC** sts are knitted, **CC** sts are slipped.*
R5: With **MC**, (k1, sl1wyf) to end.
*On the next row **CC** sts are knitted, **MC** sts are slipped.*
R6: With **MC** (k1, sl1wyf) to end.

3-NEEDLE BIND OFF
Each ssk is worked with 1 body st and 1 lining st, then bound off with the previous ssk.
Bind off (RS): Ssk, *ssk, pso to bind off; work from * until no Back Hem sts remain.

FRONT HEM
Work as Back Hem.

STEP 12: SLEEVES
Place 59 (59, 61, 63, 65) [65, 67, 67, 73, 73] Sleeve sts from holder back on larger (3 mm / US 2.5) needle. Join **MC** at right side of gap, p&k5 (6, 6, 6, 8) [8, 8, 10, 11, 11] sts along the first half of the underarm cast on, pm, p&k6 (7, 7, 7, 9) [9, 9, 11, 12, 12] sts more along second half of underarm, knit to m.

70 (72, 74, 76, 82) [82, 84, 88, 96, 96] sts

REFER TO BOX E FOR ROUND INSTRUCTIONS
Work **Rnd 1** to 5 cm / 2" from underarm.

SLEEVE DECREASES
Work **Decrease Rnd**.
68 (70, 72, 74, 80) [80, 82, 86, 94, 94] sts

Continue with **Rnd 1**, working **Decrease Rnd** every 15 (15, 13, 11, 9) [9, 8, 7, 8, 8]th round again x 5 (5, 6, 7, 9) [9, 10, 11, 10, 11].
58 (60, 60, 60, 62) [62, 62, 64, 74, 72] sts

Work to 30.5 (30.5, 31.5, 31.5, 32) [32, 32.5, 32.5, 33.5, 33.5] cm / 12 (12, 12.5, 12.5, 12.5) [12.5, 12.75, 12.75, 13.25, 13.25]" from underarm or 2.5 cm / 1" from desired sleeve length.

STEP 13: CABLE CUFF
The cable is worked and attached sideways to Sleeve stitches. Begin by winding on 12 sts perpendicular to the cuff, using the working yarn.

LEFT CUFF
Sl1 to LN, using smaller (2.75 mm / US 2) needle and Provisional Winding Cast On, wind on 12 sts onto LN.
The cable is knitted back and forth; on RS rows ssk the last cable st with 1 or 2 Cuff sts. Attach to approx every 4 of 5 Cuff sts; that is, ssk 3 times, then sssk (using 2 Cuff sts). Alternate the two cable crossings on every 14th row.

R1 (RS): K10, p1, k2tog.
R2 (WS): Sl1wyf, k1, p9, sl1wyf.

REFER TO BOX F FOR THE CABLE REPEAT
Work 3 complete cable repeats around cuff, work another half repeat (Rows 1 – 14) or until 1 Cuff st remains, ending with a WS row. If necessary make an additional (or omit one) sssk to accommodate the final cable repeat.

On a RS row, graft sts with provisional sts to close the cable, working a final ssk when grafting the final 2 sts.
Alternatively, close with a 3-Needle Bind Off from WS.

Verdite

Work cable repeats around neck to Centre Back (see BOX G), stop at Centre Back.

LEFT HALF

From Centre Back, continue with working yarn to pick up sts for Left Half of collar to Centre Front, p&k approx 28 (29, 31, 32, 33) [35, 36, 37, 37, 39] sts to Left Shoulder, approx 34 (35, 38, 39, 40) [41, 41, 41, 43, 44] sts from Shoulder to 1 st before Centre Front.
Approx 62 (64, 69, 71, 73) [76, 77, 78, 80, 83] sts

Slip provisional sts to working needle, remove and discard slip knot, work and attach cable along Left Front to Centre Back as follows.

R1 (RS): Sl1wyb, p1, k9, sl1wyf.
R2 (WS): K1, p9, k1, p2tog.
Work **Rows 1 & 2** again x 5.

Work cable repeats around neck to 1 st before Centre Back (see BOX H).

On a RS row, graft sts with provisional sts to close the cable, working a final ssk when grafting the final 2 sts.
Alternatively close with a 3-Needle Bind Off from WS.

NOTES

The cable collar is worked in two halves.

When joining yarn at Centre Front to pick up first half of Neck, use a long yarn end and leave the main ball at Centre Front for casting on and working the first half of the cable.

Begin by picking up & knitting sts from RS around the neck, starting 1 stitch before Centre Front going clockwise across Right Shoulder and picking up inside an entire selvedge stitch. Then wind on stitches to work and attach a cable (as for Cuff) from Centre Front along Right Front to Centre Back.

From Centre Back, pick up sts over Left Shoulder to Centre Front, work cable from the provisional stitches at Centre Front along Left Front to Centre Back. Graft or close with a 3-Needle Bind Off at Centre Back where it will be less obvious if you end up with an incomplete cable repeat – and you will have a perfectly centred cable in Front.

FINISH

Weave in loose ends. Soak and block lightly to measurements, taking care to pin out collar and cuff cables.

RIGHT CUFF
Work as Left Cuff.

STEP 14: CABLE COLLAR

RIGHT HALF
With 2.75 mm (US 2) circular needle and 1 st to the right of Centre Front, from RS attach **MC**, p&k approx 36 (37, 40, 41, 42) [43, 43, 43, 45, 46] sts along Right Front to Right Shoulder, approx 28 (29, 31, 32, 33) [35, 36, 37, 37, 39] sts from Shoulder to Centre Back, stop at Centre Back.
Approx 64 (66, 71, 73, 75) [78, 79, 80, 82, 85] sts

The Neck Cable is worked like the Cuff Cable but with 2 additional rows between Cable Crosses. Work and attach the Cable from Centre Front along Right Front to Centre Back as follows:

Provisional Cast On: Sl1 to LN, using the already attached ball of yarn wind on 12 sts onto LN.
R1 (RS): K10, p1, k2tog.
R2 (WS): Sl1wyf, k1, p9, sl1wyf.

BOX G

CABLE REPEAT ALONG RIGHT FRONT TO CENTRE BACK

R1 (Cable Cross 1, RS): K1, sl3 to CN1, hold to **back**, sl3 to CN2, hold to **front**, k3, k3 from CN2, k3 from CN1, p1, ss(s)k.
R2 (WS): Sl1wyf, k1, p9, sl1wyf.
R3 (RS): K10, p1, ss(s)k.
R4: Sl1wyf, k1, p9, sl1wyf.

Work **Rows 3 & 4** again x 6.

R17 (Cable Cross 2): K1, sl3 to CN1, hold to **back**, sl3 to CN2, hold to **back**, k3, k3 from CN2, k3 from CN1, p1, ss(s)k.
R18: Sl1wyf, k1, p9, sl1wyf.

Work **Rows 3 & 4** again x 7.

BOX H

CABLE REPEAT ALONG LEFT FRONT TO CENTRE BACK

R1 (Cable Cross 1, RS): Sl1wyb, p1, sl3 to CN1, hold to **front**, sl3 to CN2, hold to **back**, k3, k3 from CN2, k3 from CN1, sl1wyf.
R2 (WS): K1, p9, k1, p2(3)tog.
R3 (RS): Sl1wyb, p1, k9, sl1wyf.
R4: K1, p9, k1, p2(3)tog.

Work **Rows 3 & 4** again x 6.

R17 (Cable Cross 2): Sl1wyb, p1, sl3 to CN1, hold to **back**, sl3 to CN2, hold to **front**, k3, k3 from CN2, k3 from CN1, sl1wyf.
R18: K1, p9, k1, p2(3)tog.

Work **Rows 3 & 4** x 7.

Photo © Friederike Winter

Verdite

Legend:

- Sleeve increases
- Body increases
- Neck increases
- Front cast on
- Underarm cast on
- Gather

Sizes (columns, by group): 32, 34, 36, 38, 40, 42, 44, 46, 48, 50

Each size column has sub-columns labelled: Sleeve increases · Body increases · Neck increases

Rows from Cast On (left and right margins): 21, 23, 25, 27, 29, 31, 33, 35, 37, 39, 41, 43, 45, 47, 49, 51, 53, 55, 57, 59, 61, 63, 65, 67, 69, 71, 73, 75, 77

Short Rows: 4

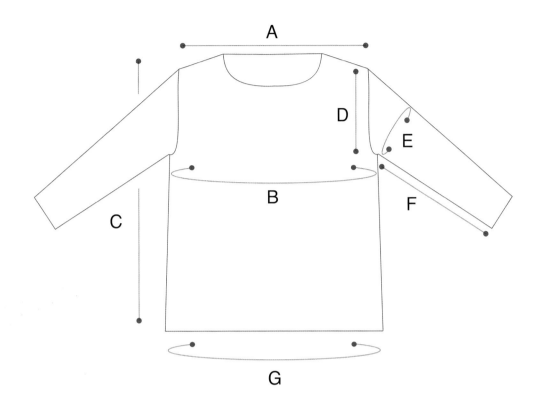

VERDITE GARMENT MEASUREMENTS

	32	34	36	38	40	42	44	46	48	50
A – Shoulder width (cm)	32	33	34.5	36.5	37	39	40.5	41.5	43	44.5
in	12.5	13	13.5	14.25	14.5	15.25	16	16.25	17	17.5
B – Bust (cm)	92.5	96	101	107.5	116	119	124	129	134	139
in	36.5	37.75	39.75	42.25	45.75	46.75	48.75	50.75	52.75	54.75
C – Length (cm)	65	65	65	67	67	67	67	68	68	68
in	25.5	25.5	25.5	26.5	26.5	26.5	26.5	26.75	26.75	26.75
D – Armhole depth (cm)	19.5	19.5	20	20.5	20.5	20.5	22	22	23	23
in	7.5	7.5	8	8	8	8	8.5	8.5	9	9
E – Sleeve circumf (cm)	29	30	31	31.5	34	34	35	36.5	40	40
in	11.5	11.75	12.25	12.5	13.5	13.5	13.75	14.25	15.75	15.75
F – Sleeve seam (cm)	33	33	34	34	34.5	34.5	35	35	36	36
in	13	13	13.5	13.5	13.5	13.5	13.75	13.75	14.25	14.25
G – Hem circumf (cm)	94	97.5	102.5	111	119	122.5	127.5	132.5	137.5	142.5
in	37	38.5	40.25	43.75	46.75	48.25	50.25	52.25	54.25	56

Aranaranja brings you the futuristic style of Fubarite at an aran gauge. Alpaka Walk, a vibrant felted alpaca/merino blend from Dibadu, creates an extravagantly plush stand-up turtleneck. The cording below the waist is quietly understated, yet holds its own against the bold, textured cuffs and provides vertical detailing to contrast with the horizontal lines of the cuffs and collar. The citrussy orange colour will brighten any day. And, just for fun, there is a contrasting hidden lining.

The cording allows you to sneak in extra increases for a more relaxed fit, and instructions on how to achieve this are supplied.

Aranaranja

tailored aran turtleneck

TO FIT SIZE

81 (86, 91, 97, 102) [107, 112, 117, 122, 127] cm
32 (34, 36, 38, 40) [42, 44, 46, 48, 50] inches

TURTLENECK

Folded textured rib collar, knit sideways

FIT

Tailored shoulders and slight waist shaping, slight positive ease

YARN

Dibadu Alpaka Walk (Aran-weight, felted, 50% alpaca, 50% merino,
199 m (218 yds) per100 g); Kürbiscreme 5 (6, 6, 6, 6) [7, 7, 7, 8, 8] skeins
Scrap (approx 30 m / 35 yds) of **CC** in Sport – Aran
Sample **CC**: Alpaka Walk Aran, Rubin (red)

APPROX YARDAGE

1000 (1050, 1100, 1150, 1200) [1250, 1300, 1400, 1450, 1500] m
1100 (1150, 1200, 1300, 1300) [1350, 1450, 1500, 1600, 1650] yds

ALTERNATIVE YARN SUGGESTIONS

Cascade Eco+, Vahva/Paksu Pirkkalanka

NEEDLES & NOTIONS

5 mm (US 8) circular needle, 80 – 100 cm (32 – 40")
or size to obtain gauge
4 mm (US 6) circular needle, 60 – 100 cm (24 – 40") x 2
Stitch holders; stitch markers

BLOCKED GAUGE

18 sts x 24 rows on 5 mm (US 8) needle = 10 cm / 4"

SAMPLE SIZE

Size 40 with Middling bust darts weighs 518 g / 18.25 oz

Photo © Alexis Borsboom

STEP 1: CAST ON & RIGHT BACK SHOULDER

With **MC**, using longtail cast on, and 5 mm (US 8) needle, cast on 62 (64, 66, 68, 70) [72, 74, 76, 78, 80] sts.

Setup Row (WS): P13 (14, 15, 15, 16) [18, 18, 19, 20, 20], turn.
R1 (RS): Sl1^, pm, k7 (8, 9, 9, 9) [11, 11, 11, 12, 12], turn.
R2 (WS): Sl1^, purl to m, rm, p1^, p1, turn.
R3: Sl1^, pm, k4 (4, 5, 5, 5) [6, 6, 6, 6, 6], turn.
R4: Sl1^, purl to m, rm, p1^, p1, turn.
R5: Sl1^, pm, knit to last 2 sts (working any sl1^ as k1^), sl1wyb, k1.
R6: Purl to m, rm, p1^, p1, turn.
R7: Sl1^, pm, knit to last 2 sts, sl1wyb, k1.
R8: Purl to m, rm, p1^, purl to end.

62 (64, 66, 68, 70) [72, 74, 76, 78, 80] Back sts.

STEP 2: LEFT BACK SHOULDER

R1 (RS): K1, sl1wyb, k11 (12, 13, 13, 14) [16, 16, 17, 18, 18], turn.
R2 (WS): Sl1^, pm, p7 (8, 9, 9, 9) [11, 11, 11, 12, 12], turn.
R3: Sl1^, knit to m, rm, k1^, k1, turn.
R4: Sl1^, pm, p4 (4, 5, 5, 5) [6, 6, 6, 6, 6], turn.
R5: Sl1^, knit to m, rm, k1^, k1, turn.
R6: Sl1^, pm, purl to end (working any sl1^ as p1^).
R7: K1, sl1wyb, knit to m, rm, k1^, k1, turn.
R8: Sl1^, pm, purl to end.

STEP 3: WORKING ACROSS BACK

R1 (RS): K1, sl1wyb, knit to m, rm, k1^, knit to last 2 sts, sl1wyb, k1.
62 (64, 66, 68, 70) [72, 74, 76, 78, 80] Back sts
R2 (WS): Purl.
R3: K1, sl1wyb, knit to last 2 sts, sl1wyb, k1.
R4: Purl.

Work **Rows 3 & 4** again x 0 (0, 1, 1, 1) [1, 2, 2, 2, 2].
Work **Row 3** once more.
Final Row (WS): Purl to last 2 sts, p2tog, pm, p&p5 (5, 6, 6, 6) [6, 7, 7, 7, 7] sts along edge (for first half of Left Sleeve Cap).

5 (5, 6, 6, 6) [6, 7, 7, 7, 7] Left Cap sts
61 (63, 65, 67, 69) [71, 73, 75, 77, 79] Back sts

Slide stitches off needle tips to rest on the cable.
Set these stitches aside, continue to next step without turning.

STEP 4: LEFT FRONT SHOULDER

nM1 = neck increase
Setup Row (WS): Loop cable, p&p12 (13, 14, 14, 15) [17, 17, 18, 19, 19] sts (for Left Front Shoulder) in the cast on of Left Back Shoulder, *and remember to pick up second st in line with faux seam.*
12 (13, 14, 14, 15) [17, 17, 18, 19, 19] Left Front sts
R1 (RS): K8 (8, 9, 9, 10) [11, 11, 12, 12, 12], turn.
R2 (WS): Sl1^, purl to end.
R3: K4 (4, 4, 5) [5, 5, 6, 6, 6], turn.
R4: Sl1^, purl to end.
R5: Knit to 2 sts before loop (working any sl1^ as k1^), sl1wyb, k1, turn.
R6: Purl.
R7: Knit to 2 sts before loop, sl1wyb, k1, turn.
R8: Purl.
R9: K2, nM1R, knit to 2 sts before loop, sl1wyb, k1, turn.
13 (14, 15, 15, 16) [18, 18, 19, 20, 20] Left Front sts
R10: Purl.
Work **Rows 9 & 10** again x 1 (1, 2, 2, 2) [2, 3, 3, 3, 3].
14 (15, 17, 17, 18) [20, 21, 22, 23, 23] Left Front sts

BOX A

sM1 = sleeve increase   **nM1 = neck increase**

RS ROWS

R1: K2, nM1R, (knit to 1 st before m, sl1wyb, sm, sM1L, knit to m, sM1R, sm, sl1wyb) twice, knit to last 2 sts, nM1L, k2

WS ROWS

R2: Purl.

R4: P2, nM1Lp, purl to last 2 sts, nM1Rp, p2.

Final Row (RS): K2, nM1R, knit to 2 sts before loop, ssk, pm, p&k5 (5, 6, 6, 6) [6, 7, 7, 7, 7] sts (for second half of Left Sleeve Cap), knit to m, sm, k1, sl1wyb, knit to last 2 sts, ssk, pm, p&k5 (5, 6, 6, 6) [6, 7, 7, 7, 7] sts (for first half of Right Sleeve Cap).

10 (10, 12, 12, 12) [12, 14, 14, 14, 14] Left Cap sts
5 (5, 6, 6, 6) [6, 7, 7, 7, 7] Right Cap sts
14 (15, 17, 17, 18) [20, 21, 22, 23, 23] Left Front sts
60 (62, 64, 66, 68) [70, 72, 74, 76, 78] Back sts

Slide stitches off needle tips to rest on the cable.
Set these stitches aside, continue to next step without turning.

STEP 5: RIGHT FRONT SHOULDER

nM1 = neck increase

R1 (RS): Loop cable, p&k12 (13, 14, 14, 15) [17, 17, 18, 19, 19] sts (for Right Front Shoulder) in the cast on of Right Back Shoulder, *and remember to pick up second st in line with faux seam.*
12 (13, 14, 14, 15) [17, 17, 18, 19, 19] Right Front sts
R2 (WS): P8 (8, 9, 9, 10) [11, 11, 12, 12, 12], turn.
R3: Sl1^, knit to end.
R4: P4 (4, 4, 4, 5) [5, 5, 6, 6, 6], turn.
R5: Sl1^, knit to end.
R6: Purl to loop (working any sl1^ as p1^), turn.
R7: K1, sl1wyb, knit to end.
R8: Purl to loop, turn.
R9: K1, sl1wyb, knit to last 2 sts, nM1L, k2.
13 (14, 15, 15, 16) [18, 18, 19, 20, 20] Right Front sts
R10: Purl to loop, turn.
Work **Rows 9 & 10** again x 1 (1, 2, 2, 2) [2, 3, 3, 3, 3].
14 (15, 17, 17, 18) [20, 21, 22, 23, 23] Right Front sts
Work **Row 9** once more.
15 (16, 18, 18, 19) [21, 22, 23, 24, 24] Right Front sts
Final Row (WS): Purl to 2 sts before loop, p2tog, pm, p&p5 (5, 6, 6, 6) [6, 7, 7, 7, 7] sts (for second half of Right Sleeve Cap), purl to end.

10 (10, 12, 12, 12) [12, 14, 14, 14, 14] sts for each Sleeve Cap
14 (15, 17, 17, 18) [20, 21, 22, 23, 23] sts for each Front
60 (62, 64, 66, 68) [70, 72, 74, 76, 78] Back sts

STEP 6: SLEEVE CAPS & BODY

You will now increase for the sleeves and neck.
(See Helpful Table for an overview of all increases.)

REFER TO **BOX A** FOR ROW INSTRUCTIONS
Work **Rows 1 & 2** x 1 (1, 2, 1, 1) [1, 1, 1, 1, 1].
12 (12, 16, 14, 14) [14, 16, 16, 16, 16] Sleeve sts
15 (16, 19, 18, 19) [21, 22, 23, 24, 24] sts for each Front

Works **Rows 1 & 4** x 2 (2, 1, 2, 2) [2, 2, 2, 2, 2].
16 (16, 18, 18, 18) [18, 20, 20, 20, 20] Sleeve sts
19 (20, 21, 22, 23) [25, 26, 27, 28, 28] sts for each Front

STEP 7: JOIN FRONTS TO KNIT IN THE ROUND

Joining Row-Round 1 (RS): K2, nM1R, (knit to 1 st before m, sl1wyb, sm, sM1L, knit to m, sM1R, sm, sl1wyb) twice, knit to last 2 sts, nM1L, pm (=Nm), k2, *(turn work over over so WS is facing) borrow last st for cast on loop,* crochet cast on 21 (21, 21, 21, 21) [19, 19, 19, 19, 21] sts, *replace loop onto LN (make a final chain st but not around the needle), turn work over so RS is facing,* join to Left Front, knit to m, sm.

You are now at Left Front Sleeve.

18 (18, 20, 20, 20) [20, 22, 22, 22, 22] Sleeve sts
61 (63, 65, 67, 69) [71, 73, 75, 77, 79] Front sts
60 (62, 64, 66, 68) [70, 72, 74, 76, 78] Back sts
Joining Round 2: Knit to Nm, rm, ssk, knit to end of cast on, make loop in bar and place on LN, k2tog (the first st of Left Front and the loop), knit to 1 st before m.

18 (18, 20, 20, 20) [20, 22, 22, 22, 22] Sleeve sts
60 (62, 64, 66, 68) [70, 72, 74, 76, 78] Front sts
60 (62, 64, 66, 68) [70, 72, 74, 76, 78] Back sts

STEP 8: SLEEVE & BODY INCREASES
Continue to work sleeve increases and also introduce body increases.
The round begins 1 stitch before Left Front Sleeve marker.

REFER TO **BOX B** FOR ROUND INSTRUCTIONS
Work **Rnds 1 & 2** x 9 (10, 9, 9, 8) [9, 8, 9, 8, 9].
36 (38, 38, 38, 36) [38, 38, 40, 38, 40] Sleeve sts

SIZE 32 ONLY
Work **Rnds 1 & 4**.
40 Sleeve sts

BOX B

sM1 = sleeve increase   bM1 = body increase

ODD (SLIP-STITCH) ROUNDS
   Rnd 1: (Sl1wyb, sm, sM1L, knit to m, sM1R, sm, sl1wyb, knit to 1 st before m) twice.

   Rnd 3: (bM1L, sl1wyb, sm, sM1L, knit to m, sM1R, sm, sl1wyb, bM1R, knit to 1 st before m) twice.

EVEN (PLAIN) ROUNDS
   Rnd 2: Knit.

   Rnd 4: (K1, sm, sM1L, knit to m, sM1R, sm, knit to 1 st before m) twice.

   Rnd 6: (bM1L, k1, sm, sM1L, knit to m, sM1R, sm, k1, bM1R, knit to 1 st before m) twice.

ALL SIZES

INTRODUCE BODY INCREASES
Work **Rnds 3 & 2** x 0 (0, 0, 2, 3) [3, 3, 3, 3, 3].
40 (38, 38, 42, 42) [44, 44, 46, 44, 46] Sleeve sts
60 (62, 64, 70, 74) [76, 78, 80, 82, 84] Front sts
60 (62, 64, 70, 74) [76, 78, 80, 82, 84] Back sts

Work **Rnds 3 & 4** x 2 (3, 3, 2, 2) [2, 2, 1, 1, 1].
48 (50, 50, 50, 50) [52, 52, 50, 48, 50] Sleeve sts
64 (68, 70, 74, 78) [80, 82, 82, 84, 86] Front sts
64 (68, 70, 74, 78) [80, 82, 82, 84, 86] Back sts

Work **Rnds 3 & 6** x 0 (0, 0, 0, 0) [0, 0, 1, 2, 2].
48 (50, 50, 50, 50) [52, 52, 54, 56, 58] Sleeve sts
64 (68, 70, 74, 78) [80, 82, 86, 92, 94] Front sts
64 (68, 70, 74, 78) [80, 82, 86, 92, 94] Back sts

Work **Rnd 3**.
50 (52, 52, 52, 52) [54, 54, 56, 58, 60] Sleeve sts
66 (70, 72, 76, 80) [82, 84, 88, 94, 96] Front sts
66 (70, 72, 76, 80) [82, 84, 88, 94, 96] Back sts

Final Rnd: Knit to 2 sts before Left Front Sleeve m.

STEP 9: SEPARATING SLEEVES & BODY
Separation Rnd 1: *Pm, k2, rm, place all sts to next m on holder (= sleeve sts), rm, *(turn work over so WS is facing) borrow last st for cast on loop,* crochet cast on 5 (5, 6, 7, 7) [8, 9, 9, 9, 9] sts, pm, cast on 4 (4, 5, 6, 6) [7, 8, 8, 8, 8] sts, *replace loop onto LN (make a final chain st but not around the needle), turn work over so RS is facing*, knit to 2 sts before m, work from * to * once more, knit to m.

You are now at Left Front Sleeve.

75 (79, 83, 89, 93) [97, 101, 105, 111, 113] Front sts
75 (79, 83, 89, 93) [97, 101, 105, 111, 113] Back sts

Separation Rnd 2: *Rm, ssk, knit to m, sm, p1, knit to end of underarm cast on, make loop in bar and place on LN, k2tog (next st and loop), knit to m*, work from * to * once more.
74 (78, 82, 88, 92) [96, 100, 104, 110, 112] Front sts
74 (78, 82, 88, 92) [96, 100, 104, 110, 112] Back sts

STEP 10: BODY & SHAPING
Continue in stocking stitch over body stitches only.
The round begins under Left Sleeve.

Note: *Two stitches under each arm are worked in a cord pattern that creates a faux side seam (TwSl on alternate rounds).*

AT THE SAME TIME
Please read through the entire step before proceeding, as a few things happen at the same time or overlap.

- Optional Bust Darts
- Waist Shaping (begins before or just after the darts, depending on where you place them)
- Decorative cords on lower body

REFER TO **BOX C** FOR ROUND INSTRUCTIONS

Work **Rnds 1 & 2** to 5 cm/ 2" from underarm.

AT THE SAME TIME OPTIONAL BUST DARTS
Optional Bust Darts may be placed here or a bit lower. See BOX D.
   Note: *If you are trying to stretch your skeins, this is a good place to set the body aside to work the sleeves before finishing the body.*

AT THE SAME TIME WAIST SHAPING
Note: *For a more relaxed fit, refer to BOX E (see next page) for shaping*

At 5 cm / 2" from underarm, begin waist shaping.

WAIST DECREASES
Work Decrease **Rnd 3 & Rnd 2**.
72 (76, 80, 86, 90) [94, 98, 102, 108, 110] Front/Back sts

Continue with **Rnds 1 & 2**, working **Decrease Rnd 3** on the next 10 (10, 12, 12, 12) [12, 12, 12, 14, 14]th rnd.
70 (74, 78, 84, 88) [92, 96, 100, 106, 108] Front/Back sts

Work **Rnds 2 & 1** x 4 (4, 5, 5, 5) [5, 5, 5, 6, 6].

INTRODUCE CORDS ON FRONT **&** BACK

On the next round, add 3 cords in Front and 3 in Back evenly spaced along the round, for a total of 8. One cord each is at centre Front and Back.

Next Rnd: Sm, TwSl, k16 (17, 18, 19, 20) [21, 22, 23, 25, 25], {pm, TwSl, k15 (16, 17, 19, 20) [21, 22, 23, 24, 25]} x 2, pm, TwSl, k16 (17, 18, 19, 20) [21, 22, 23, 25, 25], sm, TwSl, k16 (17, 18, 19, 20) [21, 22, 23, 25, 25], {pm, TwSl, k15 (16, 17, 19, 20) [21, 22, 23, 24, 25]} x 2, pm, TwSl, k16 (17, 18, 19, 20) [21, 22, 23, 25, 25].
Work **Decrease Rnd 3 & Rnd 2**.
68 (72, 76, 82, 86) [90, 94, 98, 104, 106] Front/Back sts

BOX C

BODY **&** SHAPING
Rnd 1: Knit.

Rnd 2: (Sm, TwSl, knit to m) to end of round.

Decreases and increases are made on plain knit rounds.
Decrease Rnd 3: Sm, (k2, k2tog, knit to 2 sts before m, ssk) twice. *4 sts decreased*

Increase Rnd 4: Sm, k2, RLI, knit to Centre Back m, LLI, sm, k2, RLI, knit to side m, LLI, sm, k2, RLI, knit to Centre Front m, LLI, sm, k2, RLI, knit to side m, LLI. *8 sts increased*

Increase Rnd 5: (Sm, k2, RLI, knit to side m, LLI) twice. *4 sts increased*

BOX D

OPTIONAL BUST DARTS
Place your darts at approx 5 (6, 10, 10) cm / 2 (2.25, 4, 4)" from underarm or where desired:
For placement of darts, see Hints & Tips
(Remember to place them in Front!)

Smallish (Middling, Busty, Wowza!)
Worked over 8 (12, 16, 20) rows, adds approx 3.5 (5, 6.5, 8.5) cm / 1.5 (2, 2.5, 3.25)"

R1 (RS): Sm, knit to m, sm, knit to 22 (22, 26, 30) sts before left underarm m, turn.
R2 (WS): Sl1^, pm, purl to 24 (24, 28, 32) sts before right underarm m, turn.
R3 (RS): Sl1^, pm, knit to m, rm, k1^, k5 (4, 3, 3), turn.
R4: Sl1^, pm, purl to m, rm, p1^, p5 (4, 3, 3), turn.
Work **Rows 3 & 4** again x 2 (4, 6, 8).

Final Row (RS): Sl1^, pm, knit to m, rm, knit to m.
Resume working in the round.
Next Rnd: Sm, TwSl, knit to m, sm, TwSl, knit to 1 st before m, k1^, rm, k1^, knit to m.

WORK STRAIGHT

Work Rnds 1 & 2 for 4 (4, 5, 5, 5) [5, 5, 5, 5, 5] cm / / 1.5 (1.5, 2, 2, 2) [2, 2, 2, 2, 2]"

WAIST INCREASES

Increases take place at each side, at Centre Front, and Centre Back.

Work **Increase Rnd 4 & Rnd 2**.

72 (76, 80, 86, 90) [94, 98, 102, 108, 110] Front/Back sts

Continue with **Rnds 1 & 2**, working another **Increase Rnd 4** on the next 14 (14, 14, 18, 18) [18, 18, 18, 18, 18]th rnd.

76 (80, 84, 90, 94) [98, 102, 106, 112, 114] Front/Back sts

Work to 31.5 (31.5, 32.5, 33, 34) [34, 35, 34, 35, 35.5] cm / 12.5 (12.5, 12.75, 13, 13.5) [13.5, 13.75, 13.5, 13.75, 14]" from underarm or to 2.5 cm / 1" from desired length.

BOX E

WIDER BODY

Follow the general instructions and BOX C Rounds but make just one Decrease round and make more Increase rounds. Increases take place at each side, at Centre Front, and Centre Back.

At 5 cm / 2" from underarm, work **Decrease Rnd 3** & **Rnd 2**.

72 (76, 80, 86, 90) [94, 98, 102, 108, 110] Front/Back sts

Continue with **Rnds 1 & 2**, working **Increase Rnd 5** on every 10 (10, 12, 12, 12) [12, 12, 12, 14, 14]th rnd x 2.

76 (80, 84, 90, 94) [98, 102, 106, 112, 114] Front/Back sts

INTRODUCE CORDS ON FRONT & BACK

Next Rnd: Sm, TwSl, k17 (18, 19, 21, 22) [23, 24, 25, 26, 27], {pm, TwSl, k17 (18, 19, 20, 21) [22, 23, 24, 26, 26]} x 2, pm, TwSl, k17 (18, 19, 21, 22) [23, 24, 25, 26, 27], sm, TwSl, k17 (18, 19, 21, 22) [23, 24, 25, 26, 27], {pm, TwSl, k17 (18, 19, 20, 21) [22, 23, 24, 26, 26]} x 2, pm, TwSl, k17 (18, 19, 21, 22) [23, 24, 25, 26, 27].

Work **Rnd 2.**

Continue with **Rnds 1 & 2**, working **Increase Rnd 4** on every 18 (18, 20, 20, 20) [20, 20, 22, 22, 22]th rnd x 2.

84 (88, 92, 98, 102) [106, 110, 114, 120, 122] Front/Back sts

Work to Hem and work Lined Hem (STEP 11).

84 (88, 92, 98, 102) [106, 110, 114, 120, 122] Front/Back Lining sts

Do not cut the yarn.

Note: *If you are adding length, you may wish to include one more round of increases.*

STEP 11: LINED HEM

LINING

Hem lining stitches are picked up on WS (see Tutorial section). Slide stitches off needle tips to rest on the cable.
Take working **MC** to WS. With smaller (4 mm / US 6) needle on WS and going counterclockwise, p&k sts in every bar *between* all sts, take **MC** to RS.

76 (80, 84, 90, 94) [98, 102, 106, 112, 114] Front/Back Lining sts

Join DK (or Sport or Fingering) **CC**.
On WS (along inside of sweater and downwards, knit 5 rounds.
Cut **CC**.
Slide sts off needle tips to rest on cable, set Lining sts aside.

HEM

With **MC** and 4 mm (US 6) needle, work 6 rnds as set (with cords), or to *slightly* longer than Lining, take **MC** to WS.

LINING

With **MC**, knit one round, take **MC** to RS.

Note: *If necessary, work an additional hem-round to make hem slightly longer before binding off.*

BIND OFF

Weave in any loose ends at hem.
From RS, bind off hem sts together with lining sts using 3-Needle Bind Off and keeping an even tension.

STEP 12: SLEEVES

Place 50 (52, 52, 52, 52) [54, 54, 56, 58, 60] Sleeve sts from holder back on larger (5 mm / US 8) needle. Join **MC** at right side of gap, p&k4 (4, 5, 6, 6) [7, 8, 8, 8, 8] sts along the first half of the underarm cast on, pm, p&k5 (5, 6, 7, 7) [8, 9, 9, 9, 9] sts more along second half of underarm, knit to m.

59 (61, 63, 65, 65) [69, 71, 73, 75, 77] sts

REFER TO **BOX F** FOR ROUND INSTRUCTIONS

Work **Rnd 1** to 5 cm / 2" from underarm.

SLEEVE DECREASES

Work **Decrease Rnd**.

57 (59, 61, 63, 63) [67, 69, 71, 73, 75] sts

BOX F

Continue with **Rnd 1**, working **Decrease Rnd** every 11 (10, 9, 8, 8) [7, 7, 7, 7, 6]th round again x 6 (7, 8, 9, 9) [11, 11, 11, 11, 12].
45 (45, 45, 45, 45) [45, 47, 49, 51, 51] sts

Work to 36 (36, 37, 38, 38) [38, 38, 39, 39, 39] cm /14.25 (14.25, 14.5, 15, 15) [15, 15, 15.25, 15.25, 15.25]" from underarm or 11 cm / 4.25" from desired sleeve length.

SIDEWAYS RIB CUFF
The cuff is worked sideways and attached clockwise on every RS row. Attach to approx 3 of every 4 sleeve sts (attach into 1st, 2nd, then into 3rd & 4th together with an sssk).
After the winding cast on, begin with a RS.

Sl1 from RN to LN. Onto LN, provisionally wind on 26 sts.
R1 (RS): Ksk, (p2, yo, p1, yo) x 7, p1, ssk (last cuff st with one sleeve st).
Rows 2, 4, 6 (WS): Sl1wyf, k1, (p3tog, k2) x 7, sks.
R3: Ksk, (p2, yo, p1, yo) x 7, p1, ssk (last cuff st with one sleeve st).
R5: Ksk, (p2, yo, p1, yo) x 7, p1, sssk (last cuff st with 2 sleeve sts).
Keep working **Rows 1 – 6** until 1 sleeve st remains, ending with a RS row.
Final Row (WS): Sl1wyf, k1, (p3tog, k2) x 7, sl1wyf, p2togtbl.

Join the cuff with a 3-Needle Bind Off from RS, working the final bind off together with the final sleeve st.

STEP 13: SIDEWAYS RIB COLLAR
The folded collar is worked inside out (RS of rib is on inside) and attached at the end of every RS row, going counterclockwise.
Beginning at Left Shoulder, pick up and attach collar on WS around the back, then along front.
Along Back, attach to every second row in the slanting parts, and 4 of every 5 stitches along the straight parts. Along Front, attach to 2 of every 3 rows in the slanting parts and every stitch along the cast on.
Approx 72 (72, 72, 76, 76) [72, 76, 76, 76, 80] sts

With **MC** and 4 mm (US 6) needle, provisionally wind on 33 sts.
R1 (RS): Ksk, (p2, yo, p1, yo) x 9, p2, sl1wyf, yb, p&k1, sl2 to LN, ssk.
R2 (WS): Sl1wyb, (k2, p3tog) to last 5 sts, k2, sks.
Keep working **Rows 1 & 2** until 1 collar pick up remains, ending with a RS row.
Final Row (WS): Sl1wyb, (k2, p3tog) to last 5 sts, k2, sl1wyf, p2togtbl.

Join the collar from its RS (inside of collar) with a 3-Needle Bind Off (see Tutorial section), working the final bind off together with the final picked up collar st.

FINISH
Weave in loose ends. Soak and block lightly to measurements, taking care not to stretch the collar and cuff ribbing.

Rows from Cast On

Short Rows

Sleeve Increases | Body Increases | Neck Increases

This is a sizing chart with columns grouped by size (32, 34, 36, 38, 40, 42, 44, 46, 48, 50), each with "Sleeve Increases", "Body Increases", and "Neck Increases" sub-columns, and outer columns labeled "Rows from Cast On" (odd rows 15–59).

Legend:

- Sleeve Increases
- Underarm cast on
- Body Increases
- Neck Increases
- Front cast on

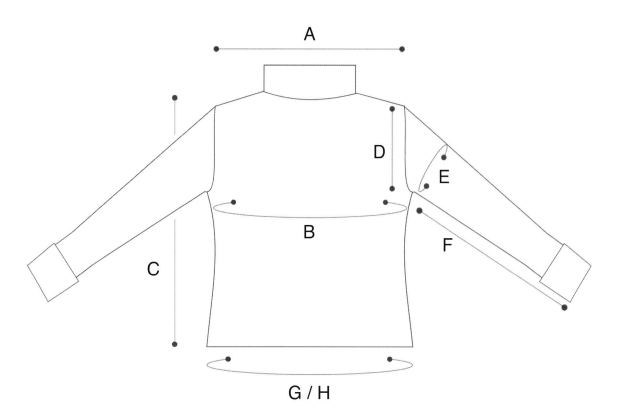

ARANARANJA GARMENT MEASUREMENTS

	32	34	36	38	40	42	44	46	48	50
A – Shoulder Width (cm)	33.5	34.5	35.5	36.5	38	39	40	41	42	43.5
in	13.25	13.5	14	14.25	15	15.25	15.75	16.25	16.5	17.25
B – Bust (cm)	82	86.5	91	98	102	106.5	111	115.5	122	124.5
in	32.25	34	35.75	38.5	40.25	42	43.75	45.5	48	49
C – Length (cm)	54	55	56	57	58	59	60	60	61	62
in	21.25	21.75	22	22.5	22.75	23.25	23.5	23.5	24	24.5
D – Armhole depth (cm)	18	19	19	19.5	19.5	20.5	20.5	21.5	21.5	22
in	7	7.5	7.5	7.5	7.5	8	8	8.5	8.5	8.5
E – Sleeve circumf (cm)	33	34	35	36	36	38.5	39.5	40.5	41.5	43
in	13	13.5	13.75	14.25	14.25	15.25	15.5	16	16.25	17
F – Sleeve seam (cm)	47	47	48	49	49	49	49	50	50	50
in	18.5	18.5	19	19.25	19.25	19.25	19.25	19.75	19.75	19.75
G – Hem circumf (cm)	84.5	89	93.5	100	104.5	109	113.5	118	124.5	126.5
in	33.25	35	36.75	39.25	41.25	43	44.75	46.5	49	49.75
H – Hem with extra sts (cm)	93.5	98	102	109	113.5	118	122	126.5	133.5	135.5
in	36.75	38.5	40.25	43	44.75	46.5	48	49.75	52.5	53.25

This is a versatile and elegant laceweight version of Mayhem cardigan with the same overlapping fronts, and a squarish, slightly swingy shape that is easy to wear. It can look formal or entirely casual with its set-in tailored sleeves. The easy four-row stitch pattern makes for compulsive knitting.

This is the DK version of Black Basalt, an everyday wardrobe staple, your 'always-reach-for' basic cardigan.

The blue cardigan features a more generous neckline and a more rear-warming length. An optional contrasting triangle detail on the cuff adds interest without making a big statement.

Tutorials

Tutorials :: Ziggurat Steps

The Ziggurat Steps are usually the same in all Ziggurat patterns.
Pullovers and Cardigans differ only a little.
A few Ziggurat pullovers start with the collar and proceed differently, but still follow the same principle.

Some zigging and zagging builds and shapes each shoulder, and also creates lovely sleeve caps for the no-sew set-in sleeves. Short rows shape the shoulders and the curving back neckline.

Steps 1 – 3 are the same for Pullovers and Cardigans.
Steps 4 & 5: CARDIGANS add a Buttonband (4a) that is knitted along with the Fronts.

STEP 1 Cast on stitches for Back and knit Right Back Shoulder.

STEP 2 Knit Left Back Shoulder.

STEP 3 Knit back and forth across the Back.
These rows create the Sleeve Cap edges – fewer rows make a narrower Sleeve Cap, more rows make a wider Sleeve Cap.
At the end of Step 3: Pick up stitches for the first half of Left Sleeve Cap (see Tutorial for Picking Up Stitches).

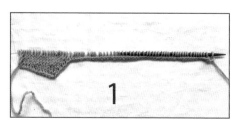

1. Cast on & Right Back Shoulder.

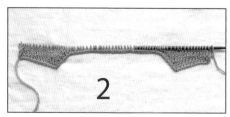

2. Left Back Shoulder done.

3. Working back and forth across the back.
Final Row (WS): Pick up & purl stitches for first half (A) of Left Cap.
NOTE: Pick up & purl is done from Right Side. (See Step 3 detail for picking up sts.)

STEP 3 DETAIL

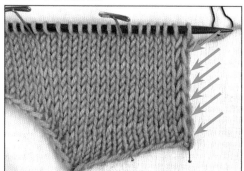

1. Final Row (WS – pick up is worked from RS)
The arrows point to the line of slipped stitches that will frame the cap. (The outermost edge stitch has rolled under and is not visible.) Pick up next to the slipped stitches and inside the complete outermost stitch.

2. Work from left to right. Keep the loops loose so you can see where to pick up next. Pick up & knit stitches and place loops on LN. Note the double bars between the picked up & knitted stitches. Also note that there is nothing between the slipped faux seam stitches and the picked up loops.

3. All stitches have been picked up & knitted and placed on LN. Time to tighten them up. This completes Step 3.

TIP The trick to get neat Caps is to keep edge stitches nice and snug. After working the three first stitches on any row, go back and pull on those three stitches to tighten them up a little. Do this from the first row in Step 1.

PICKING UP CAP STITCHES ON A WS ROW FROM RS

The first cap stitch pick up takes place on a WS (at the end of Step 3, see detail on previous page). Turn work over to work from RS. Work from Left to Right. As stitches are picked up & knitted, place them on LN. Keep stitches long and loose until all stitches are picked up. This makes it easier to see where the next and following stitches will be picked up. When all Cap stitches have been picked up, go back and tighten them by tugging and tightening until all sit snugly on LN.

STEP 4 (WS continued but working from RS) Loop cable, pick up stitches for Left Front Shoulder and knit Left Front. CARDIGANS: Cast on for Buttonband. At the end of Step 4:
Pick up stitches for second half of Left Sleeve Cap, knit all the way around to Right Shoulder, pick up stitches for first half of Right Sleeve Cap.
STEP 4a *CARDIGANS: Knit and attach Buttonband around the neck to Right Shoulder.*
STEP 5 Loop cable, pick up stitches for Right Front Shoulder and knit Right Front.
At the end of Step 5: Pick up stitches for second half of Right Sleeve Cap, work around to Left Front.

The tricksy bits are over. All stitches sit on one circular without loops. Markers are in place for the increases that begin in the next step.

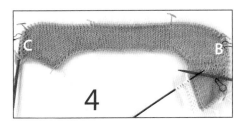

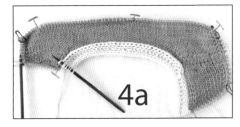

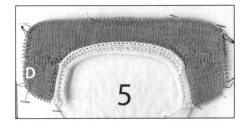

4. (WS continued but working from RS) Loop cable, pick up & knit stitches (from RS) for Left Front Shoulder. On final row: Pick up & knit stitches for second half of Left Cap (B), knit across the back to Right Shoulder, pick up & knit stitches for the first half of Right Cap (C).
CARDIGANS: Cast on Buttonband stitches to work Buttonband along with Left Front Shoulder.

4a. CARDIGANS only: Before Working Step 5, knit and attach the Buttonband around the back neck to Right Shoulder.
Start at the provisional cast on at Left Shoulder.
CC Buttonbands: Use the ball already attached in Step 4.
MC Buttonbands: Join new MC.

5. Continuing from where you stopped in Step 4, loop cable, pick up & knit Right Shoulder sts.
CARDIGANS only: knit Buttonband sts, then knit Buttonband along with Right Front.
Final Row: Make decrease, pick up & purl stitches for second half of Right Cap (D), purl across the Back and around to Left Front.
At the end of this step, the tricksy bits are over and all stitches sit happily together on the circular needle without loops.

STEP 4 DETAIL

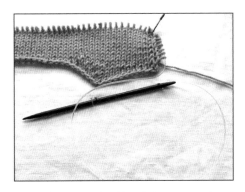

1. To pick up Front Shoulder stitches you need to LOOP the circular cable.

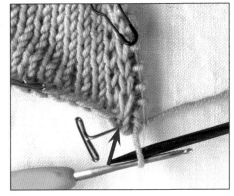

2. You are working from Left to Right.
The only tricky thing here is to make sure that the SECOND stitch for Left Front Shoulder is picked up at the bottom of the slipped-stitch column (pink arrow). For the first stitch it is not necessary to have two strands of yarn on the outside. Only take care not to distort the last Cap stitch nor the second Shoulder stitch that goes at the bottom of the slipped stitch column.
A crochet hook can be used to fetch the yarn. (Especially with thinner yarns it may be easier to use a hook.)

Tutorials :: Ziggurat Steps

STEP 4 DETAIL (CONTINUED)

3. Left Front Shoulder The important second stitch has been picked up at bottom of the slipped stitch column.

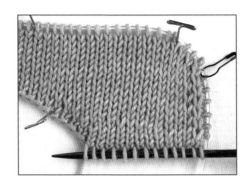

4. Pick up & knit for Left Front is complete. CARDIGANS with Buttonband: Cast on stitches for Buttonband at this point. See Buttonband Tutorial.

5. Photo shows how the chain from the cast on ends up on the Wrong Side (except on the Vaudeville Tunic, where it is a Right Side feature).

6. Final Row (RS) Picking up & knitting stitches for the second half of Left Cap is more straightforward than the previous pick up.

7. Second half of Left Cap Needle tip is inserted inside the complete outermost stitch (2 strands of yarn). Pick up & knit the first stitch here. Pink arrow points to placement of second stitch, next to the "V" of the faux seam stitch.

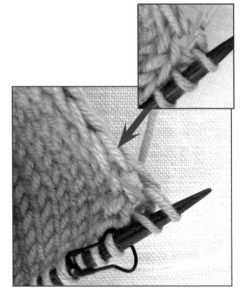

8. Second half of Left Cap Two stitches picked up & knitted. Pink arrow points to placement of third stitch, next to the "V" of the faux seam stitch. Blue arrow points to double bar between stitches.

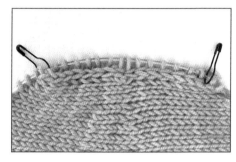

9. All stitches for the second half of the Left Cap have been picked up.

Slide stitches from first half to LN tip to knit them. The markers are in place for sleeve increases (later, in Step 6).

A judgement call: If there is a clear gap before LN stitches, pick up & knit an additional stitch, keeping the faux seam column tidy.

What to do with the extra stitch? Either nothing, or omit the M1R Sleeve Cap increase on the first Increase Row in Step 6.

10. Both halves of Left Sleeve Cap stitches sitting on the cable (markers in place for sleeve increases in Step 6). Ready to knit across Back to Right Sleeve Cap.

11. Step 4 is complete: Stitches for first half of Right Cap have been picked up and moved to sit on the cable. Ready for Step 5.

STEP 5 DETAIL

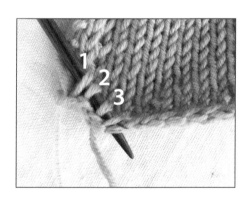

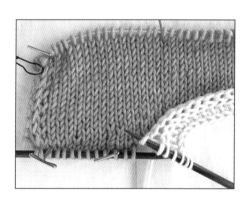

1. **Step 5:** Loop cable, pick up & knit stitches in Right Front shoulder. Again, it is the SECOND stitch that needs careful placing at the bottom of the faux seam column (pink arrow). Blue arrow points to where the first stitch goes – usually in the knot from the cast on (use a crochet hook to wiggle into it). Alternatively, find another spot for the first stitch that neither distorts the Cap stitches nor the next, SECOND stitch.

2. Three stitches picked up & knitted. Needle tip is inserted through double bars of the next cast on stitch to pick up & knit a fourth stitch. (Use a crochet hook if you find that easier.)

3. Right Front Shoulder pick up is complete. Knit Right Front. CARDIGANS: Knit Buttonband along with Right Front.

Tutorials :: Ziggurat Steps

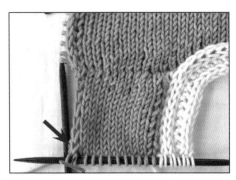

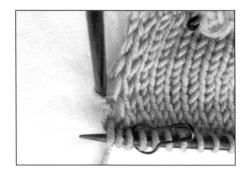

4. Final Row (WS) seen from RS. Again the picking up is done from RS, going from left to right and placing loops on LN. Pick up stitches next to the slipped faux seam column and inside the complete outermost stitch.

5. Final Row (WS) working from RS. Three stitches have been picked up & knitted and placed on LN. RN is inserted to pick up & knit a fourth stitch. Note the double bars between stitches. Also note the empty space between needle and the faux seam stitch.

6. The picking up for Right Sleeve Cap is complete. Time to tighten the stitches on LN. Turn work over to WS to complete the Final WS row.

A GENERAL NOTE ON PICKING UP CAP STITCHES

When picking up, insert needle tip (or crochet hook) next to the first complete slipped stitch (the faux seam stitch) and also inside the complete outermost stitch, fetch the yarn and place the loop on LN.

Continue to pick up & knit along the edge, inside the outermost stitch and next to the slipped stitch column, making sure there are two bars of yarn between the picked up stitches and two strands of yarn outside them.

Keep loops loose until the picking up is complete. If you tighten stitches as you go, the fabric gets distorted. This makes it difficult to see where to pick up the next stitch.

Note: If space seems tight and you cannot find a way to fit in all stitches, try picking up the first stitch closer to the marker.

This is a judgement call. Sometimes I start with the second 'V' which is the first *complete* slipped stitch, sometimes with the first 'V' if it looks better visually or to squeeze in an extra Sleeve stitch.

SPECIAL CASE: WAYS TO MODIFY

The usual Cap pick up & knit, picks up next to every slipped (or faux seam) stitch. In some patterns more stitches are picked up.

You can also pick up more stitches than instructed, to add more room in the upper sleeve.

SPECIAL CASE: PICKING UP ON A WS ROW

(Step 3 Final Row & Step 5 Final Row) The pick up & purl on WS rows is always made from the RS. Turn work over to work from RS. Work from left to right to pick up & knit stitches and place loops on LN. Again, keep the loops loose so you can see where to pick up next.

The completed pick up for the Right Cap seen from WS. (The yarn end is from the cast on in Step 1.)

The completed pick up for the Right Cap seen from RS.

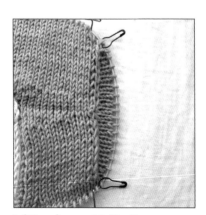

Left Cap a few rows into Step 6.

MODIFICATION POSSIBILITIES

NECKLINE

To make the neckline deeper:

Spread out the neck increases and cast on to join fronts later (the exact number of rows is up to you).

BUST

To accommodate a larger or smaller bust size than your Ziggurat size:

Note the total number of back stitches for 1–2 sizes up or down. For a larger bust, pencil in extra body increases either by starting them earlier and/or squeezing in some extra every-row increases toward the end.

For a smaller bust, omit some every-row body increases and/or start the increases later.

SLEEVE

To create a wider upper sleeve:

Add sleeve increases on WS rows towards the end.

Another way to add more width for sleeve:

The usual Cap pick up & knit, picks up next to every slipped (or faux seam) stitch. You can also pick up more stitches than instructed to add more room in the upper sleeve.

ARMHOLE DEPTH

To shorten the armhole depth without changing any other measurements:

Squeeze some of the last increases together. That is, add Sleeve increases to WS rows and perhaps start the body increases earlier than indicated, and/or make more every-row body increases.

HOW TO DETERMINE ARMHOLE DEPTH (CM)

Total Rows from Cast on minus the Short Rows divided by row gauge.

For size 38 in the sample Helpful Table columns (see page 195):

10 cm = 26 rows

1 cm = 2.6 rows

Rows from Cast On to Underarm Cast On = 58

Short rows = 4

Armhole depth = (58-4)/2.6 = 20.5 cm

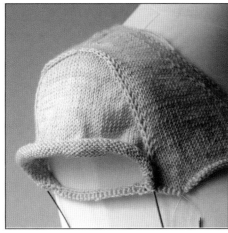

The nicely sculpted sleeve caps at the end of Step 7. All increases are complete and Sleeves have been separated from Body. Design: Sweet Laurel cardigan (SweetGeorgia DK, Laurel)

Design: Chatoyant with underarm gusset (Walk Collection DK Luxe, Cement).

Shoulder with Sleeve Cap and Neck increases in progress.
Rohrspatz & Wollmeise Pure (Gioia, Natur, 13AL)

Tutorials :: Helpful Table

USING THE HELPFUL TABLE IN STEP 6
INCREASING FOR SLEEVE CAP, FRONT NECK, AND BODY

Everything you need to knit a Ziggurat sweater is written out in the pattern instructions.
The Helpful Table is provided only for extra convenience, to be helpful!
I created it as a visual aid for my own design process and it became a trademark feature of all Ziggurat patterns from the start.

The Helpful Table can be your good friend, especially if you wish to modify a Ziggurat pattern. Or design your own. But also just for carefree knitting.

The stitch counts in the squares reflect the total after completing a particular row (or round, when working in the round).

When working flat:
  Odd rows = RS
  Even rows = WS

Most increases take place on RS/odd rows.
Sleeve Cap faux seam stitch is slipped only on RS/even rows.
Most WS/odd rows are plainly purled (blank squares).

All Helpful Tables are colour coded the same way, which is also reflected in the written instructions.

- **Red** squares and red font: **Sleeve increases**
- Green squares and green font: Neck increases
- **Blue** squares and blue font: **Body increases**
- Yellow squares: Front cast on
- Orange squares: Underarm cast on
- Pink squares and pink font: Buttonholes

nM1	neck increase	1 or 2, sometimes 3 stitches in from front edge (mostly 2 sts in)
sM1	sleeve increase	Between the sleeve markers, next to marker
bM1	body increase	1 or 2 stitches away from sleeve marker (mostly 1 st away)
L	Left-leaning	The photo illustration opposite indicates where to use Left-leaning or Right-leaning for each increase.
R	Right-leaning	

WHERE to slip the faux seam stitches for Sleeve Caps

Sl1wyb 4 times per Row/Round:
Next to (outside) each sleeve marker Slip faux seam st on RS rows only
(and/or every second round)

Because all Ziggurats proceed in the same manner, once you have made it through Step 5, most of Step 6 can be knitted by glancing at the Helpful Table every now and then.
It tells you, for example, how many sleeve increases you need to make before body increases begin, how many neck stitches you should have before joining to knit in the round or turning the Buttonbands for cardigans, and so on. And because all Right Side rows are usually the same, and most Wrong Side rows are plainly purled, you can knit away without consulting the instructions until something new needs to happen – increases on WS rows, joining to knit in the round, and so on.

WHERE

All increases are written out in the instructions and they are made in virtually the same place in all ZIggurat patterns.

This means that once you have knitted one Ziggurat pattern, you will be familiar with the rhythm of the rows or rounds and where to place any increases.
It also means that the Helpful Table is even more helpful; for with the knowledge of where a particular increase is made, you can read off the Helpful Table on which rows or rounds to make it and how often.
See BOX on next page for how to read the table.

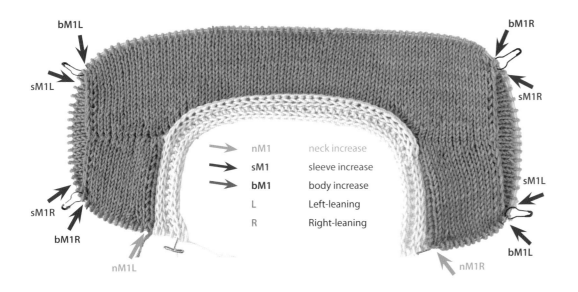

nM1	neck increase		
sM1	sleeve increase		
bM1	body increase		
L	Left-leaning		
R	Right-leaning		

HOW TO READ THE TABLE

Reading size 38 in our table, we see that after 4 neck increases on every RS row, a final increase is made on the next WS row where stitches are cast on for Fronts (actually picked up in Buttonband tabs as this is a cardigan). You will need to refer to the written Buttonband instructions.

After that it is plain sailing until there are 38 Sleeve stitches as you keep making Sleeve increases on every RS row and purl every WS row (making no increases). On the following RS row, start a 3-row buttonhole (refer to pattern for buttonhole instructions).

When the buttonhole is complete, there are 42 Sleeve stitches (Row 47 from cast on).

Continue to make sleeve increases until there are 46 sleeve stitches (Row 51 from cast on). On the next RS row, make sleeve increases and body increases. There are now 48 sleeve stitches and 80 back stitches. Over the next 4 rows make sleeve and body increases on every row. There are now 56 sleeve stitches and 88 back stitches. Purl a final row without increases. On the next RS row separate sleeves from body stitches and cast on 12 stitches for each underarm.

Legend:
- Sleeve increases
- Body increases
- Neck increases
- Front pick up
- Underarm cast on
- Buttonhole

Rows from Cast On	Short Rows	Sleeve increases (36)	Body increases (36)	Neck increases (36)	Sleeve increases (38)	Body increases (38)	Neck increases (38)
65	4						
63							
61					**38**		
59					12		
57		**36**			56	88	
		10			54	86	
55		56	86		52	84	
		54	84		50	82	
53		52	82		48	80	
		50					
51		48	80		46		
		46					
49		44	78		44		
47		42			42		
45		40			40		
43		38			38		
41		36			36		
39		34			34		
37		32			32		
35		30			30		
33		28			28		
31		26	12		26	12	
			12	29		12	30
29		24		28	24		29
27		22		27	22		28
25		20		26	20		27
23		18		25	18		26
		36			**38**		
21							

Tutorials :: Hints & Tips

HINTS & TIPS

SIZING & FIT

For best fit, choose size based on your **shoulder width less 1 cm / 0.25 "** (see Schematic and Table of Measurements for each pattern).
Base your initial choice on a fitted shoulder Ziggurat, then select the size of a semi-dropped shoulder Ziggurat based on that.

That said, if you normally wear a standard size 44 and it usually fits you, then choose that size also for your Ziggurat sweater. If shop-bought clothes are typically too big over the shoulders but fail to accommodate your bust, then choose a Ziggurat one or two sizes smaller than your bust size, based on your shoulder measurement. Conversely, if standard sizes tend to be too baggy over the bust and body but tight in the shoulders, choose a Ziggurat one or two sizes larger than your bust size based on your shoulder measurement, and then adapt for a narrower body.

TRY IT ON!

Try your Ziggurat on every now and then! I suggest trying on the sweater for fit about 5 cm (1") after the underarm cast on to make sure you are on the right track.
The beauty with all top down knitting is that you can try on for size sooner rather than later to get at least an approximate idea of the fit.
It may require one or two trials to get it right.
Much will also depend on the yarn. A drapey, stretchy yarn is more forgiving but can also expand too much over time. This is something you will learn how to gauge and estimate only with practice.
For the more casual and relaxed sweaters in this book exact fit is less important, but you should still choose your size with care.
Another useful gauge is to place your sweater in progress flat on top of a favourite finished and worn sweater. There is always a sweater that fits just so. Sammelsurium and Filijokus (an earlier design) are my trusted guides for fitted shoulder sweaters, and Messing About in Boats for semi-dropped shoulders.

GAUGE & SWATCHING

Yes, swatches can be lying liars. Nevertheless, always swatch unless you are on very familiar terms with a particular yarn and already know how it behaves.

Ideally, measure your swatch both before and after blocking. That way you will know by how much it will grow. If you are armed with the knowledge that your row gauge will grow by 20% after wet blocking, you can better judge, for example, when to bind off your sleeve. The stitch gauge is more easy to adjust up or down for size than row gauge.
Row gauge is important because it determines armhole depth. This is is why all increases and shaping in the patterns have been calculated for you, so you can simply cast on and knit. It may require some consdered calculations and references to the Helpful Table to adjust for a different row gauge. But it is also a raison d'être for the Helpful Table – it is a tool for knitters who wish to make their own calculations and adjustments. Features (other than armhole depth) also determined by row gauge are more easily adjusted as you go. Try on your sweater to check where your bust darts will end up, whether pockets will sit at a comfortable height, and where your waist lands.

GAUGE & DRAPE

So yes, gauge is important and any given needle size is only a suggestion. You may need to go up or down one or more sizes to obtain gauge.
Even more important than gauge is the fabric. Your knitted fabric should feel good and move well. A yarn may indeed be nudged into a specified gauge. But do not force it into a stubbornly dense fabric nor one that is too floppy to keep its shape.
This book presents a wide range of gauges and yarn weights to increase the likelihood of you finding a good match for yarn, gauge, and design. Experienced knitters are encouraged to play with the designs and apply the gauge and stitch counts of one design to the style and features of another for an even wider variety of choice.

ADJUSTING FOR BUST SIZE

Follow the instructions for your chosen shoulder size through Step 5. Before working Step 6, notice the difference between the number of final back stitches in the size you are knitting and in the size that corresponds to your ideal bust size. If your bust size is larger than the size you are knitting, you should add more body increases to create the extra space needed. Add the extra body increases to rounds where they are not currently indicated, at a rate of 1 increase-round for every 2 stitches of difference. You can do this by starting body increases on an earlier row/round than suggested and/or make some **every**-row/round body increases where there are none in the pattern. If your bust size is smaller than the size you are knitting, make fewer body increases (that is, start them later, or spread them out – make them on only every second row/round where a pattern instructs every row/round).

Tutorials :: Hints & Tips

OPTIONAL BUST DARTS

If your sweaters tend to ride up in front, you will probably benefit from adding bust darts. Most of the patterns include optional bust darts; these instructions can be used to add bust darts to any sweater as long as you take the issue of placement into consideration.

To determine which bust darts to make, measure from your mid-shoulder down your back to your underbust line (where a bra would sit). Also measure from the same point on your shoulder down your front, over your bust and down to your underbust line. If the front measurement is no more than 5 cm/2″ longer than the back measurement, you probably do not need to add bust darts

Choose Smallish if the difference between front and back is 5–7.5 cm/2–3″, **Middling** if the difference is 7.5–10 cm / 3–4″, **Busty** if the difference is 10–12.5 cm / 4–5″, and **Wowza!** if the difference is 12.5–15 cm / 5–6″. The dart should start approximately at the level of the pointiest part of your bust – begin the darts sooner or later if necessary as only approximate guidelines in each pattern are given.

Note: For heavier yarns or yarns with significant drape, you may want to place the darts higher than you normally would. A heavier garment will lengthen with wear and your darts may end up droopy rather than perky.

JAPANESE SHORT ROWS are sometimes a less conspicuous choice for bust darts when the yarn is light and knits up with very clear stitch defintion. See Tutorial section.

YARDAGES

All yarn requirements include a 15% margin of security to account for gauge and other individual knitting quirks. In many cases you can make do with less yarn than stated. For additional guidance and for the brave I have indicated how much each sample weighs, which for some designs amounts to an entire skein less than recommended.

MAKING YOUR SKEINS STRETCH

If you are unsure that you have sufficient yarn for the project, or are cutting it close, you can finish the sleeves before finishing the body. There is an indication in each pattern for this. When knitting with hand-dyed yarn, it is a good idea to save a portion of your first skein for the sleeves, to avoid visible joins of skeins at the start of the sleeves.

UNTANGLE SKEINS OFTEN

To save time and stay sane, when working with multiple skeins, stop to untangle them often.

BLENDING IN SKEINS THAT DIFFER IN COLOUR

The very thing that makes hand-dyed yarns so attractive also means they can be unpredictable in their behaviour. Knitters love that unpredictability; the subtle shifts and surprises that emerge add considerably to the pleasure of already pleasurable knitting. However, it can sometimes spell trouble for larger projects – unexpected, sharp transitions in the middle of a sleeve, or across a chest or midriff.

Dyers routinely suggest that we alternate skeins to avoid this problem. I do not particularly fancy alternating skeins. So I usually wing it and knit happily along until trouble (sometimes) appears.

The solution is to ease the new skein in gently.

A clever way to transition from one colour or dye lot to the next is by knitting with skein A, and gradually introduce second skein B using the following striping sequence.

BAAAA – 1 round of B, 4 rounds of A
BBAAA – 2 rounds of B, 3 rounds of A
BBBAA – 3 rounds of B, 2 rounds of A
BBBBA – 4 rounds of B, 1 round of A

Each section of the sequence can be repeated one or more times. Knitter, friend and tech editor Charlotte Monckton taught me this nifty technique. It has come in handy also for several of the sweaters in this book. The Fubarite sleeves were knitted this way. Jolt of Blue also blends in quite different shades of blue. The sleeves of the Vaudeville Tunic are visibly different as one of four skeins was much darker.

By easing in a new and different skein you can still make it work.

NEATNESS

For neat and pleasing sleeve caps and any edges in general, but especially on details such as the triangle inserts on the sleeve, on every row, work 3 stitches then tighten them gently before continuing the row. This removes extra slack that can make edges sloppy.

KNIT WITH ABANDON

For all the detail and intricate instructions I have worked out for myself and for you, I encourage you to knit with abandon and off piste. Go for it!

Tutorials :: Cast On

LONGTAIL CAST ON

This is the cast on used for the initial cast on in Step 1 for all Ziggurat sweaters. You can use a different cast on but note that it may make it more difficult to pick up stitches for the Front Shoulders in Steps 4 and 5.

NOTE: I start with a slipknot rather than a simple loop. The slipknot provides an excellent spot for the sometimes tricky first stitch to pick up for the Ziggurat Front Shoulder.

1. Make a slipknot with a long tail (approx 3.5 times the shoulder width) and place this on the needle.

Insert thumb and index finger as shown.

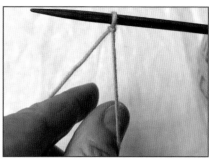

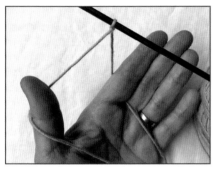

2. Shorter end of yarn runs around the thumb. Ball end of yarn runs around index finger.

3. Lock in yarn ends with the other fingers. This is the basic position. Return to this position after each new stitch cast on.

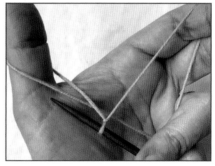

4. Bring needle to front of thumb loop.

5. Insert needle from below into thumb loop.

6. Fetch near strand of index finger loop. Bring it back through thumb loop.

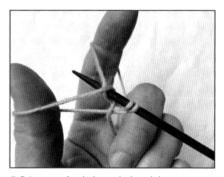

7. Bring yarn back through thumb loop.

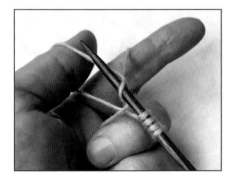

8. Slip thumb loop over fetched strand and off needle.

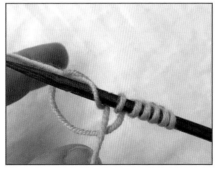

9. Tighten the new stitch around the needle.

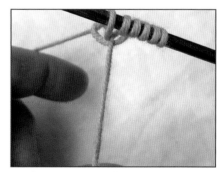

10. Insert thumb and index finger between strands to tighten the new stitch around the needle. Return to basic position and repeat until required number of stitches are on the needle.

Tutorials :: Cast On

WINDING PROVISIONAL CAST ON

This is the simplest cast on imaginable.

Even if it may look a little peculiar.

It is my preferred cast on for sideways collars, cuffs, and hems.

It is also the cast on used to introduce the Ziggurat buttonband on cardigans with buttonbands.

I suggest you do not substitute a different provisional cast on. Why?

Most provisional cast ons create an initial row of knit stitches.

With the Winding Cast on you can start any stitch pattern directly into the provisional loops. This is useful for lace and other stitch patterns where you may not want a solid knitted row to interrupt the pattern.

For Ziggurats the cast on usually extends from a knitted row or round and you (mostly) use the working yarn to wind on stitches.

You will need an additional smaller circular for winding on and holding the provisional stitches.

N1: Working needle

N2: Additional smaller needle (becomes holder for provisional stitches).

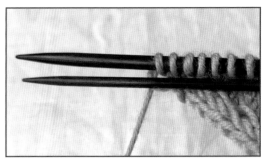

1. Place a second smaller needle below working needle. Needles are parallel.

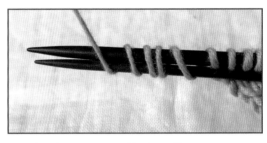

2. Wind working yarn around both needles. Going from under to front, and over to the back.

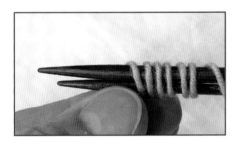

3. At the desired number of stitches, pinch yarn against the needles to hold it in place while turning needles to face in the opposite direction.

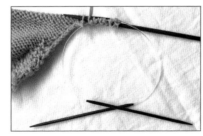

4. The additional circular can be quite short. After a few rows, the provisional stitches can be placed on a smaller stitch holder or a removable marker if the circular gets in your way.

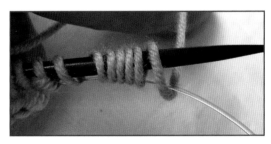

5. Pull on bottom needle to slide bottom of loops onto its cable. Bring yarn up under provisional cable and hold in place to knit the first stitch.

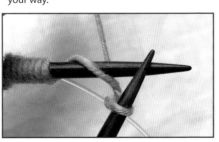

6. To knit the first stitch, insert right tip of working needle into the first loop to fetch yarn through the space between cable and left tip of working needle.

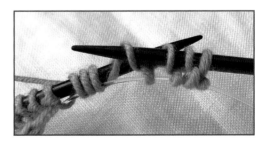

7. Work the first loop as if it were a normal stitch. The first stitch will feel a little awkward as it is not yet anchored properly.

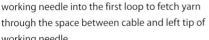

8. Work all wound-on loops according to pattern.

CROCHET CAST ON PERFECTED

The crochet cast on makes for neat necklines and underarm cast ons. And buttonholes.
No gaps, no holes.

NOTE: *In all Ziggurat patterns using the crochet cast on, the pattern instructs you to cast on one more stitch than is required. This extra stitch is decreased on the next round or row.*

Most Ziggurat crochet cast ons start with the last knitted stitch at the end of a RS Row or for an underarm cast on where Sleeve Cap begins.

1. Turn work over to WS. Using a crochet hook, borrow the first stitch to make the initial loop for casting on. Place working yarn behind knitting needle. This is th ebasic position. Keep crochet hook in front. Working yarn goes behind knitting needle after each new stitch.

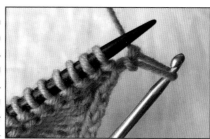

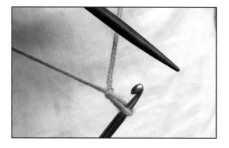

Note: To start a crochet cast on that is not an extension of knitted fabric, first make a slipknot.

2. Fetch yarn and pull it through the loop. The yarn goes over and around the knitting needle.

3. Place yarn behind knitting needle. Tighten the cast on stitch around the needle. Keep loop on crochet hook long – this makes it easier to fetch and pull yarn through for each new cast on stitch.

4. After final stitch has been cast on: Leave yarn in front.

5. Make a chain stitch but not around the needle.

6. Place this stitch on needle. You have now replaced the loop borrowed at the start.

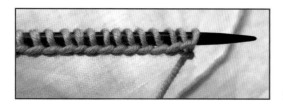

Done.

CROCHET CAST ON NEXT ROUND (OR ROW)

When the Crochet Cast On is complete:

IN THE ROUND

Turn work over to work from RS, join to Left Front (or other side of Sleeve).
On this round the gaps before and after the cast on are closed.

1. Next Round: Knit to marker, remove marker.

2. Ssk to close the gap. *1 stitch decreased*

3. Gap closed.

4. Knit to end of cast on.

5. Make a loop with bar at end of cast on, place on Left Needle.
K2tog (the loop and next stitch) to close the gap.

6. K2tog (the loop and next stitch) to close the gap.

7. Gap at far end of cast on closed.

WORKING FLAT

If working flat, your next row will likely be a WS row.
If so, purl to 1 stitch before cast on, sl1, make a twisted loop and place on Left Needle, sl1 back to LN, p2tog, purl to 2 stitches before marker, p2tog tbl.

Tutorials :: Picking Up Stitches

PICKING UP FOR A LINING
PICK UP ON WRONG SIDE WITH WRONG SIDE FACING

Use an additional circular needle 1–2 sizes smaller than the working needle to pick up stitches and to knit the lining.

Lining stitches are picked up on the WS in bars between stitches, in front of the cable, and going from bottom up.

The picking up round can be knitted with MC or CC yarn.
Most often I tend to use the MC yarn as this is most likely to be invisible from the RS.
However, it depends on the yarn. Heavier yarns may add bulk, so for Aran and some DK sweaters it may be better to use the lighter CC lining yarn for the pick-up round.
If the MC yarn has a halo or is a bit hairy, it is likely to disguise the CC pick up. You will need to experiment!

For the Ziggurats in this book only the linings for Aranaranja and Fubarite were picked up with CC. All others were picked up with MC, including the Aran weight sweaters.

PICKING UP USING MC YARN

In the round
for cuff of a sleeve or hem of a pullover
Slide stitches onto the cable. Take working MC yarn to WS.
From WS and going counterclockwise along the inside of the sweater, pick up & knit a stitch in every bar between all stitches, take MC to RS.

Working flat
for a cardigan hem
End with a RS row. Slide stitches onto the cable. Take working MC yarn to WS.
With a smaller circular, working yarn, and going from right to left, pick up & knit a stitch in every bar between all stitches, take MC to RS.

For a contrasting lining, join CC on the next round or row to knit the lining (on the inside and, going counterclockwise if working in the round).

1. Slide stitches onto cable.
Turn work over to WS.

2. The needles identify the bars between stitches and in front of the cable.

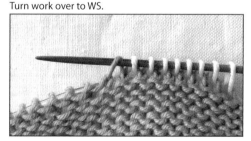

3. Pick up & knit into the bars indicated above. This is what the pick up looks like with a contrasting yarn. 8 stitches have been picked up & knitted, the needle tip is inserted into the next bar to pick up & knit a 9th stitch.

4. View from top.

Tutorials :: Picking Up Stitches

PICKING UP FOR A TUCK & SOME POCKETS
PICK UP ON **WRONG** SIDE WITH **RIGHT** SIDE FACING

Work from Right Side and pick up into bars behind the cable, going into loops from the top.

1. Slide stitches onto cable. Work from Right Side.

2. Pick up & knit in the bars between stitches BEHIND the cable, going in from the top. The needle tips are inserted into those bars to identify them clearly.

3. Pick up & knit in the bars between stitches BEHIND the cable, going in from the top.

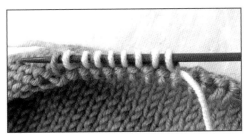

4. View from top.

PICKING UP ON RIGHT SIDE OF FABRIC
PICK UP ON **RIGHT** SIDE WITH **RIGHT** SIDE FACING

This technique is used to pick up stitches for the double-knitted details on:

- Dusala cardigan

It is also used to pick up stitches for pockets with buttonband edgings (Pocket 3D in Pocket Tutorials) on:

- Black Basalt cardigan
- Jadeite cardigan

1. Slide stitches on working needle onto its cable. Pick up and knit a second layer in the bars between stitches IN FRONT of the cable, going in from the bottom. The needles are inserted into those bars to identify them clearly.
A crochet hook can be used to fetch any uncooperative bars.

2. Five CC stitches have been picked up, the needle tip is inserted into the next bar to pick up & knit a sixth stitch.

Tutorials :: Bind Off

STRETCHY BIND OFF

This is a good bind off to finish a rolled hem or neckline.
It can be used also on a rolled cuff.

Setup: Knit 1.
Step 1 Knit 1 (2 sts on RN).

Step 2 Insert LN into the front legs of the 2 sts.

Step 3 Complete the k2tog tbl with RN.

Repeat from Step 1 until all stitches are bound off.

THREE-NEEDLE BIND OFF

This bind off has several virtues.
It is naturally elastic while also being tidy and
provides a simple and elegant finish to lined hems
and cuffs.

Place needles parallel and with tips pointing in the
same direction.

Step 1 K2tog by knitting through 1 stitch from each
needle.

Step 2 K2tog (1 stitch from each needle) again.

Step 3 Pass stitch over and off needle to bind off.

Stitch has been bound off.
Repeat from Step 1.

INCREASES

Like many or most knitters I have developed a preference for certain types of increases for certain purposes. These are the three different increases used in Ziggurat patterns.

The increases suggested in the patterns are just that, suggestions.

If you intend to replace the suggested directional increases with your own preferred increases, then for the sake of symmetry I recommend that you use another directional increase.

M1L & M1R
MAKE 1 LEFT & MAKE 1 RIGHT

These are made into the horizontal bar between stitches.

This is my preferred increase for **Sleeve** caps and **Body** increases (toward underarm).
Sleeves: The increases are made leaning in towards the sleeve.
This is a matter of taste and sometimes a matter of the yarn. Some yarn bases look more sculpted leaning away from the faux seam. For some sweaters you may want a less pronounced faux seam.
Body: The increases are made leaning away from the faux seam at the Sleeve Caps. For every-row (or round) increases, you may want to try the FL1/BL1 increase instead. Some knitters prefer this to minimize gapping. I waver and for some sweaters and yarns use the one, for some the other.

The important things are to consistently use the same type of increase and to ensure that the pairs of increases mirror each other – both should lean inward or both outward.

Other uses in Ziggurat sweaters:
- Often but not always used for neck increases
- Often used for Waist Shaping
- M1L is used for the Optional Rear Shaping

M1L – Make 1 Left
1. Insert LN from front into bar between stitches. Knit into back leg of the lifted bar.

M1L
2. Done.

M1Lp – Make 1 Left Purl
1. Insert LN from front into bar between stitches.

M1Lp – Make 1 Left Purl
2. Purl into back leg of the lifted bar.

M1R – Make 1 Right
1. Insert LN from rear (*Rear for Right*) into bar between stitches.

M1R
2. Knit into Front leg of the lifted bar.
Use your left index finger to push on the twisted loop (toward you) to create a little extra space for the RN.

M1R
3. Done.

M1Rp – Make 1 Right PURL
1. Insert LN from rear (*Rear for Right*) into bar between stitches. Purl into front leg of lifted bar.
Done.

Tutorials :: Increases

LLI & RLI

LIFTED (OR RAISED) INCREASE

Worked into a stitch on a previous row/round.

Uses in Ziggurat sweaters:
- Sometimes used for Neck Increases
- Sometimes used for Waist Shaping

LLI – Left-Leaning Lifted Increase

1. Lift the stitch 2 rows below the last stitch on RN.

2. Lift the loop onto LN. The left leg of the lifted loop faces front. Knit into the back leg.

3. Complete

RLI – Right-Leaning Lifted Increase

1. Lift the stitch below next stitch: Insert RN from behind into the right leg of the stitch below.

2. Lift the loop onto LN, knit the loop. The lifted stitch overlaps the next stitch slightly.

3. Knit the next stitch as usual.

FL1 & BL1

BACKWARD LOOP INCREASE / FORWARD LOOP INCREASE

A very simple increase. Similar to a cable cast on, this increase is made by looping the working yarn. One advantage of the loop increase is how it behaves when increases are stacked on every row. Other types of increases can distort the fabric or produce unsightly gapping when increasing on every row or round. I am grateful to Ravelry knitter TexasGabi for teaching me this.

Uses in Ziggurat sweaters:
- An alternative to M1L/M1R for **Body** increases

 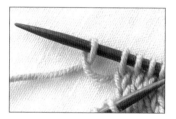

FL1 – left-leaning

1. Make a loop with long yarn end layered on bottom. Insert RN from behind to place loop on RN.

2. Tighten. Done. On the next row or round, knit or purl this loop as a normal stitch.

BL1 – right-leaning

1. Make a loop with long yarn end layered on top. Insert RN from front to place loop on RN.

2. Tighten. Done. On the next row or round, knit or purl this loop as a normal stitch.

DECREASES

These are the directional decreases used in Ziggurat patterns – and in most any knitting, for that matter.

RIGHT-LEANING DECREASES

This is the simpler of the directional decreases.

On RS rows: K2tog.
On WS rows, the corresponding decrease is p2tog.
Making a p2tog on the wrong side results in a right-leaning decrease on the RS of the fabric.

K2tog
Knit 2 stitches together.

P2tog
Purl 2 stitches together.

LEFT-LEANING DECREASES

On RS rows: Ssk.
On WS rows, the corresponding decrease is p2tog tbl.
There are many version of this decrease. The version I prefer produces an exact mirror of the ssk.

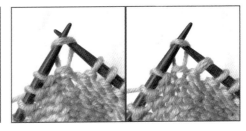

SSK – slip, slip, knit
1. Slip 1 stitch knitwise, slip 1 stitch knitwise.

SSK
2. Insert LN from left to right into front legs of the 2 slipped stitches. Knit them together through the back.

P2tog tbl –
purl 2 sts together through the back loop(s)
1. Slip 1 stitch knitwise, slip 1 stitch knitwise.

P2tog tbl
2. Insert LN from Right to Left, going into second, then first stitch.

P2tog tbl
3. Stitches are mounted in the correct order on LN – first stitch (arrow) below second.

P2tog tbl
4. Purl the 2 stitches together.

Tutorials :: Short Rows

TURNING ON A KNIT ROW

1. RS: Knit to point for turning. Turn work over to work from WS.

2. Slip 1 purlwise with yarn in front (yarn is already in front).

3. Pull on the yarn – up and round the back until 2 legs show. Keep pulling yarn behind, around and downwards.

4. Arrows point to the 2 legs of the slipped stitch. Take yarn to front between needles to purl next stitch as usual, while keeping the tension on the slipped stitch. Work to end of row or to next point of turning.

TURNING ON A PURL ROW

1. WS: Purl to point for turning. Turn work over to work from RS.

2. RS: Take yarn to front. Sl1 purlwise with yarn in front.

3. Pull on yarn up and over and down until 2 legs show. Keep pulling yarn behind, around and downwards.

4. Arrows point to the 2 legs of the slipped stitch. Knit next and following stitches as usual, while keeping the tension on the slipped stitch. Work to end of row. Next row: WS.

GERMAN SHORT ROWS

The German Short Row is my favourite and until recently only short row technique.

It is simple and straightforward.

It produces neat, well nigh invisible shaping, as on a Ziggurat shoulder, just as an *example*.

My German knitting friends look askance at the name German Short Row. I am not sure who named it, but it seems to be the common way to refer to this technique among Anglo knitters.

Incidentally, Germans call the stitch on which everything turns a *Doppelmasche* (a double stitch), which makes perfect sense.

ABBREVIATIONS

The abbreviations I use (invented by Steph Boardman, the original Ziggurat technical editor):

sl1^   With yarn in front, sl1 pwise, pull on yarn over and behind needle until both legs of st show

k1^   Knit through both legs of the short row stitch (sl1^) from prev row as if it were a normal, single stitch

p1^   Purl through both legs of the short row stitch (sl1^) from prev row as if it were a normal, single stitch

WORKING THE SL1^ ON RS

1. Knit to the sl1^-stitch. Treat it as a single stitch. Knit this stitch through both legs, taking care to go through the centre of the interlocking legs.

2. Done.

WORKING THE SL1^ ON WS

1. Purl to the sl1^-stitch. Treat it as a single stitch. Purl this stitch through both legs, taking care to go through the centre of the interlocking legs.

2. Done.

JAPANESE SHORT ROWS

The Japanese Short Row is more fiddly than the German but also more precise.

I suggest using this method for bust darts made in shiny or bright yarns where perhaps the German or any other short row would disrupt the fabric in more obvious ways.

The photos and instructions are arranged in the order you would work the Japanese Short Rows for Ziggurat bust darts in the round.

ABBREVIATIONS

Jsl1	Sl1, hang removable marker on working yarn, knit/purl next stitch with marker hanging on WS between this stitch and the slipped stitch
Jk1	Knit to gap, pull on marker to place loop untwisted onto LN, k2tog (next stitch and loop), remove marker
Jp1	Purl to gap, sl1, pull on marker to place loop untwisted onto LN, sl1 to LN (the previously slipped st), p2tog (slipped st and loop), remove marker

1. RS: Knit to the point for turning.
Turn work over to work from WS.

2. Jsl1 on WS: Hang a removable stitch marker on the working yarn, slip 1 purlwise with yarn in front, purl next stitch while making sure that the marker sits on the yarn between the slipped stitch and next stitch.

3. Marker is hanging on yarn between slipped stitch and next stitch.
Purl to next point for turning.
Turn work over to work from RS.

4. RS: Hang a removable marker on working yarn on WS, behind needle.
Slip 1 stitch purlwise with yarn in back. Knit next stitch while making sure that the marker sits on yarn between the slipped stitch and the next stitch.

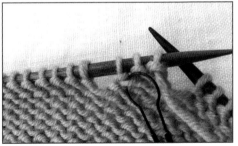

VIEW from WS after 1 more st knitted: Marker hangs on yarn between the slipped stitch and next (knit) stitch.

5. Knit to the gap.
The marker sits on WS between the last 2 stitches on RN.
Take yarn to front (RS), pull on marker to make loop available.

Tutorials :: Short Rows

6. Keep yarn to front, place loop on LN, with its right leg to front (untwisted), remove marker.

7. Take yarn to back between needles as shown.

8. Take yarn to back, knit 2 stitches together (the loop and the next stitch). Jk1 is done.
If working bust darts you will now repeat Steps 1 & 2 before continuing with Step 9.

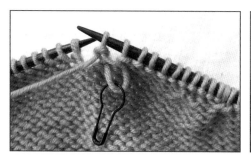

9. WS: Purl to the gap.
The marker sits between the last 2 stitches on RN.

10. Slip 1 stitch purlwise (pink arrow).
Pull on marker to make loop (blue arrow) available.

11. Place loop (blue) on LN with its right leg to front, going in front of the slipped stitch (pink) on RN, remove marker.

12. Slip the slipped stitch back to LN.
Blue arrow points to loop stitch.
Pink arrow points to slipped stitch.

13. Purl 2 stitches together (the slipped stitch and the loop).
Jp1 is done.

14. Repeat from Step 3 to work as many short rows (and as many stitches after each turn) as directed in the pattern.

15. On the first normal round after the Bust Dart is completed, you will come across an unworked Jsl1. This final Jk1 is worked differently than that in Steps 5–8:
Knit to the gap, pass loop behind next stitch and place loop on LN, remove marker, knit 2 stitches together (next stitch and loop).

BUTTONBANDS

Most Ziggurats feature this Buttonband. I have tried variations but keep coming back to this one because it just works and works well for all weights of yarn.
(The Sweet Laurel cardigan does have a slight variation. Try it!)

It may seem unusual to knit the Buttonband with the same size needles as the Body. Not to worry. The slipped stitches in the Buttonband keep it all together at the right tension.

THE GIST

In Step 4 provisional stitches are cast on to introduce the Buttonband which is knitted along with Left Front, then knitted and attached around the Back Neck up to the Right Shoulder (Step 4a), from where it is knitted along with Right Front (Step 5). Now the Buttonband is knitted along with Body and any increases for Fronts and Sleeves (Step 6).

At the desired neck depth (or where instructed in the pattern) you create the overlap of Fronts and also the first buttonhole. At this point Front stitches are set aside and you work the 8 Buttonband stitches. You are preparing extended bits of Buttonband along whose lower edges stitches are then picked up – both to create the vertical Buttonbands and to add the number of required Front stitches to match the Back. (This corresponds to the cast on for joining to knit in the round on pullovers.)
The photos show a contrasting Buttonband for clarity. Most cardigans in the book do not have contrasting Buttonbands.

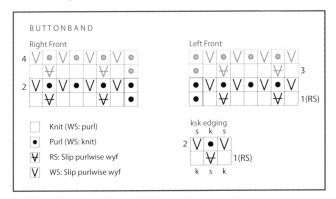

COLOUR JOIN

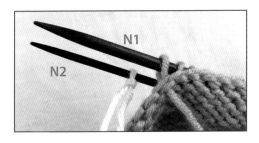

1. Continuing on the WS row:
Place a CC slipknot on an additional circular (N2).
Place N2 below working needle (N1).
Note: For cardigans with MC Buttonbands, wind on stitches with working MC without first adding a slipknot. Wind on 8 sts (see Tutorial for Winding cast on). Work the loops according to pattern as if they are normal stitches.
Cardigan Buttonband **R1 (RS):** K1, sl1wyf, k3, sl1wyf, k1, p1. *8 sts.*
This first row locks the loops in and creates the provisional stitches on N2 cable.

2. Part of Row 1 completed.

3. At the colour join always lay old (white) colour over new (yellow), bring new up from under.

4. Buttonband is worked along with Left Front.

5. Lay old (yellow) yarn over new (white), bring new yarn up from under.

6. The colour join viewed from WS.

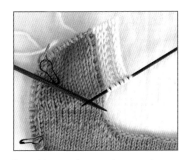

Step 4 is complete, ready to work Step 4a.

Tutorials :: Buttonbands

Step 4 is complete, ready to work Step 4a.

Step 4a

1. **N1:** Work the provisional stitches on **N2** according to pattern:
Slide off and discard slipknot.
R1 (RS): K2tog, sl1wyf, k3, sl1wyf, k1tbl. *7 sts*
Attach the Buttonband along Back Neck on every RS row. Attach to approx 3 of 4 stitches.

For MC buttonbands: Join new MC.
For CC buttonbands: Use already attached CC.

Step 4a

2. Pick up & knit 1 st in Back Neck, place on LN.

Step 4a

3. Place the picked up stitch on LN, k2tog (picked up stitch and Buttonband stitch)

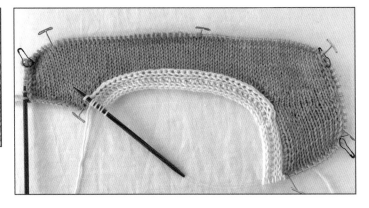

Step 4a

4. Knit and attach Buttonband around Neck up to 1 stitch before Right Shoulder. End with a WS row.
Step 4a is complete.

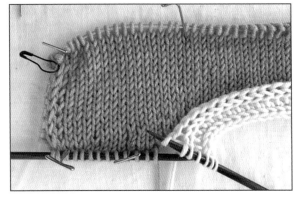

Step 5:

Pick up & knit Right Front Shoulder stitches, with CC pick up & knit 1 new stitch in Buttonband, work the 7 Buttonband stitches.
8 Buttonband sts
Continue to work Buttonband along with Right Front.

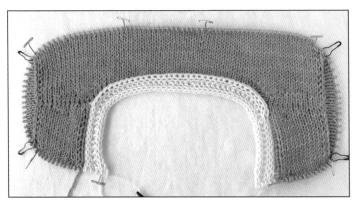

Step 5 is complete and also a few rows of Step 6, where Buttonbands continue along with Sleeve and Neck increases in the next step.

BUTTONBANDS & CENTRE FRONTS CAST ON (PICK UP)

 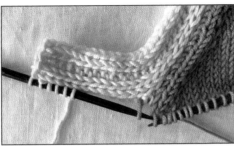 

1. LEFT BUTTONBAND Set Front stitches aside. Knit an extension of the Buttonband (to length stated in each pattern).
Bind off.
1 stitch remains after binding off the edge.
Note: For the Dusala Cardigan with two **CC**, proceed a little differently. See below.

2. LEFT BUTTONBAND Pick up & knit 5 sts for Buttonband. *6 BB sts*
MC Buttonband: Continue to pick up & knit stitches up to Front stitches on LN.
For **CC** Buttonband: With MC and going from left to right, pick up & knit stitches up to the Buttonband. Lay **CC** over MC, and work the next RS row with MC to Right Front.

3. LEFT BUTTONBAND Pick up & knit 5 sts for Buttonband. *6 BB sts*
For **CC** Buttonband: With MC and going from left to right, pick up & knit stitches up to the Buttonband. Lay **CC** over MC, and work the next RS row with MC to Right Front.

DUSALA BUTTONBAND Buttonband **CC1**-stitches are bound off, but before final stitch is bound off, join CC2 for a smooth transition to the vertical Buttonband.
The vertical Buttonband stitches are picked up with **CC2**. MC stitches are picked up going from Left to Right to meet the Buttonband.

4. LEFT BUTTONBAND Pick up & knit 5 sts for Buttonband. *6 BB sts*
MC Buttonband: Continue to pick up & knit stitches up to Front stitches on LN.
(here done with white **CC**)

  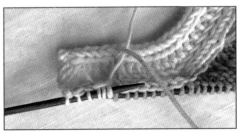

1. RIGHT BUTTONBAND Set Front stitches aside. Knit an extension of the Buttonband as for Left Buttonband, but make a BUTTONHOLE 5 rows before binding off.

2. RIGHT BUTTONBAND This is a WS row.
Turn work over to work from RS, going from left to right to pick up & knit 5 sts for Buttonband. *6 BB sts*
MC Buttonband: Continue to pick up & knit stitches up to Front stitches on LN.
For **CC** Buttonband: With MC from RS, pick up & knit stitches up to the Buttonband.

3. RIGHT BUTTONBAND MC Buttonband: Turn work over to WS, purl to Left Front Buttonband.
For **CC** Buttonband: Turn work over to WS, lay **CC** over MC, bring MC from under and purl to Left Front Buttonband. Make 2 increases in Left Front Buttonband. *8 Left BB sts*
On next RS Row: Make 2 increases. *8 Right BB sts*

Tutorials :: Buttonholes

BUTTONHOLE ROWS WORKED IN THE RIGHT BUTTONBAND

1. BUTTONHOLE
BR1 (RS): Sl1wyf, k1, bind off 2 sts, ksk.

2. BUTTONHOLE
BR2 (WS): (Sl1wyf, k1) twice.

3. BUTTONHOLE
BR2 (WS): Turn work over to RS to cast on stitches.
Borrow the last st to start the crochet cast on.
(See Crochet Cast On Tutorial)

4. BUTTONHOLE
3 stitches are cast on, borrowed loop replaced onto
LN. *9 sts*

5. BUTTONHOLE
Turn work back to continue the WS row (k1, sl1wyf).

6. BUTTONHOLE
On this row, the buttonhole is secured (in the same
way as for Centre Front and Underarm Cast Ons),
BR 3 (RS): Sl1wyf, sl1 kwise, pick up a twisted loop in
bar before cast on, pass 2 sts back to LN (twisted loop
and sl st), ssk, sl1wyf, k2,
k2tog, sl1wyf, k1. *8 sts*

7. Work 2 more Butttonband rows, then bind off from
WS.
1 st remains.

Additional buttonholes in the vertical
Buttonband are made over three rows in the
same manner. The buttonholes are placed
slightly off-centre on purpose. It minimises
gapping and the buttons remain nicely centred
when the cardigan is buttoned up.

DOUBLE KNITTED CC DETAIL

Design featuring this detail:
- Dusala cardigan

MATERIALS
CC1: Q.E.D. (grey)
CC2: Grünfink (green)

For Dusala cardigan, a **CC2** rectangle is worked over 16 sts at Centre Back. Do not let my imagination limit yours – this detail can be placed wherever you please.

Below the first rectangle, two smaller **CC2** rectangles are worked over 7 sts each, two rows below the **CC2** rectangle.

16-STITCH RECTANGLE
CC = CC2

Setup Row (RS): Work to 8 sts before Centre Back, pm (= Bm1) join **CC** (k1**CC** in bar between sts, k1**MC**) x 16, pm, (= Bm2) with **MC**, work to end of row (or BB).

R2 (WS): Work to Bm2, sm, p1**MC**, cross yarns, (p1**CC**, k1**MC**) x 15, p1**CC**, yf (to WS), cross yarns, sm, with **MC** work to end of row (or BB).

R3: Work to Bm1, sm, cross yarns, (k1**CC**, p1**MC**) x 15, k1**CC**, cross yarns, with **MC** k1, sm, with MC work to end of row (or BB).

R4: As Row 2.

Work **Rows 3 & 4** once more. Cut **CC2**.

Next Row (RS): Work to m, sm, k32, sm, work to end of row.

Final Row (WS): Work to CBm2, sm, (p2tog) x 16, sm, work to end of row.

Work 2 rows according to pattern.

1. Two layers are created, with **CC** sts being picked up in bars between **MC** sts.

CC is held to RS and passed in front of **MC**.
MC is held to WS.

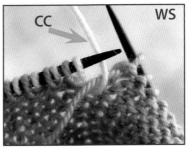

2. Cross yarns before the first **CC** stitch and after the last **CC** stitch: Lay **MC** over **CC**, take **CC** to RS (catch **MC** from below and up around)

3. **DOUBLE KNITTING**
Keep **MC** to WS, **CC** to RS and take care not to cross the yarns/ layers.
WS double-knitting continental style: run **MC** over index, **CC** over middle finger to keep the layers apart.

4. On WS at the END of **CC** detail: Take both yarns to WS, leave **CC** on WS, take **MC** across **CC**, work to end of row.

5. On RS at the BEGINNING of **CC** detail:
Lay **MC** over **CC**, with **CC** catch **MC** (from below and up around), k1**CC**, p1**MC**) x 15, k1**CC**.

On RS, **CC** is always kept in front of **MC**.

Tutorials :: Double-Knitted Detail

TWO **7**-STITCH RECTANGLES

CC = CC1

Setup Row (RS): Work to Bm1, join **CC** (k1**CC** in bar between sts, k1MC) x 7, k2, (k1**CC** in bar between sts, k1MC) x 7 sm, with **MC**, work to end of row (or BB).

R2 (WS): Work to Bm2, sm, p1MC, cross yarns, (p1**CC**, k1MC) x 7, p2MC, (p1**CC**, k1MC) x 6, p1**CC**, yf (to WS), cross yarns, sm, with **MC** work to end of row (or BB).

R3: Work to Bm1, sm, cross yarns, (k1**CC**, p1**MC**) x 7, k2MC, (k1**CC**, p1**MC**) x 6, k1**CC**, cross yarns, k1MC, sm, with MC work to end of row (or BB).

R4: As Row 2.

Work **Rows 3 & 4** once more. Cut **CC1**.

Next Row (RS): Work to m, sm, k32, sm, work to end of row.

Final Row (WS): Work to Bm2, rm, (p2tog) x 16, rm, work to end of row.

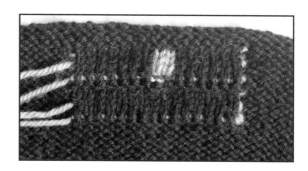

ZIGGURAT TUCKS

IN THE ROUND

Tuck Rounds create additional layers for the Ziggurat Tuck.

The layers created are initially worked as an accordion fold.

After a few rounds, there is enough fabric to work Body and Tuck stitches as a single layer with N1.

The moves may seem intricate but are nevertheless straightforward once you make them.

Use an additional long circular (N2), 1 – 2 sizes smaller than the needle used for the body.

N1: Layer 1 with Body sts

N2: Tuck sts

    Layer 2: 5 sts x 2

    Layer 3: 10 sts.

RS: Work stitches with RS of garment facing towards you.

WS: Work stitches with WS of garment facing towards you.

BASIC TUCK

Tuck Rnds 1 & 2 create 2 additional layers behind the Body stitches.

Tuck Rnd 1:

    N1: Knit to 5 sts before Centre Back, pm (=Tm), sl10, pull on RN tip to slide sts onto cable.

    N2 (Layer 2): With working yarn and directly after Tm (before the first slipped st), in bars between the slipped sts (behind the cable), p&k5 sts, skip one bar, p&k5 more sts, pull on tips to slide sts onto cable.

    N1: Work to end of round.

    N2 (Layer 2): Loop cable, sl5 onto other tip of **N2** *(needle tips are facing each other; there are 5 sts on each tip)*, pull on tips to slide sts onto cable.

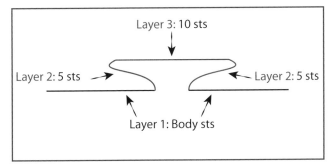

Layer 3: 10 sts
Layer 2: 5 sts — Layer 2: 5 sts
Layer 1: Body sts

1. Tuck Rnd 1: 10 sts slipped

2. Tuck Rnd 1 (Layer 2): Pick up & knit first stitch in this bar.

3. Tuck Rnd 1 (Layer 2): The first 5 sts picked up & knitted in bars between stitches. One bar is skipped. Tip is inserted in bar for the first of next 5 to be picked up & knitted

4. Tuck Rnd 1: 10 stitches have been picked up & knitted for Layer 2. Stitches rest on the cable.

5. Tuck Rnd 1: Needle tip pulled to present the stitches at other end of N2.

6. Tuck Rnd 1: 5 stitches slipped to RN, dividing Layer 2 into two halves.

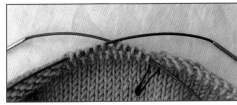

7. Tuck Rnd 1: Both needle tips pulled, all stitches rest on N2 cable.

Tutorials :: Tucks

Tuck Rnd 2

N1: Work to Tm, sm, k5, pull on tip to slide sts onto cable, turn work over to work from WS.

N2 (Layer 2) WS**:** K5, turn work over to work from RS.

N2 (Layer 3) RS**:** Loop cable, starting in bar before first st, p&k5 sts in bars between sts and behind the cable, skip one bar, p&k5 more sts, turn work over to work from WS.

N2 (Layer 2) WS**:** Loop cable, k5, slide sts onto cable, turn work over to work from RS.

20 Tuck sts

N1 (Layer 1) RS: Work to end of round.

Tuck Rnds 3 – 6

N1 (Layer 1) RS: Work to Tm1, sm, k5, slide sts sit onto cable, turn work over.

N2 (Layer 2) WS: Loop cable, k5 (from centre out), turn work over to work from RS.

N2 (Layer 3) RS: Loop cable, k10, turn work over to work from WS.

N2 (Layer 2) WS: Loop cable, k5 (to centre), slide sts onto cable, turn work over to work from RS.

N1 (Layer 1) RS: Work to end of round.

On the next round work all sts with N1:

Tuck Rnd 7

N1: Work to Tm, rm, k5, k5 (from N2), pm (=Tm1), k10, pm (=Tm2), k5 (no sts remain on N2), knit to end of rnd.

All stitches are on **N1**.

1. Tuck Rnd 2: First 5 stitches on N1 (Layer 1) worked, ready to turn over to work Layer 2 from WS.

2. Tuck Rnd 2 (WS): Arrows point to first 5 stitches (Layer 2) to be knit with N2.

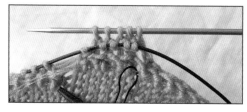

3. Tuck Rnd 2: Picking up stitches for Layer 3. The first 5 stitches have been picked up.

4. Tuck Rnd 2: Layer 3 with 10 sts on N2 is complete.

5. Tuck Rnd 2 (Layer 2): Five stitches knitted to centre. Layer 2 is done for this round.

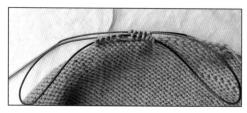

6. The loops of N2 look like this while Layer 1 is worked with N1.

7. Tuck Rnd 2 (Layer 1): Final 5-stitch leg of the accordion fold; continue with N1 to complete the round.

TRIANGLE TUCK

Tuck Rnds 1 – 10 create a double-knitted triangle that precedes and provides stitches for the Tuck. The layers created are initially worked as an accordion fold. After a few rounds, there is enough fabric to work Body and Tuck stitches as a single layer with N1.
Use an additional long circular (N2), 1 – 2 sizes smaller than the needle used for the body.

N1: Layer 1 with Body sts
N2: Tuck sts
CC: Small scrap of weight similar to or slightly lighter than yarn for body

RS: Work stitches with RS facing toward you.
WS: Work stitches with WS facing toward you.

TUCK TRIANGLE

Tuck Rnd 1: Knit to 5 sts before Centre Back, pm (=Tm), k5, with **CC** M1L, with **MC** knit to end of round.
1 CC st

Tuck Rnd 2: Knit to Tm, sm, k5, k1**CC**, with **MC** knit to end of round.

Tuck Rnd 3: Knit to Tm, sm, k4, with **CC** M1R, yf, k1**MC**, yb, k1**CC**, yf, k1**MC**, yb, with **CC** M1L, yb, with **MC** knit to end of round.
3 CC sts

Tuck Rnd 4: Knit to Tm, sm, k3, sl7, with **CC** M1L, yb, turn work over, sl1**CC**wyf, (sl1**MC**wyb, p1**CC**) x 3, sl1**MC**wyb, turn work over, with **CC** M1R, yb, leave **CC** in back, (k1**MC**, sl1**CC**wyb) x 4, with **MC** knit to end of round.
5 CC sts

Tuck Rnd 5: Knit to Tm, sm, k2, with **CC** M1R, yf, (k1**MC**, yb, k1**CC**, yf) x 5, k1**MC**, **MC**yb, with **CC** M1L, yb, leave **CC** in back, with **MC** knit to end of round.
7 CC sts

Tuck Rnd 6: Knit to Tm, sm, k1, sl15, with **CC** M1L, yb, turn work over, sl1**CC**wyf, (sl1**MC**wyb, p1**CC**) x 7, sl1**MC**wyb, turn work over, with **CC** M1R, yb, leave **CC** in back, (k1**MC**, sl1**CC**wyb) x 8, with **MC** knit to end of round.
9 CC sts

Tuck Rnd 7: Knit to Tm, sm, with **CC** M1L, yf, (k1**MC**, yb, k1**CC**, yf) x 9, k1**MC**, yb, with **CC**, M1L, yb, leave **CC** in back, with **MC** knit to end of round.
11 CC sts

1. Tuck Rnd 1 complete.

2. Tuck Rnd 3 complete.

3. Tuck Rnd 4 in progress. There are 4 CC stitches; a 5th is still to be created.

4. Tuck Rnd 4 (WS) in progress.

5. Tuck Rnd 8 complete.

6. Tuck Rnd 9: Separation of layers in progress.

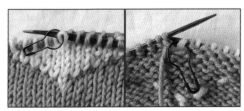

7. Tuck Rnd 9: Separating layers (in progress).
Centre stitch put on removable marker and pulled to WS.

Tutorials :: Tucks

Tuck Rnd 8: Knit to Tm, sm, sl21, turn work over, (p1CC, sl1MCwyb) x 10, p1CC, turn work over, leave **CC** in back, (sl1CCwyb, k1**MC**) x 11, with **MC** knit to end of round, cut **CC**.
11 CC sts

Continue with **MC** only.
On the next round, knit Body sts with N1, knit Tuck sts with a second circular needle (N2).

N1: Body sts (held to front), working **CC** sts.
N2 (2.75 mm / US 2): Tuck sts (held to back), working **MC** sts between CC sts.

k1N1 = k1 with N1
k1N2 = k1 with N2

Note for throwers: Pass the yarn under N2.

Tuck Rnd 9: Knit to Tm, sm, (k1N1, k1N2) x 5, place next CC-st on a removable marker and hold to WS, (k1N2, k1N1) x 5.
   N2: Pull on tips to slide sts onto cable.
   N1: Work to end of round, pull on tips to slide sts onto cable.
   N2: Loop cable, sl5 *(needle tips are facing each other; there are 5 sts on each tip)*, pull on tips to slide sts onto cable.

Tuck Rnd 10:
   N1: Knit to Tm, sm, k5, pull on tips to slide sts onto cable, turn work over to work from WS.
   N2 (Layer 2) WS: K5, turn work over to work from RS.
   N2 (Layer 3) RS: Loop cable, p&k10 sts in **MC** bars between sts and behind the cable, turn work over to work from WS.
   N2 (Layer 2) WS: Loop cable, k5, pull on tips to slide sts onto cable, turn work over to work from RS.
   20 Tuck sts
   N1 (RS): Sm, knit to end of round.

The Tuck is now set up in three layers.

N1: RS Layer 1 with Body sts
N2: Tuck sts
   Layer 2: 5 sts x 2
   Layer 3: 10 sts
The layers are worked as an accordion fold.

After approx 6 additional rounds there will be enough fabric to work Body and Tuck sts as a single layer with N1.

8. Tuck Rnd 9: Separation complete.
N1 holds Layer 1 stitches.
N2 (red cable) holds Layer 2 stitches.

9. Tuck Rnd 9 (Layer 2): Needle tip pulled to present the stitches at other end of N2.

10. Tuck Rnd 9 (Layer 2): 5 stitches slipped to Right Needle, dividing Layer 2 into two halves.

11. Tuck Rnd 10: First 5 stitches on N1 (Layer 1) worked, ready to turn over to work Layer 2 from WS.

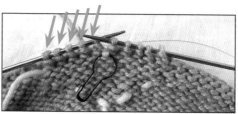
12. Tuck Rnd 10 (Layer 2). WS: Arrows point to first 5 stitches to be knit with N2.

13. Tuck Rnd 10: Picking up stitches for Layer 3.
4 stitches picked up & knitted, the 5th is ready to be picked up through next bar and the CC-st on holder.

14. Tuck Rnd 10: CC1-st has been knit together with the fifth bar to make the 5th st on Layer 3, needle tip is inserted into next bar to be worked.

Tuck Rnd 11:

N1 (Layer 1)**:** Knit to Tm, k5, pull on tips to slide sts onto cable, turn work over to work from WS.

N2:

Layer 2 (WS): K5, turn work over to work from RS.

Layer 3 (RS): Loop cable, k10, turn work over to work from WS.

Layer 2 (WS): Loop cable, k5, pull on tips to slide sts onto cable, turn work over to work from RS.

N1 (Layer 1) RS**:** Knit to end of round.

Work **Tuck Rnd 11** again x 5.

On the next round work all sts with **N1**:

Next Tuck Rnd: Knit to Tm, rm, k5, from N2, k5, pm (=Tm1), k10, pm (=Tm2), k5 (no sts remain on N2), knit to end of rnd.

All sts are on **N1**.

15. Tuck Rnd 10 with 3 Layers. Layer 1 on N1 (transparent cable) in front) with Body sts. (The 10 Tuck sts of Layer 1 are worked in separate halves.) Layer 2 on N2 cable (red cable) with 5 sts x 2 (worked in separate halves). Layer 3 on N2 (needle tip) with 10 sts picked up & knitted.

16. Tuck Rnd 10.
N2 (Layer 2) WS: Five stitches knitted to centre. Layer 2 is done for this round.

17. Tuck Rnd 10 (Layer 1): Working with N1 from RS again. All tuck stitches have been knit; ready to work to end of round.

18. Tuck Rnd 10 complete. Viewed from above.

19. After a few rounds: All stitches are on N1.

Tutorials :: Pockets

SPECIES OF ZIGGURAT POCKET

THREE METHODS OF POCKET CONSTRUCTION ARE USED IN THIS BOOK

1. AFTERTHOUGHT Pocket: A separate pouch is knitted on the inside resulting in a triple layer pocket.
2. Slim LINING FLAP: Knitted onto the body separately and then attached while knitting the body, resulting in a single layer on the inside.
3. Slim DOUBLE-KNITTED: Integrated with knitting of body, resulting in a single layer on the inside.

THE POCKETS CAN HAVE THREE STYLES OF EDGING — OR NO EDGING

A. NO EDGING
    - Mayhem DK cardigan (flap lining)
    - Rabalder (flap lining)

B. I-CORD(ish) EDGE knitted on last – can be worked with provisional stitches from the setup of the Double-Knitted Pocket (3) or onto an Afterthought Pocket (1)
    - Sweet Laurel Cardigan (Double-Knitted)
    - Black Basalt (teal sample with Afterthought Pocket)

C. EDGING knitted separately, then attached over a few rows or rounds – can then continue as a Flap Pocket (2) or a Double-Knitted Pocket (3)
    - Vaudeville Tunic (Double-Knitted with Welt)
    - Sammelsurium (Flap with Welt)
    - Coucou Tunic (Flap with Cable)

D. BUTTONBAND edge that is picked up, knitted, and integrated with the knitting of a Double-Knitted Pocket (3)
    - Black Basalt
    - Jadeite

KNITTING FLAT OR IN THE ROUND

The double-knitted pockets in this book are all knitted flat, including the mini pocket for the Vaudeville Tunic – the tunic is knitted flat from the point where double-knitting for the pocket begins.

This does not mean that you cannot choose a double-knitted pocket for a pullover in the round, only that you will need some additional patience and manoeuvres to make it happen.

The flap pocket is a good slim pocket alternative when knitting in the round. The afterthought pocket works for all kinds of knitting, in the round or flat. Note that not all possible combinations of pocket construction and edgings are described on the following pages.

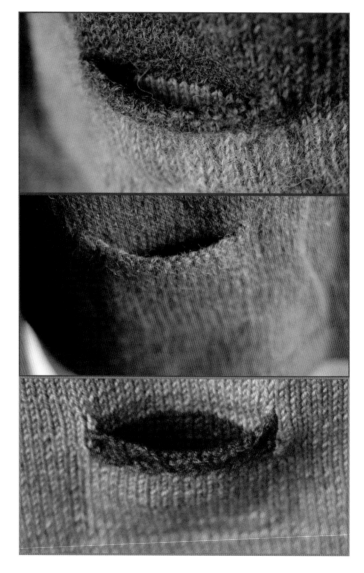

Åsa Tricosa Ziggurats :: 16 elegantly seamless knits

222

1A: afterthought pocket – no edging

The afterthought pocket is knitted after the body has been completed. While knitting the body, waste yarn is knitted into the fabric as a placeholder to mark the pocket opening.

The simplest version is worked without an edging.

MATERIALS & NEEDLE PLACEMENT

N1: 1 small circular needle for picking up stitches
N2: 1 or 2 circular needles, 1 – 2 sizes smaller than needle used for the body
Short piece of waste yarn
CC yarn, same weight or slightly lighter than garment yarn

STITCH COUNTS

Counts and instructions are based on a pocket that is 30 sts wide and where the waste yarn is worked into 30 sts. Adjust as appropriate to fit your sweater and pocket.

POCKET PLACEMENT

Knit to pocket position, with a short piece of waste yarn, k30 (or to desired width of pocket), slip these 30 sts back to LN, with working yarn knit same 30 sts again. Continue round or row according to pattern.

POCKET LINING

Thread a smaller circular needle (N1) through each stitch below the waste yarn, picking up in the right leg of each 'V'.

Loop the cable (or use a second circular), continue to thread through every stitch above the waste yarn.
Make sure you catch every stitch.

30 sts along upper edge
30 sts along lower edge

Remove waste yarn.

With N2 join CC at right side of lower edge, with CC k30 (to end of lower edge sts), p&k1 in the gap, loop cable, k30 along top edge, p&k1 in the gap.
2 x 31 sts
Rnd 1: Loop, p31, loop, k30, p1.
Rnd 2: (Loop, k30, g1) twice.
Work **Rnd 2** to desired depth.

Push your pocket through the opening to WS.
Close with a 3-Needle Bind Off.

1. N1 is threaded through every stitch along lower edge, cable looped, and first stitch picke up for upper edge.

2. Waste yarn removed. N2 and **CC**: Stitches knitted along bottom. Arrow points to gap where a stitch is to be picked up and knitted.

3. Knit the lining in the round with 1 garter stitch at each side, On the first round, purl the lower edge.

4. The lining is closed with a 3-Needle Bind Off on the WS.

5. The finished pocket from RS.

Tutorials :: Pockets
1B: afterthought pocket with slanting i-cord edging

This pocket features a contrasting slanting top and i-cord-ish edge.

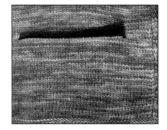

MATERIALS & NEEDLE PLACEMENT
N1 & N2: Circular needles 1 – 2 sizes smaller than needle used for Body
N3: A double pointed needle 1– 2 sizes smaller than working needle
Crochet hook in size similar to N1
CC yarn, same weight or slightly lighter than garment yarn
Stitch markers

STITCH COUNTS
Counts and instructions are based on a pocket that is 33 sts wide and where the waste yarn is worked into 33 sts. Adjust as appropriate to fit your sweater and pocket.

PLACEMENT OF POCKET
Mark the pocket placement with waste yarn as for Simple Afterthought Pocket (Pocket 1A).

PICKING UP THE POCKET STITCHES
Pick up as for Simple Afterthought Pocket without edging, but use two circulars. Thread N1 through each stitch below the waste yarn, picking up in the right leg of each 'V'.

With N2 thread through every stitch above the waste yarn.
Make sure you catch every stitch.
N2: *33 sts along upper edge*
N1: *33 sts along lower edge*
Remove waste yarn.

PICKING UP MORE STITCHES (SEE PICKING UP STITCHES TUTORIAL)
With MC and starting at right end of pocket opening to work sts behind N1, loop cable on N2, with N2 p&k1 st in the bar before the first st, then along lower edge and from WS (that is, behind the sts on N1), p&k sts in bars between sts, p&k1 final st in horizontal bar after final st. *34 sts*
Loop cable to work sts on N2, k33 sts, p&k1 st in the gap.
N2: *68 Lining sts*
Slide edging sts on N1 onto its cable and set aside.

Picking up pocket lining stitches behind what later will become the edging (yellow stitches on red cable). Contrasting lining yarn used here for visibility.

LINING
The last stitch on each half (the 'gap stitch') is worked as a garter stitch (g1) to create a better fold that makes the pocket lie flat on the inside.

Rnd 1: Loop, p34, loop cable, k33, p1.
Rnd 2: (Loop, k33, g1) twice.

Work **Rnd 2** to desired depth of pocket.

Close pocket with a 3-Needle Bind Off.

Stitches on N1 are set aside for later. Lining pouch is knitted in the round (N2) as for Pocket 1A.

1B: afterthought pocket with slanting i-cord edging

FINISH POCKET EDGES

Work the stitches on N1.

Refer to BOX for attaching technique.

LEFT POCKET

Join new MC (or CC for a contrasting edge).

R1 (RS): Attach first stitch to Front fabric, knit to last st, attach last stitch.

R2 (WS): Attach first st, p11, turn.

R3: Sl1^, knit to last st, attach last st.

R4: Attach first st, p5, turn.

R5: Sl1^, knit to last st, attach last st.

R6: Attach first st, purl to last st, working any sl1^ as p1^, attach last st.

I-CORD-ISH EDGING LEFT POCKET

Work the edging with N3.

R1 (RS): With working yarn, p&k2 sts in consecutive bars above first st, place on LN, sl1, BL1, ssk.

R2 (WS): Sks.

R3: K1, sl1wyf, ssk.

R4: Sks.

Tip: WS Rows 2 & 4 can be worked backwards (from left to right) – this obviates the need to turn work over between rows (see BOX).

Work **Rows 3 & 4** until 1 st remains on N2.

Final Row (RS): (Ssk) twice, cut yarn.

With crochet hook pull each of the 2 remaining sts, one at a time and with one bar between them to WS. On WS, chain stitch the top st through the bottom st, fetch yarn end from RS through to WS, secure final stitch with yarn end, weave in end.

RIGHT POCKET

Right Pocket mirrors the Left Pocket slant.

Join new MC (or CC for a contrasting edge).

R1 (RS): Attach first st, k11, turn.

R2 (WS): Sl1^, purl to last st, attach last st.

R3: Attach first st, k5, turn.

R4: Sl1^, purl to last st, attach last st.

R5: Attach first st, knit to last st, working any sl1^ as k1^, attach last st.

R6: Attach first st, purl to last st, attach last st.

I-CORD-ISH EDGING RIGHT POCKET

Work as for Left Pocket.

RIGHT SIDE

ATTACHING AT START OF ROW

Sl1, take bar between stitch columns (bar immediately above first) and place onto LN, sl1 to LN, ssk – slipped st and bar.

ATTACHING AT END OF ROW

Knit to last st, place bar in column above last st of N2 onto LN, k2tog – bar and last st.

WRONG SIDE

ATTACHING AT START OF ROW

Sl1, place next bar up from previously attached st onto LN, sl1 to LN, p2tog.

ATTACHING AT END OF ROW

Purl to last st, place next bar up onto LN, p2tog tbl.

WORKING WS ROWS FROM RS

Work **Rows 2 & 4 from RS:** Sl1wyb, p1 backwards (take yarn to front and manoeuvre the yarn so you make a normal p1), then slip the final st wyb.

1. Start of RS Row: Sl1, pick up bar (between stitch columns) above the slipped st and place on LN

2. Sl1 from RN to LN, join CC to ssk the slipped stitch and the picked up bar together.

Tutorials :: Pockets

1B: afterthought pocket with slanting i-cord edging

3. End of RS Row: Knit to last stitch, pick up horizontal bar above the last stitch, place bar on LN, k2tog (bar and last stitch).

7. I-cord Bind Off: Pick up & knit 1 stitch each in the 2 bars shown, place on LN.

4. Start of WS Row: Slip 1 stitch, pick up horizontal bar (arrow) above previous picked-up bar, place bar on LN.

8. The 2 picked-up stitches placed on LN.

5. Start of WS Row: Slip 1 stitch from RN to LN, p2tog (first stitch and bar).

9. Slip 1 stitch, make 1 (BL1 – blue arrow), then ssk (white arrows) next 2 stitches.

6. End of WS Row: Purl to last stitch, pick up horizontal bar above previously picked-up bar, place bar on LN, p2tog tbl (see Decrease Tutorial).

10. Work and attach the 3-stitch edging until 1 Edging stitch remains on LN. (Ssk) twice. 2 stitches remain on RN.

11. Pull each of the 2 remaining sts, one at a time (and with one bar between them) to WS. On WS, chain stitch the top st through the bottom st, fetch yarn end from RS through to WS, secure final stitch with yarn end, weave in end.

On the Mayhem cardigan, this hidden pocket is worked into a broken rib stitch pattern. The rib holds the opening in place so no edging is required. On Rabalder, which is knitted in the round and in plain stocking stitch, a narrow rib edging holds things in place (see BOX for instruction).

The flap technique can be used with other stitch patterns and edgings. Experimenting is encouraged.

Designs featuring this pocket:
- Mayhem cardigan
- Rabalder

MATERIALS & NEEDLE PLACEMENT

N1 (MC): Body sts (needle size and yarn weight as per pattern)
N2 & N3 (CC): 1 – 2 sizes smaller than N1; Lining sts

CC yarn, same weight or slightly lighter than garment yarn
Stitch markers

LPm = Left Pocket marker   RPm = Right Pocket marker

MAYHEM POCKET INSTRUCTIONS (FOR TWO POCKETS)

This pocket is worked over 17 sts and 20 rows. Make it wider and/or deeper as you wish.

A = width of pocket
B = number of stitches beween Side marker and Pocket

The sample pocket below fits and gives the stitch counts for Mayhem DK Cardigan in broken rib stitch pattern.

A = 17
B = 8 (10, 13, 15, 18) [20, 18, 23, 20, 23] sts

End with a WS rib row on your garment.

LEFT POCKET LINING

R1 (RS): K37 (37, 39, 39, 41) [41, 47, 47, 55, 55] (to A+B sts from Left side m), adjust to end on a p-rib column, slide N1 sts onto the cable, using a smaller needle (N2), join CC and k16 (A-1).

Work only the Lining sts on N2 as follows:
R2 (WS): K1, M1L, purl to last st, M1L, sl1wyf. *18 (A+1) sts (2 sts increased)*
R3 (RS): Knit to last st, sl1wyf.
R4 (WS): K1, purl to last st, sl1wyf.
Work **Rows 3 & 4** again x 6 – or to desired depth of pocket.
Work **Row 3** once.
Final Row (WS): K1, purl to last 2 sts, p2tog. *17 (A) sts (1 st decreased)*

Slide stitches onto the cable, set N2 aside.

With N1 and working MC, *(turn work over so WS is facing) borrow last st for cast on loop*, crochet cast on 17 (A) sts, replace loop onto LN *(make a final chain st but not around the needle)*, join to Body sts on far side of Lining, k1, pm (LPm2), knit to Right Side m, sm, k8 (10, 13, 15, 18) [20, 18, 23, 20, 23] (B) adjust to end on a p-rib column.

RIGHT POCKET LINING

With N3 work Right Pocket lining as for Left Pocket; when Lining is complete, set Lining sts aside.

RABALDER FLAP POCKET KNITTED IN THE ROUND

RIGHT POCKET LINING

Rnd1: Sm, g1, knit to m, sm, g1, k15 (15, 15, 19, 19) [19, 19, 25, 25, 25], pm (RPm1), k2, using smaller (4 mm / US 6) needle (N2), join new MC (MC2), k15. *15 Lining sts*
Work Lining as described for Mayhem Pocket (and decrease 1 st on final row), set the 16 Lining sts aside.
With working MC, crochet cast on 15 sts, work to end of rnd.

JOIN LINING TO BODY

On the first two rounds, work the 15 pockets stitches in rib as follows.
Rnd 1: Sm, g1, knit to m, sm, g1, knit to RPm1, sm, ssk, p1, (k1, p1) x 7, make loop in bar and place on LN, k2tog, pm (RPm2) knit to m.
Rnd 2: Sm, g1, knit to m, sm, g1, knit to RPm1, sm, attach, p1, (k1, p1) to 1 st before RPm2, attach, sm, knit to m.
Continue in plain stocking stitch, attaching on every second round.

CLOSING THE POCKET

Close the pocket by knitting body and lining sts together:
Next Rnd: Sm, g1, knit to m, sm, g1, knit to RPm1, rm, k2tog (1 body st with 1 lining st) to RPm2, rm, knit to end of rnd.

Tutorials :: Pockets

2A: flap pocket – no edging

With MC on N1 crochet cast on and place marker as for Left Pocket, knit to end of row.

JOINING LINING TO BODY

The Lining is joined to the Body on every RS row.

Note: fetch yarn through both legs of the slipped edge-stitch of the lining.

Next Row (WS/knit): P1, *knit to Pm2, sm, sl1 pwise, make twisted loop in cast on bar and place on LN, sl1 back to LN, k2tog (last st and loop) k16 (A-1), pm (Pm1), ssk (last cast on st and first Body st)*, work from * to * once more, knit to last st, p1.

R1 (RS/rib): K2, rib to LPm1 (last st is a p1), sm, *k2tog (next Body st with edge-stitch of Lining, going through both legs of this slipped st), rib to 1 st before Pm2 (last st is a p1), k2tog (next Body st with edge-stitch of Lining), sm*, rib to RPm1, sm, work from * to * once more, rib to last 2 sts, k2.

R2 (WS/rib): P2, rib to last 2 sts, p2 (no attaching).

R3/knit: Knit to LPm1, sm, *k2tog (next Body st with edge-stitch of Lining, going through both legs of this slipped st), knit to 1 st before Pm2, k2tog (next Body st with edge-stitch of Lining), sm*, knit to RPm1, sm, work from * to * once more, knit to end of row.

R4/knit: P1, knit to last st, p1 (no attaching).

Work **Rows 1 – 4** again x 3.

Work **Rows 1 & 2** once more.

CLOSING THE POCKETS

Close the pockets by knitting body and lining sts together:

Next Row (RS): Knit to LPm1, rm, *k2tog (1 body st with 1 lining st) x 17 (A), rm*, knit to RPm1, rm, work from * to * once more, knit to end.

1. The pocket lining is knitted first.

Cast on stitches to make a bridge across the flap.

2. Continue to knit body as before.

The lining edges are attached to the body on every RS row.

3. (Near edge) When attaching the lining, insert needle through both legs of the slipped edge stitch to fetch the yarn and k2tog (body stitch with edge stitch).

4. Far edge) K2tog – body stitch together with edge stitch of lining flap, again going through both legs of the slipped stitch.

5. When the Body layer is level with the flap, or just a tad longer, the two layers are knitted together from RS on a plain (knit) row.

Finished pocket seen from WS.

Finished pocket seen from RS.

2C: flap pocket with prepared edging

This pocket begins with a separately prepared edging. The short edges of the edging are attached over 3 rounds and stitches are picked up to bridge the gap across the flap lining. Alternatively, the gap is bridged by a prepared welt that has live stitches. From this point the pocket is knitted as Flap Pocket 2A, but in the round.

Designs featuring this pocket:
- **Coucou tunic** with cable edge
- **Sammelsurium** with welt edge

COUCOU: MATERIALS & NEEDLE PLACEMENT
N1 and **MC**: Body (needle size and yarn weight as per pattern)
N2 and **CC**: 1–2 sizes smaller than **N1**
N3 (for Welt edge) dpn or circular; same size as N2 or smaller)
CC yarn, same weight or slightly lighter than **MC**
Stitch markers

LPm = *Left Pocket marker*   RPm = *Right Pocket marker*
A = width of pocket
B = number of stitches beween Side Seam and Pocket

The sample pocket below fits and gives stitch counts for the **Coucou tunic**. For a wider pocket, you need to work more repeats of the cable edging.
A = 20 sts
B = 22 (24, 26, 26, 30) [30, 36, 36, 40, 40] sts
C6   Place 5 sts on CN and hold in back, k1, sl first st from CN to LN, k4 from CN, k1

COUCOU: PREPARE POCKET CABLE EDGE
With **N2**, using **CC** and longtail cast on, cast on 7 sts.
R1 (RS): Knit. *7 sts*
R2 (WS): Purl.
Work **Rows 1 & 2** once more.
R5: C6, k1.
Work **Row 2** once.

Work previous 6-row sequence x 3.
Work **Rows 1 & 2** once.

Bind off 4 sts, k2tog, pso to bind off final st, do not cut the yarn, pull on the final loop to make it really big for later use.

COUCOU: ATTACH CABLE TO THE BODY
The cable edging short ends are attached 1 stitch at a time along either side and on every round (attaching into every second edge stitch). Stitches are picked up along the long edge of the cable to bridge the gap across the flap lining.

Round A: Work to Right side marker, sm, work 22 (24, 26, 26, 30) [30, 36, 36, 40, 40] sts, pm (= RPm1), sl1 kwise, place Edging with bind-off edge pointing to the right, from RS of Edging, insert crochet hook inside the first bound off st to fetch working **MC**, psso. Place Edging's enlarged remaining bind-off loop on WS, continue on **MC** sts, k20.

Attach cast on edge of Edging: From RS, insert crochet hook inside the first cast on st to fetch working **MC** and place on LN, k2tog (the next body st with the fetched st), pm (= RPm2), work to end of round.

Round B: Work to RPm1, sm, sl1 kwise, from RS of edging, insert crochet hook inside the 3rd bound off st to fetch working **MC**, psso, continue on **MC** sts, k20, from RS of cable, insert crochet hook inside the 3rd cast on st to fetch working **MC** and place on LN, k2tog (the next body st with the fetched st), sm, work to end of round.

Work **Round B** once more, attaching the Edging short edges 1 st further along each short edge.

Next Round: Work to RP1m, sm, sl1 kwise, from RS of cable, insert crochet hook inside the final bound off st to fetch working **MC**, psso. Pull on needle tip to let sts rest on cable, set this needle (**N1**) aside for now.

SAMMELSURIUM: PREPARE WELT (SEE POCKET 3C)
With 3.25mm (US 3) circular needle (N2), **MC**, and using Provisional Winding Cast on, wind on 17 sts.
R1 (RS): Loop cable, knit the wound loops to end. *17 sts*
(17 provisional sts rest on the cable and are not worked at this time)
R2 (WS): Purl.
Work **6 rows more** of stocking stitch, ending with a WS row.
Slide provisional sts onto a spare needle (N3), fold Welt double with RS

2C: flap pocket with prepared edging

facing out, N2 in front of N3, tips parallel and pointing in the same direction. With N2 knit the two layers together, working 1 stitch from N2 and 1 st from N3 for each k2tog. *17 sts*

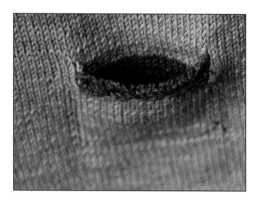

SAMMELSURIUM: ATTACH WELT TO THE BODY

Attach the Welt over the final 3 rounds of **MC** as follows:

Rnd 1 (N1): Knit to Right side marker, sm, k15 (15, 15, 20, 20) [20, 25, 25, 25, 25] sts, pm (Pm1), place Welt with folded edge facing towards top of pullover, RS facing up.

Sl1 kwise, insert RN tip into outer corner of Welt to fetch yarn through both layers, psso (if Welt has slipped behind work, swing it between needle tips to front of work, then continuing along body sts, k15, then insert RN tip into upper far corner of Welt going through both layers), fetch yarn through both layers, place st on LN, pass next body st over and off LN, slip resulting st to RN, pm (Pm2), work to end of round.

Rnd 2: As Rnd 1 but now attach Welt through stitch above previously attached edge stitch (and slip instead of place markers).

Rnd 3: As Rnd 2.

All stitches in Rnd 4 are worked with N1.

Rnd 4: With CC1, knit to Pm1, sl next st onto N2, ssk, (one body st tog with first Welt st, then continue along Welt sts on N2; knit to last st, sl1, set N1 aside (no sts remain on N2).

Pull on N1 to slide sts onto cable.

FLAP LINING

Coucou: The lining is worked back and forth onto the body over 22 sts with CC and N2 behind the cable edging.

R1: Place remaining Edging CC-loop on RN of N2, with attached CC, k19, M1L, k1, turn. *22 sts*

R2: K1, purl to last st, sl1wyf.

Sammelsurium: The CC2 lining is worked over 15 body sts behind the Welt.

R1 (RS): With N2, CC2, and starting 1 st after Pm1, k14, sl1wyf. *15 sts*

R2 (WS): K1, M1Lp, purl to last st, M1Lp, sl1wyf. *17 sts*

Coucou & Sammelsurium:

R3: Knit to last st, sl1wyf.

R4: K1, purl to last st, sl1wyf.

Work **Rows 3 & 4** again x 9 or to desired depth of pocket.

Cut CC (or leave attached for later adjustment of pocket depth). Slide sts onto cable, set N2 aside.

Coucou:

With **N1** and already attached **MC**, p&k20 sts along long edge of Edging, attach final st of Edging, sm, work to end of round.

Sammelsurium

Rnd 1 (N1) continued: Sl last Welt st to LN, k2tog, sm, work to end of rnd.

ATTACH POCKET LINING

The lining is joined to the body on every second round.

Note: *Fetch yarn through both legs of the slipped edge stitch (see Pocket 2A).*

Sammelsurium (welt edge):

Rnd 1 (attachm-rnd): With CC1, knit to Pm1, sm, k2tog (next Body st with edge-stitch of Lining, going through both legs of this slipped st), knit to 1 st before Pm2, k2tog (next Body st with edge-stitch of Lining), sm, work to end of round *and pay attention to the g1-st along sides and to waist shaping.*

Rnd 2: Knit to Pm1, sm, make twisted loop in bar between sts and place on LN, k2tog (body st together with loop), work to end of round.

Work **Rnds 1 & 2** until body is level with lining or just slightly longer.

CLOSE POCKET

Body sts on **N1** and lining sts on **N2** are joined with ssk (Coucou) or k2tog (Sammelsurium), working 1 st from **N1** and 1 st from **N2** for each ssk/k2tog as for Pocket 2A.

3B: double-knitted pocket with slanting i-cord edge

For this pocket provisional stitches are wound on to bridge the Front layer over a Lining layer. The two layers are interlaced on the first WS row, then double-knitted on subsequent rows.
The provisional cast on also provides stitches for the i-cord edge which is knitted last.

Design featuring this pocket:
- Sweet Laurel cardigan

MATERIALS

N1 and **MC**: Body (needle size and yarn weight as per pattern)
N2 & **N3**: 1 – 2 sizes smaller than N1
N4 & N5: Smaller (and short) for provisional winding cast on
MC yarn for Body, 2 additional balls of **MC** for pocket linings
Stitch markers

NEEDLE PLACEMENT

N2 and MC2: Left Pocket (at start of RS rows)
N3 and MC3: Right Pocket (at end of RS rows; buttonhole side)
N4 : Left Pocket provisional top edge sts
N5: Right Pocket provisional top edge sts

LPm = Left Pocket marker   RPm = Right Pocket marker

Refer to Box (on next page) for double-knitting and crossing yarns.

A = width of pocket
B = number of stitches beween Buttonband and pocket

The sample pocket below uses the stitch counts for the Sweet Laurel Cardigan where
A = 29 (29, 33, 33, 33) [33, 33, 33, 33, 33]
B = 5 (7, 7, 7, 9) [9, 9, 12, 12, 12]

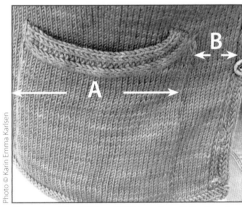

Illustration of A (width) and B (distance from Buttonband)
Note: The photo shows pocket 3D.

R1 (RS): BB, sm, k5 (7, 7, 7, 9) [9, 9, 12, 12, 12] (B), pm (LPm1), k1, with N2 and new MC (MC2), k29 (29, 33, 33, 33) [33, 33, 33, 33, 33] (A), pull on N2 to slide sts onto cable, set N2 aside.

  N1: With MC and using N1 & N4 for provisional cast on, wind on 29 (29, 33, 33, 33) [33, 33, 33, 33, 33] (A) sts, k1, pm (LPm2), knit across back (according to pattern) to 36 (38, 42, 42, 44) [44, 44, 47, 47, 47] (A+B+2) sts before BB, pm (RPm1), k1, with N3 and new MC (MC3), k29 (29, 33, 33, 33) [33, 33, 33, 33, 33] (A), pull on N3 to slide sts onto cable, set N3 aside.

  N1: With MC and using N1 & N5 for provisional cast on, wind on 29 (29, 33, 33, 33) [33, 33, 33, 33, 33] sts (A sts), k1, pm (RPm2), knit to m, sm, BB.

On the following WS Row, Pocket sts are interlaced with Body sts for double knitting (DK).
MC is used for RS layer, MC2/3 are used for WS/lining layer.
All sts are worked with N1, which transfers all sts from N2 & N3 to N1.

R2 (WS): BB, sm, purl to RPm2, sm, *sl1, twist bar and place loop on LN, sl1 to LN, p2tog, cross yarns *, (p1MC3, p1MC) to last MC3-st, p1MC3, cross yarns, p2togtblMC, sm, work to LPm2, sm, work from * to * once more, (p1MC2, p1MC) to last MC2-st, p1MC2, cross yarns, p2tog tblMC, sm, purl to m, sm, BB.

R3: BB, sm, knit to LPm1, sm, k1, cross yarns, (k1MC2, k1MC) to last MC2-st, k1MC2, cross yarns, k1MC, sm, work to RPm1, sm, k1, cross yarns (k1MC3, k1MC) to last MC3-st, k1MC3, cross yarns, k1MC, sm, knit to m, sm, BB.

3B: double-knitted pocket with slanting i-cord edge

R4: BB, sm, work to RPm2, sm, p1, cross yarns, (p1**MC3**, p1MC) to last **MC3**-st, p1**MC3**, cross yarns, p1MC, sm, work to LPm2, sm, p1, cross yarns, (p1 MC2, p1MC) to last MC2-st, p1 MC2, cross yarns, p1MC, sm, work to m, sm, BB. Work **Rows 3 & 4** again x 14 or to desired depth of pocket, while paying attention to final buttonhole placement in relation to the hem.

CLOSE POCKET

Next Row (RS): BB, sm, work to LPm1, rm, k1, (k2tog) x 28 (28, 32, 32, 32) [32, 32, 32, 32, 32] (A-1), rm, work to RPm1, rm, k1, (k2tog) x 28 (28, 32, 32, 32) [32, 32, 32, 32, 32] (A-1), rm, knit to m, sm, BB.

FINISH POCKET EDGES

Work the provisional stitches on N4 (Left Pocket) and N5 (Right Pocket) as for Pocket 1B.

DOUBLE KNITTING (DK)

Work stitches alternately from RS & WS layer.

It is important to keep the layers separate and to only cross yarns/ layers at the beginning and end of the pocket.

For this pocket the DK section always begins and ends with MC2/3.

RS

MC is held to front (toward you) and is used for RS layer, MC2/3 is held to back and used for WS layer.

WS

MC is held to back (RS), MC2/3 is held to front (WS).

CROSSING YARNS

Both yarns to WS, MC2/3 over **MC**, take **MC** to RS.

1.
N1 (tips) shows Body stitches
N2 (cable) holds what becomes the lining

2.
Winding on stitches to bridge across the lining layer with the help of an additional short circular (N4)

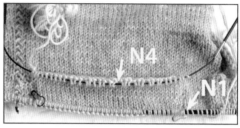

3.
N4: Holds provisional stitches
N1: Holds the interlaced Body & Lining stitches

4.
A few short rows are worked with the provisional stitches to make slanting upper edge before being finished with an attached i-cord.
(The pocket edging here was finished before the pocket was complete.)

3C: double-knitted pocket with welt edging

The sample pocket features a plain stocking stitch folded edge, a Welt, which is attached while knitting the body in the round. Any Edging can be attached using the method below, including a sideways knitted cable (as on the Coucou Tunic), or a Welt with, for example, a ribbed or striped outside, and plain inside.

The pocket itself is double-knitted while knitting flat (back and forth), but can also, with some extra slipping and manoeuvres, be knitted in the round. The Vaudeville Tunic, which features this pocket, has side slits, which allow the pocket to be knitted flat as the Front and Back are finished separately.

Designs featuring this pocket:
- Vaudeville tunic
- Sammelsurium pullover (welt of 3C used with pocket 2C)

MATERIALS & NEEDLE PLACEMENT

N1 and **MC**: Body (needle size and yarn weight as per pattern)
N2: Smaller circular for Welt
N3 (1 – 2 sizes smaller than N1): Briefly used for Pocket Lining
MC yarn for Body
MC & **CC1** for Welt
CC2 for Pocket Lining
Stitch markers

RPm = Right Pocket marker

Refer to Box for double-knitting and crossing yarns.

A = width of pocket
B = number of stitches beween Side seam and pocket

The sample pocket fits and gives the stitch counts for the Vaudeville tunic, where
A = 25 sts
B = 22 (22, 25, 24, 24) [24, 26, 26, 28, 28] sts

PREPARE THE WELT (FOLDED EDGING)

Work with **MC** and **CC1** (lime).
With N2, **CC1,** and using Winding Provisional Cast On, wind on 25 (A) sts.
Loop cable to work 5 rows of plain stocking stitch, cut **CC1**.
Working from opposite end (the provisional sts), remove and discard slipknot. With new **MC**, work 6 more rows of plain stocking stitch.

Weave in yarn ends before closing the Welt.
Slide **CC1** sts to N3, fold piece double (wrong sides together) so that **MC** sts lie on top of **CC1** sts, needle tips parallel and pointing in the same direction.
With **MC**, knit the two layers together as follows:
(K2tog) to end (for each k2tog work 1 **MC** st & 1 **CC1** st). *25 (A) Welt sts*

ATTACH WELT

The Welt short ends are attached on every round, 1 stitch at a time along either side and going through both layers.

The completed Welt before it is folded with RS facing out. MC and CC1 stitches are then knitted together to close the Welt.

Vaudeville pocket knitted flat (after the Welt is attached while knitting in the round, before the side slits).
Circle marks the almost invisible points of attachment.

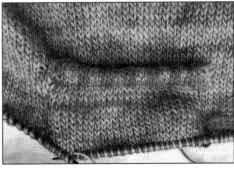

Knitted in the round – requires some additional slipping and manoeuvering on every other round, but quite doable.

Tutorials :: Pockets

3C: double-knitted pocket with welt edging

Rnd A (N1): K22 (22, 25, 24, 24) [24, 26, 26, 28, 28] (B) sts, pm (= RPm1), sl1 kwise. Attach right edge of Welt: Place Welt with **MC** facing out and folded edge pointing towards top of garment. At top of Welt, 1 st in from side edge and going through both layers, insert crochet hook to fetch working **MC**, place on RN, sl2 to LN, k2tog tbl (slipped st and fetched st), k23 (A-2) Front sts.

Attach left edge of Welt: From RS, insert crochet hook 1 st from edge, go through both layers to fetch working **MC**, place on LN, k2tog (the next Front st with the fetched st), pm (= RPm2), work to end of round.

Rnd B (N1): Work to RPm1, sm, sl1 kwise, from RS of Welt, insert crochet hook 1 row below previously attached st to fetch working **MC**, place on RN, sl2 to LN, k2tog tbl, knit to 1 st before RPm2, from RS of Welt, insert crochet hook 1 row below previously attached st to fetch working **MC**, place on LN, k2tog (the next Front st with the fetched st), sm, work to end of round.

Work Round **B** again x 2: On each round attach the Welt short edges 1 row below previously attached st.

POCKET LINING SETUP
Work with **MC** and **CC2** (Teal).
Setup Round:
  N1: Knit to RPm1, sm, sl1 kwise, from **N2** sl1, knit the 2 sl sts tog tbl (slide sts on **N2** onto cable).
  With N3 and **CC2**, k23 (A-2) Front sts (from **N1**), p&k1 in bar.
  Set N3 aside. *24 (A-1) Lining sts*
  N1: Knit to last st from **N2**, knit final st on **N2** tog with next st on **N1**, k1, sm.
  No sts remain on **N2**.
  N1: With **MC**, knit to end of round

For Vaudeville: Return to main pattern now.
Instructions for working pocket flat (back & forth) for other patterns continue below.

SET UP DOUBLE KNITTING
*The first row is worked with MC only. Front and Lining stitches are interlaced as all stitches on N3 are worked onto **N1**.*
R1 (RS): Knit to RPm1, sm, (k1 from **N1**, sl1wyf from N3) to 1 st before RPm2, cross yarns, k1, sm, knit to end.
R2 (WS): Purl to RPm2, sm, p1MC, cross yarns, (p1CC, p1MC) to last CC, p1CC, cross yarns, p1MC, sm, with **MC** purl to end.
R3: Knit to RPm1, sm, k1MC, cross yarns, (k1CC, k1MC) to last CC, k1CC, cross yarns, k1MC, sm, with **MC** knit to end.
R4: Purl to RPm2, sm, p1MC, cross yarns, (p1CC, p1MC) to last CC, p1CC, cross yarns, p1MC, sm, with **MC** purl to end.
Work **Rows (3 & 4)** again x 8 (or to desired depth), cut CC.

CLOSE POCKET
Next Row (RS): Knit to RPm1, rm, k1, k2tog (1 **MC** st with 1 **CC** st) to m, rm, knit to end.

First row of Lining stitches (teal) knitted before they are interlaced with Front stitches for the double-knitted pocket.

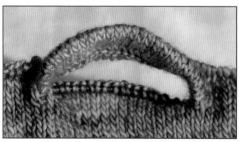

First row of Lining stitches knitted (viewed through attached Welt).

3D: double-knitted & buttonband edging

WORKED FLAT & WITH MUCH PATIENCE

This pocket starts with an edging that is picked up in the front fabric and knitted first. Stitches are picked up along the edging. The edging is then attached to the Front over the next few rows. Finally, pocket and front sts are interlaced for double-knitting.

Do take the time to untangle yarn and needles often – on every row, even. For sanity.

Designs featuring this pocket:
- Black Basalt cardigan
- Jadeite cardigan

MATERIALS & NEEDLE PLACEMENT
N1 and MC: Body
N2 & N3 (1 – 2 sizes smaller than N1)
MC, MC2, MC3
Stitch markers

NEEDLE PLACEMENT
N1 and MC: Body (needle size and yarn weight as per pattern)
N2 and MC2: Left Pocket (at start of RS rows)
N3 and MC3: Right Pocket (at end of RS rows; buttonhole side)

LPm = Left Pocket marker
RPm = Right Pocket marker
A = width of pocket
B = number of stitches beween Buttonband and pocket
BB = Buttonband

Right Pocket edge with a few short rows done
(at left bottom).
The pocket edgings are first attached only at one end. The far end is attached one stitch at a time over several rows.

The prepared Right pocket edging: 5 sts sit on a holder (transparent cable at right), stitches are picked up & knitted along the slipped-stitch edge toward Centre Front.

PREPARE POCKET EDGES

R1 (RS): BB, sm, knit to BB, sm, BB.

Pick up for pocket edges (see Picking Up Stitches tutorial):
Slide all N1-sts onto cable.

At B sts
Blue:	7 (7, 7, 9, 9) [9, 9, 12, 12, 12] sts
Black:	5 (5, 6, 6, 9) [9, 9, 11, 11, 11] sts
Jadeite:	5 (5, 5, 7, 7) [7, 9, 9, 11, 11] sts

in from Left BB

With N2 and new MC (MC2), p&k6 sts in the next 6 bars between sts for Left Pocket. At
B+6 sts
Blue:	13 (13, 13, 15, 15) [15, 15, 18, 18, 18] sts
Black:	11 (11, 12, 12, 15) [15, 15, 17, 17, 17] sts
Jadeite:	11 (11, 11, 13, 13) [13, 15, 15, 17, 17] sts

before Right BB

With N3 and new MC (MC3), p&k6 sts in bars between sts for Right Pocket.

R2 (WS): BB, sm,

purl B sts
Blue:	p7 (7, 7, 9, 9) [9, 9, 12, 12, 12]
Black:	p5 (5, 6, 6, 9) [9, 9, 11, 11, 11]
Jadeite:	p5 (5, 6, 6, 9) [9, 9, 11, 11, 11]

pm (RPm2), cross yarns (see BOX), p6, cross yarns, purl to

B+6 sts before BB
Blue:	13 (13, 13, 15, 15) [15, 15, 18, 18, 18] sts
Black:	11 (11, 12, 12, 15) [15, 15, 17, 17, 17] sts
Jadeite:	11 (11, 12, 12, 15) [15, 15, 17, 17, 17] sts

before BB

Cross yarns, p6, cross yarns, pm (LPm1), purl to BB, sm, BB.
Set N1 with Body sts aside for now.

LEFT POCKET EDGE
Work only MC2 sts on N2.

Setup Row (WS): (Sl1wyf, M1L, sks, M1L, sl1wyf, k1. 8 sts
R1 (RS): Sl1wyf, ksk, k1, ksk.
R2 (WS): (Sl1wyf, k1) x 4.

Tutorials :: Pockets
3D: double-knitted & buttonband edging

> **CROSSING YARNS**
> Both yarns to WS, lay MC over MC2/3, take MC2/3 to RS

Work **Rows 1 & 2** again

    x A-4

Blue:	x 29
Black:	x 26 (26, 26, 29, 29) [29, 29, 29, 29, 29]
Jadeite:	x 22 (22, 22, 22, 22) [24, 24, 24, 24, 24]

Work **Row 1** once more.

Next Row (WS): P2tog, p1, k1, p1, p2togtbl, slide these 5 sts to a holder (or leave on circular if not too short), p1, in slipped sts along pocket edging, p&p

    A-2 sts

Blue:	31 sts
Black:	28 (28, 28, 31, 31) [31, 31, 31, 31, 31] sts
Jadeite:	24 (24, 24, 24, 24) [26, 26, 26, 26, 26] sts

STITCH COUNT

5 + A-1 sts

Blue:	5 + 32 sts
Black:	5 + 29 (29, 29, 32, 32) [32, 32, 32, 32, 32] sts
Jadeite:	5 + 25 (25, 25, 25, 25) [27, 27, 27, 27, 27] sts

RIGHT POCKET EDGE

Work only MC3 sts on N3.
Setup Row (WS): P1, sl1wyf, M1L, sks, M1L, sl1wyf. 8 sts
R1 (RS): Ksk, k1, ksk, sl1wyb.
R2: P1, (sl1wyf, k1) x 3, sl1wyf.

Work **Rows 1 & 2** again

    x A-4

Blue:	x 29
Black:	x 26 (26, 26, 29, 29) [29, 29, 29, 29, 29]
Jadeite:	x 22 (22, 22, 22, 22) [24, 24, 24, 24, 24]

Next Row (RS): Ssk, k3, k2tog, slide these 5 sts to holder (or leave on circular if not too short), k1, in slipped sts of pocket edging, p&k

    A-2 sts

Blue:	31 sts
Black:	28 (28, 28, 31, 31) [31, 31, 31, 31, 31] sts
Jadeite:	24 (24, 24, 24, 24) [26, 26, 26, 26, 26] sts

STITCH COUNT

5 + A-1 sts

Blue:	5 + 32 sts
Black:	5 + 29 (29, 29, 32, 32) [32, 32, 32, 32, 32] sts
Tumult:	5 + 25 (25, 25, 25, 25) [27, 27, 27, 27, 27] sts

AT THE SAME TIME POCKET & BODY & BUTTONHOLES

While working the pockets, also work Box C Basic **Rows 1 & 2** with Buttonbands, buttonholes and Body sts as instructed in garment pattern, including g1 at the side 'seams' (not noted in the instructions below).

CONTINUE OVER BODY & POCKET STS

N1, N2, & N3 are worked in the specific sequence described below. After finishing with each needle, slide sts onto the cable.

N1 R1 (RS): BB, sm, knit to LPm1, sm, cross yarns (see BOX), knit to RPm2, cross yarns, sm, knit to BB, sm, BB.

    N2 R1: K2, turn.
    N2 R2: Sl1^, p1.

N1 R2 (WS): BB, sm, purl to RPm2, cross yarns, sm, purl to LPm1, cross yarns, sm, purl to BB, sm, BB.

N3 R2: P2, turn.	**N2 R3:** K1, k1^, k1, turn.
N3 R3: Sl1^, k1.	**N2 R4:** Sl1^, p2.

N1 R3: BB, sm, knit to LPm1, sm, cross yarns, knit to RPm2, cross yarns, sm, knit to BB, sm, BB.
N3 R4: P1, p1^, p1, turn.
N3 R5: Sl1^, k2.

N1 R4: BB, sm, purl to RPm2, sm, cross yarns, sm, purl to LPm1, cross yarns, sm, purl to BB, sm, BB.
On next row join one stitch of the far end of Left Pocket edging – slide the leftmost st from holder (the stitch at the upper edge of the edging).

N1 R5: BB, sm, knit to LPm1, sm, cross yarns,
    knit A sts

Blue:	k33
Black:	k30 (30, 30, 33, 33) [33, 33, 33, 33, 33]
Jadeite:	k26 (26, 26, 26, 26) [28, 28, 28, 28, 28]

from holder sl1 MC2 to LN, k2tog (1 MC2 with next **MC**), pm, (LPm2), knit to RPm2, cross yarns, sm, knit to BB, sm, BB.

N3 R6: P2, p1^, p1, turn.	**N2 R5:** K2, k1^, k1, turn.
N3 R7: Sl1^, k3, turn.	**N2 R6:** Sl1^, p3, turn.

On next row join one stitch of the far end of Right Pocket edging – slide the rightmost st from holder (the stitch at the upper edge of the edging).

N1 R6: BB, sm, purl to RPm2, sm, cross yarns,

purl A sts
  Blue: p33
  Black: p30 (30, 30, 33, 33) [33, 33, 33, 33, 33]
  Jadeite: p26 (26, 26, 26, 26) [28, 28, 28, 28, 28]

from holder sl1MC3 to LN, p2togtbl, pm (RPm1), purl to LPm2, sm, sl1, from holder sl1MC2, sl2 from RN to LN, p2tog, purl to LPm1, cross yarns, sm, purl to BB, sm, BB.

N1 R7: BB, sm, knit to LPm1, sm, cross yarns, knit to 1 st before LPm2, from holder sl1MC2 to LN, k2tog, sm, knit to RPm1, sm, sl1 kwise, from holder sl1MC3 kwise, sl2 to LN, k2togtbl (that is, ssk 1**MC** with 1**MC3**), sm, knit to RPm2, cross yarns, sm, knit to BB, sm, BB.

N3 R8: P3, p1^, p1, turn.	**N2 R7:** K3, k1^, k1, turn.
N3 R9: Sl1^, k4, turn.	**N2 R8:** Sl1^, p4, turn.

N1 R8: As Row 6 (slip instead of place markers).

On the following RS row, Left Pocket sts are interlaced with Body sts for double knitting (DK).
MC and MC2 switch places. MC is held to front and used for RS layer, MC2 is held to back and used for WS/lining layer.
*All sts are worked with **N1**, which transfers all sts from **N2** to **N1**.*
Crossing yarns also changes (see Box).
N1 R9: BB, sm, knit to m, sm, cross yarns, starting with MC2 and WS layer, DK-k4, k1MC2, k1^MC, DK-k to 1 st before m, from holder sl1MC2 (final holder st) to LN, k2tog, sm, knit to RPm1, sm, sl1 kwise, from holder sl1MC3 kwise, sl2 to LN, k2togtbl, knit to RPm2, cross yarns, sm, knit to BB, sm, BB.

On the following WS row, Right Pocket sts are interlaced with Body sts for double knitting.

MC and MC3 switch places.
MC is used for RS layer, MC3 is used for WS/lining layer.
*All sts are worked with **N1**, which transfers all sts from **N3** to **N1**.*

N1 R10: BB, purl to m, sm, cross yarns, begin with MC3 and WS layer, DK-p4, p1MC3, p1^MC, DK-p to 1 st before m, cross yarns, from holder sl1MC3 (final holder st) to LN, p2togtbl, sm, purl to LPm2, sm, p1, cross yarns, beginning with MC2, DK-p to m, cross yarns, sm, purl to BB, sm, BB.

All sts are now on N1.

R11: BB, sm, knit to m, sm, cross yarns, beginning with MC2, DK-k to 1 st before m, cross yarns, k1MC, sm, knit to RPm1, sm, k1, cross yarns, beginning with **MC3**, DK-k to m, cross yarns, sm, knit to BB, sm, BB.

R12: BB, sm, purl to RPm2, sm, cross yarns, beginning with **MC3**, DK-p to 1 st before m, cross yarns, p1MC, sm, purl to LPm2, sm, p1, cross yarns, beginning with MC2, DK-p to m, cross yarns, sm, purl to BB, sm, BB.

Don't forget buttonhole placement and the g1 at the sides.

Work **Rows 11 & 12** to length suggested in pattern or to desired length, taking hem into account.

FINISHING THE POCKETS
Next Row (RS): Ssk, k3, k2tog, p1, rm, knit to m, rm, (k2tog) to LPm2, rm, knit to RPm1, rm, k1, (k2tog) to 1 st before RPm2, sl1, rm, sl1 back to LN, k2tog, rm, knit to m, rm, p1, ssk, k3, k2tog. Cut MC2 and **MC3**.

Tutorials :: Pockets

3D: double-knitted & buttonband edging

ATTACHING RIGHT POCKET EDGING

1A. View from RS but working from WS to attach first holder stitch.

WS: Orange sts (blue arrow) on red cable are the picked-up edge stitches. Leave these aside.
Attach holder stitches, beginning with the stitch (yellow arrow) furthest away from red cable.

1B. WS: Slip 1 stitch from holder to LN.
Take care to mount the slipped stitch properly (right leg to front).

1C. WS: Prepare for p2tog tbl.
Slip 1 stitch knitwise (the holder stitch – yellow arrow).
Slip 1 more knitwise (blue arrow).

1D. WS: Prepare for p2tog tbl.
Insert LN from right to left, going into second, then first stitch.

1E. WS: Prepare for p2tog tbl.
Stitches are mounted in the correct order for completing the p2tog tbl.
Purl the 2 stitches together.

2A. RS: Knit to marker, slip marker, slip 1 stitch knitwise (blue arrow) , from holder slip 1 stitch knitwise (yellow arrow).

2B. RS: Slip the 2 stitches to LN, knit them together through the back loop (= an ssk).

3. Attach 2 more stitches over the next 2 rows in the same manner.
1 stitch remains on the holder.

4. WS: Edging and body stitches are interlaced for double-knitting. Attach final holder stitch with a p2tog tbl as before. No stitches remain on holder.

5. Right Pocket seen from RS: Done.

3D: double-knitted & buttonband edging

ATTACHING LEFT POCKET EDGING

1A. RS: Attach first holder stitch.
Stitches on red cable (blue arrow) are the picked-up edge stitches. Leave these aside.
Attach holder stitches, beginning with the stitch (yellow arrow) furthest away from red cable.

1B. RS: Slip 1 stitch from holder to LN.

1C. RS: Knit 2 stitches together (the slipped holder stitch and next stitch), pm, (=LPm2)

2A. WS: Purl to LPm2, sm, slip 1 stitch (blue arrow), from holder slip 1 stitch (furthest away from red cable – yellow arrow).

2B. WS: Slip the 2 stitches back to LN, purl them together.
3. Attach 2 more stitches over the next 2 rows in the same manner.
1 stitch remains on the holder.

4. RS: Edging and body stitches are interlaced for double-knitting. Attach final holder stitch as before:
Slip to LN, k2tog.
No stitches remain on holder.

5. Left Pocket: Done.

Acknowledgements

Like every knitter, I stand on the shoulders of fellow knitters. In particular, the Ziggurat method is indebted to and inspired by Tuulia Salmela's Tailored Sweater Method.

I also want to thank my impressive and generous test knitters, sample knitters, cheerers on in my Ravelry group, random knitters, inspiring friends past and present, designers, the Erfurt knitters, and the knitters in the Tiefthal Knitting Group led by textile artist Dr. Monika Besser; and also the inspiring and enthusiastic Ziggurateers at the knitting retreats hosted by Les Soeurs Anglaises and Hand Herz Seele.

They include:

Barbara Angermann, Jen Arnall-Culliford, Catherine Aspinall, Rachel Atkinson, Sally Atkinson, Laura Aylor, Liesel Bach, Sarah Bachman, Martina Behm, Melanie Berg, Iris Birkemeyer, Dianne Blackett, Stephanie Boardman, Susan Bromiley, Anne Brooker, Sarah Browning, Chris Browse, Irmtraud Brunke, Susi Bull, Heidi Capatos, Heather Corbishley, Susan W Davis, Kim Denise, Eva Doggen, Julia Duffield, Andrea Dular, Maria-Theresia Dünser, Katja Embacher, Mary Fellman, Natalie Fergie, Fabian Fiedler, Rotraud Fiedler, Daien Forrest, Christine Gandre, Diane Goldenring, Beth Graham, Judit Gummlich, Ute Haasler, Annette Hähn, Naima Hakim, Marjan Hammink, Jerry Harlow, Anne Hein, Jeni Hewlett, Maria Higgs, Sue Hill, Karen Hoffberg, Merrian Holland, Sarah Holmes, Diane Hughes, Vicky Hutchings, Anne Kamsvaag, Helen Keijser, Tea Kekkonen, Ann Kingstone, Beatrice Klünder, Constance Knoflick, Jessica Krop, Jo Lakey, Marianne de Lapérouse, Julia Lauder, Liz Lawrie, Christine Lazik, Carol Lindquist, Jane Lithgow, Jana Lütz, Nina Machlin Dayton, Brita MacKey, Stina MacKey-Söderman, Susan Maddock, Hanna Maciejewska, Emma Magnano-Prime, Victoria Magnus, Nancy Marchant, Merryn McArthur, Brita Melendez, Mica & Jo, Concetta Miniello, Naoko Ogawa, Elaine Osborne, Elisabetta Pierantoni, Meg Prescott, Thurid Riehe, Michaela Rißmann, Nuala Sheehan, Carol Silberfeld, Jan Sims, Katharina Sokiran, Moira Strachan, Susan Stevens (Fleegle),Kim Suhre, Michele Sung, Dani Sunshine, Nicola Susen, Carol Temple, Judith Thiery, Ann Thorpe, Harriet Topping, Jo Torr, Ann Turbervill, Sascha Uetrecht, Michaela Utsch, Jacqui Walker, Jane White, Chantal Wikberg, Emily Williams, Friederike Winter, Barbara Wolfe, Anke Wulffen, Soo-hoon Yeo, Bettina Zander, Elaine Zoe, and more!

I owe so much gratitude to sample and test knitter Alexis Borsboom, to sample knitter Ursula Freund, and to Sabine Bach, Gabriele Dietrich, Friederike Winter, and Annabel Young, patient, exacting, creative, and inspiring test knitters par excellence. I wish to thank all test knitters, present and past.

Some of the loveliest photographs stem from Annabel's generous retreats on Hvalø. The Petrichor photographs were taken at the creative oasis Les Soeurs Anglaises, hosted by Katie Elliott Armitage & Susie Bolton Nash.

Anne Kamsvaag taught me how to create a reliable what:if formula for the recurring short-row calculations. Thank you!

Another special thank you goes to Steph Boardman (technical editor) and Nic Blackmore (graphics artist) for helping make presentable my first sprawling design instructions way back when, and Nic for helping me visualise the beginnings of a book.
My consistency tsarinas are technical editors Kitty Wunder and Cathy Susko at knit1tech2.

They are in excellent company: Without the crucial editing, checking, and encouragement by Jeannette Gustavus, Charlotte Monckton and Maria Skrzypiec in way too many late-night crunch sessions this book would not exist. Nor would it without the firm herding and project management talents of the latter two.

Ewa Opalinska Shephard has made this a more beautiful book than I had ever hoped possible, and is also a member of the crucial late-night team, The Four Graces!

Thank you!

Yarn Support :: Links & Resources

Yarn Support

Not least, I wish to thank the wonderful dyers and yarnistas for generously supporting this book with their beautiful yarns:

Barbara Wolff, Dibadu	www.dibadu.de
Cordula & Nicole, DyeForYarn	www.dyeforyarn.com
Jessica James-Thomson, Ginger Twist Studio	www.gingertwiststudio.com
Emma Boyles, The Little Grey Sheep	www.thelittlegreysheep.co.uk
Estelle Hughes, Midwinter Yarns	www.midwinteryarns.com
Danica Mäder Jully, Nature's Luxury	www.naturesluxury.com
Deborah Moore, Outlaw Yarn	www.outlawyarn.com
Sarah & Jonathan Lewis, Purlescence	www.purlescence.co.uk
Christine Biedermann, Rauwerk	www.rauwerk-wolle.de
Helen Lockhart, Ripples Crafts	www.ripplescrafts.com
Claudia Hoell-Wellmann, Rohrspatz & Wollmeise	www.rohrspatzundwollmeise.de
Ce Persiano, The Uncommon Thread	www.theuncommonthread.co.uk
Cathrin Walk, Walk Collection	www.walkcollection.com
Cascade	www.cascadeyarns.com
Malabrigo Yarn	www.malabrigoyarn.com

A special thank you goes to Rohrspatz & Wollmeise, with whom I have a creative and ongoing collaboration.

And thank you to every knitter who has commented, knitted, modified, invented, sent suggestions, found errors, or lavished praise.

Links & Resources

Åsa Tricosa photo tutorials	www.asatricosa.com/category/howto
Beyond Measure (Beautiful notions)	www.shopbeyondmeasure.co.uk
Buttonalia (Ceramic buttons)	www.etsy.com/shop/buttonalia
Charlotte Monckton (Technical editing)	www. charlottemonckton.co.uk
Dan Lepard On Bread (Good bread)	www.danlepard.com
Edinburgh Yarn Festival (Hand-knitting show)	www.edinyarnfest.com
Hand Heerz Seele (Kreativ retreat)	www.handherzseele.de
Herr U am Amalienpark (Berlin yarn shop)	www.herr-u.de
Hvalø Gård (Idyllic island creative retreats)	www.hvalogard.com
knit1tech2 (Technical editing)	www. knit1tech2.com
KuniBag Hamburg (Handmade bags)	www.kunibag.de
Les Soeurs Anglaises (Creative workshops)	www.lessoeursanglaises.com
The Loopy Ewe (Colorado yarn shop)	www.theloopyewe.com
mylys (Hamburg yarn shop)	www.mylys.de
Nancy Marchant (Brioche knitting)	www.briochestitch.com
Ottolenghi (Good food)	www.ottolenghi.co.uk
Purlescence (UK yarn shop)	www.purlescence.co.uk
Ravelry (Knitting community)	www.ravelry.com
Sommerfuglen (København yarn shop)	www.sommerfuglen.dk
WollWerkstatt Kiel (for Holz & Stein needles)	www.wollwerkstatt-kiel.de
Yarn Over Berlin (Berlin yarn shop)	www.yarnoverberlin.de
Yllo Tyll (Uppsala yarn shop)	www.yllotyll.com
Zing Creative (Graphic & web design)	www. zingcreative.eu

Index

Index

knit
with
abandon !